FROM ROMANTICISM TO SURREALISM

SEVEN SPANISH POETS

From Romanticism to Surrealism

Seven Spanish Poets

ROBERT G. HAVARD

BARNES & NOBLE BOOKS
TOTOWA, NEW JERSEY

Published in Great Britain by
University of Wales Press, 1988

First published in the USA 1988 by
BARNES & NOBLE BOOKS
81 ADAMS DRIVE
TOTOWA, NEW JERSEY, 07512

Library of Congress Cataloging-in-Publication Data

Havard, Robert.
  From romanticism to surrealism: seven Spanish poets
by Robert G. Havard.
    p. cm.
  Bibliography: p.
  Includes index.
  ISBN 0-389-20810-8
1. Spanish poetry—20th century—History and criticism.
2. Spanish poetry—19th century—History and criticism.
3. Romanticism—Spain.
4. Surrealism (Literature)—Spain.
I. Title.
PQ6187.H38 1988   88-23244
861'.62'09—dc19   CIP

Typeset and printed in Great Britain
at The Bath Press, Avon

TO DORRIT

Contents

Preface

Few countries can rival Spain for poets, especially in the post-Romantic era when Spanish poets of genuine stature have appeared with increasing frequency. This book looks at seven of them, six poets and one poetess, and its twofold purpose is to introduce the non-specialist English reader to them and provide the Hispanist with an in-depth study of each. To this end a consistent pattern is followed: each chapter begins by focusing on one key poem by the poet in question and then opens out into a broader discussion of his or her work, the guiding principle being that to know one poem well makes the rest more accessible. Also, since I accept Pedro Salinas's view that all great poets have a 'tema vital', a vital or binding theme, the initial discussion of a single poem frames the issue to be developed in each case. Each chapter thus has a definite point of view and argument to state, but, I trust, by virtue of the centrality of the issue taken up, avoids being blinkered. A constant concern is the relationship between a poet's vital theme and his way of expressing it, for this, I believe, is where we find his poetics. Here 'poetics' is not intended in the restricted sense of rules which govern composition but refers more conceptually to that point of intersection between a poet's view of reality and his view of language. The justification for this is found in the modern poet's heightened consciousness of and esteem for the medium in which he works: not just a vehicle for thought, poetry, in our agnostic age, has come to be regarded as an interpretative tool, even a revelatory medium, and it is in the practice of poetry that the poet seeks to discover meaning and the self. This discovery is pursued, broadly speaking, with either an intellectual or an emotional bias, and, not surprisingly, all these poets of the era from Romanticism to Surrealism can be profoundly metaphysical or else intensely subjective. Thus, analysis of the poets considered here is frequently informed by reference to contemporary thought and psychoanalytical theory, two contexts in which the poets might be compared with their European counterparts. The first two poets represent Romanticism, albeit belatedly, the last two Surrealism, in their case progressively, while the three in the middle are less securely labelled by such tags as 'modernist'—in the case of Machado—and 'pure' poets, Guillén and Salinas. But though this book traces the evolution of Spanish poetry since about the middle of the nineteenth century, and indeed goes as far as to argue a spiritual connection between Romanticism, Surrealism and what these two movements enclose, it is in the end much more a book about poets than literary movements. The ones selected are in my opinion the seven best Spanish poets of the era, though the choice is purely personal and omissions are not hard to find. What was originally conceived as a book on ten poets shrank to its present size when I thought it wiser to confine myself to those poets who said most to me and about whom I felt I had something new to say.

I wish to express my gratitude to the British Academy for two grants which allowed me to visit Madrid and Galicia in connection with the writing of certain parts of the book, also to Mr John Rhys, Director of the University of Wales Press, for his helpful advice, and Mrs Margaret Parry, a most diligent secretary.

I

Gustavo Adolfo Bécquer

The Transcendental Poetics of Romanticism

> Los invisibles átomos del aire
> en derredor palpitan y se inflaman;
> el cielo se deshace en rayos de oro;
> la tierra se estremece alborozada.
> Oigo flotando en olas de armonía
> rumor de besos y batir de alas;
> mis párpados se cierran . . . ¿Qué sucede?
> ¿Dime? . . . ¡Silencio! . . . ¡Es el amor que pasa!¹
>
> (The invisible atoms of the air
> pulsate all around and burst into flame;
> the sky dissolves in golden beams;
> the earth trembles overcome with joy.
> I hear floating on waves of harmony
> a sound of kisses and a beating of wings;
> my eyelids close . . . What is happening,
> Will you tell me? . . . Silence! . . . It is love passing!)

Modern Spanish poetry, by common consent, begins with Gustavo Adolfo Bécquer (1836–70), the author of one slim collection of verse, *Rimas* (*Rhymes*), published posthumously in 1871. But modern as he undoubtedly is, especially in terms of technique, Bécquer is also a poet of exquisite sensitivity whose temperament is at core Romantic, this being immediately recognizable in the above poem where he converts the physical atoms of the cosmos into an imaginative and emotional register while, in the last line, he assumes the role of poet-seer for humanity. Exalting the imagination and the extra-sensory faculties of perception, Bécquer also brings a new dimension to the Romantic tradition by focusing attention on the intrinsic powers of poetry and by making poetry very often the subject of his poem. His unprecedented ambition was to make the language of his poem one and the same substance as the ethereal realms of the imagination, which is to say, he wished to capture in words nothing less than the ineffable spirit of poetry, 'Espíritu sin nombre, / indefinible esencia' (p. 444) ('Nameless spirit, indefinable essence'), as his fifth *rima* begins. Not even San Juan de la Cruz, the sixteenth-century mystic, had aspired to such poetic spirituality, for the saint disclaimed control over the poems he wrote—or which were written through him—while Bécquer, a modern secular visionary struggles openly and tormentedly with what in his first *rima* he calls 'el rebelde, mezquino idïoma' (p. 439) ('the rebellious, mean language'). His earnest spirituality is indicative of his Romantic pedigree, while his reflexivity or acute consciousness of the medium in which he works gives him the stamp of a modern poet. Not until Bécquer had poetry been the subject of poetry, at least not so conspicuously and at least not in Spain. Never before had poetry—in this sense, poetic feeling—been treated with the religious awe and fervour that we find in the first handful of the eighty or so pieces that compose the *Rimas*. In the tenth *rima*, quoted above, poetry is still very much the subject as the poet closes his eyes and rapturously senses the cosmic spirit of love, which is to say, for Bécquer, feeling, inspiration, poetry.

This *rima* is a fine example of the way Bécquer's pure, unadorned language leads us into what can only be called a transcendental experience. In his revealing prose commentary, *Cartas literarias a una mujer* (*Literary Letters to a Lady*), there is a passage which Bécquer seems to have written with the same experience in mind:

> Sin embargo, yo procuraré apuntar, como de pasada, algunas de las mil ideas que me agitaron durante aquel sueño magnífico, en que vi al amor, envolviendo a la Humanidad como en un flúido de fuego, pasar de un siglo en otro, sosteniendo la incomprensible atracción de los espíritus, atracción semejante a la de los astros, y revelándose al mundo exterior por medio de la poesía, único idioma que acierta balbucear algunas de las frases de su inmenso poema.   (p. 671)

> (Nevertheless, I will try to set down, in passing, some of the thousand ideas that stirred me during that magnificent dream, in which I saw love, enveloping Humanity as in a fiery fluid, moving from one century to the next, sustaining the incomprehensible attraction of spirits, an attraction like that of the stars, and revealing itself to the exterior world

through poetry, the only language which manages to babble some of the lines of its immense poem.)

Not only is love described as an 'immense poem', but, Bécquer argues, it is something which can only be made intelligible to us in the material world through poetry. Poetry is thus both transcendence and that which communicates transcendence; the way and the goal, in true mystic fashion, have become one. The same equation is explicit a few pages later in the *Cartas* when a third element is introduced:

> El amor es poesía; la religión es amor. Dos cosas semejantes a una tercera son iguales entre sí ... La religión es amor, y porque es amor es poesía.   (p. 678)

> (Love is poetry; religion is love. When two things are like a third they are themselves alike ... Religion is love, and because it is love it is poetry.)

Here we have the key connection that Béquer's poetry makes: *poetry = love = religion*, which essentially is a connection between poetic reflexivity and transcendentalism. It is true that the transcendence of poetry lies strictly in poetic *feeling* and that the power to communicate transcendence is a less certain attribute of poetic *language*, but let us overlook the small print for the moment and recognize the large theme, namely, the transcendental nature of poetry. This is the pivotal issue which links Bécquer to the poets who followed him and to the Romantics who preceded him: on the one hand, the Romantic tradition of transcendentalism, which Bécquer continues; on the other, modern reflexivity, which he begins. All the other poets discussed in this book share Bécquer's acute awareness of his medium, and, with it, his vocational urge as a poet to discover himself—his own Self—within that medium, his will to unearth meaning by virtue of his activity as a poet. In short, Bécquer's significance lies in his redirecting the transcendental impulse of Romanticism towards the medium of poetry itself, a theme which the present chapter will examine.

But let us first assert that poetry's concern with transcendence and the Self is very much a product of Romanticism. The new trajectory poetry was taking in the nineteenth century had been noted in England by Matthew Arnold, who, having the example of Wordsworth much in mind, spoke of 'the high destinies of poetry' and forecast that 'most of what now passes with us for religion and philosophy will be replaced by poetry'.[2] The reason for this was to be found in the decline of formal religion, which Arnold lamented, and in the consequent need of individuals to discover an alternative meaning to life, which, Arnold felt sure, could only be done in the meditative medium of poetry. Arnold was observing a phenomenon that had begun with the Romantics and, at his time of writing, shortly after Bécquer's death, was still gathering momentum throughout Europe. All the poets discussed here, though they come from Catholic Spain, confirm his thesis: from Rosalía de Castro, with her uneasy faith, to the agnostic Guillén and the atheistic Alberti, the central issue is a quest for meaning in relation to the Self, whether this is metaphysically or psychoanalytically adumbrated. Even in the most orthodox figure, Antonio Machado, religion plays second fiddle to metaphysics, while in Bécquer, as the above poem already shows, the transcendental force pervading the cosmos has more to do with poetry than with God. For Bécquer, 'La religión es ... poesía' ('Religion is ... poetry'), and when he concludes his eighth *rima* '¡ ... yo llevo algo / divino aquí dentro!' (p. 449) ('I bear something / divine here within!'), he refers to the gift of poetry not of faith. Indeed, his first *rima* opens with a stanza which shows just how much poetry has usurped the place of religion and how completely religious zeal is subsumed in this alternative transcendentalism:

> Yo sé un himno gigante y extraño
> que anuncia en la noche del alma una aurora,
> y estas páginas son de ese himno,
> cadencias que el aire dilata en sombras.   (p. 439)

> (I know a hymn, gigantic and strange,
> that announces a dawn in the soul's night,
> and these pages are of that hymn,
> cadences that the air dilates in shadows.)

As an evangelist of poetry Bécquer was to win many disciples, but, while the message he brought was new, what we need to recognize is that the ground had been well prepared by earlier writers of lofty aspiration, even if they were, in the main, prophets of doom. Thus, to understand Bécquer's emergence on the Spanish scene as a poet-visionary, to appreciate how it was that twentieth-century Spain should have so completely fulfilled what Arnold called 'the high destinies of poetry', it is necessary to look back for a moment at Romanticism proper where the seeds of agnostic transcendentalism and a concomitant quest for the Self were sown. In looking back we shall need to keep in mind the point which all commentators on Romanticism assert, namely that Romanticism is the watershed in the history of man's spiritual and intellectual development, there having occurred at the end of the eighteenth century a definite change in the climate of ideas, a certain metaphysical crisis which involved, to quote the hispanist D. L. Shaw, 'the apparent collapse of previously established values, whether these rested on religion or Rationalism'.[3] Rationalism's mechanistic universe, its view of nature as a well-regulated clock that would tell the time whether man were present or not, was no longer sufficient. There was dissatisfaction too with the watchmaker God, even in Spain, and a need for something more intimate, more relevant to the individual soul. The individual and his soul, this is the crux, and from it stems the cult of the imagination, of the mysterious, the irrational and what we now call the unconscious. This is precisely the emphasis of Bécquer's tenth *rima*, quoted above, with its magical landscape of irridescent shafts of light that change as quickly as human feelings. But let us remember too that the movement away from reason, from machine to man, from sense to sensibility, from data to dream, was a reaction against the old order, a revolt against the forces of spiritual oppression. And with what ecstasy Bécquer embraces the liberation of the spiritual self, looking inwards to make sense of what lies outside:

> mis párpados se cierran ... ¿Qué sucede?
> ¿Dime? ... ¡Silencio! ... ¡Es el amor que pasa! (p. 449)

> (my eyelids close ... What is happening?
> Will you tell me? ... Silence! ... It is love passing!)

For many commentators the revolt is still going on and the Romantic aesthetic prevails today. We shall be better able to judge if this is the case in Spain and better able to understand Bécquer's transcendental poetics if we cast an eye first at some of his more significant predecessors in Romantic Spain.

Though Romanticism is often considered to have been a relative failure in Spain—a failure usually attributed to a conservative, 'churchy' country's resistance to new ideas, or else to men of letters having been distracted by the Peninsular War and the ensuing oppressive regime or Ferdinand VII—there are nevertheless several major Spanish figures who express the genuine ethos of this European-wide movement. They do not necessarily belong to the period after 1833, a date which marks the death of Ferdinand and, with the return of the liberal exiles, Romanticism's official opening. One can go back as far as José de Cadalso, who died in 1782, and find an incipient Romanticism in his *Noches lúgubres* (*Lugubrious Nights*), a work whose subtitle acknowledges Edward Young's *Night Thoughts* as its inspiration and whose topic is that of a crazed lover who disinters the body of his dead mistress, evidence enough of Cadalso's religious disquiet and of his protagonist's impatient, near suicidal melancholy. This graveyard theme will echo through the nineteenth century down to Bécquer, notably in *rimas* 70 and 73. The latter has the famous refrain:

> ¡Dios mío, qué solos
> se quedan los muertos!   (p. 486)
>
> (My God, how lonely
> lie the dead!)

and a desperate, near agnostic, last stanza which begins:

> ¿Vuelve el polvo al polvo?
> ¿Vuela el alma al cielo?
> ¿Todo es vil materia,
> podredumbre y cieno?
> ¡No sé; pero ... (!)   (p. 488)
>
> (Does dust return to dust?
> Does the soul fly up to heaven?
> Is everything base matter,
> putrefaction and slime?
> I know not; but ... (!))

However, interesting as such parallels are, my purpose is not to provide an exhaustive account of the influence of Romanticism on Bécquer, far less to discuss the movement as a whole, but only to trace the emergence in the Romantic era of what we have called agnostic transcendentalism. To this end we can dispense with the bulk of those who appeared between Cadalso and the tragic Mariano José de Larra—a writer who did in fact commit suicide—and turn our attention to three seminal figures, two poets and a painter: Meléndez Valdés, Goya and Espronceda. In looking at the first two of these we disregard the 1833 demarcation and that simplistic view of Spanish Romanticism as a nicely packaged import from abroad, a kind of express delivery that followed the lifting of tariffs. What really matters is that these three figures pin-point crucial phases in the transition from rational neo-classical thinking to the rebellious and even ungodly values of Romanticism.

The first, Meléndez Valdés, was for the most part a poet of bucolic and anacreontic odes, a man of neo-classical training who had imbibed the theory of 'The Great Chain of Being' as expressed in Pope's *Essay on Man*.[4] Yet Meléndez had heard Cadalso read his *Noches lúgubres* to him as a student in Salamanca, and in 1794, having left his Chair of Classics and entered the less tranquil arena of law and politics, Meléndez sent a new kind of poem to his mentor Jovellanos which he entitled 'A Jovino: el melancólico' ('To Jovino: The Melancholy'). It contained the lines:

> Sí amigo, sí: mi espíritu insensible
> del vivaz gozo a la impresión süave,
> todo lo anubla en su tristeza oscura,
> materia en todo a más dolor hallando
> y a este fastidio universal que encuentra
> en todo el corazón perenne causa.[5]

> (Yes, friend, it is true: my spirit, insensible
> to the seductive impression of vigorous joy,
> clouds everything in its dark sadness,
> for all matter prompts only more sorrow
> and this universal disaffection which my heart
> finds in all things as perennial cause.)

Meléndez's 'fastidio universal' ('universal disaffection') is indicative of an utter pessimism, a spiritual malaise, anguish, *Angst* or *angustia*, which is born of a metaphysical crisis and which, remarkably, is unalleviated by faith. In such a poem it is no longer a question of the mind recording its perceptions of nature, as the anacreontic Meléndez had done in accordance with Locke's sensualist theory; rather, the poet's own emotional disposition takes absolute precedence and determines the value of sensations and the way they are experienced.

On one occasion the traumatic change which took place in Meléndez is telescoped into a single poem, 'La tarde' ('The Evening'), from the 1797 edition of his poems. A simply conceived poem, its subject being the darkening contours of a landscape as it moves into dusk and night, 'La tarde' is also the most revealing poem of its time, for, effectively, in this particular nightfall we move from the eighteenth into the nineteenth century. It opens with some thirty lines of picturesque and vapid images which fully illustrate why neo-classical poetry is so little read today. The first four lines will suffice to provide the flavour:

> Ya el Héspero delicioso
> entre nubes agradables,
> cual precursor de la noche,
> por el occidente sale . . .[6]
>
> (Now delicious Hesperus,
> like the night's precursor,
> amidst pleasant clouds
> appears in the west . . .)

Despite occasionally showing Meléndez's eye for detail, the poem continues in this decorative vein, predictable in its diction and sentimental in its images of peasant homes with smoking chimneys and homeward-plodding animals after Gray. This is, in short, a kind of poetry which the practised Meléndez could almost have written in his sleep, and the effect is equally soporific. All of which is strictly in keeping with the secure world of neo-classicism and its methodized, tidy-garden nature, as is the tranquil philosophical conclusion to which we are painstakingly led:

> Todo es paz, silencio todo,
> todo en estas soledades
> me conmueve . . .
> El verde oscuro del prado,
> la niebla que en ondas se abre
> . . . me enajenan y me olvidan
> de las odiosas ciudades . . .
>
> (All is peace, all quiet,
> and everything in these solitudes
> moves my heart . . .
> The dark green of the meadow
> the mist that opens in waves
> . . . transport me away forgetful
> of the hateful cities . . .)

Had the poem ended here it would have been utterly unremarkable, but, with happy inconsistency, Meléndez changes to a new mood that shatters his smug Horatian calm. First, he takes up Rousseau's theme, 'Liberal naturaleza' ('Plentiful nature'), and this sense of nature's abundance—which prompted an unlikely but apt comparison with the modern vitalist Jorge Guillén[7]—is the first step in an extraordinary change of mood which turns from observation to participation and from objective distance to the immediacy of spontaneous physical contact with a landscape now dramatically foreshortened at nightfall. As though reacting against his erstwhile complacency, Meléndez suddenly surrenders control to the unpredictable forces of nature:

> Yo me abandono a su impulso:
> dudosos los pies no saben
> do se vuelven, do caminan,
> do se apresuran, do paren.

> (I abandon myself to its impulse:
> uncertain my feet know not
> where they turn, where they tread,
> where they hurry, or where they will stop.)

The lines that follow are Meléndez's freshest and deserve ample quotation. They vividly recall moments from Wordsworth, notably *The Prelude*, as the poet, struck by a sense of awe and presence in nature, becomes a fugitive amid the ominous shapes of his landscape:

> Cruzo la tendida vega
> con inquietud anhelante,
> por si en la fatiga logro
> que mi espíritu se calme.
> Mis pasos se precipitan;
> mas nada en mi alivio vale,
> que aun gigantescas las sombras
> me siguen para aterrarle.
> Trepo, huyéndolas, la cima,
> y al ver sus riscos salvajes,
> '¡Ay!', exclamo, '¡quien cual ellos
> insensible se tornase!'
> Bajo del collado al río,
> y entre sus lóbregas calles
> de altos árboles el pecho
> más pavoroso me late.
> Miro las tajadas rocas
> que amenazan desplomarse
> sobre mí, tornar oscuros
> sus cristalinos raudales.
> Llénanme de horror sus sombras,
> y el ronco fragoso embate
> de las aguas más profundo
> hace este horror y más grave.

(I cross the outstretched plain
with breathless anxiety,
to see if by tiring myself
I manage to calm my soul.
My steps rush on;
but no respite comes,
for the gigantic shadows still
pursue and terrify me.
I climb the crest in flight,
and, on seeing its wild crags,
'Alas!', I exclaim, 'If only I
could turn as insensible as they!'
I go down from the height to the river,
and amidst its dark alleys
of towering trees my heart
beats more fearfully.
I see the sheer-cut rocks,
which threaten to tumble down
on me, turn their crystalline
torrents to dark.
Their shadows fill me with horror,
and the raucous thunder
of the dashing waters deepens
my horror and makes it more grave.)

This fine sequence has the ring of real rather than bookish experience. The edifice of reason and restraint has collapsed in the mysterious, terrifying darkness and a new poem has emerged of quite different tension, a tension much helped by the forceful enjambments in the tight *romance* or ballad form. Amongst Meléndez's contemporaries only Jovellanos, in 'Fabio a Anfriso' ('Fabio to Anfriso'), came close to attaining such immediacy; but Jovellanos's poem is in the heavier hendecasyllable and lacks the pulse of Meléndez's ballad. The latter part of 'La tarde' fully justifies McAndrew's praise of Meléndez's nature poetry as 'the golden milestone' on the road to 'individualism' in Spanish poetry.[8] By the poem's end, with the picturesque details of the early verses now scarcely remembered, we sense that the poet, through the real experience of fear, has almost unwittingly discovered his true self in the dark. It may be excessive to say that it is the dark of his unconscious which he finds, but we can at least recognize that his anxiety has an inner as well as an outer source: 'Así azorado y medroso / al cielo empiezo a quejarme / de mis amargas desdichas ...' ('Thus alarmed and fearful / I begin protesting to heaven / at my bitter wretchedness ...'). Meléndez avoids the temptation to moralize a second time, nor could he have, logically, for, as he runs from crags to tree-trunks and beating water, his anguished cries and faltering steps in the dark are a perfect emblem of his confusion and of man's uncertain entry into the nineteenth century.

If Meléndez was two poets in one, Goya, more emphatically, was two artists. He too lived through the Napoleonic catastrophe and was likewise hounded out of Spain for his liberalism to die in Bordeaux in 1828. But the change in Goya had come long before, in 1792 to be precise, a year in which he suffered a mysterious illness and perhaps a mental breakdown which left him deaf, pessimistic and reclusive. Possibly his new mood owed something to the excesses of the French Revolution and to the humiliating turn Spanish affairs had taken under the detested Godoy, Queen María Luisa's ambitious young lover. But in any event, one thing is plain: the seductive colours and round forms of the rococo artist who had painted such canvases as *The Sunshade* and *The Meadow of San Isidro* in the 1770s and 80s gave way to the sombre configurations of a man now less interested in harmony than in truth. It was a painful truth that Goya expressed in the disturbing and often nightmarish images of successive series of drawings, *Los caprichos* (*The Caprices* or *Fantasies*), *Los desastres de la guerra* (*The Disasters of War*), *Disparates* (*Absurdities*), and finally the *Pinturas negras* (*Black Paintings*), gruesome works which lined the walls of his country house, the Quinta del Sordo (Deaf Man's Estate), outside Madrid. While the rococo canvases of idyllic country scenes were neo-classical in conception, and, as Edith Helman suggests, probably inspired in some cases by specific poems of Meléndez in anacreontic mode,[9] the new Goya of the 1790s shows much the same inner terror as the man who shouted in the dark at heaven in 'La tarde'. Goya would still paint to commission, it is true, and many portraits of royalty and friends—including Jovellanos and Meléndez—were still to come. But now there were the private works too, increasingly so after 1800,[10] and in these, as Goya explained in a letter accompanying a batch of them to the Academy in 1794, he could 'hacer observaciones a que regularmente no dan lugar las obras encargadas, y en que el capricho y la invención no tienen ensanches'[11] ('make observations which it is normally not possible to make in commissioned pictures which leave no scope for fantasy and invention').

Fantasy and invention, not neo-classicism's reason and imitation, these are the values which characterize the new works which came more from an inner need than a need for artistic acclaim. Goya was well aware of the kind of world he was entering by giving vent to fantasy, as is indicated by the famous caption to *capricho* 43,

'El sueño de la razón produce monstruos' ('The sleep of reason produces monsters'). In this etching, originally intended as frontispiece to the whole series, the hideous bats and owls that fly above a tormented sleeping artist fully reflect Goya's stated intention to 'exponer a los ojos formas y actitudes que sólo han existido hasta ahora en la mente humana'[12] ('make visible forms and attitudes which hitherto have only existed in the human mind'). Goya was breaking new ground. This is true even if we allow for the influence of Hieronymus Bosch, the fifteenth-century Flemish painter known as 'El Bosco' in Spain, many of whose best works were in the royal collection and familiar to Goya in his capacity as Painter to the Royal Chamber. Quite simply, Bosch had painted visions of hell while Goya was now depicting a hell on earth. As in Bosch, however, Goya's cat-faced lawyers, donkey-headed statesmen (which refer no doubt to Godoy),[13] decrepit hags, lascivious prostitutes and the increasingly distorted human limbs of the *Caprichos* all show how the Spaniard's disillusionment found release in fantasy. His despair deepened with the terrible events of 1808–14 which prompted *Los desastres de la guerra*. Rape, hanging, garrotting, impalement, famine, mutilation, castration: these are the topics treated in plates which depict face after emaciated face and pile upon pile of butchered corpses in what is the most harrowing account of the effects of war. Though the source is again specific, a universal dimension is apparent in the plates' captions, for instance: 'Nothing, that's what it is' (no. 69), where the word 'Nada' ('Nothing') is scratched on a sepulchral slab by a half-buried man; 'They do not know the way' (no. 70), the comment on a group of disoriented human beings tied pathetically together by a rope; 'And nothing can be done' (no. 15), the caption to a mass execution; 'Sad forebodings of what is to come' (no. 69 and frontispiece), which refers to a haggard man on his knees looking upwards in despairing supplication at a black, godless sky. This is no mere war reportage. Far less is it to be dismissed as anti-French propaganda; in many plates Spaniards inflict worse atrocities on fellow Spaniards than do the French soldiers. Nor is it even a question of war bringing out the worst in man. Rather, we sense that for Goya the horrors of war epitomize man's elemental nature and render transparent something which is always there.

The *Disparates*[14] and *Pinturas negras* take us further into Goya's hellish world. The twenty-two dreamlike etchings of the former are often more facially grotesque than the *Caprichos* and more senselessly cruel than the *Desastres*. Sexual imagery continues: a man carries off a woman on a winged monster; a stallion raises a woman from the ground by its teeth; a struggling couple are tortuously joined together at the shoulders in tragic bondage. But the most disturbing and universal theme is found in the plates that show huddles of people against a dark, empty sky. One such plate has a group sitting on an enormous dead branch with a vast horizon-less void all around them. The same sense of limbo and mute terror dominates the *Pinturas negras* where blackness of space is the overriding theme. This terrible darkness is painted with a frenetic brush, suggesting the artist's urgency, his neurosis even. The menace in *The Witches' Sabbath*, the repulsiveness of *Two Old People Eating Soup*, the insane ferocity of two men fighting in quicksand in *Duel with Cudgels*, the hysteria in the series of massed, grimacing and syphilitic faces, all this is set against an incomprehensible and uncomprehending spatial void which is ultimately more unnerving than the figures themselves. There is no source of light in these pictures. Even in the daylight scene of *The Dog*, where the dumb head of a dog looks forlornly into a sky that fills three parts of the canvas, the source of light is undifferentiated. All we have is the void, usually a solid mass of darkness, and it is this which gives real if irrational context to the depravity, the panic and the despair. In two famous paintings, *The Collossus* and *Saturn Devouring One of His Children*, the sky is filled with a destructive giant. Again there is no hope of redemption and no sympathy. The ogre gods seem only to mirror man's baseness, the might of the colossus suggesting his lust for power and the cannibalism of Saturn his convulsive tendency to self-destruction. In the absence of reason and the absence of God, man's own demonic image is projected into the sky. Or else there is the void.

No doubt there was a cathartic element in the *Pinturas negras* which served to release anxieties and tensions in Goya, much as the spiteful, bilious imagery of Lorca and Alberti would serve them therapeutically in Surrealist works we shall meet at the end of this book. The therapy would seem to have been successful, for Goya went on to produce serene works in his French exile. But he was over eighty when he painted *The Milkmaid of Bordeaux* and perhaps, after his repeated illnesses, simply glad to be alive. For young Spaniards of the day like Larra and Espronceda there was less hope of serenity. Larra, whom we only mention in passing, was in fact best known as a journalist. His most moving article, 'El día de difuntos de 1836' ('All Soul's Day, 1836'), which describes the ritual exodus of Madrilenians on 2 November towards the outlying cemetery, is in its mood highly reminiscent of Goya's *The Pilgrimage of San Isidro*, one of the most macabre of the *Pinturas negras*. Larra's theme, that the existing citizens are themselves already dead and that the city they leave behind is in fact the 'horrible cementerio' ('horrible cemetery'), continues the necrophobic despair Cadalso and Goya showed in the face of the void. So does his conclusion, 'Mi corazón no es más que otro cementerio. ¿Qué dice? Leamos ... "¡Aquí yace la esperanza!"'[15] ('My heart is but another sepulchre. What does it say? Let's read ... "Here lies hope!"'), which gives some measure of the mental torment that within three months would drive Larra at the age of twenty-nine to make the ultimate Romantic gesture of committing suicide.

But it is the poet José de Espronceda who crystallizes this desperate and rebellious anguish. Espronceda also died young, burnt out at thirty-four by a hectic life that had begun with an in-transit birth in Extremadura in 1808 when his parents were fleeing French-occupied Madrid for the safety of liberal Cadiz. This set the tone for a remarkably nomadic life which took him as a revolutionary-minded youth to Lisbon, London, Brussels and Paris during Ferdinand's 'ominous decade', 1823–33. These were years when Espronceda fought as well as wrote for the liberal cause, and when he also had a tempestuous affair with a certain Teresa Mancha whom he finally abducted from her husband and brought back briefly to live with him in Spain under the amnesty of 1834. Much taken with Byron's poetry and personality, Espronceda first wrote rapturously about freedom and then splenetically about erotic love, alcohol and debauchery in the mid-1830s. Then came his epic dramatic poem, *El estudiante de Salamanca* (*The Student of Salamanca*), which, like his unfinished *Diablo mundo* (*Hellish World*), integrates the themes of anguish and rebellion. In *El estudiante*, the nearest thing Spanish Romanticism proper has to a masterpiece, the decisive issue, as Pedro Salinas and Joaquín Casalduero have argued,[16] is the transcendental aspiration of its daring but world-weary protagonist.

A projection of Espronceda's personality, the student is described alternatively as a 'Segundo don Juan Tenorio' ('Second Don Juan Tenorio'), which recalls Tirso de Molina's Golden Age prototype, and a 'Segundo Lucifer' ('Second Lucifer'), which links him rather more meaningfully with the *Sturm und Drang* ethos of Goethe's *Faust*. Certainly the student is much more than a revival of the Golden Age hero, much more than a dueller and an abuser of women. When he sets out in the fourth and final part to pursue what he believes to be the figure of a woman, it is not merely another conquest he is after. The unseen woman has taken on symbolic values and his pursuit of her has come to signify a desperate human need to attain the unattainable, know the unknowable, a need born of his chronic dissatisfaction with the human lot. Warned by his quarry that to continue his pursuit would be an offence against God, the student goes on regardless, accepting this ultimate challenge and receiving in the process Espronceda's highest praise and some of his best lines:

> Grandïosa, satánica figura,
> alta la frente, Montemar camina,
> espíritu sublime en su locura,
> provocando la cólera divina:
> fábrica frágil de materia impura,
> el alma que la alienta y la ilumina,
> con Dios le iguala, y con osado vuelo
> se alza a su trono y le provoca a duelo.

> Segundo Lucifer que se levanta
> del rayo vengador la frente herida,
> alma rebelde que el temor no espanta,
> hollada sí, pero jamás vencida:
> el hombre que en fin en su ansiedad quebranta
> su límite a la cárcel de la vida,
> y a Dios llama ante él a darle cuenta,
> y descubrir su inmensidad intenta.[17]

> (Illustrious, satanic figure,
> with head held high, Montemar presses on,
> sublime spirit in his madness,
> provoking the wrath of the divine:
> fragile fabric of impure matter,
> the soul which infuses and enlightens him
> makes him God's equal, and in audacious flight
> ascends to his throne and challenges him to duel.

> Second Lucifer, lifting up
> his wounded brow from the vengeful beam,
> rebellious soul whom fear does not alarm,
> humiliated he may be, but never vanquished:
> a man who out of desperation finally breaks
> the confines of life's prison
> and calls God to account before him,
> striving thus to uncover his greatness.)

Mad, despairing, yet unbowed, Montemar incarnates the tortured spirit of Romanticism. His madness rails against the eighteenth-century totem of Reason which demanded moderation and compliance in all things, just as Espronceda as a poet flouts all the old rules for harmony and decorum in a work that is vertiginously unbalanced, unchronological, polymetric and hybrid in genre. Montemar is mad like Don Quixote because he wants more from life. But he is mad too in the modern sense of being neurotic, his neurosis coming from the uncertainty, unfulfilment and unutterable longing which constitutes his existential condition. His madness is ultimately *sublime*, for he seeks to transcend the limitations of this world and break out of 'la cárcel de la vida' ('life's prison'), a recurring image which for Victor Brombert lies at the heart of all modern sensibility since the Romantics.[18] The key that opens the prison door, says Espronceda, is held by God alone, and this, paradoxically, makes God man's gaoler, religion his fetters. Inevitably, then, Espronceda confronts his gaoler head on, and with inevitable consequences. Bécquer, as we shall see, in the second wave of Romanticism, adopts more subtle ploys to get out of what is essentially the same prison. His master stroke was the equation, *religion = love = poetry*, for it allowed the key of freedom to pass from the first to the last of these three elements, something the poet could struggle with on rather more equal terms.

The three figures we have considered under the heading of Romanticism illustrate an increasing spiritual disquiet and frustration. From the timorous Meléndez, shouting at heaven in the unnerving dark, to the sorely troubled Goya who depicts man's baseness against an empty backdrop which calls the role and even existence of God into question, finally to the radical Espronceda, where the worm turns as man asserts himself against God, there is a growing sense of dissatisfaction with the old order and a craving need for new answers. The dissatisfaction is clearest in Goya, while Espronceda is clearest on the theme of man's indomitable will to transcend, with or without God. Ultimately, however, Espronceda's transcendental aspiration is just that, an aspiration, and it provides no real answers. This is partly because man's projection of himself in the student is satanic, not unlike Goya's ogres, and this emphasizes frustration rather than positive transcendental values. It is also because of the sleight of hand at work in the poem, for the student is in fact already dead in the fourth part when he makes his challenge; consequently the only answer which the poem provides is the enigma of death itself, a veritable wall. All we can say about Espronceda's transcendentalism, apart from noting the terrible craving involved, is that in it the nature of ultimate reality is deemed in the end unknowable. Espronceda takes us beyond the natural and rational boundaries of this world only to arrive immediately at an impasse. His death-bound transcendentalism is stillborn.

It is Bécquer who leads us through the impasse, and he does so essentially by reasserting the primacy of the spiritual self. Bécquer takes us forward by first taking one step back, into the real world. He elevates man by stressing his spiritual faculty, above all as a poet. This new emphasis on spirituality is one trend of the mid-nineteenth century, bringing to mind for instance the Pre-Raphaelite movement in England, notably Christina Rossetti. At the same time the emphasis on poetry, and the attribution of potentially transcendental powers to the medium, is another feature of the age that we find in a very different poet like Baudelaire. However, the decisive linking of spirituality and poetic reflexivity is perhaps most apparent in a contemporary German poet with whom Bécquer is always associated, Heinrich Heine, fifteen of whose poems appeared in Spanish translation in 1857.[19] Noteworthy in Heine is that his concern for the higher reality of dream and imagination never entails dissociation from the real world; indeed Heine, rejecting Romanticism's tendency towards dissociation, compared the poet to the classical giant Antaeus, 'strong and mighty so long as he stands on real ground'.[20] This attachment to the real while simultaneously seeking out dream is shared by Bécquer, as the tenth *rima* quoted at the beginning of this chapter fully illustrates. Like Heine, Bécquer projects man as a supersensible medium and subject of spirituality. At the same time he brings spirituality down to earth by equating it with poetic feeling. Thus the fifth *rima*, which begins 'Espíritu sin nombre, / indefinible esencia' ('Nameless spirit, / indefinable essence'), and in which the speaking voice is the voice of poetry itself, concludes with the important assimilation:

> Yo soy el invisible
> anillo que sujeta
> el mundo de la forma
> al mundo de la idea.

> Yo, en fin, soy ese espíritu,
> desconocida esencia,
> perfume misterioso
> de que es vaso el poeta.   (p. 447)

(I am the invisible
ring which binds
the world of form
to the world of idea.

I am, finally, that spirit,
unknown essence,
mysterious perfume
for which the poet is a vessel.)

In making poetry the key link between the material and non-material
worlds, Bécquer transfers the issue of transcendentalism from the
problematic relationship God-man to the not unproblematic question
of how the spiritual essence of poetry can be contained within the
material poem. In so doing he also transfers the frustration which
was once vented against God to the frustration the poet experiences
with his medium, language. This is a decisive moment in the development of what we have called agnostic transcendentalism, which is
simply intended to convey the idea of a committed search for a deeper
reality by some means other than orthodox religion. Let us now
see the form it takes in Bécquer.

The first *rima*, as we have already glimpsed, proclaims poetry as
'un himno gigante y extraño' ('a hymn, gigantic and strange') which
has the power to lead man out of his darkness, 'que anuncia en
la noche del alma una aurora' ('that announces a dawn in the night's
soul'), a darkness which, in historical terms, is nothing other than
the prison and catacombs of Romanticism. But after this trumpeting
start Bécquer continues in the poem's two remaining stanzas to spe-
cify with amazing precision the practical possibilities of writing such
poetry, and he becomes increasingly pessimistic:

Yo quisiera escribirlo, del hombre
domando el rebelde, mezquino idïoma,
con palabras que fuesen a un tiempo
suspiros y risas, colores y notas.

Pero en vano es luchar; que no hay cifra
capaz de encerrarlo, y apenas, ¡oh hermosa!,
si teniendo en mis manos las tuyas,
pudiera al oído contártelo a solas.   (p. 439)

(I should like to write it, controlling
the rebellious, mean language of man,
with words that were at once
sighs and laughter, colours and notes.

But it is useless to struggle; for no cipher
can contain it, and scarcely, my beauty,
even holding your hands in mine,
could I whisper it in your ear when alone.)

Several points may be isolated in this extremely dense poetic manifesto. To begin with we note the verb 'quisiera' ('I should like'), where the subjunctive mood in Spanish already anticipates the unlikelihood of the wish being fulfilled. The reasons for such pessimism are then given: language is 'rebelde' ('rebellious'), never saying quite what the poet wants it to say; it is also 'mezquino' ('mean'), not having the resources to say what he wants it to say; finally, it is 'del hombre' ('of man'), which implies that it is too worldly or practical for spiritual matters and also perhaps—anticipating Bergson— that its reference is generic rather than individual, spirituality of course being very much centred on the individual. Bécquer commits himself to the idealistic poetic programme of controlling or taming— 'domando'—language. And the ideal language he envisages is one which has extraordinary elasticity, 'palabras que fuesen a un tiempo / suspiros y risas, colores y notas' ('words that were at once / sighs and laughter, colours and notes'). This partly recalls Baudelaire's theory of *correspondences* and the concept of synaesthesia, but also, if we allow full force to the words 'a un tiempo' ('at once'), it again anticipates Bergson's stress on simultaneity, that is, the argument which holds that while human thoughts and emotions are simultaneous in occurrence language is by nature sequential and separative. These are points we shall return to shortly, but for the moment let us simply note that they lead to a conclusion of muted despair in the last stanza: there is really no possibility of finding a poetic register or 'cifra' ('cipher') that will convey spirituality or feeling, poetic feeling, for the latter is not at all linguistic or poematic. If feeling, Bécquer adds, is scarcely expressible in the physical-cum-linguistic intimacy of two lovers when alone, what chance has the poet with words on the page? Here the poem—a proem, in effect— ends on a note that prepares us for the consistent use of love throughout the *rimas* as a point of metaphorical reference for the transcendental nature of poetry.

The ideas stated with such terse precision in the proem are expanded upon in the *rimas* that immediately follow. Specifically, the second *rima* develops the notion of randomness and hence elusiveness, as we see in its first and last stanzas where again the speaking voice is the spirit of poetry:

> Saeta que voladora
> cruza arrojada al azar,
> sin adivinarse dónde
> temblando se clavará ...
>
> eso soy yo, que al acaso
> cruzo el mundo, sin pensar
> de dónde vengo, ni adónde
> mis pasos me llevarán.   (p. 440)
>
> (A flying arrow
> that speeds from an aimless shot,
> not knowing where
> tremulously it will thrust ...
>
> such am I, crossing the world
> at random, not thinking
> whence I come, nor whither
> my steps will lead.)

This radically new emphasis upon motility—which was to have a marked influence upon Pedro Salinas—is also apparent in the poem's three intervening stanzas which focus in turn on a falling leaf, a breaking wave and flickering light. Notable in this pattern of imagery is the cosmic and god-like dimension which is attributed to feeling, reminding us again of the tenth *rima*. But the most telling connection with the proem comes from the sense of tantalizing elusiveness which motion suggests. Developing this, the third *rima* then distinguishes between what comes to the poet by way of inspiration and by way of reason. Naturally the first of these is closer in kind to the random spirit of poetry, and in one stanza Bécquer evokes the delicate concept of a poem in a nascent mental state, that is, prior to the moment when the inspirational source is regulated by reason into linguistic form:

> ideas sin palabras,
> palabras sin sentido,
> cadencias que no tienen
> ni ritmo ni compás   (p. 441)
>
> (ideas without words,
> words without meaning,
> cadences that have
> neither rhythm nor measure)

This would seem an ideal state for language since it closely approximates the elasticity valued in the proem. But it is an incubescent, germinal phase in which, strictly, language is as yet unborn, unformed. Linguistic form, as the second half of the poem explains, will be chiselled out only when the poet brings his rational faculties to bear on the matter. And this, as we can imagine, is where the problems start. Indeed Bécquer concludes the *rima* by suggesting a fundamental incompatibility between *inspiration* and *reason*, an incompatibility which can only be resolved by 'el Genio' ('Genius'):

> Con ambas siempre en lucha
> y de ambas vencedor,
> tan sólo el Genio puede
> a un yugo atar las dos. (p. 443)

> (With both ever struggling
> and conqueror of both,
> only Genius can
> tie the two to one yoke.)

There is, in short, a world of difference between *la inspiración* and *la razón*, between the source material of poetry, feeling, and its end product, the poem. The metamorphosis involved in the making of a poem is almost total, being essentially one from motion to fixity: the multiple, random and simultaneous impulses of feeling, which are like pulsating atoms or electrons in the mind of a sentient being, have to submit to the rational appratus of language with all its grammatical, syntactical and lexical logic, a logic which is hard and fast like that of a graph or 'cifra' ('cipher'). This is what Jorge Guillén described as the 'Capital contradicción' ('capital contradiction') in Bécquer's poetry,[21] the contradiction between spirit and matter, feeling and form. But is there no way out of this in-built contradiction, no way in which language, poetic language, can be used and adapted so as to give at least an indication of what the poet felt in that pure inspirational stage? If Bécquer did not think so he would not have had such a high opinion of poetry and would not have dedicated himself so completely to the pursuit of that mystical muse he calls 'Genio' ('Genius'). We can at least say that the *Rimas* as a whole represent a bold undertaking which has this goal in mind. But if we are to understand the procedure Bécquer adopts in his undertaking we shall need to look very closely at his language, that is to say, his use of words. In what follows I shall consider Bécquer's use of words in two broad categories: words as individual units of meaning and words as groups in a syntactical flow of meaning. In the first of these categories interest focuses on the texture of Bécquer's vocabulary, its lexical patterns, and on the role of metaphor as a contribution to meaning. In the second category, which will be considered more fully, the issue is the extent to which Bécquer manages to adapt the sequential logic of language to his random, unstructured, inspirational source. In both these areas of his language we are fortunate that discussion has already been well advanced by two fine critical appraisals.

It was J. M. Aguirre who first isolated what we now recognize as a fundamental characteristic in Bécquer's diction, its evanescent quality.[22] No doubt this will have struck the present reader in several of the *rimas* already quoted, notably again in the tenth, but it is very clear in the magnificent fifteenth *rima* which begins:

> Cendal flotante de leve bruma,
> rizada cinta de blanca espuma,
>   rumor sonoro
>   de arpa de oro,
> beso del aura, onda de luz,
>   eso eres tú.
>
> Tú, sombra aérea, que cuantas veces
> voy a tocarte te desvaneces
> como la llama, como el sonido
> como la niebla, como el gemido
>   del lago azul.   (p. 453)
>
> (Floating gauze of light mist,
> curling ribbon of white foam,
>   sonorous murmur,
>   of a golden harp,
> kiss of breeze, wave of light,
>   such are you.
>
> You, airy shadow, who, whenever
> I seek to touch you, disappear
> like the flame, like the sound,
> like the haze, like the sigh
>   of the blue lake.)

Bécquer's diction is nothing if not systematic in evoking the elusive quality of the object of his quest, 'Tú' ('you'). Lightness and insubstantiality is suggested by virtually every noun—'Cendal' ('gauze'), 'bruma' ('mist'), 'cinta' ('ribbon'), 'espuma' ('surf'), 'rumor' ('murmur'), 'beso' ('kiss'), 'onda' ('wave'), 'sombra' ('shadow'), 'llama' ('flame'), 'sonido' ('sound'). 'niebla' ('haze') and 'gemido' ('sigh')— which, as phenomena, seem all to be on the point of disappearing.

The adjectives, which are plentiful, make the nouns they describe even more tenuous, especially 'flotante' ('floating'), 'leve' ('light'), 'rizada' ('curling') and 'aérea' ('airy'). This is also true of the adjectival nouns, 'beso del aura' ('kiss of breeze') and 'onda de luz' ('wave of light'), where potentially concrete nouns are de-substantialized by the nouns associated with them. Clear patterns emerge: almost all the objects introduced have a mobile quality; several are strictly non-visual and refer to liquid or semi-liquid objects of indeterminate form. In all, the two stanzas create an impression of lightness, motion and insubstantiality, which is to say, evanescence. The complete pictorial representation is reminiscent of a Turner seascape in which air, clouds and water seem to merge indistinguishably. This in turn is a very precise correlative for the elusiveness which Bécquer attributes to the essence of 'tú' ('you'), an elusiveness which is in keeping with the volume's theme of frustrated love but which above all invokes the spirit of poetry.

Similar observations can be made of the next two stanzas which form the second half of the poem. Here, in a pattern which exactly parallels the first two stanzas, Bécquer attempts to describe with equal commitment the essential quality of the 'yo' ('I'), that is, himself, the earnestly searching lover and poet:

> En mar sin playas, onda sonante;
> en el vacío, cometa errante;
> largo lamento
> del ronco viento,
> ansia perpetua de algo mejor,
> eso soy yo.

> ¡Yo, que a tus ojos, en mi agonía,
> los ojos vuelvo de noche y día;
> yo, que incansable corro y demente
> tras una sombra, tras la hija ardiente
> de una ilusión!   (p. 454)

> (In a shoreless sea, a crashing wave;
> in empty space, a wandering comet;
> long lament
> of the hoarse wind,
> perpetual longing for something better,
> such am I.

> I, who towards your eyes, in my agony,
> turn my eyes by night and day;
> I, who untiringly and demented run
> after a shadow, after the ardent daughter
> of an illusion!)

Again we note the systematic use of images that have no form or contour: 'Mar sin playas' ('shoreless sea'), 'vacío' ('empty space'), 'viento' ('wind') and 'sombra' ('shadow'). The first two mentioned depict a boundless area in which the poet-lover pursues his goal, lost, alone and hopelessly undirected. His 'agony' and 'demented' state of mind recall Espronceda, especially in its combination of anguish and vagueness: 'ansia perpetua de algo mejor' ('perpetual longing for something better'). This, like many other Bécquer poems and above all like his prose *leyenda* ('legend') entitled *El rayo de luna* (*The Moonbeam*), has essentially the same format as *El estudiante de Salamanca*, namely the pursuit of an unattainable goal symbolically represented by the female 'tú'. Though the latter seems to take on more personalized form in the last stanza with the image of 'ojos' ('eyes'), this soon dissolves into 'sombra' ('shadow') and 'ilusión' ('illusion') and we are left in little doubt that the 'hija ardiente' ('ardent daughter') for whom Bécquer searches is less a real person than the airy, intangible muse of poetry.

This fifteenth *rima*, in somewhat extreme form, typifies the work as a whole both in terms of its diction and in terms of the metaphorical use made of the love theme. As regards diction, there are admittedly more concrete poems to be found, but the texture of Bécquer's language is predominantly light and evanescent as J. M. Aguirre has shown by focusing on a clutch of his favourite nouns, most of which in fact appear in *rima* fifteen. This texture is to be found in almost all the early *rimas*, notably numbers 8, 9, 10 and 13, and in a great many of the later ones, for instance 52, 66 and 72. We can agree with Aguirre that the essential characteristic of Bécquer's diction is its extraordinary imprecision, the result of a highly selective process which concentrates on the attributes of formlessness and motion. The aim of this process, so admirably achieved, may be very simply described: it is to destabilize language. As distinct from the normal tendency of language, Bécquer's language seeks not to define, particularize or fix the object or concept described, but rather to expand on its vagueness by means of an accumulation of images which suggest its limitlessness and ultimate ineffability. The very same destabilizing intent is at work in the central metaphor and allegorical system of the *Rimas*, that is, in Bécquer's purposeful intermingling of the theme of love with the theme of poetry.

Quite simply, as we are told in the brief *rima* 21, the *amada* ('beloved') is poetry:

> "¿Qué es poesía?", dices mientras clavas
> en mi pupila tu pupila azul.

"¿Qué es poesía? ¿Y tú me lo preguntas?
  Poesía ... eres tú."   (p. 456)

('What is poetry?', you say as you pierce
  my pupil with your blue pupil.
'What is poetry? You ask me such a question?
  Why, poetry ... is you'.)

Similarly, *rima* 34 describes the *amada* in these terms:

Ríe, y su carcajada tiene notas
  del agua fugitiva;
llora, y es cada lágrima un poema
  de ternura infinita.   (p. 464)

(She laughs, and her laughter has the music
  of fleeing water;
she cries, and each tear is a poem
  of infinite tenderness.)

Simple as these poems are, they pose an almost unanswerable question: is woman or poetry their true subject? Is poetry used as metaphorical reference to endow the love theme with greater spirituality, or, vice versa, is woman primarily a metaphor of the muse, 'fuente eterna de poesía' ('eternal source of poetry'), as the above poem goes on to say? The question is unanswerable in that form because both alternatives apply simultaneously, and because they apply to varying degrees in different poems. Many poems, I suggest, would be extraordinarily trite if we did not accept that Bécquer intended both levels at once. This is true of *rimas* 17 and 23, and of the following *rima* 11:

"Yo soy ardiente, yo soy morena,
  yo soy el símbolo de la pasión;
de ansia de goces mi alma está llena.
  ¿A mí me buscas?" "No es a ti, no".

"Mi frente es pálida; mis trenzas, de oro;
  puedo brindarte dichas sin fin;
yo de ternura guardo un tesoro.
  ¿A mí me llamas?" "No; no es a ti".

"Yo soy un sueño, un imposible,
  vano fantasma de niebla y luz;
soy incorpórea, soy intangible;
  no puedo amarte." "¡Oh, ven; ven tú!".   (p. 450)

('I am fiery, I am dark,
  I am the symbol of passion;
a longing for pleasure fills my heart.
  Is it me you seek?' 'No, it is not you'.

'My brow is pale; my tresses, golden;
I can bring you endless joy;
I safeguard a treasure of tenderness.
Is it me you call?' 'No, it is not you'.

'I am a dream, an impossible,
imaginary phantom of mist and light;
I am incorporeal, I am intangible;
I cannot love you'. 'Oh, come, come, you!')

The poem virtually obliges a metaphorical reading that allows the theme of poetry as its subject. It is not that the poem makes no contribution to the volume's love theme, but rather that the whole thrust of the last stanza coincides with the ideas found in *rimas* 2, 5 and 15 which, significantly, were published for the first time in the same year as the above, 1866.[23] In particular, the theme of elusiveness and intangibility recalls the diction of *rima* 15, and we cannot help but think that Bécquer has the aspirations and tribulations of poetic composition in mind. In this context we might further speculate that the first two female symbols—and the first is explicitly described as a *symbol*—are rejected for poetic reasons. The first is the *morena* (the sultry female, dark of hair and skin), a common topic in poetry of the oral tradition; the second is by contrast the fair-haired and pale beauty associated with the upper classes and frequently found in courtly poetry. It would not be excessively fanciful to believe that Bécquer here intends to suggest a rejection of two well known types of poetry—the traditional and the cultured—and that his earnest wish is for an as yet unknown poetic idiom. The central point, however, is that as we read this *rima*—and so many others—we read on two levels at once and we follow two different narrative lines, the search for love and the search for poetry. While the metaphor *amada-poesía* ('beloved-poetry') is by no means original, and indeed is frequent in Renaissance poetry, it is doubtful whether in Spanish poetry it has ever been quite so prominent in a work or so forcefully sustained. Only Pedro Salinas, as we shall see, gives such equal and convincing treatment to both elements in the metaphor. And he does so for exactly the same purpose as Bécquer: to destabilize the connotative power of language by means of the twofold reference and, thereby, to create the sensation of fluid simultaneity which reflects the free and spontaneous experience of feeling.

But if Bécquer's diction and metaphorical system are perfectly in accord with the theme of poetry's elusiveness and in accord with

the ideals announced in the proem, there is one further area of his
language where concordance is less evident: his syntactical grouping
of words. It was Carlos Bousoño who showed most clearly that Bécquer's way of constructing a poem is extraordinarily deliberate, patterned and, in a word, parallelistic.[24] This will already have been
noticed in the above *rima*, number 11, with its triptychal system,
and was even more evident in *rima* 15 where stanzas three and four
exactly parallel stanzas one and two and lead to the precise equations
'eso eres tú ... eso soy yo' ('such are you ... such am I'). Similarly,
when Bécquer attempts to define the spirit of poetry in *rima* 5, he
adopts a system of repetition based on eighteen stanzas beginning
with the object of definition, 'yo' ('I'), and evolving with strict syntactical parallels: 'Yo soy el fleco de oro ... Yo soy la ardiente nube
... Yo soy el invisible anillo ... ' ('I am the golden fringe ... I
am the burning cloud ... I am the invisible ring ...'). There is
a marked tendency to compress words into formula: *rima* 4 is based
on repetition of the connective pattern 'mientras ... habrá poesía'
(p. 443) ('as long as ... there will be poetry'), *rima* 8 on 'Cuando
miro ... me parece' (p. 448) ('When I look at ... it seems to me')
and the *rima* 'A Elisa' ('To Elisa') on 'Para que (tú) ... hice mis
versos yo' (p. 496) ('So that you might ... did I write my poems').
Bousoño finds that no less than a third of the *rimas* have a strict
parallelistic form, while many more have repetition of a less regular
kind, and he suggests that we cannot help but be amazed by the
high frequency of this *mathematical* procedure in a poet as emotive
as Bécquer. Indeed there does seem to be a contradiction here
between subject-matter and treatment, between the random quality
of Bécquer's quest and the densely structured form of the *Rimas*.
It is, in short, paradoxical that the poet who exclaimed despairingly
in his *Cartas*, '¡El orden! ¡Lo detesto!' (p. 671) ('Order! I detest it!'),
should rely so heavily in the making of his poems on the very thing
that is so alien to his temperament and to feeling generally.

This blatant contradiction is for me the most revealing feature
in the *Rimas*. Different attempts can be made to rationalize it. First,
we would agree with Bousoño that the reiterative technique of parallelism functions essentially as an intensifier. Indeed, repetition
creates a mood of urgency and insistence which is compatible with
the notion of a quest. But while this is undoubtedly an important
correlative function of language in the *Rimas*, it is one, we note,
which relates to the poet's aspiration and not to the crucial and
elusive object of his quest. Second, we might argue that repetition

is one of the most basic and primitive techniques in composition, that it is the very source of rhythm and song, and that by indulging in it so heavily Bécquer seeks to evoke a primordial or pristine aura that is itself suggestive of the pure spirit of poetry. But here we are left with the uneasy feeling that Bécquer's poems are rather too elaborate and sophisticated in their architecture for such a purpose. Finally, it might be argued that parallelism does create in some way a sense of simultaneity, or, in Bergson's terms, of *duration* as opposed to linear succession, for clearly in a poem's repetition of syntactical forms the past is restated or echoed even as the poem moves on. This is something we shall have to bear in mind when we look in a moment at a densely structured poem. For the present, however, it does not seem that this or any of the above points resolves the fundamental contradiction in the *Rimas* between random feeling and systematic language.

To take the issue further we need to recall the proem and the approach to language projected there: it consisted of 'controlling' ('domando') the 'wayward' ('rebelde') and 'mean' ('mezquino') nature of language so as to compress poetic spirituality within a kind of formula, 'cifra'. We can see immediately that syntactical patterning is in practice the main discipline in the *Rimas* and that the parallelisms conform to the 'cifra'. Yet in that same *rima* Bécquer rejected such a formulistic course as futile, aware no doubt that to emphasize order would only accentuate the incompatibility of language and feeling: 'Pero en vano es luchar; que no hay cifra / capaz de encerrarlo' (p. 439) ('But it is useless to struggle; for no cipher / can contain it'). Why, then, persist with form, and why so insistently? The answer is perhaps already there in Bécquer's pessimism, and perhaps above all in the adjective 'mean' ('mezquino'), which we can take to refer to the rational rather than spiritual orientation of language in its communicating capacity. If language is 'mean', as Bécquer says, if it is by nature bound to the material, rational world, then it might be argued that it no longer matters to the poet whether his language is more or less systematic, more or less logical, for it will in any case be too systematic, too logical and too rational. Thus, finally, we postulate two distinct theories about Bécquer's use of highly structured language, a distinction based upon the opposition between the adjectives 'rebelde' ('wayward') and 'mezquino' ('mean'). First, structure reflects an attempt to control a medium he considers wayward, at least semantically in its individual parts or diction, and from this structure there results a rhythmic impression of insistency which correlates the poet's determination to reach his quest. Secondly, structure, an excess of structure, reflects an over-reaction on the poet's part to his unhappy awareness that the mean logic of language is in any case irradicable, for, specifically, language is bound to adopt the enumerative, linear form of syntax. From here it is only a short step to appreciate why Bécquer resorts to the most ironical course of exaggerating the formal and logical features of language: it is a means of bringing out into the open the very adversary he would conquer.

In this last context the most revealing of Bécquer's poems are those in which the linguistic order of a parallelistic structure is first created and then destroyed. This process of construction and deconstruction is found for instance in *rima* 52:

Olas gigantes que os rompéis bramando
en las playas desiertas y remotas,
envuelto entre las sábanas de espuma,
   ¡llevadme con vosotras!

Ráfagas de huracán que arrebatáis
del alto bosque las marchitas hojas,
arrastrado en el ciego torbellino,
   ¡llevadme con vosotras!

Nubes de tempestad que rompe el rayo
y en fuego ornáis las desprendidas orlas,
arrebatado entre la niebla oscura,
   ¡llevadme con vosotras!

Llevadme, por piedad, a donde el vértigo
con la razón me arranque la memoria . . .
¡Por piedad! . . . ¡Tengo miedo de quedarme
   con mi dolor a solas!   (pp. 472–3)

(Gigantic waves that break roaring
on deserted and remote beaches,
enveloped in sheets of foam,
   carry me away with you!

Hurricane winds that tear off
the tall wood's withered leaves,
dragged along by the blind whirlwind,
   carry me away with you!

Storm clouds where lightning flashes
and adorns with fire the loosened fringes,
abducted by the dark mist,
   carry me away with you!

> Carry me away, for pity's sake, to where giddiness
> might strip me of reason and memory . . .
> For pity's sake! . . . I am afraid
> to remain alone with my grief!)

As we can plainly see, the first three stanzas are organized very
carefully on the basis of syntactical parallelisms, having identical
punctuation and almost identical distribution of parts of speech:
the first line of each (in the Spanish) takes the form of noun-subject,
adjectival development, relative and finally verb; the second line
of each gives the respective locations; the third lines begin in each
case with an adjective formed out of a past participle—'envuelto',
'arrastrado', 'arrebatado' ('enveloped', 'dragged along', 'abducted')—which refers to the poet who appears in the refrain. Strongly
foregrounded in this way, the participles are the centrepoint of all
three stanzas, connecting the principal and extremely mobile image
of each stanza with the poet and his aspirations. In all cases the
participles are followed by preposition, article, noun and adjective,
the only variation being a change of order to adjective and noun
in stanza two. The fourth line in each stanza is of course a straightforward repetition of the refrain. Plainly, then, the poem is constructed on the basis of an extremely rigorous patterning of words.
However, this edifice of logic and order is hauled down in the fourth
and last stanza where the poet turns directly to his own predicament.
Here a new rhythmic pattern is in force as we see from the different
punctuation, an additional exclamation, repetition of 'por piedad'
('for pity's sake'), two sets of suspension marks and enjambment
into the last line which is no longer the refrain. The change completely
disrupts the pattern which had been so carefully established and
indeed it suggests metaphorically the sense of vertigo or giddiness
which the poet yearns for in place of 'razón' ('reason') and 'memoria'
('memory'). In short, the syntactical presentation of this *rima* reflects
both the orderly 'razón' Bécquer detested and—at the end—the
anarchic freedom, 'vértigo', he desired.

Similar disruptions are to be found in other *rimas*, though often
the point is not made until well into the final stanza. Suspension
marks again alert us in the fourth and last stanza of the extremely
parallelistic *rima* 67:

> ¡Qué hermoso es, cuando hay sueño,
> dormir bien . . . y roncar como un sochantre . . .
> y comer, y engordar! ¡Y qué desgracia
> que esto solo no baste!   (p. 481)

(How sweet it is, when one is drowsy,
to sleep well ... and snore like a choirmaster ...
to eat, and grow fat. And what a pity
that this alone is not enough!)

The first line continues the pattern of the three previous stanzas—
'¡Que hermoso es ...' ('How sweet it is ...!')—and it is not until
we come to the suspension marks in the second line that we begin
to realize that the rhythm is changing. The poem's thematic complacency is then fully shaken by the additional exclamation in line
three and its force is underlined by a change in the order of verse
length: whereas the first three stanzas had consisted of three hendecasyllables and one heptasyllable, with the latter at line three, the
last stanza reverses this by having the heptasyllable last, thereby
giving more bite to the conclusion. Exactly the opposite happens
in the last line of *rima* 43 where a longer line at the end disrupts
the pattern established in the two previous stanzas. Here again the
disruption is thematically relevant, for the extra length of 'y que
en aquella noche envejecí' (p. 469) ('and on that very night I grew
old') is clearly a syntactical metaphor of the poet's ageing or extra
years. This technique of disruption—very often a sharp shock—is
not unlike Heine's renowned practice of *Stimmungsbrechung*, which
is defined as 'the breaking of the sentiment at the close of the poem'
or 'the negation or the ridiculing, in the concluding lines, of the
mood produced by the poem'.[25] Indeed, there is a sting in the tail
of *rima* 43 when it ends bitterly on 'envejecí' ('I grew old'), and
there is irony in the conclusion of *rima* 67, '¡Y qué desgracia / que
esto solo no baste!' ('And what a pity / that this alone is not enough!'),
which in fact recalls Heine's poem 'Wahrhaftig' ('Sincerely') and
its ending: 'But songs and stars and flowers and pretty eyes and
moonlight and sunshine may all be very pleasurable, but they don't
make a world, not nearly'.[26] Irony is found too at the end of the
short *rima* 35:

¡No me admiró tu olvido! Aunque de un día,
    me admiró tu cariño mucho más;
porque lo que hay en mí que vale algo,
    eso ... ¡ni lo pudiste sospechar!   (p. 464)

(Your leaving was no surprise! Though it lasted just one day,
    your affection surprised me a good deal more;
for what there is in me that is of any worth,
    that ... you could not have had an inkling of!)

The real surprise in the poem is the way the poet turns on his *amada* in the last line, accusing her of superficiality even in the affection she had shown him. Yet he too is guilty of shallowness, as we find in the surprising end to *rima* 39:

> Sé que en su corazón, nido de sierpes,
> no hay una fibra que al amor responda;
> que es una estatua inanimada; pero . . .
> ¡Es tan hermosa!   (p. 466)

> (I know that in her heart, that nest of serpents,
> there is not a single fibre that responds to love;
> that she is an inanimate statue; but . . .
> She is so beautiful!)

In both the last two poems mentioned the change of mood is announced by the rhythmic jar of a single isolated word—'eso . . . ' ('that . . .'), 'pero . . . ' ('but . . .')—together with suspension marks and the following exclamation. Finally the same features are to be found in plenty at the conclusion of *rima* 42 which describes the poet's mood after the departure of his *amada*. The third and last stanza reads:

> Pasó la nube de dolor . . ., con pena
> logré balbucear breves palabras . . .
> ¿Quién me dio la noticia? . . . Un fiel amigo . . .
> ¡Me hacía un gran favor! . . . Le di las gracias.   (p. 468)

> (The cloud of grief passed . . ., painfully
> I managed to stammer a few short words . . .
> Who broke the news to me? . . . A faithful friend . . .
> He did me a great favour! . . . I thanked him well.)

Here, as irony turns to sarcasm, the halting rhythm conveys the sense of the poet's spluttering rage and, at the same time, suggests the disintegration of his world in tatters.

It is tempting to conclude that Bécquer is indebted to Heine, especially with regard to the practice of *Stimmungsbrechung*. Yet very great differences exist between the two poets, as Dámaso Alonso has pointed out.[27] Essentially Bécquer is a more earnest poet than Heine, and, as already indicated, his earnestness is above all apparent in his insistent rhythms and in his tight forms and parallelistic structures, not to be found in Heine. The result is that when Bécquer employs a disruptive technique akin to *Stimmungsbrechung* not only is the mood of the poem ruptured but—even more importantly—the entire linguistic logic underlying the poem is sabotaged. For a last example of this we turn to one of the most famous and most densely structured *rimas*, number 53:

> Volverán las oscuras golondrinas
> en tu balcón sus nidos a colgar,
> y otra vez con el ala a sus cristales
>   jugando llamarán;
> pero aquellas que el vuelo refrenaban,
> tu hermosura y mi dicha al contemplar;
> aquellas que aprendieron nuestros nombres,
>   ésas . . . ¡no volverán!
>
> Volverán las tupidas madreselvas
> de tu jardín las tapias a escalar,
> y otra vez a la tarde, aun más hermosas,
>   sus flores se abrirán;
> pero aquellas cuajadas de rocío,
> cuyas gotas mirábamos temblar
> y caer, como lágrimas del día . . .,
>   ésas . . . ¡no volverán!
>
> Volverán del amor en tus oídos
> las palabras ardientes a sonar;
> tu corazón, de su profundo sueño
>   tal vez despertará;
> pero mudo y absorto y de rodillas,
> como se adora a Dios ante su altar,
> como yo te he querido . . . desengáñate:
>   ¡así no te querrán!   (pp. 473–4)

(The dark swallows will again [literally 'return to'] hang their nests on your balcony, and once again with their wings on its windows
    playfully will knock;
but those that halted their flight,
seeing your beauty and my joy;
those that learnt our names,
    those . . . will not return!

The thick honeysuckles will again [literally 'return to'] climb the walls of your garden, and once again at evening, lovelier than ever,
    their flowers will open;
but those brimful of dew,
whose drops we saw tremble
and fall, like the day's tears . . .,
    those . . . will not return!

Passionate words will again [literally 'return to'] ring of love in your ears;
your heart, from its deep slumber

> perhaps will awaken;
> but mute and spellbound and kneeling,
> as one worships God before his altar,
> as I have loved you ... don't fool yourself:
> that way you will not be loved!)

Stimmungsbrechung is very clear in the last stanza, but we note how much more effective it is now that it involves the breaking of a rigorously parallelistic structure. For the most part the last stanza continues the parallelisms established in the first two stanzas, and how appropriate the reiterative system is to the poem's theme of seasonal repetition. Specifically, the first two lines are again contained within the formula 'Volverán ...' ('will return ...') plus an infinitive at the end; the fourth line ends in a future tense as before; the fifth begins with 'pero' ('but'), and there is no variation in line length. Yet the poem's real argument is that seasonal repetition is in fact an illusion or deception, for within the seeming reality of the same birds returning and the same plants regenerating is found the actual reality of change: they are simply not the same swallows nor the same honeysuckles that return each year. Since repetition is then an illusion, reaction against the poem's repetitive system is essential, and when Bécquer turns to the experience of love in the last stanza we find that his reaction is poignant. As to structural differences, however, we note that the third line of the last stanza does not begin as before with 'y otra vez' ('and once again'), and though the fifth line begins as it should with 'pero' ('but'), its rhythm is changed decisively by the following three adjectives which act as intensifiers, as we see by comparison:

stanza 1	pero aquellas que el vuelo refrenaban (but those that halted their flight)
stanza 2	pero aquellas cuajadas de rocío (but those brimful of dew)
stanza 3	pero mudo y absorto y de rodillas (but mute and spellbound and kneeling)

We are conditioned to expect a phrase such as 'pero aquel amor mío ... no volverá' ('but that love of mine ... will not return'), but this is in fact understood as we read the third line above and instinctively apply to the poet its three adjectives—'mudo', 'absorto', 'de rodillas' ('mute', 'spellbound', 'kneeling')—adjectives which derive added force from the rhetorical device of cumulation and the repetition of the connective 'y' ('and'). The tone of desperation is sustained by a further intensive repetition, 'como ... como ...' ('as ... as ...'), which had not occurred previously, and we may be surprised to find a noun, 'altar' ('altar'), in the place previously reserved for an infinitive. The second 'como' introduces 'yo' '(I') for the first time and with telling effect, while the suspension marks that follow again indicate variance in rhythm and give striking isolation to the bitter, climactic and staccato 'desengáñate' ('don't fool yourself'). To complete the disruption '¡así no te querrán!' ('that way you will not be loved') replaces the established refrain.

By these various techniques Bécquer manages to create a cataclasmic effect at the end of several of his poems, an effect which goes far beyond *Stimmungsbrechung*. The denouement of dissonance is appropriate on various thematic levels, notably in the context of disappointed love and the ensuing spiritual disorientation. At the end of such poems we have a rhythmic and indeed visual metaphor of the poet's disintegrating world. But also in these poems, where, as we might say, the norm has been ruptured, Bécquer expresses most accurately his own rebelliousness, the essential Romantic aspiration towards freedom. And it is as much a rebellion against his medium of language as it is against his subject-matter. The final impression in these poems is that the poet, having restrained himself so long through the mathematical strictures of form, becomes, towards the poem's end, aware of its insufficiency, aware of the artificial nature of orderliness. His last futile act, within the context of metaphorical syntax, is to strike out at the deceit of language within which 'he had perforce imprisoned himself. In a parallelistic poem the act of disruption will seem violent, born of frustration. In a less densely structured poem, such as *rima* 10 with which we began, the disruptions will seem fuelled by a transcendental ideal:

> mis párpados se cierran ... ¿Qué sucede?
> ¿Dime? ... ¡Silencio! ... ¡Es el amor que pasa!
>
> (my eyelids close ... What is happening?
> Will you tell me? ... Silence! ... It is love passing!)

In either case the fragmentation is symptomatic of the impossible task Bécquer set himself: to find an idiom that would synthesize love, religion and poetic feeling in a pure, random state. If language itself could only 'balbucear algunas de las frases de su inmenso poema' (p. 671) ('babble some of the lines of its immense poem'), it is hardly surprising that Bécquer sometimes stammered. But the poets who followed him caught his every word.

II

Rosalía de Castro

The Poetics of *Saudades*

Yo no sé lo que busco eternamente
en la tierra, en el aire y en el cielo;
yo no sé lo que busco, pero es algo
que perdí no sé cuándo y que no encuentro
aun cuando sueñe que invisible habita
en todo cuanto toco y cuanto veo.

Felicidad, no he de volver a hallarte
en la tierra, en el aire ni en el cielo;
¡aun cuando sé que existes
y no eres vano sueño![1]

(I know not what I seek unceasingly
on earth, in the air and in heaven;
I know not what I seek, but it is something
I lost I know not when and which I cannot find,
though I dream it dwells invisibly
in all I touch and all I see.

Happiness, I am never to find you again
on earth, in the air or in heaven;
even though I know you exist
and you are no vain dream!)

Rosalía de Castro, Spain's greatest female poet, expresses an authentic Romantic *Angst* via an emotional register her fellow Galicians
have long held to be part of their collective Celtic psyche and which

they denote by a word which has no proper equivalent in Castilian, *saudades* (also *soidades, soidás*). What Galicians mean by *saudades*—briefly, a kind of unutterable longing—is largely indicated in the above part-poem from *En las orillas del Sar* (*On the Banks of the Sar*), Rosalía's only substantial volume in Castilian and our main concern in this study.

As we can see, however, the lines also bear close comparison with Bécquer's cosmopolitan concepts in that they depict a search for something elusive and indefinable which dreams or visionary moments come closest to grasping. The first point to be made about Rosalía, then, is that she is at once an ethnic poet, Galician to the core, and a poet whose work coincides unaffectedly with a broader European ethos. What distinguishes her subjectivism from Bécquer's is that the *saudades* complex stipulates an emotional response to the *patria chica* or small homeland, Galicia, and this leads to an evocation of the *patria* in the real terms of its landscape, topography, climate and even aspects of the social problems which its people face. Thus *En las orillas del Sar* sets Rosalía apart as the first major Spanish poet of place, anticipating Antonio Machado in this regard. Herein lies Rosalía's considerable appeal, for the rain that falls in her poems as surely as it falls in Galicia is not only symbolic but also wet, and, by the same token, the apparently ethereal emotionalism of her *saudades* is offset by the same register's earthbound locative force, not to be found in Bécquer. That she was a woman who wrote as a woman only enhances the specific and universal dimensions of her work, and with some poignancy.

Rosalía's life as a woman and as a Galician is the substance of her poetry, especially the volume she published one year before her death, *En las orillas del Sar* (1884), in which she meditates on her often tragic life and on the sufferings of her *patria* in such a way as to interfuse the two. But, intensely personal and deeply moving as her poetry is, it is not, I wish to show, the formless indulgence of a weak-minded female. Here the question of an ethereal emotionalism as opposed to sharply defined themes and artistic rigour is one that needs to be put in perspective at the outset. Certain prejudices persist and, in this connection, the first stanza above has been the most quoted in all Rosalía's work doubtless because the hopeless despair and apparent indefiniteness of its repeated 'Yo no sé lo que busco' ('I know not what I seek') is thought to enshrine the imprecision of *saudades*. This standard view is borne out by a Galician encyclopaedic-dictionary which, after listing various definitions of *saudades*, conforms to the rubric by concluding:

La *saudade*, en realidad, es un sentimiento inexplicable, que no se sabe de donde viene, ni se alcanza a donde va, ni se comprende lo que persigue ... Esta imprecisión es precisamente lo que caracteriza la *saudade*.[2]

(*Saudades*, in fact, is an indescribable emotion, for one knows not from where it comes, nor whither it goes, nor does one understand what it pursues ... This imprecision is precisely what characterizes *saudades*.)

The spirit of this conclusion may not be misplaced, but one cannot help feeling that its commentator rather delights in the cultivation of *saudades* as an impenetrable mystique. Such a mystique has always surrounded Rosalía, though not always to her advantage, for while she is revered by some as an almost saintly personification of Galician values and Galician identity, others take a dim view of what they have been encouraged to regard as vague emotionalism, seeing this as but a short step from lachrymose sentimentality. My point, quite simply, is that *saudades* is not nearly as lacking in precision as we are led to believe, at least not when seen in context. In its entirety the context of *En las orillas del Sar* provides a rigorous account of what Rosalía's *saudades* consists of, namely and most notably a problematic attitude towards the *patria*, towards love and towards God. Not only are these very definite thematic concepts, but, I shall argue, it is the absolute integration of the three as frustrated ideals which determines what should be considered the psychological complexity rather than the imprecision of *saudades*, at least in Rosalía's case.

The poem quoted above typifies this. If we consider it more closely we shall find that the mystification of its first stanza largely disappears with the following stanza's disclosure that it is in fact 'Felicidad' ('Happiness') which Rosalía seeks, that, furthermore, happiness is something which she knows exists, which is no more illusion, which she once experienced though no longer can. We are thus dealing here with the most basic of all human issues, the striving for spiritual well-being, for psychical wholeness, the Utopian quest for self. The reverse of this is frustration, a prerequisite of *saudades*, and our first task is to see where and why Utopian happiness is denied. The volume as a whole will provide the full account, in which psychological sense it is far more compelling than Bécquer's *Rimas*, but already a clear indication of the areas of Rosalía's frustration is found in the line which with slight variation appears in both stanzas above, 'en la tierra, en el aire y en el cielo' ('on earth, in the air and in heaven'). Vaporous as the line may seem at first, I suggest that its list of three—earth, air, heaven—corresponds exactly to Rosalía's three central preoccupations as already mentioned, the *patria*, love and God respectively, the one symbolic noun 'aire' ('air') being intermediate just as ideal love for Rosalía is located between heaven and earth. It was, in fact, in her homeland, in love and in God that Rosalía once knew happiness, but by the time of *En las orillas del Sar* these have turned into problematic fixations. The decisive point poetically, however, is that the fixations each contribute with remarkable cohesion and even with the above line's compressed simultaneity to the total sense of longing and loss which is Rosalía's *saudades*. It is this interlocking which is so characteristic of *saudades* and of Rosalía's poetic manner generally. Later I shall try to show that the vigorous integrational energy of *saudades* is what gives form to *En las orillas del Sar*. Before we can accept this, however, before we can allow that deep psychological forces may generate their own artistic form, we need to know something of Rosalía's life and circumstance prior to the composition of her major work.

Rosalía was born an illegitimate child in 1837 in Santiago de Compostela, Galicia's spiritual capital, her mother Teresa de Castro being of good Galician stock and her father a seminarian who later became a priest. Santiago, we remember, takes its name from St James the patron saint of Spain whose bones according to tradition were discovered there in the ninth century, since when it has been the Peninsula's most important shrine, revered by pilgrims in the Middle Ages and retaining even today an austere air in the vicinity of its imposing cathedral. In this setting the full stigma of Rosalía's birth can be appreciated, for if illegitimacy was no small matter anywhere in nineteenth-century Spain it was surely a catastrophe in zealous Santiago, as its repercussions in Rosalía's work confirm. Rosalía's early years, as a result, were spent not with her mother in Santiago but in the country, at Oruño probably, where she was raised by family confidants and where she learnt the oral folklore that was to be such a feature of her Galician volumes. Joining her mother in her early teens, Rosalía studied at Santiago's Lyceum where she learnt French and took part in the city's newly flourishing cultural activities. Her arrival in the capital soon after 1850 coincided with the upsurge in Galician nationalism, the movement here as in Catalonia and the Basque Country owing much to Romanticism's libertarian ideals. Young poets were once again writing in Galician, that gentle language so suited to lyricism which had been Spain's foremost poetic medium in the thirteenth century when Provençal troubadours trod the pilgrims' *ruta de Santiago* and when even the King of Castile,

Alfonso X, the Wise, wrote his poems in Galician. Among the poets Rosalía would have known in Santiago was the dashing Aurelio Aguirre whose promising career was cut short by his drowning at the age of twenty-four. Indeed, according to Machado da Rosa, her most informed biographer, Rosalía was courted for a time by Aurelio and the relationship ended when she unaccountably lost her honour to another, anonymous male, an event which obliged her to leave Galicia for Madrid.[3] This theory of a disastrous second affair, partly assembled as it is from textual indices, is too speculative for many observers however, for whom Rosalía's sudden flight to Madrid is only to be explained by the increasing social embarrassment of her birth. What can be said with certainty is that the theme of sexual temptation, of guilt and remorse, juxtaposed with idealistic notions of love, is one of the most powerful and lasting in Rosalía's work.

In Madrid in 1856 Rosalía lived with her aunt Carmen Lugía de Castro who occasionally held literary soirées at her home. The guests may well have included Bécquer, but almost certainly Manuel Murguía, a rising figure in the Galician revival who was soon to be Rosalía's husband. In 1857 Rosalía published her first slim volume of verse, La flor (The Flower), a rather sentimental collection which Murguía reviewed favourably in La Iberia while claiming no knowledge of its author. Despite its faults, the volume develops a sense of personal anguish which gives a foretaste of her mature work, the anguish embracing a religious crisis, 'la fe perdida' (p. 222) ('lost faith'), a sense of unwarranted persecution, 'La risa y el sarcasmo por doquiera / que fuera yo mi corazón palpaba' (p. 219) ('Laughter and sarcasm wherever / I went did my heart sense'), and an embittered feeling of isolation:

> ¡Sola era yo con mi dolor profundo
> en el abismo de un imbécil mundo!   (p. 219)

> (Alone was I with my profound grief
> in the abyss of an imbecile world!)

As regards the love theme, the volume's last and longest poem, 'La rosa del camposanto' ('The Graveyard Rose') deals with a young woman's passion, vanity and jealousy, while 'Un recuerdo' ('A Memory') deals with the theme of sexual temptation leading to betrayal and despair. Such topics may well echo Rosalía's personal experience, specifically an unfortunate liaison, but the issue is clouded by the fact that she somewhat naively adopts the literary mask of a bereft Romantic heroine, as popularized by Espronceda, and while literary fashion and personal experience are not of course mutually exclusive it is hard to tell where one ends and the other begins. Ultimately the most salient index of autobiographical content in *La flor* is its recurring tone of bitterness, for not only is this to be prominent in her mature work but it is also an emotion which the literary Romantic heroine is traditionally above.

The year after *La flor* came out Rosalía married Manuel Murguía and the couple returned to Galicia where their first child was born in 1859. After nearly a ten year gap six more children followed by 1877, though the last died at birth and one of Rosalía's two sons died of a fall before his second birthday, his burial being the subject of a moving poem in *En las orillas del Sar* (p. 576). Rosalía's husband was a man of extremely small physical stature and reputedly of difficult temperament. The conspicuous absence of conjugal poems in her work tends to support the widely held view that the marriage was not a happy one. But Murguía was an important figure in the Galician revival who is best remembered for his voluminous history of Galicia and for critical works on Galician writers. As editor of a Galician periodical in Madrid and as government archivist in Simancas, Murguía spent much time away from home. Rosalía accompanied him on one of his trips in 1861 and it was in Simancas on the dry Castilian *meseta* that, consumed with homesickness for her green Galicia, she began the volume that would endear her to her fellow Galicians, *Cantares gallegos* (*Galician Songs*). The composition of such songs as 'Adiós ríos, adiós fontes' (p. 304) (Goodbye rivers, goodbye springs) and 'Airiños, airiños aires, / airiños da minha terra' (p. 308) (Breezes, little breezes, / breezes of my land) began as a form of distraction, but Murguía encouraged Rosalía to pursue this evocative strain and then publish her songs as a collection in 1863. Often, as in the following delightful piece which names a country church some miles south of Santiago, the song simply expanded upon a snatch of a popular ditty and even the ancient technique of *leixa-pren*—interlocking stanzas through partial repetition—was used:

> Campanas de Bastabales,
> cando vos oyo tocar,
> mórrome de soidades.

> Cando vos oyo tocar,
> campaniñas, campaniñas,
> sin querer torno a chorar.

Cando de lonxe vos oyo,
penso que por min chamades,
e das entrañas me doyo.

Dóyome de dor ferida,
qu' antes tiña vida enteira
y oxe teño media vida ...   (pp. 294–95)

(Bells of Bastabales,
when I hear you ring,
I die of saudades.

When I hear you ring,
little bells, little bells,
I can't help but cry.

When I hear you from afar,
I think it is for me you call,
and I suffer deep inside.

I suffer a wounded pain,
for once I had a whole life
and today I have but half ...)

The emotional directness and haunting musicality of these songs—
much aided as the latter is by the nasal vowels and 'sh' final *s* of
Galician—makes *Cantares gallegos* a rare poetic experience which can
be enjoyed by anyone with a knowledge of Spanish who has a Galician
or even Portuguese grammar at his side. The volume's total commitment to subjectivity places it firmly within the ambit of Romanticism,
though its roots in *saudades* are more ethnic and perennial. Homesickness, as the above poem shows, is a prominent feature in *saudades*,
in which sense it is particularly close to another Celtic phenomenon
of psychical complexity, Welsh *hiraeth*. We also see from the fourth
stanza that *saudades* describes suffering in terms of a loss of wholeness,
but while the poem goes on to instance love as the cause of this
dismemberment the treatment is traditional, lyrical and generic,
which is to say that Rosalía surrenders to the mood of *saudades* rather
than engages in the self-analysis characteristic of her later work.

Later in the same year, 1863, Rosalía published a small volume
of poems in Castilian, *A mi madre* (*To My Mother*), her mother having
died the year before. The loving and sympathetic regard in which
Rosalía held her mother is here transparent, 'Yo tuve una dulce
madre ... más tierna que la ternura' (p. 245) ('I had a sweet mother
... more tender than tenderness'), though one also senses a compen-
satory factor by which Rosalía seeks to surmount the absence of
a father figure or alternatively tries to bear her mother's cross. It

was, however, *Cantares gallegos* which brought Rosalía to her people
and which made her the focal point of the Galician cultural revival.
So successful was the volume that she felt 'obrigada a que non fose
ò primeiro y ò último' (p. 413) ('obliged that it should not be the
first and last') of her works in Galician. Hence, after trying her
hand at a number of prose works in the 1860s and following another
stay at Simancas in 1870, Rosalía began to write the poems of *Follas
novas* (*New Leaves*). When it appeared in 1880, she could say in its
prologue 'pagada va á deuda en que me parecía estar c'o á minha
terra' (p. 413) ('the debt which it seemed to me I owed my country
is now paid'), and it does seem that Rosalía felt pressured to write
this volume. Nevertheless, despite the fact that the new poems were
again 'escritos n'ò deserto de Castilla' (p. 409) ('written in the desert
of Castile'), *Follas novas* is quite different in tone. Longer in the writing, more reflective in its mood and ambitiously innovative in its
versification, *Follas novas* is the 'dolorosa epopeya' (p. 413) ('tragic
epic') of a mature and complex woman, a woman who is an individual
as well as a Galician. While Galicia, as Rosalía says, had been 'ò
obxeto, á alma enteira' ('the purpose, the entire spirit') of *Cantares
gallegos*, it is now 'ò fondo d'o cuadro' (p. 411) ('the background
of the picture') and it is the poet's own personality which is to the
fore. The treatment of Galicia itself is also different, for though aspects
of the folkloric remain there is a more actual and sociological depiction of the region which suffered so greatly from the curse of the
minifundia, that practice of subdividing land which, with the dramatic
population growth of the nineteenth century, resulted in farms too
small to sustain a family. The ensuing mass emigration of Galicians
is treated in the book's last section entitled 'As viudas d'os vivos
e as viudas d'os mortos' ('The Widows of the Living and the Widows
of the Dead') and in fact the entire book is dedicated to the Galician
Welfare Society in Havana. The poem '¡Pra a Habana!' ('To
Havana!') concludes:

> Este vaise y aquel vaise,
> e todos, todos se van;
> Galicia, sin homes quedas
> que te poidan traballar.
> Tês, en cambio, orfos e orfas
> e campos de soledad,
> e nais que non teñen fillos
> e fillos que non tén pais.
> E tês corazons que sufren
> longas ausencias mortás,

viudas de vivos e mortos
que ninguén consolará.   (p 523)

(This one leaves, that one leaves.
and all of them, all of them leave;
Galicia, you are left without men
who can work your soil.
You have instead orphaned girls and boys
and fields that are solitary,
and mothers who have no sons
and sons who have no fathers.
And you have hearts that suffer
long absences without end,
widows of the living and of the dead
whom no one can console.)

The tone is no less heartfelt than in *Cantares gallegos* but there is the added immediacy of its speaker being a witness to a contemporary phenomenon. Moreover, that Rosalía should focus the theme of exile on orphans and widows of the living—both experiences being close to her core—is indicative of her growing tendency to empathize at the most personal level with the suffering of her *patria*. Similarly, the more intimate poems of *Follas novas*, as from its second book '¡Do íntimo!' ('From Within!'), are more particular than before. Nowhere is Rosalía's terrible persecution complex more evident than in 'Ladraban contra min, que camiñaba' (p. 432) ('They Howled at Me as I Walked By'), for the abuse suffered by the woman in this poem surely compares with the kind of taunts which Rosalía herself once had to endure as the illegitimate daughter of a priest. Thus the tragic mood which pervades *Follas novas* is something which, on the one hand, stems from within,

Teño un mal que non ten cura,
un mal que naceu comigo   (p. 491)

(I have a sickness that has no cure,
a sickness that was born with me.)

and which at the same time finds specific correlation in the tragic circumstance of her homeland. This identification of land and spirit relates Rosalía to the 1898 Generation while her emphasis upon suffering prefigures *Modernismo*. Her kinship with the early Machado can be verified by comparing her poem 'Un-ha vez tiven un cravo / cravado no corazón' (p. 418) ('Once I had a thorn / pierced in my heart') with Machado's famous 'Yo voy soñando caminos' ('I go dreaming paths') which also develops the thorn motif. In both poems the thorn is extracted, but, as opposed to feeling relief, both poets conclude that suffering, though unwanted, is better than no feeling at all. For Rosalía suffering was to be such an all consuming presence in her life that by the time of *En las orillas del Sar* it was, paradoxically, almost cherished:

> pero conmigo llevaba todo:
> llevaba mi dolor por compañía. (p. 653)
>
> (but with me I had everything:
> I had my suffering for company.)

There was good reason too why suffering became the key note in *En las orillas del Sar*: by 1884 when it appeared Rosalía was already dying a slow and painful death from cancer of the uterus. Thus a spectre lies over her greatest volume which was written, as its title poem says, 'al acabarme' (p. 574) ('in the process of dying'), and a layer of physical pain lies upon the mental anguish of one who had experienced a loss of faith, bereavement of children and, it seems, the torments of sexual guilt. But physical pain is in any case endemic in *saudades* where emotional suffering is so acute as to be psychosomatic, and it is this persistent bodily sting which separates Rosalía from Bécquer and from Machado and which distinguishes *saudades* from its simpler Castilian cousin, *soledades* ('loneliness'), this latter word being the title of Machado's first volume of poems. As to Rosalía's reasons for turning to Castilian in her last work which, ironically, expressed her *saudades* most fully and profoundly, briefly it could be said that these might have included an ambition to reach a wider audience, but almost certainly uppermost in Rosalía's mind was the need to discover her own poetic voice free from the trappings of *folklorismo*. *Follas novas* had made strides in this direction, which is why it was less well liked in Galicia than *Cantares gallegos*. But Rosalía had a lot more to say about herself. No amount of badgering from Murguía, she tells him in a letter of 1881, could make her write another volume in Galician (p. 1551). Her antipathy towards the conservative Galician oligarchy was most marked in her later years, as Catherine Davies shows, and no doubt Rosalía wished to rise above their pettiness as well as prove her worth to those in Madrid who had neglected her largely because of the political implications of her regionalism.[4] But the surprising point is that Castilian was to prove a wise choice aesthetically too, for while Galician had been apt for poems about the *patria* written in exile, Castilian was now apt for poems written in her homeland by a poet who had come to feel distanced from the very things she had once loved. The thematic line 'Cual si en suelo extranjero me hallase' (p. 572) ('as if I were on foreign soil') is indicative of the alienation which pervades *En las orillas del Sar*, and thus it is Castilian which conveys both the hardness of Rosalía's new mood and the necessary distance and separation of *saudades*.

It is time now to take closer stock of what *saudades* means. The dictionary definition, which as we saw earlier ended by stressing its imprecision, provides in fact a detailed account of its many possible manifestations:

> **Saudade** *s.f.* Recuerdo, nostalgia, añoranza. // Ansiedad moral que los gallegos llevamos dentro de nosotros mismos y que es herencia de raza. // Esperanza de un bien futuro que se anhela y se juzga irrealizable. // Deseo vehemente y atormentado de lo imposible e indefinido. // Añoranza, pena causada en el ánimo por la ausencia de la patria, de la tierra nativa y de la aldea en que uno nació / Morriña ...[5]

> (**Saudade** *fem. n.* Reminiscence, nostalgia, longing. // A moral anxiety which we Galicians carry inside ourselves and which is a racial heritage. // Hope of a future happiness which one longs for but deems unrealizable. // A vehement and tormented desire for the impossible and undefined. // A yearning, a spiritual grief caused by the absence of the homeland, of the native land where one was born; Homesickness ...)

The above not only indicates the range of *saudades* but provides a good working introduction to virtually all Rosalía's themes and affective units in *En las orillas del Sar*. From the points we have made about Rosalía's life it will already be appreciated that the notions itemized above as a moral anxiety, a vehement desire and of course homesickness have very specific application as regards her religious dilemma, her passionate nature and her concern for the *patria*. It is inappropriate to describe such emotions as vague; indeed, when broken down to its component parts *saudades* refers to typical and identifiable human experiences, even if, for a variety of reasons, they are ones to which Galicians are especially prone. What is genuinely peculiar about *saudades*, I had earlier begun to suggest, is not so much that its affective units are more deeply felt in Galicia, true as this may be, but rather that the variety of experiences involved is there integrated into one whole. Castilian does not have a term to cover the collective force of *saudades* because the Castilian mind does not integrate its separate units, nor for this reason do Bécquer's *Rimas* have the psychical cohesion of *En las orillas del Sar*. In Bécquer, as we have seen, the insistent rhythms, repetitions, parallelisms, triptychal poems and general narrative definition all combine to help frame an elusive subject. In Rosalía, on the other hand, despite her undoubted metrical virtuosity, no such purposeful use of form is apparent. Instead, however, in compensation for the lack of a formal structuralizing system, it is the complex of *saudades* itself which integrates *En las orillas del Sar*, the complex being a highly systematic one in its own right which operates, as we shall see, through a set of continually shifting equivalents and oppositions. Thus while Bécquer's mode is formal in an external sense and decidedly antagonistic *vis-à-vis* his sensibility, Rosalía's poetic system, based on *saudades*, is internal and psychical and quite inseparable from her sensibility. The point is that when Rosalía embarks upon one or another of her cherished themes a second and usually a third theme is instantly present in her thoughts and there ensues that characteristic simultaneity and synthesis which leads either, through equivalents, to empathy, or, through opposition, to dilemma. This may be better understood with the help of a diagram which, comprising the three major components of Rosalía's *saudades* on which we have insisted, serves as a paradigm for the thematic content and involuted psychical tension of *En las orillas del Sar*:

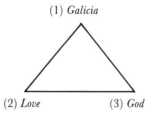

(1) *Galicia*

(2) *Love*　　　(3) *God*

The three points represent Rosalía's fixations; as the loci of her past joy they are areas in which she has suffered a profound sense of loss and which hence now represent her Utopian ideals. The paradigm's main purpose, however, is to illustrate structural integration. Briefly: if we take one of the points, for instance, (3) *God*, we shall find that her thoughts on this issue are inseparable from her thoughts on the other two points; inseparable, that is, from her depiction of herself as a sinful woman of passion—(2) *Love*—and from her pantheistic perception of the Galician landscape, (1) *Galicia*, a perception rooted in a druidic or Celtic paganism. Her thoughts on religion therefore closely integrate with her other two fixations which in effect are at odds with Christian orthodoxy. To take another example, this time one of equivalents rather than opposition: when Rosalía speaks of the depopulation of Galicia, 'pobres desheredados / para quienes no hay sitio en la hostigada patria' (p. 602) ('poor disinherited people / for whom there is no place in the scourged homeland'), this finds a strong religious parallel in her portrayal of herself as one outcast from heaven, 'me destierran del cielo' (p. 574) ('I am banished from heaven'), the person who has lost faith being 'desheredado' (p. 586) ('disinherited'). The link gives rise to such equations as:

> Desierto el mundo, despoblado el cielo (p. 578)
>
> (The world deserted, heaven depopulated)

and:

> abismo arriba, y en el fondo, abismo . . .
>
> (abyss above, and deep down, an abyss . . .)

This finds a further ready correlative in the remaining point of the paradigm through Rosalía's frequent reference to orphanhood—as in the above poem's 'huérfana y sin arrimo' (p. 578) ('orphaned and unsheltered')—for here as elsewhere orphanhood reflects her own experience and the tragic consequences of love. If we now turn to this last point, *Love*, we find that Rosalía's treatment of it owes much to the images of her distinctively Galician landscape which, in the case of trees and various types of liquid imagery, seem openly virile and phallic at times. The seductiveness of a green landscape with its 'frutos salvajes' (p. 587) ('wild fruits') corroborates the notion of earthly delights and carnal temptation. This irrepressible theme is represented in the religious context by the many appearances of the devil, 'Carne, tentación, demonio, / ¡oh! ¿de cuál de vosotros es la culpa?' (p. 583) ('Flesh, temptation, devil, / oh, which of you is to blame?') and of Mephistopheles, 'el perenne instigador oculto / de la insidiosa duda' (p. 639) ('the perennial dark instigator / of insidious doubt'). Thus Rosalía's treatment and conception of love has sharp correspondence in the other points of the paradigm and is psychologically inseparable from them. Finally, the corollary of the devil is of course Christ, a figure Rosalía responds to more readily than the abstract notion of God. No doubt this is because Christ's 'cruento martirio' (p. 629) ('bloody martyrdom') relates to that of her Galician people, 'este pueblo sufrido, que espera / silencioso en su lecho de espinas' (p. 590) ('this suffering people, who wait / silently on their bed of thorns') and because 'el Mártir de

Gólgota' (p. 597) ('the Martyr of Golgotha') finds resonance in Rosalía's own pronounced martyrdom complex which appears everywhere from the first poem's 'mi sien por la corona del mártir agobiada' (p. 575) ('my temple heavy with the martyr's crown') to the last poem's 'me resigno a seguir con mi calvario' (p. 656) ('I am resigned to bearing my cross'). The motives for this are complex and certainly include her physical suffering, but prominent amongst them as always is her acute sense of victimization in love. In general, pain, religion and sexuality are so embroiled in the issue of martyrdom as to require psychoanalytical explanation of what is sublimation and what is masochism.

From this brief account it will be apparent that the possible equivalents and oppositions in the paradigm can proliferate mesmerically. The following recasting may help us see more clearly the points so far mentioned:

(1) *Galicia*
  i. suffering people
  ii. disinheritance/depopulation
  iii. landscape: eroticism; paganism

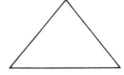

(2) *Love*   (3) *God*
  i. martyrdom/victimization   *i. Christ's martyrdom*
  ii. disinheritance/orphanhood   *ii. empty heaven/abyss*
  iii. sensuality/sin   *iii. Mephistopheles*

Needless to say, the interconnecting process takes many more forms. It is so pervasive as to be fundamental to Rosalía's articulatory system, for, in addition to being an almost instinctive source of metaphor through cross-reference, it is also, more importantly, a determining factor in the structuring of her thoughts. This is the vital point to which my comments have been leading, and we can now at last begin to appreciate it by turning to the very first stanza in the volume's title poem, a stanza which provides an admirable introduction to the work as a whole:

A través del follaje perenne
que oír deja rumores extraños,
y entre un mar de ondulante verdura,

amorosa mansión de los pájaros,
desde mis ventanas veo
el templo que quise tanto.   (p. 571)

(Across the perennial foliage
in which strange sounds are heard,
and amid a sea of undulating greenery,
the loving mansion of birds,
from my windows I see
the church I loved so well.)

Typifying Rosalía's skill in giving physical dimension to her dilemma, the stanza depicts her as spatially isolated from her once beloved church. But as she looks out from her house and takes in the mass of foliage before her, certain associations of the latter suggest that the distance between Rosalía and her church is not merely spatial. First, the strange sounds to be heard in the greenery of line two allude to the occult powers of a dynamic and mythological nature which the poem will later clarify:

lleno aún de las blancas fantasmas
que en otro tiempo adoramos.   (p. 573)

(still full of the white phantoms
which in times past we worshipped.)

Her alienation from the church is thus implicitly explained in the first instance by the persistence of pagan values in her sensibility, that is, by a nostalgic attachment to the remote and nebulous Celtic past. For the second part of the explanation we need look no further than line four which, in the form of another descriptive parenthesis, discreetly introduces the love theme. This too will soon be developed, for instance in stanza four:

de un ser amado el recuerdo
que de negras traiciones y dichas
inmensas nos habla a un tiempo.   (p. 571)

(the memory of a loved one
speaks to us of black treasons and joys
untold at one and the same time.)

The leafy greenery distancing Rosalía from her church is thus redolent with the very things which undermine her Christian faith and it constitutes a psychological divide she cannot cross. What is admirable about the stanza is the way it effortlessly integrates the three elements of her struggle within its single sentence, thereby rendering them as unbroken as the landscape itself. Her helpless plight in the

face of these contradictory yet indivisible elements is then accurately
described in the following stanza which links back to the first through
an echo of *leixa-pren* in its opening line:

> El templo que tanto quise . . .
> pues no sé decir ya si le quiero,
> que en el rudo vaivén que sin tregua
> se agitan mis pensamientos,
> dudo si el rencor adusto
> vive unido al amor en mi pecho.   (p. 571)

> (The chuch so well beloved . . .
> which I can no longer tell if I love,
> for in the cruel oscillation endlessly
> racking my thoughts,
> I doubt if sullen rancour
> lives joined to love in my heart.)

'Vaivén' ('oscillation') is an exact word for Rosalía's mental processes as she swings continuously from positive to negative, from
hope to despair and from love to bitterness, one thought giving rise
to an instant association which in turn dissolves just as quickly into
another equivalent. It is apt too for the rhythm in which her thoughts
are linguistically structured, for the oscillation is endless—literally
'truceless,' ('sin tregua')—as we see in the syntactical continuity
of both stanzas, the first with its parenthetical asides and the second
somewhat convoluted as befits Rosalía's puzzlement, confusion and
doubt. Such oscillation is not far removed in spirit from the ancient
leixa-pren technique which, as we saw in the song of Bastabales, essentially refuses to separate one emotive concept from the next. But
while traditional *leixa-pren* in light and sonorous tercets is one thing,
it is an altogether different achievement to sustain an organic to-ing
and fro-ing in a poem of twenty expansive stanzas which gives besides
such a complete montage of the poet's emotional life. This is the
key to Rosalía's unassumingly complex poem in which she invites
us to accompany her—'Bajemos, pues' (p. 573) ('Let us go down,
then')—on a meditative amble through the natural environs of Padrón where she spent her last years, and in which she leaves her
house—'cárcel estrecha y sombría' (p. 572) ('dark and narrow prison')—in an attempt to cross the divide, only to fail and return
home more dispirited than ever. The points between which the pen-
dulum swings on this reflective journey include: firstly, the uncompli-
cated joy of youth when she wore 'la venda celeste / de la fe' (p. 572)
('the celestial blindfold / of faith') as opposed to her present mood

of spiritual emptiness, 'mi alma en su desierto' (p. 575) (my soul in its desert); secondly, the contrast between her once innocent 'quejas amantes' (p. 573) (sweetheart tiffs) and her now terrifying 'sed devoradora / y jamás apagada que ahoga el sentimiento' (p. 574) ('devouring and unquenchable thirst that drowns feeling') and her bitter 'hambre de justicia' (p. 575) ('hunger for justice'); finally, above all, the contrast between her once uninhibited delight in a paradisal nature and her actual discomfort at its very beauty, this being the ultimate and painful paradox which causes her to return home:

> porque con su alegría no aumente mi amargura
> la blanca luz del día.   (p. 575)

> (so that the day's white light
> not increase my bitterness with its joy.)

The poem's timescale thus constantly fluctuates between 'antes y ahora' (p. 575) ('before and now'), 'un tiempo ... y hoy' (p. 573) ('once ... and today'), between 'entonces' (p. 572) ('then') and the six times repeated 'ya' ('now'). Similarly there is fluctuation between reality and dream, for while an impressive plasticity is generated by the placenaming of woodland, hills and streams—'Trabanca', 'La Torre', 'Fondóns', 'Presa' and 'Miranda'—and by the detailed observation of 'vencejos', 'armiño', 'abubilla', 'nenúfar' (swifts, stoat, hoopoe, waterlily), there is too a counter-texture of immaterial symbols which speak of 'sombra vana ... esperanza muerta ..., flor ... que no crece' (p. 573) ('vain shadow ... dead hope, flower ... which doesn't grow') and which even superimposes wintry desolation upon what is in fact a glorious day in May. This is no artistic confusion, but rather, rich poetic complexity, the point being that Rosalía's inner self is so laid waste as to be out of joint with the spring landscape which was once her joy and is even now burgeoning all around her. Landscape in this instance, then, is used not merely as an objective correlative, for while its greenery correlates Rosalía's erstwhile joy and while a second symbolic layer evokes her present ravaged spirit, the decisive function of landscape here is to point out by contrast the change in Rosalía's emotional life. This poignant contrast stems from the paradox of being homesick when at home—'cual si en suelo extranjero me hallase' (p. 572) ('as if I were on foreign soil')—an excruciating form of *saudades* in which Rosalía is tantalized by having all she cherishes close at hand without ever being able to grasp it. In such a plight reality and dream interfuse with torment-ing effect, as we saw in our first poem:

> aun cuando sueñe que invisible habita
> en todo cuanto toco y cuanto veo ...
> ... ¡aun cuando sé que existes
> y no eres vano sueño!   (p. 621)

> (though I dream it dwells invisibly
> in all I touch and all I see ...
> ... even though I know you exist
> and you are no vain dream!)

Present reality is illusory because in Rosalía's mind it no longer matches its past splendour, 'perdió su azul tu cielo, el campo su frescura, / el alba su candor' (p. 574) ('your sky lost its blue, the countryside its freshness, / the dawn its innocence'), and because the past psychical reality for which she searches is no more than spectral in the landscape before her. Yet at the same time her senses confirm with teasing precision that reality in itself has not changed, '¡Oh tierra, antes y ahora, siempre fecunda y bella!' (p. 574) ('Oh land, before and now, ever fecund and beautiful!'). By means of this sustained paradox Rosalía's title poem gives remarkable sub-stance to the phantom motility of her mental states, while the poem's artistry shapes her apparent desultoriness and suggests the indivisi-bility of her emotional life.

It will be clear by now that such indivisibility, summarized in the term *saudades* and realized poetically through oscillation, is in this reader's view paramount among the virtues of *En las orillas del Sar*. At the same time it is equally clear that the component parts of Rosalía's dilemma have yet to be seen in sharp definition. Our only remedy is to focus in turn on each of her three fixations, the *patria*, love and religion, while keeping one eye alert for their intergra-tional tendencies. Beginning with the apex of our paradigm, a superb example of Rosalía's evocation of a distinctively Galician topography is found in the poem which follows the title poem. The first of its three stanzas offers a striking land- and seascape as viewed across a typical Galician *ría* or fiord-like estuary. Such a vista was very familiar to Rosalía since Padrón is at the head of the Arosa *ría*:

> Los unos altísimos,
> los otros menores,
> con su eterno verdor y frescura,
> que inspira a las almas
> agrestes canciones,

> mientras gime al rozar con las aguas
> la brisa marina, de aromas salobres,
> van en ondas subiendo hacia el cielo
> los pinos del monte.   (p. 575)

> (Some quite tall,
> others shorter,
> with their eternally fresh verdure,
> which inspires in one's heart
> rustic songs,
> while the sea breeze of salty smell
> moans on skimming the water,
> in waves they go climbing skyward
> the pines of the mountain.)

This delightful intermingling of land and sea is much aided by imagery, notably the transferred epithet of the pines rising 'in waves' and the interlocking agent of the breeze which ruffles water and pines alike. But the strong impression of permeable unanimity owes most to the stanza's syntax which integrates the two elements within its one sentence, the varying length of line and linguistic unit suggesting choppiness within the overall fluidity. As subtle as it is complex, the syntax distances the initial adjectival phrases referring to height, greenery and freshness from the noun they describe, 'pinos' ('pines'), which is kept back until the end. Between, the water imagery of lines six and seven seems to pick up the fresh green tones of the land and, in all, the stanza offers a spatial analogy of the *ría*, land-sea-land. The delayed subject of the pines is reached triumphantly and with religious overtones in the final ascension, but rather than being Christian, these overtones give a sense of the primeval and procreative force of nature rising from the sea, a chthonic emphasis which is reinforced by the next stanza's reciprocal downward motion: 'De la altura la bruma desciende / y envuelve las copas / perfumadas' (p. 576) ('From above the mist descends / and envelops the perfumed treetops'). This earth-orientation is clinched in the third and final stanza where the values seem entirely pagan and pantheistic:

> El viajero rendido y cansado
> que ve del camino la línea escabrosa
> que aún le resta que andar, anhelara,
> deteniéndose al pie de la loma,
> de repente quedar convertido
>   en pájaro o fuente,
>   en árbol o en roca.   (p. 576)

> (The traveller, weary from exertion,
> seeing the rugged contour of the road

            he still has left to walk, would wish,
            as he stops at the foot of the hill,
            to be completely changed of a sudden
                into bird or spring,
                into tree or rock.)

Once again we have a single-sentence stanza in which integration is the key theme, namely, in this instance, a wish to merge with nature. The wish, ostensibly prompted by tiredness, is set in an unmistakably allegorical context which implies the tribulations of life's journey. For Rosalía, significantly, it is nature and not a Christian heaven which offers the prospect of comfort and peace. Nor is it difficult to see why: the communion of nature is innocent, physical and, above all, anonymous, with no moral strings attached. As to the stanza's syntax, it captures the idea of mergence in the interrupted progress of its main clause, 'the traveller ... would wish ... to be changed ... into rock', but this complexity is resolved with the resounding generic simplicity of the last two appropriately brief lines, their lucidity suggesting the hoped-for resolution of Rosalía's dilemma.

The earth-orientation of the above poem is double-edged, for while it appears in a negative sense to be a kind of suicidal flight from identity, it also evidences the positive attraction which nature in all its vitality held for Rosalía. One of the most appealing and distinctive features of *En las orilla del Sar*, nature's animation is so pronounced at times as to go beyond the bounds of conventional Romantic ideology and tread the threshold of Celtic superstition. Here we remember that Rosalía's husband Murguía was a prominent figure in the *Cova céltica* or Galician Celtic Society and that his historical works put much emphasis on Galicia's Celtic substratum as it survives in archaeology and legend. The Celts themselves were a highly religious race who deified aspects of nature, as Rosalía recalls:

            esas selvas agrestes, esos bosques
            seculares y hermosos, cuyo espeso
            ramaje abrigo y cariñosa sombra
            dieron a nuestros padres, fueron siempre
            de predilecto amor, lugares santos
            que todos respetaron.   (p. 594)

            (those wild woods, those ancient
            and lovely forests, whose dense
            foliage gave shelter and loving shade
            to our ancestors, were always
            specially loved, holy places
            respected by all.)

Similarly in 'Los robles' ('The Oaks') she addresses the tree, 'tú, sacra encina del celta, / y tú, roble de ramas añosas' (p. 590) ('you, holy holm oak of the Celt, / and you, oak of aged branches'), while in 'A la luna' ('To the Moon') she refers to moon worship: 'en donde un tiempo el celta vigoroso / te envió sus oraciones' (p. 638) ('where once the sturdy Celt / sent you his prayers'). When in '¡Volved!' ('Return!') Rosalía deals with the modern Celtic theme of depopulation, she beseeches her countrymen to return and attacks them at their most vulnerable point:

> yo os lo digo y os juro
> que hay genios misteriosos
> que os llaman tan sentidos y amorosos
> y con tan hondo y dolorido acento,
> que hacen más triste el suspirar del viento . . .   (p. 602)

> (I say to you and I swear
> that there are mysterious spirits
> who call out for you so tender and lovingly
> and with such a deep and sorrowful voice,
> that they make the wind's sighing even sadder . . .)

The magical powers which the ancient Celts attributed to nature still function and Rosalía suggests that the Galicians who leave lose a lot more than land. The point that nature has the power of articulation is clearest in the lovely poem which begins:

> Dicen que no hablan las plantas, ni las fuentes, ni los pájaros,
> ni el onda con sus rumores, ni con su brillo los astros.
> Lo dicen; pero no es cierto, pues siempre, cuando yo paso,
> de mí murmuran y exclaman:
> —Ahí va la loca, soñando
> con la eterna primavera de la vida y de los campos . . .   (p. 626)

> (They say that plants don't speak, nor springs, nor birds,
> nor the wave with its rumbling, nor the stars with their sparkle.
> That's what they say; but it's not true, for whenever I pass by
> they chatter about me and cry:
> 'There goes the madwoman, dreaming
> of the eternal springtime of life and the countryside . . .')

This is quite unlike the kind of articulation which Bécquer gives nature when, for instance in the fifth *rima*, it is the voice of poetry which appears to speak through nature, or, in the tenth, the voice of love. It is only superficially like that found in Machado too, for, as we shall see, the various items of landscape with which he converses are essentially symbolic representations of his alter ego. In Rosalía ancient lore outweighs literary device and, in short, we do in fact feel that nature speaks. A closer comparison might be made with another Celt, the modern Welsh poet Dylan Thomas, for in his poems such as 'Especially When the October Wind' we find the same surprising articulation of 'oaken voices', 'vowelled beeches', 'dark vowelled birds' and 'spider-tongued and loud hill of Wales'. In Rosalía, as in Thomas, it is difficult to say where historical evocation ends and irrational belief begins, there being a strong suspicion that they overlap. For Rosalía, at least, the magical and folkloric world of her ancestors held a double attraction: it offered a retreat from Christian orthodoxy with its inevitable reminders of moral rectitude, and, at the same time, it was an idealized source of Galician identity located nostalgically in the remote past. The felling of trees in '¡Jamás lo olvidaré!' ('Never shall I forget!') is thus a very literal '¡Profanación sin nombre!' (p. 594) '(Profanation beyond words!'), while the desecration of the 'árbol patrio' ('national tree') in 'Los robles' ('The Oaks') is seen as wilful destruction of a people's ethnic values leaving Galicia as barren as the plains of Castile. Here the tree is a passionate focus of all Rosalía's aspirations: 'Árbol duro y altivo ... ¡Yo te amo!' (p. 589) ('Hard and proud tree ... I love you!'). When the poem ends on an appeal for the tree's return, the point is not only ecological but intensely nationalistic and the superstition is more than whimsical:

> ¡Torna presto a poblar nuestros bosques,
> y que tornen contigo las hadas
> que algún tiempo a tu sombra tejieron
>   del héroe gallego
>   las frescas guirnaldas!   (p. 591)

> (Come back soon to inhabit our woods,
> and may the fairies come with you
> who once in your shadow spun
>   the Galician hero's
>   fresh garlands!)

Harsh economic reality underlies the linked themes of Galicia's depopulation and the laying waste of its forests, but much as this twofold dismemberment of the *patria* provides a most tangible source of Rosalía's *saudades*, it also has bearing upon her personal dilemma. Already we have seen how her religious unease is implicit in her treatment of nature and it will not have escaped notice that many images in the same poems carry more than a suggestion of eroticism,

conscious or not. The point was made by Rof Carballo when commenting on Rosalía's lack of a father figure:

> El Animus de Rosalía ha de proyectarse formando imágenes varoniles
> ingenuas o fantásticas ... Esa Ausencia radical, en lo más hondo de
> su estructura psíquica, es determinante de su vida. Será una vagabunda
> en busca de su Animus.[6]
>
> Rosalía's Animus has to project itself by forming ingenuous or fantastic
> masculine images ... That radical Absence, in the deepest level of her
> psychic structure, is decisive in her life. She will always be a vagabond
> searching for her Animus.)

No knowledge of Freud or Jung is needed to perceive this, for instance,
in her tree and liquid imagery. Both have an energizing vigour: 'El
árbol salvaje le daba sus frutos, / la fuente sus aguas de grata frescura'
(p. 587) ('The wild tree gave her its fruits, / the spring its waters
of welcome freshness'). The tree is sometimes overtly linked with
love, 'el pino aguarda inmóvil / los besos inconstantes de la brisa'
(p. 580) ('the still pine awaits / the breeze's fickle kisses'), and again
when its destruction signals the end of love: 'Ya no entonan en ellas
los pájaros / sus canciones de amor' (p. 589) ('The birds no longer
sing their songs of love on them', i.e. on the bare slopes). Liquid
imagery is used with equal directness, especially maritime images
which are a Galician specialty:

> Sedientas las arenas, en la playa
> sienten del sol los besos abrasados,
> y no lejos las ondas, siempre frescas,
> ruedan pausadamente murmurando.
> Pobres arenas de mi suerte imagen ...   (p. 584)
>
> (Thirsty grains of sand on the beach
> feel the burning kisses of the sun,
> while nearby the ever fresh waves
> tumble slowly and ripple.
> Poor sands, the image of my fate ...)

The link between sexual frustration and the sea has a long history
in Galicia and Portugal which goes back to the *cantigas de amigo*
(*lovers' songs*) and its subgenre *barcarolas* (*sailor songs*) in which young
females lamented the absence or even death of their lover at sea.
The following is an example from medieval Galicia:

> Ondas do mar de Vigo,
> se vistes meu amigo!
> E ai, Deus, se verrá cedo!
> ... Se vistes meu amigo,

o por que eu suspiro!
E ai, Deus, se verrá cedo!⁷

(Waves of the sea of Vigo,
if you saw my lover!
Oh, God, may he come back soon!
... If you saw my lover,
the one for whom I pine!
Oh, God, may he come back soon!)

The same traditional motifs are used by Rosalía to express the fugitive nature of love, 'las ondas que besan la playa / y que una tras otra besándola expiran' (p. 656) ('the waves that kiss the beach / and which one after another on kissing it die'), or, more typically, to convey that same terrible mix of loneliness and passion:

Del mar azul las transparentes olas
    mientras, blandas, murmuran
sobre la arena, hasta mis pies rodando,
tentadoras, me besan y me buscan.
... Mas cuando ansiosa, quiero
seguirlas por la líquida llanura
... huyen, abandonándome en la playa ...   (p. 628)

(Transparent waves of the blue sea,
    gentle as they ripple
on the sand, come breaking at my feet
and alluringly seek me and kiss me.
... But when, anxiously, I try
to pursue them on the liquid plain
: .. they flee, abandoning me on the beach ...)

This recurring motif aptly conveys both the idealism and the bitter disillusion which compose Rosalía's view of love.

Like the totem tree, then, the liquid imagery of Galicia's sacred rivers and seashores is a simultaneous projection of Rosalía's religious and sexual aspirations. In the case of liquid imagery the link is more particular since the idea of thirst has obvious application in both contexts. Thirst frequently alludes to physical passion, as in the remorseful poem which begins:

Sed de amores tenía, y dejaste
    que la apagase en tu boca,
¡piadosa samaritana!   (p. 646)

(He had a thirst for love, and you let
    him quench it on your mouth,
pious Samaritan!)

Here Rosalía chastises a woman who innocently gave her favours and then found herself 'sin honra' ('dishonoured'). That she identifies with the woman is plain from the line 'pero yo sé también, pecadora / compasiva' ('but I know too, compassionate / sinner'), and what Rosalía knows full well is that the male will not return but move on to another as birds of passage take to another stream when they have sullied the water of the last. The poem's several religious references insinuate a discrepancy between the Christian ethic of love and what the Church expects of women, while the ironic tone indicates Rosalía's distaste for the Church's uncharitable attitude towards those who have sinned, as it were, in good faith. The frequency of the thirst motif is largely explained by its facility for transposing into religious analogy, and here we bear in mind that Rosalía's sense of guilt is directly proportionate to her need for salvation. The mixture is often implicit:

> La venturosa copa del placer, para siempre
> rota a mis pies está ...   (p. 606)

> (The happy cup of pleasure, for ever
> lies broken at my feet ...)

But often the idea of a liquid rite clearly fuses religion and sexuality:

> —¡La copa es de oro fino,
> el néctar que contiene es de los cielos!—
> dijo, y bebió con ansia
> hasta el último sorbo de veneno.   (p. 653)

> ('The cup is of fine gold,
> the nectar it holds is from heaven!'
> she said, and drank it eagerly
> down to its last drop of poison.)

This fine cup inevitably recalls the sacramental chalice, but all idealism is shattered by the word 'veneno' ('poison') which, poignantly withheld until last, conveys the sense of a cruel deception as well as the remorse experienced in the aftermath of passion. In accord with the liquid pattern, Rosalía then describes the deceived female as one whose blood is 'emponzoñada' ('poisoned')—a motif which occurs elsewhere, 'Emponzoñada estás' (p. 616) ('Now you are poisoned')—and it is clear that passion is the complete antithesis of the life-giving love of the Eucharist. Indeed, as the poem 'Margarita' ('Margaret') concludes, it is a perversion or corruption of ideal love: 'en medio del vaso corrompido / donde su sed ardiente se apagaba'

(p. 583) ('amidst the corrupt glass / where her burning thirst was quenched').

This last poem, 'Margarita', is in fact one of the most revealing on the theme of illicit love. It presents a graphic picture of a woman tormented at night by sexual desire. The uncontrollable force of her passion is evoked by reference to animals in the opening stanza:

> ¡Silencio, los lebreles
> de la jauría maldita!
> No despertéis a la implacable fiera
> que duerme silenciosa en su guarida.   (p. 582)

> (Be still, hounds
> of the cursed pack!
> Don't awaken the implacable beast
> who sleeps silently in his lair.)

But her passion is roused and the young woman dreams of her lover while the man of the house lies sleeping. Plagued by her conscience— 'negras hijas de la duda' ('black daughters of doubt')—and indecisive for a moment—'tiembla . . . vacila . . . con las pasiones lucha' ('trembling . . . wavering . . . she struggles against her passion')—the young woman finally goes out to meet her lover only to return at dawn distraught, 'ajado el velo . . ., en su mirar la angustia' (p. 583) ('her veil crumpled . . ., her eyes full of anguish'). The mood of the poem is one of guilt, with the female powerless before the diabolical forces of passion:

> ella, insensata,
> siguió quemando incienso en su locura
> de la torpeza ante las negras aras,
> hasta rodar en el profundo abismo,
> fiel a su mal, de su dolor esclava.   (p. 583)

> (she, senseless,
> kept up her frenzied burning of incense
> at the black altars of vileness,
> until she tumbled into the deep abyss,
> faithful to her evil, slave to her sickness.)

This is a long way from Espronceda's idealized bereft heroine. The woman herself is culpable, totally unable to deal with the forces of darkness which surround her in this as in other poems:

> Y como ahuyenta la aurora
> los vapores soñolientos
> de la noche callada y sombría,
> así ahuyenta mis malos deseos.   (p. 608)

(And as dawn banishes
the drowsy vapours
of the silent and gloomy night,
so it banishes my evil desires.)

The nocturnal is found again in the poem beginning:

De la noche en el vago silencio,
cuando duermen o sueñan las flores,
mientras ella despierta, combate
contra el fuego de ocultas pasiones.   (p. 618)

(In the vague silence of night,
when flowers sleep or dream,
as she lies awake she struggles
against the fire of hidden passions.)

The struggle is hopeless for at these times the female is visited by
'el de siempre, / fiel amigo del mal, Mefistófeles' ('the perpetual
one, / faithful friend of evil, Mephistopheles') who brings his persuasive message of instant pleasure. It is clear, then, that despite the
fluctuations from first to second and third persons of the verb, Rosalía
identifies with the dark nocturnal forces and that she characterizes
herself as a sensual female weak to the temptations of the flesh.
What is more, as we see in the following treatment of the traditional
motif of the *morena* or dark-skinned woman, it appears that this weak-
ness is fatal or inherited from birth:

A las rubias envidias
porque naciste con color moreno,
y te parecen ellas blancos ángeles
que han bajado del Cielo.
¡Ah!, pues no olvides, niña,
y ten por cosa cierta,
que mucho más que un ángel siempre pudo
un demonio en la Tierra.   (p. 645)

(You envy fair girls
because you were born with dark complexion,
and to you they seem like white angels
come down from heaven.
Ah, but don't forget, my girl,
and take it as proven fact,
that a good deal more than an angel
could a devil ever do on Earth.)

The *morena's* self-disparagement has a history which goes back to
the Song of Solomon, 'I am dark but comely', and the motif was
strong in Spain where its implications of ungodly sensuality were

intensified by, among other things, the Christian view of dark Moorish women. In Rosalía, a brunette herself, it links with that secondary
Romantic concept of woman as a tainted beauty, which Mario Praz
discusses under the heading 'The Beauty of Medusa'.[8] Certainly
Rosalía identifies with the earth-bound woman for whom salvation
is a contradiction in terms.

This leads us to the religious theme itself, the third and last point
in our paradigm, which Rosalía understandably developed with far
greater urgency in her last work. Several poems locate her in meditative mood before the Christian altar, but, while her thoughts
encompass the same grand issues as were to preoccupy Antonio
Machado—'¿Qué somos! ¿Qué es la muerte?' (p. 578) ('What are
we? What is death?')—her philosophical inquiry is coloured by a
feeling of her own unworthiness, 'impía acaso, interrogando al Cielo'
('impious perchance, questioning Heaven'), and the same poem
closes with some doctrinaire angels pointedly reminding her of sin:

> mas no olvides que al Cielo
> nunca ha llegado el insolente grito
> de un corazón que de la vil materia
> y del barro de Adán formó sus ídolos. (p. 579)

> (but don't forget that Heaven
> was never reached by the insolent cry
> of a spirit who from base matter
> and Adam's clay shaped its idols.)

The same is stated elsewhere, 'No subas tan alto, pensamiento loco
... / ni puede el alma gozar del cielo / mientras que vive envuelta
en la carne' (p. 593) ('Don't fly so high, mad thoughts ... / the
soul cannot enjoy heaven / while it lives wrapped up in the flesh'),
a basic conundrum which is more keenly felt in a volume with so
many earthly attachments. Thus, for the most part, it is the distance
between heaven and earth, the absolute polarization at the two, which
Rosalía stresses. While in the last poem she had asked almost disbelievingly '¿Es verdad que lo ves? Señor' (p. 578) ('Is it true that
you can see it, Lord?', i.e. my suffering), in another altar poem she
frankly explains how difficult it is for her to conceive a God whose
grand scale dwarfs her own existence and renders it meaningless:

> Si medito en tu eterna grandeza,
> buen Dios, a quien nunca veo,
> y levanto, asombrada, los ojos
> hacia el alto firmamento
> que llenaste de mundos y mundos ...,

toda conturbada pienso
que soy menos que un átomo leve
perdido en el Universo:
nada, en fin ..., y que al cabo en la nada
han de perderse mis restos.   (p. 628)

(If I meditate on your eternal grandeur,
benign God, whom I never see,
and I lift my eyes amazed
towards the high firmament
which you filled with worlds and more worlds ...,
all abashed I think
that I am less than a mere atom
lost in the Universe:
nothing, in short ..., and that ultimately in nothing
will my remains be lost.)

This Christian God is far removed from the human sphere and all
Rosalía identifies with. Indeed, his comprehension seems to require
hard abstract thinking as opposed to the intuitive, subjective processes which are natural to her. Yet Rosalía preserves her uneasy
faith by personalizing the abstraction, as we shall see, and by reduc-
ing it to her own sensibility. She does this in at least three ways,
the first of which is by turning to the Christ figure with whose suffering
she readily empathizes, as the continuation of the above poem convincingly shows:

Mas si, cuando el dolor y la duda
me atormentan, corro al templo,
y a los pies de la Cruz un refugio
busco, ansiosa, implorando remedio,
de Jesús el cruento martirio
tanto conmueve mi pecho,
y adivino tan dulces promesas
en sus dolores acerbos,
que cual niño que reposa
en el regazo materno,
después de llorar, tranquila
tras la expiación, espero
que allá donde Dios habita
he de proseguir viviendo.   (p. 629)

(But if, when sorrow and doubt
torment me, I run to the temple,
and at the feet of the Cross seek
refuge, anxiously imploring relief,
the bloody martyrdom of Christ
so moves my heart
and I divine such sweet promises

in his bitter wounds,
that like a child resting
in her mother's lap,
with tears dried and calm
after the expiation, I hope
that there where God dwells
am I to go on living.)

The bond of suffering which links Rosalía to Christ removes all doubt
that she herself will be found worthy. The distance of the first stanza
is bridged and its arithmetic changed into human flesh which is
as warm and close as a mother's embrace.

A second example of reduction and personalization is even more
emotional or intuitive and it centres entirely on maternal instinct.
In the poem which decribes the burial of her young son, Rosalía
asks the eternal question, '¿Es verdad que todo / para siempre acabó
ya?' (p. 577) ('Is it true that everything / is finished now for ever?').
Her rejection of such finality is based on something literally felt
inside:

> Algo ha quedado tuyo en mis entrañas
> que no morirá jamás   (p. 577)

> (Something of you remains in my innermost parts
> that will never die)

The persuasiveness of this answer owes much to the poem's setting
which has presented the child's burial in terms of a return to the
womb-like earth on a day of gentle drizzle, 'y llovía, llovía / callada
y mansamente' ('and it was raining, raining / silently and softly').
The feminine *douceur* of the rain foreshadows the regenerative power
of the earth which is then stressed, 'verde y pujante crecerá la hierba'
('green and thrusting will the grass grow'), an evocative line which
again compares with Dylan Thomas's chthonic 'the force that
through the green fuse drives the flower'. Essentially, however,
Rosalía has found her way to faith through the very things dogma
requires her to reject, namely the body and the world. This also applies in principle to a last example we may take of Rosalía's emotion-
alizing of the religious issue. The long and impressive poem 'Santa
Escolástica' ('Saint Escolastica') depicts Rosalía in a state of mental
torment as she wanders about Santiago's empty streets on a wet
and sultry April afternoon. The airless atmosphere, the cemetery-like
city at siesta time and the heavy tolling of bells are all brilliantly
evoked and serve as pointers to her depressed mood. Straying near

the Cathedral, which can be come upon suddenly from the *ruas* or narrow cobbled streets, she fears for a moment that its great bulk will topple down on her, no doubt in some form of divine retribution, and there seems no prospect at all of spiritual relief. Her mood is suicidal, for, racked with pain, guilt and doubt, she senses only the distance of salvation: 'El cielo está tan alto / y tan bajos nosotros' (p. 624) ('Heaven is so high / and we so low').

Then, seeking shelter, she stumbles more by chance through the half-open door of the chapel of San Martín Pinario, and, once inside, her mood changes abruptly to one of awe at the majestic architecture of its domes, a point registered in the poem's change from hendecasyllables to the classical and weighty line of the alexandrine. Impressed spiritually by the mystic silence, her senses roused by the smell of incense and burning candles, she turns to pray at the shadowy altar, when, with the suddenness of revelation, the sun's rays break through the mist, penetrate the church windows and light up the statue of Saint Escolastica and angels. The beauty of this vision transports Rosalía and the poem ends with her kneeling at the altar to exclaim:

> ¡Hay arte! ¡Hay poesía . . .! Debe haber cielo. ¡Hay Dios!

> (There is art! There is poetry . . .! There must be a heaven. A God!)

This conclusion has been described as 'the most joyous cry in all of Rosalía's work' and as an 'illustration of the progression towards psychic wholeness evidenced in *The Sar*'.[9] This may well be so, but let us remember that the conclusion itself is decidedly atypical of the volume as a whole and that what is typical is the manner in which it is arrived at, namely through an emotional response to physical beauty. Indeed, the response itself is unmistakably centred on the body:

> ¡Majestad de los templos!, mi alma feminina
> te siente como siente las maternas dulzuras   (p. 624)

> (Majesty of temples! My feminine soul
> feels you as it feels the maternal sweetnesses)

The heady atmosphere in the church is an evocative trigger, 'despertó en mis sentidos / de tiempos más dichosos reminiscencias largas' (p. 625) ('it awoke in my senses / copious memories of happier times'), a happiness which was no doubt not entirely otherworldly and almost certainly based on a blissful ignorance of the duality of body and spirit. Similarly, Rosalía's experience in the church is pleasurable and sensuous, and, far from resolving the duality of body and spirit in favour of the latter, it indicates the inescapability and ascendancy of the former in her psychic make-up. What is more, as compared with the account of her mental anguish in the poem's main part, where her restless and random passage through Santiago's rain-soaked streets is entirely convincing, the revelation of the statue at the poem's close is somewhat engineered, stereotyped and melodramatic, to the extent that it cannot fail to strike us as sublimation.

Here we enter the difficult waters of psychology again, though psychoanalytical interpretation has always been implicit in our discussion of Rosalía under the heading of *saudades*, which, after all, is a form of neurosis. To understand Rosalía and her *saudades* more fully we need now to develop this perspective. First we might say that for Freud of course all culture is a sublimation of sexuality, and doubtless most psychologists would see 'Santa Escolástica' as a model illustration of his thesis. But Freud's view of sublimation is two-sided and complex, as Norman O. Brown points out in his chapter entitled 'The Ambiguities of Sublimation',[10] and both its aspects are relevant to Rosalía. In principle Freud views sublimation as a form of desexualization and socialization of instinctive forces whereby an individual sacrifices instinctive pleasures in order to conform to society. His two views come when assessing whether the sacrifice is beneficial or not. If, on the one hand, the sublimations are imposed by society on the individual, they are repressive. Here, with regard· to Rosalía, we might be inclined to think that there was considerable pressure on her in Santiago of all places and that her plentiful poems on the land are perhaps an attempt to escape those pressures and even to construct an alternative mythical society, the Celtic, entirely in accord with her instinct. If, on the other hand, Freud argues, the sublimations succeed in transferring the individual's instinctive aims in such a way as they cannot be frustrated by the outer world, they are therapeutic. In this connection we recall that the three poems on religious faith which we have considered all arrive at the conclusion which society demands by virtue of transferring Rosalía's instinctive bodily pleasure to the religious context, namely the body of Christ, the earth-mother and the church. In the end it is perhaps not for us to say whether therapy or repression is uppermost in Rosalía's 'orthodox' poems, though we might be inclined to argue that one poem's conclusion is more convincing than another's because of its greater degree of transference. Certainly in my opinion the poem on the Crucifixion is much more convincing in its conclusion than the poem in the chapel. What I think we can say, however, and with some confidence, is that these few poems are prompted by the neurosis of *saudades* which is the predominant feature of *En las orillas del Sar* and that they reflect her desperate need to believe, her 'querer creer' ('wanting to believe'), as Unamuno later put it, or even her self-induced 'creer creer' ('believing one believes'). The sublimation is a wish-fulfilment which reflects Rosalía's desire to transcend her neurosis and belong, for, as Brown says, 'a neurosis isolates; a sublimation unites', and, quoting Freud: 'the religious believer by accepting the universal neurosis is spared the task of forming a personal neurosis'.[11] Thus, though a handful of 'orthodox' poems function as an escape hatch, and as such may well be joyful, it is the neurosis and the existential *Angst* of *saudades* which is the true psychic reality in *En las orillas del Sar*.

But *saudades* is not only a neurosis, in the sense of being an irreconcilable conflict of psychic forces, it is also an expression of the desire to overcome neurosis, that is, to find happiness. While orthodox and eschatological religion represents that prospect problematically in the future, the main orientation of *saudades* is to the past, and here we find a different set of values even as regards the religious. Fundamentally the difference between past and future orientation is the difference between life and death, or, in Freudian terms, the difference between the body and the spirit. For Freud the body was alive in the past or in youth while it is ever dying in the adult phase of spiritual repression and sublimation. But let us note here the relevance of Freudian psychology to the past orientation of *saudades*, nostalgia being a clear example of what Freud calls regression. The key Freudian point is that childhood is in some sense an unrepressed state, and it follows that the neurotic adult flees from a repressive society by regressing to childhood. Rosalía's fixation to the past of childhood-youth is clear in *En las orillas del Sar*, for instance in its title poem where she refers to 'aquellos días hermosos y brillantes' (p. 573) ('those beautiful and brilliant days'), and again:

> Puro el aire, la luz sonrosada.
>   ¡Qué despertar tan dichoso!
> Yo veía entre nubes de incienso
>   visiones con alas de oro
> que llevaban la venda celeste
>   de la fe sobre sus ojos ...
> Ese sol es el mismo, mas ellas
>   no acuden a mi conjuro ...
> ¡ay!, ya en vano las llamo y las busco.   (p. 572)

(The air pure, the light rosy pink.
What a joyous awakening!
I would see amid clouds of incense
visions with golden wings
that bore the celestial blindfold
of faith over their eyes . . .
That sun is the same, but they
do not answer my call . . .
Alas, in vain do I now summon and seek them.)

The evocation of childhood as a state of bliss gone for ever reminds us yet again of Dylan Thomas, for instance 'Fern Hill', and his strong orientation to the past is certainly accompanied by a terror of death. In Rosalía, as in Thomas, childhood is a state of bliss in physical things, in the earth, in the body and in the senses. The important thing is what is absent, for childhood is a paradisal ignorance of morality and mortality, the twin sisters of man's Fall. As Brown says, childhood is 'the state of nature',[12] and, just as Rosalía's poems reflect her desire to return to that unthinking timeless state—notably in the poem of the pine trees where she wished to merge with nature—other poems which show the devastation of nature and its trees are not only sociological but function as correlatives of her lost youth and of her present mutilated psyche. The paradise of childhood is recovered only fleetingly in adult life by dream-like regression, as above, or by therapeutic sublimation, as when before the Cross Rosalía feels like a child 'que reposa/en el regazo materno' ('resting / on her mother's lap'). This conforms to Freud's view that while the paradise of childhood is irrevocably lost its recovery remains man's most ardent and unconscious desire. And perhaps it is in this absolute context that we may best understand the neurosis-saudades of *En las orillas del Sar* as expressed in our first poem:

> yo no sé lo que busco, pero es algo
> que perdí no sé cuando . . .
>
> (I know not what I seek, but it is something
> I lost I know not when . . .)

It is entirely consistent, psychologically speaking, that Rosalía should say in the same poem that her goal, 'Felicidad' ('Happiness'), is both the stuff of dreams and something which she knows exists, for such an *invisible* reality accords with the notion that her instinctive means of perception have been repressed and are now confined to her unconscious. By this analysis Rosalía's search is for her unconscious and for her true self, and the dilemma her poetry describes, intensely personal as it is, has compelling psychological universality.

If we should feel slightly uneasy about having subjected Rosalía to the psychoanalyst's couch, let us remember two things: first, that Freud said it was the poets, not he, who had discovered the unconscious, that he had simply found a scientific means of exploring it, and secondly, that *En las orillas del Sar* is an extreme example of a poet subjecting herself to analysis. It is the unremitting persistence of this self-analysis which gives the volume its coherence and its form. Locked entirely 'en el rudo vaivén que sin tregua / se agitan mis pensamientos' ('in the cruel oscillation endlessly / racking my thoughts'), Rosalía's volume explores areas which the Surrealists, largely through their knowledge of Freud, would later explore more consciously. Though we cannot say that the picture Rosalía offers of herself is one of psychic wholeness or mental health, we can say that *En las orillas del Sar* goes a long way towards offering the whole picture of a neurosis called *saudades*. Its expression was no doubt therapeutic for Rosalía, while the manner in which it is expressed pleases us as readers inasmuch as the involution of the conflicting forces of 'tierra ... aire ... cielo' ('earth ... air ... heaven') creates its own artistic form. *Saudades* is the unifying complex because it contains and foregrounds these three forces which compose Rosalía's neurosis and also because it expresses her desire to overcome and transcend the neurosis. The pessimism of *saudades*, totally in accord with Freud's pessimism, stems from an awareness that such a Utopian project is unrealizable.

III

Antonio Machado

The Poetics of Time

Desgarrada la nube; el arco iris
brillando ya en el cielo,
y en un fanal de lluvia
y sol el campo envuelto.
Desperté. ¿Quién enturbia
los mágicos cristales de mi sueño?
Mi corazón latía
atónito y disperso.
. . . ¡El limonar florido,
el cipresal del huerto,
el prado verde, el sol, el agua, el iris! . . .
¡el agua en tus cabellos! . . .
Y todo en la memoria se perdía
como una pompa de jabón al viento.[1]

(The shredded cloud, the rainbow
shining now in the sky,
and in a glass bell of rain
and sun the land enclosed.
I woke up. Who breathes on
the magic windows of my dream?
My heart was beating
astonished and dispersed.
. . . The lemon grove in flower,
the cluster of cypress in the garden,
the green pasture, the sun, the water, the rainbow! . . .
the water in your hair! . . .
And all that was memory vanished
like a bubble of soap in the wind.)

First in the impressive line of major twentieth-century Spanish poets is Antonio Machado, a deeply meditative poet who expresses the literary and philosophic ideas of his age in an authentic personal voice. In his emphasis upon subjectivity and sensibility, upon what he called 'una honda palpitación del espíritu' (p. 68) ('a deep beating of one's heart'), Machado keeps faith with the Romantic ethos; indeed, he is both a visionary dreamer like Bécquer, as the above poem already indicates, and a poet of place like Rosalía, who expresses his inner self through the stark correlative of the Castilian landscape. But lying upon this deep-rooted Romanticism is the well-raked topsoil of the literary movements which influenced Machado at the turn of the century, notably Symbolism, Modernism and what was to be called *noventayochismo*, the patriotic and metaphysical concerns of Spain's Generation of 1898. Regarding these three: Symbolism was something Machado knew well from his French studies and from his stays in Paris, his familiarity going far beyond the beacons of Mallarmé and Verlaine.[2] The decadence, ennui or *hastío* ('weariness') which inform his work testify to this influence, as does his remarkable concentration, his distillation of feeling and thought into terse, enigmatic signifiers in a magnificently spare Castilian. Modernism, secondly, is evident in the early Machado's melodic prosody which, owing much to Rubén Darío, had been inspired initially by Verlaine's famous tenet, 'De la musique avant toute chose'. Though he soon rejected the virtuoso in Darío and chose to 'seguir camino bien distinto' (p. 68) ('follow quite a different path'), the musicality of his first volume, *Soledades* (*Solitudes*), 1903, was never lost, rather it became more subtle in *Galerías* (*Galleries*), 1907, and in *Campos de Castilla* (*Fields of Castile*), 1912 and 1917. Finally, as a '98 man, Machado's concern for 'the problem of Spain' was increasingly apparent by the time of *Campos de Castilla* and, furthermore, he typifies the Generation in his ambivalence: 'Tengo un gran amor a España y una idea de España completamente negativa'[3] ('I have a great love of Spain and a completely negative idea of Spain'). The key point, however, is that these three movements, Symbolism, Modernism and *noventayochismo* are all interrelated in Machado, not only the first two for their compositional concerns, but also the last since its heartfelt focus on Spain's plight is a natural extension of the subjective malaise and *fin de siècle* pessimism of the other two. In particular, the three movements find their point of intersection in Machado's overriding preoccupation—time—for here theme and technique, subjective and collective anguish meet. 'Todo

poeta supone una metafísica'[4] ('Any poet must have a metaphysic'),
Machado said, and unquestionably his centres on time. Some aspects
of time in Machado go back to the medieval tradition, but its metaphysical edge, I shall argue, derives from a modern treatment which
coincides with that of the supreme contemporary metaphysician of
time, Henri Bergson, considered by many to be the philosophic
mouthpiece of Symbolism and described by Machado as 'el filósofo
definitivo del siglo XIX'[5] ('the definitive philosopher of the XIXth
century').

The poem we are to consider first was written in 1903, published
in the review *Helios* in 1904 and subsequently given the prominent
position in *Galerías* of following the introductory poem. It is a fine
example of the unassuming way Machado creates temporal perspective, integrating what he considered the two imperatives of poetry,
'esencialidad y temporalidad' (p. 71) ('essentiality and temporality'),
a sense of inner being and a sense of time. The method is unassuming
because there seems at first little effort and less rhetorical device
involved in the listing of items in the poem's two longest sentences,
lines 1–4 and 9–12, which are sentences lacking the customary finite
verb. The verbless opening sentence is in fact a feature in Machado
and may be found for instance in poems III, V, XVI and LII,
while a near verbless listing of objects occurs in XXI and LXXI.
This suggests some purpose to Machado's technique and it is not
hard to see the bearing it has on the poem's mood. The itemizing
constitutes a plain and uninventive use of syntax and it thereby
suggests a certain lethargy on the part of the poet *vis-à-vis* his task
of composition. The speaker is thus first identified by his lack of
effort, zest, commitment, that is, by his inertia. Similarly, the absence
of finite verbs tends to divest the sequence of movement and vitality
while it also exempts the poet from direct involvement. What we
have essentially in the first four lines is a simply and even disinterestedly drawn picture in which the poet, both as creator and participa-
tor, is passive. The technique is well suited to creating a mood of
ennui or listlessness, which applies in several of the poems mentioned
above; though in the case of our first poem, which is ultimately
positive in many respects, 'will-lessness' might be a more accurate
term to describe the speaker's mood. It is the absence of the poet
and the presence of landscape which impresses us in the first four
lines, and it is only because the setting has worked upon him, rather
than he upon the setting, that he comes to life in line five—'Desperté'
('I woke up')—otherwise his sensibility, we assume, would have

remained somnolent. Paradoxically, he wakes up to a reverie of recollected thoughts, which suggests his previous state had been one of distraction in the present. He wakes up, then, to dream the past, having been roused from a kind of waking sleep in the present. This initial state of distraction or will-lessness is much in the spirit of the times. It recalls the considerable influence of Schopenhauer who held that the will was evil and that only by negating it could man attain the nirvana-like peace and serenity of ataraxia. Leconte de Lisle had dealt with similar themes in his poetry, but ataraxia was a special concern of the '98 novelists Pío Baroja and Azorín whose first major works, respectively *Camino de perfección* (*Way to Perfection*) and *La voluntad* (*The Will*), had come out only one year before in 1902. With more direct regard to the poem's time theme, however, it was Bergson who argued that will-lessness or disinterest was a prerequisite for proper recall of past experience. This, together with the temporal implications paramount in Machado's verbless sentences, is something we shall consider in a moment.

Before doing so it is as well to note the poem's striking Symbolist manner. The first four lines are ample demonstration. In the abbreviated picture of a torn cloud, a rainbow and a landscape lit up in a sunshower, we have that kind of richly suggestive and mysteriously indeterminate configuration prized by the Symbolists. The setting is a correlative of the poet's mood, no doubt, but we only sense this vaguely, intuitively at first, without the conviction that simile and allegory provide. Even after several readings the picture so effortlessly created in the opening sequence seems less an external representation of the poet's mood than something which interpenetrates totally and yet inexplicably with his inner self. It is hard to put one's finger on the point of connection, though gradually we come to sense that it has something to do with the fluidity, modulation and transience of the sunshower, that this delightful mixture of sun and rain, this purely ephemeral natural phenomenon, compares somehow with the poet's own mental fluidity, his gliding intermediacy between present and past, reality and dream. In the same context the sunshower and the shifting rainbow with its merging arcs of colour is a fine example of the hallowed Symbolist principle of synaesthesia, a synthesis of disparate elements which both evokes the idea and stimulates the sensation of simultaneity in the reader's mind. Synaesthesia typically refers to musicality and to the capacity of sound to evoke quite different sensations, and here again, in its technical aspects, Machado's poem is not wanting. Two phonemic

features stand out in the first four lines: a high incidence of 'l' and
'll' sounds, ten in all, and a similarly high incidence of dipthongs,
nine in all, four of which result from synalepha and two from the
palatal 'll' [ʎ]. While it is always hazardous to allot specific meanings
to sound patterns, it is perhaps permissible here within the spirit
of synaesthesia to suggest that these two phonemic features have
a function relevant to the poem's mood and scene. Not for nothing
is the 'l' known as a liquid phoneme, its articulation characterized
by the glide of the tongue on the palate or roof of the mouth. Similarly,
the dipthong is essentially a mixture of two sounds which glide one
into the other, the point of articulation being indeterminate between
the two points which the speech organs take up to pronounce the
vowels separately. Together these features are concordant with—and
perhaps evocative of—the physical and mental instability which the
poem semantically describes. However, what the poet ultimately
seeks to suggest through such musicality and such synaesthesia, that
is to say, through the total symbol which his poem constructs, is
nothing less than the unfathomable complexity of the human mind
as a centre of simultaneous thoughts, feelings and responses. The
important implication of this emphasis upon the simultaneous and
the changing is that the human mind, at its highest levels of operation,
is governed not by reason but by intuition. It is the intuitive self
alone which can sift the multiplicity of sensations, make sense out
of the confusion and perceive its hidden concordance. Such is the
irrational, spiritual and ultimately transcendental inclination of
Symbolism which Machado's poem shares in its lifting of our gaze
from the earth to the translucent skies of intuitive perception.

But all this is no more than background theory to a poem which
has its own very special points to make. Basically, as we have noted,
it is the natural setting depicted in the first four lines which works
upon the poet and causes him to wake up to a higher reality, a
vital recall of a cherished moment in the past. He has no control
over the recollection as we see from his puzzled question '¿Quién
...?' ('Who ...?'), from his astonishment, from the spontaneous reaction of his thumping heart and, finally, from his inability to sustain
the memory. Lines 5–8 link back to the opening sequence through
two delicate allusions: 'cristales' ('windows') links with 'fanal' ('glass
bell' or 'lantern'), while the liquid motif of rain continues with the
implicit blood of the poet's heart, reminiscent of Verlaine's simile
'Il pleut dans mon cœur / Comme il pleut sur la ville'. But the
confusion and fluid simultaneity in the second sequence is most

indebted to the choice of verbs. Between the verbless sequences of lines 1–4 and 9–12 Machado introduces three verbs in quick succession, each in a different tense. No doubt we find this quite mystifying on first reading, to the extent that we experience something of the poet's own confusion. But the tenses are very telling: the initial preterite indicates a sudden event, a jolting of the poet's sensibility; the present tense which follows has the effect of actualizing the past as an immediate experience; the final imperfect distances the poet once again as he recalls the event from the perspective of composing the poem. The tenses thus indicate gradations of 'pastness', three temporal planes and three stages in the poet's life: the true present is that of the poet at work on his poem; the near-past is his experience of the setting described in the opening sequence; the remote past is his experience of the setting described in lines 9–12. Yet the verb tenses do not conform with clinical precision to this narrative scheme, for, as we have seen, a present tense is used to describe a past event. The point is that the poet's temporal perspective on events is continually fluctuating; he looks from the perspective of the present or the near-past, or he even loses himself in an actualized remote past. The result is a sense of absolute temporal fluidity, a fluidity clinched in the ambiguity of the final imperfect—'Mi corazón latía' ('My heart was beating')—which could refer to the near or remote past, or to both at once.

Now we can see the point of omitting finite verbs in the poem's two main sentences: the resulting lack of temporal specification allows the two sequences to merge in accord with the mysterious sensation of *déjà vu*. Strictly speaking, the close similarity between the initial setting and one experienced by Machado in the past has triggered off an instant recall of that past experience, recounted in lines 9–12. The first and third sequences are thus closely paralleled, both as regards their diction, with 'sol' (sun), 'iris' (rainbow) and 'lluvia/agua' (rain/water) in each case, and as regards the technique of a verbless listing. However, there are important differences: while the first sequence is linguistically relaxed, partly as a result of the connectives *y* (and), the third sequence is intense, as a result of the exclamations, the absence of connectives and the corresponding compression of the enumeration. More details are included in the third sequence, suggesting greater vividness in the past: specific plants, trees and colours are mentioned, but above all a person of evident importance in the poet's life is introduced, 'el agua en tus cabellos' ('the water in your hair'). She is probably a young, idealized love of the poet, though she could even be his mother. Lack of specification on this point is in keeping with the poem's intimacy and private mood, while it also avoids distracting our attention from the central issue, time. The compressed enumeration vividly conveys the poet's mounting excitement as the remote past of the third sequence rapidly supplants the near-past of the first. This reaches a breathless pitch in 'iris' ('rainbow') which is the decisive link with the first sequence and the point in time when present perception gives way completely to recollection. Powerless before the rush of sensations, the poet is amazed at the fidelity of his memory, its increasing precision: 'el agua ... / ¡el agua en tus cabellos! ...' ('the water ... / the water in your hair! ...'). The introduction of an entirely new element here in the form of the beloved confirms the triumph of memory, and, with this line, the poem appropriately expands syntactically in a moment of affective colouration. Strangely, however, this exultant actualization of the past is followed almost instantaneously by termination of the memory process and restoration of the past's remoteness, 'Y todo en la memoria se perdía' ('And all that was memory vanished').

Machado's treatment of time and memory in this poem, I now wish to show, adheres very closely to Bergson's analysis. Here it should first be said that there has never been much doubt about the French philosopher's influence on Machado, only obfuscation as to when the influence began. In his brief autobiographical notes Machado says of the year 1910, 'Asistí a un curso de Henri Bergson en el Colegio de Francia' (p. 65) ('I attended a course by Henri Bergson at the Collège de France'), and Spanish critics, almost to a man, have seen fit to read this as notification of Machado's first knowledge of Bergson.[6] But such a view is unlikely in the extreme, given Machado's knowledge of French, his studious nature, his interest in metaphysics, his periods of residence in Paris at the turn of the century, his friendship with the likes of Unamuno and Jiménez, both of whom we know read Bergson at that time,[7] and, finally, given that Bergson was already well known in Spain, as is indicated by the prompt translation of his second major work *Matière et mémoire* of 1896 which was published in Madrid as *Materia y memoria* in 1900.[8] My point is that intellectual disservice is done to Machado by those who stress only the *castizo* or traditionally Spanish in him; furthermore, it may very well be that the early Machado is more Bergsonian than the Machado of post 1910. As regards a poet who could say in 1913, 'He asistido durante veinte años, casi diariamente a la Biblioteca Nacional'[9] ('For the last twenty years I have been almost daily to the National Library'), who described philosophy as 'una afición de toda mi vida'[10] ('a cherished pursuit of my entire life'), and who in poem XCV of 1907, aware of this bias, described himself as,

> Poeta ayer, hoy triste y pobre
> filósofo trasnochado,   (p. 134)
>
> (Yesterday a poet, today a sad and poor
> philosopher with hollow eyes,)

is it really likely that such a poet could still have been unaware of the reigning philosophy of his time? The evidence of Machado's life, circumstance and poetry points very strongly to his having read Bergson long before 1910, and that not unnaturally he attended Bergson's lectures out of an already well developed interest in him. The poem of 1903 which we are presently considering points in the same direction.

Taking it by stages, we can say, firstly, without fear of contradiction, that Machado's poem is very Bergsonian in its view of time as something essentially fluid. Bergson's key theme was that there are two kinds of time: the negative, inhuman time of clocks which is linear, extensive and quantitative; and the positive time of human experience which is vertical, intensive and qualitative. Linear, chronometric time is negative in the human context because it treats time as space, measuring it out, segmenting it, fracturing its flow and thereby fracturing our lives in the process. Vertical, intensive time, on the other hand, is altogether more elastic and free from constraint; in place of the other's inexorable consecutiveness it stresses simultaneity and integration, a survival or perduration of the past or pasts into the present, for which reason Bergson calls such time *duration*. While the *superficial* or *public* self lives in rational, mathematical time, it is *le moi fondamental* that lives or seeks to live in the integrated terms of duration. Here we see the metaphysical and ontological implications of time in Bergson and why for him memory was 'un problème privilégié'.[11] It follows from the above that linear time is anathema to man, and Machado is insistent on this, as we shall see; secondly, it follows that man prizes the experience of duration, but unfortunately it is also the case that the pressures of linear time are so great as to make proper experience of duration, *la pure durée*, rare indeed, which is why the above poem is of signal importance. Memory is the key and the salvation; but it is not simply a question of remembering the past, the past has to be made present, actualized, relived. Thus it is only a special type of memory which allows full recapture of pastness, the experience being intuitive, dream-like, visionary and even transcendental. Here we find what is specifically Bergsonian in Machado's poem.

In *Matière et mémoire*, which as mentioned came out in Spanish in 1900, Bergson distinguishes between two types of memory. First there is *le souvenir appris*, derived from habit, which he illustrates in the tediously repeated lesson. This, incidentally, is the subject of Machado's poem V of 1906, 'Recuerdo infantil' ('Childhood Recollection'):

> 'mil veces ciento, cien mil;
> mil veces mil, un millón'.   (p. 78)

> ('a thousand times a hundred, one hundred thousand;
> a thousand times a thousand, one million'.)

Second, there is *la mémoire par excellence*, which, in its purest form, is the sudden recollection of a unique, unrepeatable event: 'Le souvenir spontané est tout de suite parfait; le temps ne pourra rien ajouter à son image sans la dénaturer; il conservera pour la mémoire sa place et sa date'.[12] Bergson then contrasts this spontaneous recollection with attentive or willed memory, *la mémoire volontaire*, and again Machado's poems reflect his finer points. Examples of willed memory are found, for instance, in poem VI of 1903 where the poet's powers have been challenged,

> ¿Te recuerda, hermano,
> un sueño lejano mi canto presente?   (p. 79)

> (Are you reminded, brother,
> of a distant dream by my present song?)

and especially in poem VII of the same year where the poet has returned to his boyhood home in Sevilla:

> y estoy solo, en el patio silencioso,
> *buscando* una ilusión cándida y vieja:
> alguna sombra ... algún recuerdo ... dormido ...   (p. 80)

> (And I am alone, in the silent patio,
> *searching* for an old and innocent vision:
> some shadow ... some sleeping memory ...)

In the first poem, despite all promptings, the poet is unable to remember; while in the second his efforts are rewarded, 'Sí, te co-nozco, tarde alegre y clara' ('Yes, I know you, happy and clear after-noon'), but more in the qualified sense of *reconnaissance* than as pure memory of a unique event. More revealing is poem XLIX of 1907 which instances both willed and pure memory in its second part. Here Machado depicts a poet striving to remember his beloved, 'Quiso el poeta recordar' (p. 109) ('The poet wanted to remember'). He reads verses in which he had described her hair; but such effort is to no avail:

> Leyó ... La letra mata; no se acordaba de ellos ...   (p. 110)

> (He read ... The printed letter kills; he couldn't remember her hair.)

But then, much later, when he disinterestedly smells a flower, the pure memory of her comes back with a rush:

> Y un día—como tantos—, al aspirar un día
> aromas de una rosa que en el rosal se abría,
> brotó como una llama la luz de los cabellos
> que él en sus madrigales llamaba rubias olas,
> brotó, porque un aroma igual tuvieron ellos ...
> Y se alejó en silencio para llorar a solas.   (p. 110)

> (And one day, a day like any other, when smelling
> the scent of a rose that was flowering in the rose garden,
> there burst like a flame the light of her hair
> which he in his madrigals had called blond waves,
> it burst upon him because they had the same scent ...
> And he went off silently to cry alone.)

Disinterested in the beloved while he is attentive to the flower, it is this as opposed to the willed disposition which generates pure memory. Regarding these different processes and different qualities of memory, Claudio Guillén notes, summarizing Bergson: 'it is not the same thing to remember an object ... as to recapture its pastness. In the latter case the full use of memory may represent a *désintéresse-ment de la vie*, an *inattention à la vie*'.[13]

Herein lies the pertinence and meaning of dream, both for Bergson and Machado. Bergson writes: 'Pour évoquer le passé sous forme d'image, il faut pouvoir s'abstraire de l'action présente, il faut savoir attacher du prix à l'inutile, il faut vouloir rêver'.[14] Disinterest, then, at its highest level is the state of *rêve* wherein pure memory processes come into operation: 'Les images passées, reproduites telles quelles avec tous leurs détails et jusqu'à leur coloration affective, sont les images de la rêverie ou du rêve'.[15] Bergson's *rêve*, precise and central to his theory of memory, finds an exact equivalent, I suggest, in Machado's *sueño* (dream), which is the transcendental dimension of his metaphysic of time and the point on which our first poem turns:

> Desperté. ¿Quién enturbia
> los mágicos cristales de mi sueño?
> Mi corazón latía
> atónito y disperso.   (p. 119)

> (I woke up. Who breathes on
> the magic windows of my dream?
> My heart was beating
> astonished and dispersed.)

The glass windows through which this kind of vision is seen are *magic* in the sense of being totally out of the ordinary run of reality, providing the subject with a fleeting glimpse of a much higher reality. But note how insistent Machado is on the subject's will-lessness: not only do the interrogative and the idea of an independently beating heart suggest this, but also the precise adjective *disperso* (dispersed) which conveys the sense of unfocalized disinterest, involuntariness. Experiencing what Bergson calls 'images de rêve' which 'paraissent et disparaissent d'ordinaire indépendament de notre volonté',[16] the poet does in fact lose contact almost immediately with his treasured memory. This conforms precisely to Bergson's theory: 'Ce souvenir spontané, qui se cache sans doute derrière le souvenir acquis, peut se révéler par des éclairs brusques: mais il se dérobe, au moindre mouvement de la mémoire volontaire'.[17] Which is to say, when the past is actualized by the fidelity of spontaneous memory the subject wishes to respond as he would to any *present* stimulus, but such a response, or movement or act of will only destroys the conditions necessary to the memory process. Hence '¡el agua en tus cabellos! ...' ('the water in your hair! ...') is both the climactic point of actualization and the end of memory.

In all respects, then, Machado's unassuming poem, written in the casual form of an irregular sonnet, is deeply Bergsonian. It introduces us to the complex metaphysic of 'esencialidad y temporalidad' ('essentiality and temporality'), that is, to the inseparableness of the question of being and the question of time. In doing so it indicates that time, the time of recollection or *sueño* (dream), is the possible answer to man's existential dilemma which itself has been posed by time; in short, it indicates that the positive Bergsonian time of simultaneity and duration is the human counter to remorseless linear time. These are points we shall need to explore further.

Antonio Machado was born in Seville in 1875 and moved to Madrid with his family at the age of eight. There he was educated at the famous Instituto Libre de Enseñanza (Free School of Learning) which had recently been founded by the remarkable and progressive pedagogic theorist, Francisco Giner de los Ríos, a close friend of the Machado family. The man and his school were to have a profound influence on Machado, as can be seen in the unreserved admiration of his elegy, poem CXXXIX, 'A don Francisco Giner de los Ríos', which presents the great liberal thinker as a virtual messiah, his mission being that of saving Spain. Machado stresses the man's integrity, his work ethic and his belief in a new European Spain as opposed to the old 'churchy' Spain of isolation and stagnation:

> ¡Yunques, sonad; enmudeced campanas!   (p. 234)

> (Anvils, ring out; be silent bells!)

Machado, who inherited his father's liberal temperament, found Giner's school a rewarding experience. It is not the Instituto that he refers to in that poem on rote learning, 'Recuerdo infantil', but the traditional Spanish school of excessive religious orientation, as we see from the oppressive motif on the classroom wall:

> Es la clase. En un cartel
> se representa a Caín
> fugitivo, y muerto Abel,
> junto a una mancha carmín.   (p. 78)

> (This is the class. An illustration
> depicts Cain
> fleeing, and Abel dead,
> next to a crimson stain.)

Such an illustration suggests the joyless mood of nineteenth-century Spain, ravaged as it was by civil wars and fanatical Carlist traditionalism. But Machado's Instituto was *Libre* (Free) in the sense of being secular, and the man who conceived it hoped to generate a new Spain out of the young, liberated minds of his pupils. The same hope and the same sharp contrast with a stagnant past is beautifully caught in Machado's short poem, III:

La plaza y los naranjos encendidos
con sus frutas redondas y risueñas.
　Tumulto de pequeños colegiales
que, al salir en desorden de la escuela,
llenan el aire de la plaza en sombra
con la algazara de sus voces nuevas.
　¡Alegría infantil en los rincones
de las ciudades muertas! . . .
¡Y algo nuestro de ayer, que todavía
vemos vagar por estas calles viejas!　　　　　　(p. 77)

(The square and the orange trees alight
with their round and smiling fruits.
　A tumult of small schoolchildren,
bursting disorderly out of the school,
fill the air of the shaded square
with the din of their young voices.
　Youthful joy in the corners
of the cities that are dead! . . .
And something, ours once, that we can still
see idling about these old streets!)

Typically, Spain's historical plight is interwoven with a sense of
the poet's own temporal life. The '98 men tended to see the problem
in subjective terms: 'Me duele España' ('Spain grieves me'), as
Unamuno succinctly put it. For Giner de los Ríos too the answer
to the problem lay inside the individual mentality: Spain's ills could
only be cured by fresh, outward-looking minds.

　Machado was every inch the inquisitive, free-thinking Spaniard
Giner de los Ríos wanted. That he took until 1907 to qualify as
a French teacher is itself consistent with his old master's Krausist
view of education as something which concerned the whole man.
Following his schooling, the young Machado steeped himself in the
cultural life of Madrid, collaborating as a satirist from 1893 in *La
Caricatura*, contributing to the important poetry magazines *Electra*
and *Helios* from 1901, and generally befriending the emerging literary
figures of the day. He spent two periods in Paris, in 1899 and 1902,
dates which encompass the writing of *Soledades*, and there, supporting
himself mainly through translation work, he made contacts of a more
cosmopolitan kind, Oscar Wilde included. There were bohemian
times, in the company of his elder brother Manuel, but essentially
Machado's preparation for his vocation as a poet was studious. He
lived the European theme of Giner de los Ríos and his awareness
of the need to be outward-looking is evident from a letter he wrote
in 1903 to Unamuno, the Generation's major philosopher who had

steeped himself in European thought, from Kierkegaard to Bergson. Machado wrote:

> Usted, con golpes de maza, ha roto, no cabe duda, la espesa costra de nuestra vanidad, de neuestra somnolencia. Yo al menos sería un ingrato si no reconociera que a usted debo el haber saltado la tapia de mi corral o de mi huerto.[18]

> (You, beyond doubt, have smashed the thick crust of our vanity, our somnolence. I at least would be an ingrate if I did not recognise that it is to you I am indebted for having jumped the wall of my backyard or garden.)

Spain is no more than a backyard to Machado who, at this stage, is of decided European inclination. Whether he was always of the same mind is another question, for, taking up his teaching post in the Castilian mountain-town of Soria in 1907 and then, when his wife of two years died, moving on to the equally remote Andalusian backwater of Baeza in 1912, it was the traditional Spain that increasingly impressed itself on him. Little wonder that in his stupendously evocative Baezan poem of 1913, 'Poema de un día. Meditaciones rurales' ('Poem on a Day. Rural Meditations'), Machado refers to Bergson as 'un tuno' ('a rogue') and 'este endiablado judío' (p. 206) ('this diabolical Jew'). The reference is largely jocular, it is true, but not without poignancy. In Baeza, a town which imposed such a heavy sense of time, it was not easy to think along the positive Bergsonian lines of 'este yo fundamental' (p. 208) ('this fundamental self'), and though the poem ends on the same need for freedom—'¡ay! por saltar impaciente / las bardas de su corral' (p. 208) ('oh! to jump impatiently / the walls of one's backyard')—the walls seem a lot taller now. If R. S. Thomas, the Welsh poet of strikingly similar metaphysical introversion, could say 'You cannot live in the present, / At least not in Wales ... / There is only the past',[19] how true this must have been for Machado in the wasted hinterland of Spain. Besides, the metaphysic he took from his French reading was one that confirmed the value of the past.

But let us stay with the early Machado for a moment, the Machado of symbolist and modernist influence. As mentioned, *Soledades* shows considerable evidence of the prosodic innovations of Modernism. The traditional Spanish lines of eleven and seven syllables predominate, it is true, but there are also poems based on the twelve-syllable line (VI, LII, LIII), on the alexandrine (XX, XXXV, XLIX), and even on the sixteen-syllable line (IX, XIII). The point about these longer lines is that they require stress at certain specified parts of the line, a systematic measuring of beats neglected in most Spanish verse. The highly musical effects produced are relevant to Machado's temporal theme, as we shall see. First, however, let us remember that Rosalía had used alexandrines, for instance in 'Santa Escolástica', 'Majestad de los templos, mi alma feminina', also sixteen-syllable lines, 'Dicen que no hablan las plantas, ni las fuentes, ni los pájaros', and, on one occasion in *En las orillas del Sar*, an eighteen-syllable line: 'Su ciega y loca fantasía corrió arrastrada por el vértigo'. Much more ambitious than Bécquer in this field, Rosalía had an influence on Modernism which is often undervalued. Yet, on examining her lines more closely, we find that though they do indeed have the required mid-line break or hemistich, as in the three lines quoted, they are of irregular beat and would thus be classified as polyrhythmic. It was Rubén Darío, the Nicaraguan poet, who brought metrical precision to Spain in the form of the patterned beat of dactyls and trochees. His famous 'Sinfonía en gris mayor' ('Symphony in Grey Major') from his seminal volume *Prosas profanas* (*Profane Prose*) of 1896 is cast in twelve-syllable dactyls, these having a stress on the second and fifth syllable in each hemistich. Here is one of its eight stanzas:

> Es viejo ese lobo. Tostaron su cara
> los rayos de fuego del sol del Brasil;
> los recios tifones del mar de la China
> la han visto bebiendo su frasco de gin.

> (He is old that wolf. His face has been burnt
> by the scorching rays of the Brazilian sun;
> the rasping typhoons of the China sea
> have seen him drinking his flask of gin.)

The dactyl has a monotonous beat—'los récios tifónes del már de la Chína', ʋ/ʋʋ/ʋ; ʋ/ʋʋ/ʋ—which is used here to evoke a sense of tropical stupor: the old sailor is steeped equally in a monochrome grey haze and in his alcoholic-cum-narcotic oblivion. This same ennui was to find a more intimate, less exotic, treatment in Machado.

In poem VI, where the poet visits a park and is challenged by the fountain to remember a similar if not identical occasion in the past, half of the fifty-two lines are dactyls:

> Yo sé que tus bellos espejos cantores
> copiaron antiguos delirios de amores:
> mas cuéntame, fuente de lengua encantada,
> cuéntame mi alegre leyenda olvidada.   (p. 79)

> (I know that your lovely singing waters
> reflected bygone ravings of love:
> but tell me, fountain of voice enchanted,
> tell me my own happy legend forgotten.)

The first three of these lines are dactyls and the poem's insistence on this rhythm creates powerful effects. Monotony, with its implicit ennui, is again prominent: the poet's present life is stale and lacks the vigour of his past or youth, his forgotten happy legend. But there is more to it: the poet is challenged to remember his past and it is this sense of memory which is allusively created by the reiterated rhythms. No less than the repetitions and the half-line echoes—'La fuente sonaba ... La fuente cantaba', '¿Te recuerda, hermano? ... No recuerdo, hermana' (The fountain was playing ... The fountain was singing; Does it remind you, brother? ... I don't remember, sister)—the intermittently recurring dactylic beat suggests an overlapping, the past being repeated in the present. This, however, is more in the Nietzschean sense of an eternal recurrence—a topic favoured by Azorín—than in the positive Bergsonian sense of a specific moment relived such as we found in our first poem. It is the oppressive, cyclical sameness of life which comes through here, not the flash of intuition. Indeed, the insistent rhythms virtually stupefy the poet, to the extent that he is unable to remember the past. At the same time the fountain deepens his gloom by telling him that the past was no different from the present and that to think that it was somehow better or more vital is mere delusion. Thus the poem's repetitions at once suggest the texture of memory and, in the very heaviness of their rhythm, measure out the steady beat of clock time.

The same opposition between vital time or duration and clock time or linearity is found in poem XIII which is written in lines of sixteen syllables with occasional half-lines of eight syllables. Here the poet is walking one summer evening on the outskirts of a city. He hears the cicada singing its one-note song; he sees the water of a river flowing past and disappearing under the arches of a bridge; he sees the sun set, its golden colours making the hills and distant city dark. All the while he ponders on the meaning of life, *his* life, insignificant as it seems in relation to the sky above him. His heavy mood is pointed up by the cicada's song, the inexorable flow of water and the clanking of buckets that lift water in a nearby field, while the sixteen-syllable line conveys the full weight of time and the poet's own weariness:

En una huerta sombría
giraban los cangilones de la noria soñolienta.
Bajo las ramas oscuras el son del agua se oía ...

Yo caminaba cansado,
sintiendo la vieja angustia que hace el corazón pesado.
El agua en sombra pasaba tan melancólicamente.   (p. 84–5)

(In a shadowed orchard
spun the buckets of a somnolent water-wheel.
Under the dark branches the sound of water could be heard . . .

I was walking along, tired,
feeling the old anguish that makes the heart heavy.
The water in shadow passed by with such melancholy.)

Once again rhythmic repetition is the key to the poem's mood, notably in the form of paralleled hemistiches:

Bajo las ramas oscuras	(Under the dark branches)
bajo los ojos del puente	(under the spans of the bridge)
Bajo los arcos de piedra	(Under the arches of stone)
bajo los arcos del puente	(under the arches of the bridge)
Bajo los ojos del puente	(Under the spans of the bridge)
Bajo las ramas oscuras	(Under the dark branches).

And, a further pattern:

Pasaba el agua rizada	(The rippled water passed)
pasaba el agua sombría	(the shadowed water passed)
El agua en sombra pasaba	(The water in shadow passed)
el agua clara corría	(the clear water ran)
caer el agua se oía	(the water was heard falling)
el son del agua se oía	(the sound of water was heard)

The insistent imperfect tense of 'Pasaba el agua' is echoed in other verbs which form the nucleus of further hemistiches:

Vibraba el aire asordado	(The deafened air was ringing)
caminaba el sol de estío	(the summer sun was moving)
giraban los cangilones	(the water-buckets were spinning)
sonaban los cangilones	(the water-buckets were ringing)
coronaban las colinas	(the hills were being crowned)
cálido viento soplaba	(a hot wind was blowing)

All of which is interwoven with the poet's own temporal actions:

Yo caminaba cansado	(I was walking along tired)
Yo iba haciendo mi camino	(I was making my way along)
Yo . . . hacia la ciudad volvía	(I . . . was returning towards the city)

Yo pensaba . . .   (I was thinking . . .)
Y pensaba . . .   (And I was thinking . . .)

The effect is hypnotic and seductive. We feel the poet is totally integrated in his profoundly temporalized landscape. In the previous poem, ivy on the park wall and moss on the park gate had given an impression of layers of time lying upon the physical presence of objects; here too the landscape is *polvoriento* (dusty) and *soñoliento* (drowsy), with layers of dust, cloud and shadow bearing down heavily. In the other poem, the monotonous bubbling of the fountain's water suggested the tedium of life; here the irreversible flow of the river suggests the same. And the point of all this rhythmic seduction is to lull the poet into passive acceptance of the inevitable: time's passing, death. Paraphrasing Jorge Manrique, the fifteenth-century poet he so admired, Machado gives us a magnificently sombre sixteen-syllable line:

Donde acaba el pobre río la inmensa mar nos espera.   (p. 85)

(Where the poor river ends the immense sea awaits us.)

Manrique's original lines are in fact quoted in poem LVIII:

'Nuestras vidas son los ríos
que van a dar en la mar,
que es el morir'. ¡Gran cantar!
Entre los poetas míos
tiene Manrique un altar.   (p. 116)

('Our lives are the rivers
that are going to flow into the sea,
which is death'. A grand song!
Amongst my poets
Manrique has an altar.)

Acceptance of death and of life's ephemeral nature leads to the view that 'no somos nada' (p. 85) ('we are nothing'), a phrase the poet believes he hears re-echoing in the passing river. This is the pessimistic and resigned theme of Ecclesiastes, once the most influential of biblical books, which Machado quotes in poem XVIII: 'Vanidad de vanidades, / todo es negra vanidad' (p. 88) ('Vanity of vanities, / all is black vanity'). Yet not all is gloom in poem VI. A certain serenity, akin to ataraxia, accompanies the awareness of one's utter insignificance:

Y pensaba: '¡Hermosa tarde, nota de la lira inmensa
toda desdén y armonía;
hermosa tarde, tú curas la pobre melancolía
de este rincón vanidoso, oscuro rincón que piensa!'   (p. 84–5)

(And I thought: 'Lovely evening, note of the immense lyre
so full of disdain and harmony;
lovely evening, you heal the pitiful melancholy
of this vain corner, this dark corner that thinks!')

The Pythagorean allusion, *tarde = nota de la lira inmensa* (evening = note of the immense lyre), brings to mind Fray Luis de León, the most erudite Spanish poet of the sixteenth century, and this not only underlines the centrality of Machado's preoccupation but, together with the allusion to Manrique, gives a sense of historicity. More importantly, the equation also suggests that there is something valuable, after all, about the evening Machado witnesses. No more than a speck in cosmic time, the evening is nonetheless part of that larger whole, and, by implication, if its single note were missing the rhythm of the cosmos would not be quite so harmonious. Thus the equation brings a sense of duration to the fragment of time Machado experiences: no longer an isolated, measurable unit, the evening is qualitatively part of time's great flow, that is, in Bergson's terms, part of 'une durée dont les moments hétérogènes se pénétrent'.[20]

The same interpenetration is suggested later in the poem, when, with its only preterite tense, a sudden insight on the part of the poet is indicated:

Y me detuve un momento
en la tarde, a meditar ...
¿Qué es esta gota en el viento
que grita al mar: soy el mar?   (p. 85)

(And I stopped a moment
in the evening to meditate ...
What is this drop in the wind
that shouts to the sea: am I the sea?)

Here interpenetration comes from the link between 'gota' (drop) and 'mar' (sea), the former micro-dimension mingling with the latter macro-dimension just as 'nota' (note) had with 'lira inmensa' (immense lyre). But let us also observe the puzzling way in which the question is asked, for this is a virtual conundrum in itself. Syntactically the lines unravel a whole series of questions: 'What is this drop?', 'What is this drop in the wind?', 'What is this drop in the wind that shouts to the sea?', and finally, the entire unit, 'What is this drop in the wind that shouts to the sea: am I the sea?' We may wonder which question has priority. Is it 'What is this drop?' or 'am I the sea?', or indeed, is the poet asking whether the decisive factor in the whole puzzle of being is the fact that man can and does ask such questions as the latter? But the question is not merely a conundrum devised to increase our puzzlement and convey the poet's own puzzlement; much less is it a rephrasing of Descartes' *cogito ergo sum*, that triumph of reason and cold analysis which Bergson so abominated. The purpose of posing the question in this multiple way, I suggest, is to show that man asks about reality from a position inside reality; more specifically, Machado asks about time from his position inside time. Aware that on the scale of things he is but a drop of water destined for the sea, he asks the eternal question about time and death from a position of utter temporality—as a 'gota en el viento' ('drop in the wind')—wherein he experiences his movement in the flow of life. As opposed, then, to the Cartesian abstraction of a problem, Machado experiences time in terms of his total interpenetration with it, and it is this, his *sympathetic coincidence* with the subject, as Bergson says, which leads him to the absolute and intuitively insightful question within a question '¿... soy el mar?' ('am I the sea?'), where *sea* is better understood not simply as Manrique's death but as the whole summation of time. This *sympathetic coincidence* is described by Bergson in one of several passages where he distinguishes between the analytical and intuitive methods of understanding, an essay of 1903: 'Il suit de là qu'un absolu ne saurait être donné que dans une *intuition*, tandis que tout le reste relève de l'*analyse*. Nous appelons ici intuition la sympathie par laquelle on se transporte à l'intérieur d'un objet pour coïncider avec ce qu'il a d'unique et par conséquent d'inexprimable' (Bergson's italics).[21] Seen in this way, the question which springs from Machado's moment of meditation is the decisive point in the poem. It is the point when the poet is no longer an external witness, a passive observer of time's irremediable succession, but is inside time's flow, experiencing its absolute indivisibility, sensing that he is one with its interpenetrating wholeness. It is the moment in the poem, then, when Machado experiences duration, and indeed, the very way he voices his question, or questions, is itself a linguistic metaphor of duration, which is to say, a metaphor of the blending in of successions into an organic whole. The four questions are successive,

¿Qué es esta gota (?)[1] en el viento (?)[2]
que grita al mar (?)[3]: soy el mar?[4]

(What is this drop (?)[1] in the wind (?)[2]
that shouts to the sea (?)[3]: am I the sea?[4])

but the successions also form a whole. The experience is akin to
that of listening to a series of musical notes, a favourite analogy
of Bergson's: 'comme il arrive quand nous nous rappelons, fondues
ainsi dire ensemble, les notes d'une melodie'. Bergson concludes:
'On peut donc concevoir la succession sans la distinction, et comme
une pénétration mutuelle, une solidarité, une organisation intime
d'éléments, donc chacun, *représentatif du tout*, ne s'en distingue et
ne s'en isole que pour une pensée capable d'abstraire' (italics mine).[22]
It is because the interpenetration is so complete that the single note is
representative of the whole and the drop of water equivalent to the sea.

Such moments of insight and such experiences of duration are
comparatively rare and necessarily fleeting, however, for our consciousness, as Bergson says, is overwhelmingly geared towards experiencing time as a consecutive as opposed to a simultaneous reality,
that is, as an exterior spatialized line to be segmented as opposed
to an interior indivisible flow. This Bergsonian view provides a clear
interpretation of an important poem whose brevity might otherwise
have proved most enigmatic, poem **XXXV**:

> Al borde del sendero un día nos sentamos.
> Ya nuestra vida as tiempo, y nuestra sola cuita
> son las desesperantes posturas que tomamos
> para aguardar ... Mas Ella no faltará a la cita.   (p. 97)

> (At the side of the path one day we sit down.
> Now our life is time, and our sole preoccupation
> is the desperate postures we take up
> to wait ... But She will not miss the appointment.)

Time here is devitalized and empty, a yawning gap in which man
merely waits for his date with death. The trouble is, as the first
line shows, the poet has ceased to experience life's flow: motion has
been fractured and rendered static by his passivity. In such a frame
of mind death is seen as a release from torment, a new beginning,
'una mañana pura' (p. 91) ('a pure morning'), as poem **XXI** ortho-
doxly puts it. Thus spatialization of time through such images as
the *camino* and *sendero* (road, path) occurs in poem after poem. Emphasis falls typically on distance and separation, as in poem **LXXIX**
where Machado complains of 'la amargura de la distancia' (p. 126)

('the bitterness of the distance') which separates him from the sunset of death. But though this negative, Manrique-based view predominates, Machado frequently struggles against it. In poem LXXXIV, for instance, he wishes he could prolong his view of ephemeral flowers:

¡quién pudiera
soñar aún largo tiempo en esas pequeñitas
corolas azuladas que manchan la pradera,
y en esas diminutas primeras margaritas!   (p. 129)

(Would that I could
dream a while longer of those tiny
bluish corollas that sprinkle the meadow
and of those minute early daisies!)

The things of this world, which Manrique said were 'de cuán poco valor' ('of such little value'), need to be rescued from oblivion by the dream-like human gaze and the duration it bestows. This elevation of reality through interiorization in human memory is what Machado brilliantly captures in poem CIV where he looks at the Guadarrama mountains near Madrid:

¿Eres tú, Guadarrama, viejo amigo,
la sierra gris y blanca,
la sierra de mis tardes madrileñas
que yo veía en el azul pintada?
   Por tus barrancos hondos
y por tus cumbres agrias,
mil Guadarramas y mil soles vienen,
cabalgando conmigo, a tus entrañas.   (p. 147)

(Are you, Guadarrama, old friend,
the grey and white mountain,
the mountain of my Madrid afternoons
that I used to see painted against the sky?
   Through your deep ravines,
and along your rough peaks,
a thousand Guadarramas and thousand suns
come riding with me to your heart.)

In retrospective mood the poet realizes that his perception of a familiar reality—the Guadarrama mountain range—is not a single perception but the sum of all his past experiences of the view. The thousand and more times he has seen the Guadarramas from Madrid come together and mingle with his current single view of the range. The result is a mutual enriching of both perceiver and perceived, of man the poet and the material object of the mountains. This two-way relationship anticipates the phenomenological metaphysic which Ortega y Gasset was developing at precisely this time, a metaphysic which owed something to Bergson and which, as we shall see, was to have considerable influence in different ways on Jorge Guillén and Pedro Salinas. However, the temporal element in Machado's poem is pure Bergson, and what the poem offers essentially is a further example of simultaneity triumphing over consecutiveness and of succession blending in with the organic whole of duration.

This last poem, CIV, belongs to *Campos de Castilla* (*Fields of Castile*), and it is to some of the poems of this later volume published in 1912 and, in expanded form, in 1917, that we now turn. *Campos de Castilla* is the volume which gained Machado his reputation as 'the poet of Castile' and it is also the one which links him most closely to the '98 Generation since it is here above all that he expresses his concern for the problem of Spain. The placenaming in the volume's title is found also in a number of its better known poems, 'A orillas del Duero' ('On the Banks of the Duero'), 'Por tierras de España' ('Through Spanish Lands') and 'Campos de Soria' ('Fields of Soria'), and it is especially in these earlier poems written in Soria that Machado seems more interested in evoking a real, physical sense of Spain than in using landscape for symbolic or subjective ends. However, the Guadarrama poem of 1911 has already shown that the greater naturalism which comes from placenaming need not exclude metaphysics and subjectivism. Certainly the volume's later poems written in Baeza continue to foreground the theme of time, many of them being nostalgic recollections of Soria and of his brief married life with Leonor. But even the early poems, with their naturalistic depictions of the deplorable conditions of Spanish rural life, are charged with anguish and temporality. The squalor of contemporary Spain is set against the backdrop of its past grandeur and the strength of the poems lies in the poignant sense of the past's survival despite its apparent physical decay:

> Castilla miserable, ayer dominadora,
> envuelta en sus andrajos desprecia cuanto ignora.   (p. 138)

> (Wretched Castile, all powerful yesterday,
> wrapped in rags, despises what she doesn't know.)

This justly famous alexandrine couplet which booms out twice in 'A orillas del Duero' suggests that Spain's hapless predicament stems from a perverse sense of national pride, a pride in the past which encourages scorn of modern progress. Though socially indefensible, attachment to the past is something Machado can readily empathize with. He finds an aura of stoic resilience in Spain's wasted landscapes, landscapes that are as proud as they are pitiable:

> ¡Colinas plateadas,
> grises alcores, cárdenas roquedas
> por donde traza el Duero
> su curva de ballesta
> en torno a Soria, oscuros encinares,
> ariscos pedregales, calvas sierras,
> caminos blancos y álamos del río,
> tardes de Soria, mística y guerrera,
> hoy siento por vosotros, en el fondo
> del corazón, tristeza,
> tristeza que es amor! ¡Campos de Soria
> donde parece que las rocas sueñan,
> conmigo vais! ¡Colinas plateadas,
> grises alcores, cárdenas roquedas! ...   (p. 157)

> (Silver hills,
> grey slopes, purple rocks
> through which the Duero traces
> its crossbow curve
> around Soria, dark oak woods,
> inhospitable banks of stone, bald crags,
> white roads and poplars along the river,
> Sorian afternoons, mystic and warlike,
> today I feel for you, from my heart's
> depth, a sadness,
> a sadness that is love! Fields of Soria,
> where it seems the rocks dream,
> you march with me! Silver hills,
> grey slopes, purple rocks! ...)

The land's infertility is certainly the result of generations of neglect and agricultural backwardness, yet its very harshness suggests the qualities of resolution and forbearance which gave Castile its imperial adventurers and its mystic saints. Now it appears even the rocks dream of years gone by and the entire landscape is interiorized by the poet and moves with him through a march of time in which the past endures. When the poet then exclaims,

> ¡ ... álamos de las márgenes del Duero,
> conmigo vais, mi corazón os lleva!   (p. 159)

> (poplars along the Duero's banks,
> you move with me, my heart bears you!)

we have a superb and characteristic image that is at once spatial
and psychical, the trees suggesting linear time's segmentation while
the water-flow and interiorization suggest duration.

Interiorization of landscape and therewith of Spain as an historical
reality sharpens our awareness of the poet as a being rich in time,
a being who lives in and through the aggregate of historical time.
But while historicity is prominent in the Soria poems, those of Baeza
interiorize on a more directly personal basis. In Baeza the poet is
full of nostalgia for his highland Castile and, just as Rosalía had
once felt 'Cual si en suelo extranjero me hallase' ('As if I were on
foreign soil'), Machado describes himself as 'extranjero en los campos
de mi tierra' (p. 198) ('a foreigner in my own land's tracts'). Nostalgia
leads to a more pronounced interiorization as Machado superimposes
the Castile he recollects on the actual Andalusian landscape before
him, for instance in CXVI, 'Recuerdos' ('memories'). This foreshadows the total recourse to memory found in CXXVI, 'A José María
Palacio' ('To José María Palacio'), a poem which, for its remarkably
dignified tone, is among Machado's very finest. Written in the form
of a letter to Palacio, a colleague at the Institute in Soria, the poem
is given over almost entirely to Machado's inquiring of his friend
as to whether spring has arrived yet in Soria, the point being that
in Soria spring is more tardy than in the southern Andalusian climes
whence Machado writes, 'En la estepa / del alto Duero, primavera
tarda' (p. 199) ('On the steppe / of the upper Duero, spring comes
late'). Machado's questions are largely rhetorical, however, for we
soon gather from his precise knowledge of Soria's topography, vegetation and animal life that he knows the answers full well. This
is confirmed by the interspersing of another type of sentence amid
the interrogatives, a sentence based on the future tense of probability
or conviction:

> ya habrán ido llegando las cigüeñas.
> Habrá trigales verdes . . .
>   Ya las abejas
> libarán del tomillo y el romero.
> ¿Hay ciruelos en flor? ¿Quedan violetas?
> Furtivos cazadores . . . no faltarán.   (p. 199)
>
> (The storks will have been arriving by now.
> The wheatfields will be green . . .
>   Already bees
> will be sucking on the thyme and rosemary.
> Are the plum trees in flower? Do violets linger?
> Poachers . . . will not be in short supply.)

No fewer than eleven of the poem's fourteen sentences are of these two types, there being six questions and five future-tense constructions, all of which lends an admirable sense of form. But, practically speaking, we may wonder why Machado dwells on rhetorical questions and on observations about Soria in a letter to one who had the real Soria before his eyes. This is not the empty padding or phatic communion of a writer who is at a loss for things to say. Rather, it is an example of a writer talking around, as opposed to about, certain issues which are too personal and delicate to mention directly. Focusing on the concrete topics of the weather, seasons and vegetation, Machado avoids an emotionalism that might embarrass his male friend; instead he communicates his feelings indirectly. Acute homesickness is one emotion a man might find difficult to confide in another male, yet the focus on Soria and the absence of reference to Baeza says it all. Another sensitive topic is the friendship one man feels for another, yet from the detail of Machado's observations we can safely assume that Palacio took a keen interest in the things mentioned, that the two men have spoken of such things before and even perhaps witnessed them together on walks; in short, we can assume that the letter deals with experiences and values shared by two men and, in this way, it is tacit confirmation of the regard in which Machado holds his 'buen amigo' ('dear friend'). The third and most emotive issue is kept for the poem's last sentence. Here Machado comes to the real point of his letter, a request:

> Con los primeros lirios
> y las primeras rosas de las huertas,
> en una tarde azul, sube al Espino,
> al alto Espino donde está su tierra ...   (p. 199)

> (With the first lilies
> and the first garden roses,
> on an afternoon of blue skies, go up to the Espino,
> to the high Espino where lies her earth ...)

The request is none other than that Palacio place flowers on his wife's grave. Suddenly the real reason for all the poet's inquiries about the seasons' change in Soria floods through and recharges the poem with meaning. It is especially important to the poet that young flowers be placed on the grave of one who married at sixteen and died at eighteen. Now we see too the reason for the poem's restraint, for few topics could be more fraught with sentimentality than this. Machado avoids this and his poem is all the more moving for its reserve. Only with the last word, 'tierra' (earth), a discreet synonym for 'grave', do we glimpse the depth of his feeling. From the preceding possessive 'su', which could mean either *his* or *her* grave, strictly we should not know that he was referring to his wife, though, paradoxically, the restraint is proof and we do not require biographical support to be convinced. Palacio, of course, needs no telling, and the relative lack of information at the close accords with the manner of a private letter and heightens our sense of the two friends' intimacy. The piece thus convinces both as a letter and as a poem, as an expression of sincere friendship and as an elegy to a beloved, all in all a stunning achievement.[23]

'A José María Palacio' also clearly relates to Machado's temporal theme. The poet's spatial removal from Soria radically illustrates the idea of being separated from the things one cherishes in the past. Yet the poem's entire thrust is the attempt to overcome this displacement in time and space through memory. Just as Palacio would have marvelled at the detail in Machado's recollections, we are convinced that he has crossed the divide and is effectively more in Soria than in the unmentioned Baeza. In short, not only does the past endure, it is more real to Machado than his present. This familiar theme of duration within succession is pointed up throughout by the season's cycles, by the repeated habits and migrations of animal life, by the regeneration associated with spring, and perhaps too by the implied notion of his wife's young body being forever part of the changing yet permanent landscape of Soria. Most charac-teristic is the motif of transition: winter and spring are not seen as separate units but as overlapping temporal phases in which the old still endures while the new already begins. The adverbs, 'aún' (still) and Machado's standby 'ya' (already) which occurs three times, suggest this elasticity of time, as does the synthesis of a line such as '¿Hay ciruelos en flor? ¿Quedan violetas?' ('Are the plum trees in flower? Do violets linger?'). Temporally located, then, at a moment when winter and spring interpenetrate—as was poem VII's afternoon, 'casi de primavera' (p. 80) ('almost springtime')— the Palacio poem has a markedly transitional feel which is as crucial to its theme of memory as was the sunshower setting in our initial poem. This metaphor of transition, which we first met in Rosalía's 'Santa Escolástica', is a virtual trademark in Machado and it takes reduplicated form in that very different yet equally impressive Baezan poem, CXXVIII, 'Poema de un día. Meditaciones rurales' ('Poem on a Day. Rural Meditations'), which begins:

> Heme aquí ya, profesor
> de lenguas vivas (ayer
> maestro de gay-saber,
> aprendiz de ruiseñor),
> en un pueblo húmedo y frío,
> destartalado y sombrío,
> entre andaluz y manchego.
> Invierno. Cerca del fuego.
> Fuera llueve un agua fina,
> que ora se trueca en neblina,
> ora se torna aguanieve.   (p. 203)

> (Here am I now, a teacher
> of living languages (yesterday
> a master of poesy,
> apprentice to the nightingale),
> In a damp and cold town,
> ramshackle and gloomy,
> half Andalusian, half Manchegan.
> Winter. Close to the fire.
> Outside a light rain falls,
> sometimes changing to mist,
> sometimes turning to sleet.)

Here the typical weather-based transitional metaphor of rain-mist-sleet is supported by the temperature mix of winter cold and a warm fire, also by the geographical indeterminacy of Baeza's location between Andalusia and La Mancha. But a more ironic mingling occurs too with the idea of teaching living languages in a lifeless town, and, if we suppose that the adjective *vivas* (living) is itself ironic, there is the further irony of the poet-teacher, one acutely sensitive to language yet paid to teach its tedious conjugations. These deft touches prepare us for the poem's treatment of time, though not quite as before.

Certainly the resulting fluidity is as appropriate as ever to Machado's musing solitude, 'En mi estancia ... sueño y medito' (p. 204) (In my room ... I dream and meditate); but the issue in this poem is not precisely memory and the transition from present to past, there being in effect only one, brief, personal recollection, 'y lo que yo más quería / la muerte se lo llevó' (p. 205) ('and what I loved most / death carried away'). Rather, the emphasis is squarely on the tedium of his present in Baeza, on the loud and regular 'tic-tic' of linear time from his nearby clock. In short, the poem's concern is with the existential dilemma which time poses, and it is Machado's insecurity in the face of this dilemma which the fluidity now insinuates and which the irony and self-mockery point up. The dilemma is developed through certain oppositions, the most fundamental of which is again that between the Ecclesiastes-Manrique tradition and the ideas of Henri Bergson whose first major work, *Les Données immédiates de la conscience* of 1889, is on the poet's table and is mentioned twice. First Machado effortlessly locates and interweaves the forces of negative time: the resounding tick of the clock, whose 'corazón de metal . . . mide un tiempo vacío' (p. 204) ('metal heart . . . measures out an empty time'), is echoed in the tolling of church bells and then by the increasing loudness of 'el repiqueteo / de la lluvia en las ventanas' (p. 205) ('the rain's ringing on the windows'). The rain in turn relates to the seasons' cycles, so important to the Baezan farmers, and ultimately to Manrique's graveyard sea:

¡Oh, tú, que vas gota a gota,
fuente a fuente y río a río,
como este tiempo de hastío
corriendo a la mar remota . . .!   (p. 205)

(Oh, you, ebbing away drop by drop,
fountain by fountain and river by river,
like this time so full of tedium
running to the distant sea . . .!)

While Manrique's shadow looms large, the pessimistic biblical text is directly quoted:

¿Todo es
soledad de soledades,
vanidad de vanidades,
que dijo el Eclesiastés?
. . . Todo llega y todo pasa . . .   (p. 207)

(Is all
solitude of solitudes,
vanity of vanities,
as Ecclesiastes said?
. . . Everything comes and everything passes . .)

All Machado has to sustain him in his war against linear time is metaphysical speculation, for he lacks even the farmers' closeness to the rhythm of the seasons, fatalistic as this might be. The odds are heavily stacked against him in a town like Baeza where it is impossible to feel the flow of life:

En estos pueblos, ¿se escucha
el latir del tiempo? No.
En estos pueblos se lucha
sin tregua con el reló . . .   (p. 204)

> (In these towns can one hear
> time's heart beat? No.
> In these towns one struggles
> endlessly against the clock ...)

Even to ponder on the speculations of metaphysicians seems, in this setting, no more than idle distraction:

> ¡Oh, estos pueblos! Reflexiones,
> lecturas y acotaciones
> pronto dan en lo que son:
> bostezos de Salomón.   (p. 207)

> (Oh, these towns! Reflections,
> readings, notes in the margin
> soon give over to what they are:
> yawnings of Solomon.)

What, then, is the use of metaphysics? As regards the three thinkers mentioned in the poem—Unamuno, Kant and Bergson—Machado as ever affirms his allegiance only to Unamuno: 'tu filosofía ... es la mía' (p. 206) ('your philosophy ... is mine'). But this, one suspects, is based less on hard ideas than on an empathy Machado feels with Unamuno's concern for Spain and with the anguish which pervades *Del sentimento trágico de la vida* (*On the Tragic Sense of Life*), a text which, having come out in the year Machado wrote his poem, 1913, is certainly one of the 'Libros nuevos' (p. 205) ('New books') on the poet's table. While Unamuno's tragic sense of mortality applies in Machado, the same cannot be said of his central religious dilemma which is neatly summarized in the poem as a 'querer y no poder / creer' (p. 205) ('wanting but not being able / to believe'), and, apart from the question of death, Unamuno would seem to offer little to Machado in the temporal context. It is thus Bergson's book which Machado more meaningfully, if offhandedly, picks up:

> Enrique Bergson: *Los datos*
> *inmediatos*
> *de la conciencia.* ¿Esto es
> otro embeleco francés?
> Este Bergson es un tuno;
> ¿verdad, maestro Unamuno?
> Bergson no da como aquel
> Immanuel
> el volatín inmortal;
> este endiablado judío
> ha hallado el libre albedrío

dentro de su mechinal.
No está mal:
cada sabio, su problema,
y cada loco, su tema.   (p. 206)

(Henri Bergson: *Les Données*
immédiates
de la conscience. Is this
another French fantasy?
This Bergson is a rogue,
is he not, master Unamuno?
Unlike that Immanuel,
Bergson doesn't make
an immortal jump;
the diabolical Jew
has found free will
inside his own brain-box.
That's fair enough:
every sage has his problem,
and every madcap his theme.)

Machado's ironic tone indicates scepticism, but this does not con-
ceal the fact that for him the burning issue is the possibility of being
free despite all impositions of time and space. Immanuel Kant fell
back on a priori and transcendental arguments to prove free will,
but Bergson looks no further than the human mind itself, understood
in terms of his special theory of time. In the *Essai sur les données*
immédiates de la conscience, whose title in the English translation is
Time and Free Will,[24] Bergson argues that man is free when his acts
spring from the whole of his personality: 'Bref, nous sommes libres
quand nos actes émanent de notre personalité entière, quand ils
l'expriment'.[25] As we would expect, this whole personality or fundamental self is only engaged when man experiences duration: 'L'acte
libre se produit dans le temps qui s'écoule, et non pas dans le temps
écoulé' (ibid., p. 145). The notions of duration and free will are
thus inseparable and virtually interchangeable in Bergson: 'Agir
librement, c'est reprendre possession de soi, c'est replacer dans la
pure durée' (ibid., p. 151), and 'le processus de notre activité libre
se continue en quelque sorte à notre insu, à tous les moments de
la durée ... le sentiment même de la durée vient de là' (ibid.,
p. 155). It follows from this equation that, since our experience of
duration is limited and fleeting, our experience of freedom is likewise
rare:

> Il y aurait donc enfin deux moi différents, dont l'un serait comme la
> projection extérieure de l'autre, sa représentation spatiale et pour ainsi

dire sociale. Nous atteignons le premier par une réflexion approfondie, qui nous fait saisir nos états internes comme des êtres vivants, sans cesse en voie de formation ... Mais les moments où nous nous ressaisissons ainsi nous-mêmes sont rares, et c'est pourquoi nous sommes rarement libres. (ibid., p. 151).

Bergson repeatedly stresses that freedom is a contingent rather than absolute quality of human life: 'la liberté ne présente pas le caractère absolu que le spiritualisme lui prête quelquefois; elle admet des degrés' (ibid., p. 109), and again, 'les actes libres sont rares' (ibid., p. 110). This is precisely what Machado recognizes at the end of his poem, when after having taken his evening walk and having overhead a platitudinous conversation in the nearby chemists, he returns to his room and once more picks up Bergson's book:

> Sobre mi mesa *Los datos*
> *de la conciencia*, inmediatos.
> No está mal
> este yo fundamental,
> contingente y libre, a ratos ...   (p. 208)

> (On my table *The Data*
> *of Consciousness*, immediate to hand.
> It's fair enough
> this fundamental self,
> contingent and free, at times ...)

'Poema de un día', then, for all its stress upon linear time, is a poem in which Machado recognizes duration and its concomitant freedom as a human possibility. Contingent and sporadic freedom is the consolation Machado has to settle for at the end. That *Ecclesiastes* and Manrique predominate over Bergson in no way diminishes the latter, but simply confirms his view of duration's rarity, as does the fact that real duration is the subject of relatively few of Machado's poems. Finally, however, it must be said that there is something in the casual, extemporary style of 'Poema de un día' which palpably evokes freedom, not merely as a possibility but as an imminent reality. The colloquial language and the anecdotal touches—such as the poet mislaying his glasses or going for a walk when the rain stops—point to his authentic personality as this expresses itself from moment to moment in the poem's very real day. In short, we feel that the poet, in his abstraction and in his spontaneous ease of manner, is ripe for an experience of duration, and that, to the extent that this masterly self-portrait convinces us of his uniqueness as a human being, a degree of freedom, as Bergson said, operates even here. By the poem's end this contingent freedom has virtually solved the poet's dilemma and relieved, though not banished, his anguish.

This same interconnection of time and free will is found in an enigmatic ten-line poem from CXXXI, 'Proverbios y cantares' ('Proverbs and Songs'), near the end of *Campos de Castilla*, which we now turn to by way of conclusion:

> Caminante, son tus huellas
> el camino, y nada más;
> caminante, no hay camino,
> se hace camino al andar.
> Al andar se hace camino,
> y al volver la vista atrás
> se ve la senda que nunca
> se ha de volver a pisar.
> Caminante, no hay camino,
> sino estelas en la mar.   (p. 223)

> (Traveller, your footprints
> are the road, nothing else;
> traveller, there is no road,
> the road is made by walking.
> By walking is the road made,
> and on turning one's eyes back
> one sees the path that never
> can be trod again.
> Traveller, there is no road,
> only a wake in the sea.)

The temptation is to read this sombre poem as no more than an account of Machado's nostalgia: all that is of value is in the past, which is gone for ever, and there is no road ahead. But this may not be the full picture and, at least as far as the present and future are concerned, the poem is not entirely pessimistic. We have only to recall the negative temporal value of 'camino' ('road') in so many of Machado's poems to wonder if 'no hay camino' ('there is no road') is negative in the temporal sense. In poems such as XXXV and LXXIX the road stretching ahead is a symbol of the empty time which awaits the poet, a time which is tedious, predictable and measurable. To have no road ahead, on the other hand, removes these negative values and indeed might well suggest an open-ended future, which is to say, implicitly, free will. It was precisely Bergson's argument in the *Essai* that determinists who reject the idea of free will always do so by giving a geometric representation of the process of coming to a decision: they see choice as a road which branches in two directions. The error, according to Bergson, lies in the spatial representation which only solidifies what is a dynamic and fluid inner process: 'cette figure représente une chose, et non pas un progrès' (ibid., p. 119), while, of course, 'les états de conscience sont des progrès, et non pas des choses' (ibid., p. 129). To represent choice as a road which divides in two is only relevant after the choice has been made, 'cette figure ne me montre pas l'action s'accomplissant, mais l'action accomplie' (ibid., p. 118); at the very moment of choice there is no road, 'Avant que le chemin fût tracé, il n'y avait pas de direction possible ni impossible, par la raison fort simple qu'il ne pouvait encore être question de chemin' (ibid., p. 120). In short, the spatial representation of choice devitalizes the whole issue by excluding duration and reintroducing the enemy of linear time. Returning to the poem, we find that it is this very sense of progress and duration, as opposed to solidity, which is indicated, especially in the two lines whose circular repetition seems itself an apt linguistic metaphor of simultaneity:

> se hace camino al andar.
> Al andar se hace camino . . .
>
> (the road is made by walking.
> By walking is the road made . . .)

Thus it might be said that the pessimism in Machado's poem is relieved by his awareness of time-flow, duration and, indeed, free will. Though, admittedly, here as elsewhere, such victories against time are only partial and are ultimately as fragile as his bubble of soap in the wind.

IV

Jorge Guillén

The Poetics of Being

Cuerpo veloz

En marcha.
                    ¡Más viento!
                              Libres,
Sotos, praderías, mieses,
Lomas de ondulación
Continua de muchos verdes,
Arboledas reservadas
A un paraíso inminente
Parten, me siguen, me azuzan
Y tras mi rumbo se tienden
Respirando a bocanadas
Más viento, más viento siempre
Con una acumulación
De claridad impaciente,
Que precipita a más luz
Y en rachas de gloria envuelve
Mientras, nivel sobrehumano,
Los deseos son poderes
A la vista de invasores
Esplendores en un trueque
Final.
          ¡Ay!
                    Freno, quietud.
¿Y aquel dominio celeste?[1]

(*Speeding body*

On the move.
                        More wind!
                                    Free,
Copses, meadows, cornfields,
Hillocks in continuous
Undulation of varied greens,
Woodlands set aside
For an imminent paradise
Open up, chase me, spur me
And on my track stretch out
Inhaling by the mouthful
More wind, even more wind
With an accumulation
Of impatient clarity,
Hurtling towards more light
And wrapped in gusts of glory
While, oh superhuman realm,
Desires are possessions
On beholding invading
Splendours in a switch
Supreme.
                        Oh!
                        Brakes, peace.
And that sublime dominion?)   ·

This poem, based on the exhilarating topic of a fast car ride, typifies the physical and metaphysical intensity of Jorge Guillén's great work, *Cántico* (*Canticle*), the .most intellectually challenging volume in modern Spanish poetry. Besides its customary linguistic compression, which reminds us that Guillén wrote his doctoral thesis on Góngora, there is also the challenge of conceptual meaning, for Guillén is a poet deeply attuned to modern European thought. Indeed, for Guillén, poetry is essentially a finely honed tool with which to probe the metaphysical issue of being, to unravel and define the existential puzzle of what it means to be in this world. His achievement is to have done this poetically, to have made a perfect match of poetry and metaphysics. His work might thus be seen as the culmination of two movements. On the one hand, formally, Guillén found the legacy of Góngora confirmed by the same absolute commitment to the art of poetry shown by the recent French tradition which had passed from Mallarmé to Valéry, the latter a personal acquaintance of his. From them Guillén inherited not only a high regard for technical rigour but also a belief in the mysterious power of poetic language to reveal truth. On the other hand, metaphysically, Guillén follows closely in the wake of Unamuno, Antonio Machado and especially Ortega y Gasset who had all, in their separate ways, rekindled an interest in metaphysical inquiry in Spain. While Unamuno gave a Spanish perspective to Kierkegaard's *Angst* and Machado showed poetry's efficacy in interpreting metaphysics, Bergsonism in his case, it was the eclectic Ortega who provided Guillén with a virtual compendium of philosophical issues and, specifically, a profoundly meditated and up-to-the-minute analysis of what was to be his own great theme, vitalism, an attachment to life, 'Fe de vida' ('Faith in Life'), as he subtitled *Cántico*. The wonder of it was that Guillén adapted the rigorous artistic principles of Góngora-Valéry to such metaphysical notions as Ortega spoke of, that he applied the taut form of what the French called *poésie pure*, an essentially reflexive *l'art pour l'art*, to the outgoing worldliness of vitalism. The point of connection was linguistic compression, for this, the inevitable concomitant of *poésie pure*'s eliminatory minimalism, made a perfect voice for Guillén's intense, ecstatic and exclamatory response to the real world. The above poem already evidences this and it leads us straight to the heart of Guillén's metaphysical theme.

The fast car ride of 'Cuerpo veloz' conveys all the excitement and immediacy of Guillén's contact with reality, a reality he literally rides out to meet. But let us also note at the outset that for all its thrill and urgency the poem is very finely constructed. The *romance* or ballad form in which it is cast is an apt choice for a swift narrative, while Guillén has shaped this to the round form of twenty lines. The poem is neatly framed, its jerky opening and the equally heavy lineal punctuation of its close expressing acceleration and deceleration respectively. In between, the main part of the ride is given in the headlong rush of a single eighteen-line sentence, which, with its vigorous repetitions, enjambments and elusive clausal hierarchy, conveys the sense of a continuously twisting, undulating motion. This formal technique is most expressive of the poem's deeper themes, continuation and accumulation being two recognizable and interrelated thematic terms in the poem's diction. Continuation applies to the landscape's physical unanimity and to the indivisibility of the poet's motion through it, the latter much aided by Guillén's favourite interlocking agent, air, here activated to 'viento' (wind). But continuation applies above all in the temporal sense, for the objects which the poet speeds past are not left behind, rather, 'me siguen, me azuzan / Y tras mi rumbo se tienden / Respirando' ('chase me, spur me/And on my track stretch out / Inhaling'), so that what has flashed by to the rear past remains with the poet as part of his accumulated life experience, sustaining him. The same point, we might interject, is made in the *décima* 'Profunda velocided' ('Profound Speed) where another car ride provides a stunning synthesis of time's three dimensions. The poem ends:

> ¡Mas cómo se profundiza
> La presencia escurridiza
> Del país, aunque futuro,
> Tras el límite en apuro
> Del velocísimo Ahora,
> Que se crea y se devora
> La luz de un mundo maduro! (p. 244)
>
> (But how profound becomes
> The vanishing presence
> Of even the future landscape,
> In the wake of the pressing front
> Of the breakneck Now,
> Which the light of a mature world
> Creates and devours!)

Here, as in 'Cuerpo veloz', the road ahead and the road behind are linked by the driver in his hurtling vehicle who is located in the 'velocísimo Ahora' ('breakneck Now'). This lightning present contains both the future and the past, for the emergent landscape rushes into view precisely when and as the landscape at hand vanishes phantasmagorically. 'Ahora' ('Now'), then, is that point in time when reality at once creates and devours itself in its ongoing process, 'devour' referring to the eagerness with which realty seeks to increase its store and 'create' suggesting the perpetual imminence of becoming in an open-ended future. Thus the present moment mobilizes both the past and the future, especially, as we see in 'Los nombres' ('Names'), in the supreme temporal context of human life:

> Esa pujanza agraz
> Del Instante, tan ágil
>
> Que en llegando a su meta
> Corre a imponer Después.
> Alerta, alerta, alerta,
> Yo seré, yo seré.
>
> (That unripe vigour
> Of the Moment, so agile
>
> That on reaching its goal
> It hastens to impose After.
> Look out, look out, look out,
> I will be, I will be.)

The unripe vigour of the present moment is a sign of life's urgency to be more, to be futuritively or in advance of itself, that is, to become. These points return us finally to 'Cuerpo veloz' which gives more ample expression to both past accumulation and future aspiration. Accumulation is forcefully expressed in the poem by the four times repeated 'más' ('more'), also 'muchos' ('many'), by the piled-up main sentence, by the listing of objects early on and by the incessant pluralization. Such an accumulation suggests the pléntifulness of reality, its paradisal bounty. But it is, we note, 'un paraíso inminente' ('an imminent paradise'), for there is still more to be had, more to be seen, and the poet-driver thus impatiently propels himself towards that future 'más'. At this point, in the last half dozen lines of the main sentence, Guillén makes most spectacular and even illusionist use of the car motif. With his foot down literally to the floorboards, he accelerates past the present:

> Mientras, nivel sobrehumano,
> Los deseos son poderes
> A la vista de invasores
> Esplendores en un trueque
> Final.
>   ¡Ay!
>
> (While, oh superhuman realm,
> Desires are possessions
> On beholding invading
> Splendours in a switch
> Supreme.
>   Oh!)

Reality's splendours invade at such breathtaking speed that what is desired futuritively is already possessed. The supreme 'switch' is therefore the transference of future into present, a god-like achievement which suggests a being's self-transcendence, even if, as the poem's last line indicates, the transcendence is only temporary.

What we have been describing here, with regard to time, reality and transcendence, is essentially the metaphysics of phenomenology. At least it conforms to Ortega's vitalist brand of phenomenology which straddles the early or pure phenomenology of Husserl in the first decades of the century and the later existential development given it by Heidegger. Briefly, the fundamental theme of phenomenology concerns the desire for an immediate and uncluttered perception of reality in its phenomena. In the act of directly perceiving a phenomenon, man, according to Husserl, discovers two things: the essence

of the thing perceived and the structure of his own consciousness.
Ortega had sympathetically explained Husserl's theory in an essay
of 1913, 'Sobre el concepto de la sensación' ('On the Concept of
Sensation'),[2] where the key point is that consciousness is always
'conciencia de' ('consciousness of') something. It is in his consciousness of something that man discovers his own consciousness, and,
furthermore, this consciousness is always in a sense transcendental
since it includes something which is outside the self, namely the
thing one is conscious of. Complex as this might sound, it will be
apparent that the primary thrust of phenomenology is to stress the
bond between man and reality as opposed to the emphasis upon
the thing-in-itself or the being-in-itself of other philosophies. Two
clear points emerge: first, as regards 'consciousness of' something,
we see that in phenomenology man is always inclined towards reality,
towards the things themselves, which are, says Husserl, 'intended'
by him. Second, as regards the things themselves, they are phenomena in the strictly etymological meaning of this Greek word, which
is to say, they are 'things that appear', which actively show themselves, as Ortega stressed in the manner of Husserl: 'Lo real ...
(es) lo que de él *aparece* en la conciencia, lo que de él se manifiesta
... *apariencia* (*fainómenon*)' (ibid., pp. 254–5) ('What is real ... (is)
that which *appears* in consciousness, that which manifests itself ...
appearance (*fainómenon*)'). In phenomenology, then, not only is man
purposefully inclined towards things, but things too incline towards
man in their dynamic act of appearing to him. This two-way link
is the crucial point in what we may call Guillén's phenomenological
vitalism, a point which finds acute metaphorical expression in the
moving car, as we again see in the opening lines of a third poem
on this motif, 'Vario mundo' ('Varied World'):

> Corro hacia ti, sorpresa,
> Búscame tú.   (p. 366)
>
> (I rush towards you, surprise,
> You, look for me.)

The moving car dramatically accentuates man's propensity towards
reality while it hyperbolically animates reality's *appearance* as an
oncoming rush. At the point of convergence, where phenomena and
consciousness meet at redoubled closing speed, is the instantaneous
perception, the 'Sentimiento inmediato' ('Immediate Experience'),
as Guillén years later entitled the first of two poems to Maine de
Biran in *Homenaje* (*Homage*), his third volume:

Me invade un sentimiento inmediato de vida,
Independiente así del anterior saber.
Es un bien absoluto . . .   (p. 1150)

(I am invaded by an immediate experience of life,
As such independent of prior knowledge.
It is an absolute good . . .)

Leaving aside for a moment why Guillén chose to acknowledge this rather minor precursor of modern thought rather than the modern thinkers themselves, it will be clear that the absence of a priori notions as a condition of pure perception in Maine de Biran is precisely in the spirit of phenomenology, the exclusion of prior thought being equivalent to Husserl's celebrated phenomenological reduction or bracketing off, *epoche*, as he called it. The moving car motif is again appropriate in this regard for it certainly has the effect of bracketing off the inessential, there only being time to register what is immediately perceived.

This last sentence holds largely true even of 'Vario mundo', a five-page poem in which a great many things are seen. In this, the third and last poem on the car motif which provides our introduction to Guillén's metaphysic, the poet-driver speeds eastwards at dawn in a surging journey which takes him over mountains, across an arid plain, past hamlets whose inhabitants are still lost in sleep, until, finally, he arrives at a delightful coastal region where he stops. The poem's length accommodates a copious amount of reality, '¡Cuánto mundo real!' (p. 367) ('So much real world!'), as well as its diversity, the clear theme of the title. The journey has an allegorical flavour, 'El coche se entregaba al sinuoso / Destino' (p. 368) ('The car surrendered to its sinuous / Destiny'), a sense of purpose which is intensified by the ascent to 'pasajes / Celestes' ('heavenly passageways'), by the coming of dawn and by the splendid final setting. What the poet has been in pursuit of from the outset is total reality, 'Yendo tras el mensaje / Mayor, tras el aroma total de una mañana' (p. 366) ('Going after the supreme / Message, after the complete scent of a morning'). He is eager to experience as much reality as possible, but to experience it with all the purity and uninhibited wonder of primordial man. His avidity, 'mi ansiedad de viajero' (p. 367) ('my traveller's eagerness'), compares with Adam looking upon things for the first time, and, as he is literally transported to paradise, to newness and to bounty, the modern machine even provides him with a primordial intuition of the earth's shape and wholeness:

> Sentir en la ascensión la curva de la tierra,
> Tierra de los orígenes con toros y bisontes,
> Profundo espacio entero
> Que en círculos crecientes se propaga y se cierra.   (p. 367)

> (To feel on rising up the curve of the earth,
> Earth of the beginnings with bulls and bisons,
> A profound whole space
> Which in increasing circles expands and closes.)

Such a primordial intuition had been phenomenology's goal, for, evidently, the primordial is equivalent to an absence of a priori concepts and, by the same token, Husserl's phenomenological reduction was very literally intended as a *re-ducere* or leading back. As opposed to the a priori, then, and as the key factor in man's response to reality, Guillén repeatedly stresses in 'Vario mundo' a point which the car motif again dramatically illustrates, 'sorpresa' or 'asombro' ('surprise', 'wonder'). Man is doubly astonished by the plentifulness and dynamism of reality, and, what is more, it is his reaction of surprise which makes him a worthy hero of life's drama:

> Hacia la inmensidad unida en un asombro,
> Frente al anfiteatro que reclama
> Protagonista. ¿Yo? (Yo lo soy si le nombro
> Con toda mi sorpresa.)
>   Sorpresa de viajero:
> Remotas invenciones son mías de repente.   (p. 369)

> (Towards the immensity united in a startle,
> Facing the amphitheatre that demands
> A protagonist. Me? (Indeed I am if I say so
> With absolute surprise.)
>   A traveller's surprise:
> Distant discoveries are of a sudden mine.)

The protagonist of 'Vario mundo' is hence both modern man in his car and Adam in paradise, seeing new things and seeing things anew. He is the protagonist precisely because all life converges on him, like a theatre in the round, and demands that he be its pivotal hero. This had been Ortega's point in an essay of 1910, 'Adán en el Paraíso' ('Adam in Paradise'): 'Cuando Adán apareció en el Paraíso, como un árbol nuevo, comenzó a existir esto que llamamos vida' ('When Adam appeared in Paradise, like a new tree, there began this thing we call life'), and 'VIDA' (LIFE), as Ortega then capitalizes it, is nothing other than '(E)l corazón de Adán, centro del universo, es decir, el universo íntegro en el corazón de Adán, como un licor hirviente en una copa'³ ('Adam's heart, the centre of the universe, that is, the universe integrated in Adam's heart, like a liquid boiling in a glass'). This anticipates Ortega's great theme of circumstantial being which he developed in his central text, *Meditaciones del 'Quijote'* (1914), (*Meditations on the Quixote*). There we find his most celebrated formula, 'Yo soy yo y mi circunstancia'⁴ ('I am I and my circumstance'), a statement which was to be decisive as regards Guillén's interpretation of being and a statement which leads us from pure phenomenology to an existential metaphysic. The main thrust of the formula is, quite simply, that man is inseparable from his circumstance; he is in a state of *Dasein*, or being-in-the-world, as Heidegger later put it. Furthermore, he is the supreme being or protagonist of life precisely because, as Ortega explains above, life depends upon him for its meaning, a meaning which he bestows by integrating life, by absorbing and by taking possession of his circumstance: '*mi* circunstancia' ('*my* circumstance'), says Ortega, and similarly Guillén above with another forceful possessive, 'Remotas invenciones son mías de repente' ('Distant discoveries are of a sudden mine'). Not only is the suddenness of the perception important, then, but also the possession which results from it. After this particular line in 'Vario mundo' there follows another of those extraordinary long sentences which suggest the great avalanche of reality which converges on the poet and which he instantaneously possesses. In the poem's final section the unremitting plurals culminate with the absorption and possession of reality on the part of the poet now definitively located at the pivotal centre:

> Flores. Pinturas. Lacas.
> Yo soy su amigo como si existieran ya dentro
> De mi mundo habitual . . .
>   También aquí mi capital.
> Me ciñe siempre el círculo de un mundo siempre enorme.   (p. 370)

> (Flowers. Paintings. Lacquers.
> I am their friend as if they already existed inside
> My habitual world . . .
>   My capital is here too.
> I am always surrounded by the circle of an always immense world.)

The car ride, we note, has extended the scope of man's role as integrator, linking the poet with a great variety of once unfamiliar objects and thereby increasing the store of that twofold complex, human life, as Ortega meaningfully called it. This life-enhancement is man's ethical priority, both for Guillén and Ortega, the latter having tellingly illustrated the point by focusing his *Meditaciones* on the supreme example of a man who rides out creatively in search of reality, Don Quixote. Guillén, who devoted one of *Cántico*'s longest poems to the famous knight, is himself a kind of metaphysical *caballero andante* riding out in his modern automobile, for each new sally, indeed each new poem, is a purposeful quest for meaning and an adventure aimed at enriching the human lot. Though his phenomenological acceptance of reality for what it is might seem at first more in the mould of Sancho Panza, it is his acceptance of the existential challenge to be reality's protagonist, that is, his acceptance of the responsibility to amplify and integrate to the point of transcendence that mysterious complex of being-and-reality, which characterizes him definitively as heroic. Here, in the theme of the hero, we find the ultimate connection between Ortega and Guillén. The hero, according to Ortega, is the man who unselfishly gives himself to reality, who immerses himself totally in his circumstance, just as Guillén in fact does in 'Cuerpo veloz' where the landscape opens up and surrounds the hurtling car driven so intentionally into it. But in this giving of the self to reality, Ortega argues, man paradoxically discovers himself, his true, sublime or extreme self, his 'nivel sobrehumano' (literally his 'superhuman level') as 'Cuerpo veloz' says, which is 'superhuman' for the simple reason that reality has now been annexed to the self, absorbed, possessed. Finally, then, man is heroic when he accepts this transcendental goal as his vocation in life, that is, when he makes an aspiring project of his entire being: '¡Oh potencia ya heroica ...! / Él es quien se destina' (p. 436) ('Oh power now heroic ...! / He is the one who determines his own destiny'), says Guillén in his poem on Don Quixote, 'Noche del caballero' ('Night of the Chivalrous'); and similarly Ortega in his *Meditaciones*, 'Héroe es ...´ quien quiere ser él mismo', 'el héroe quiere su destino', 'El héroe anticipa el porvenir y a él apela' (pp. 392, 394, 396) ('The hero is ... he who wants to be himself; the hero wants his destiny; the hero anticipates the future and calls it forth'). By facing up to reality in this literal way, by accepting the pivotal role as life-enhancer, by accepting the challenge to be to the maximum capacity, man meets his obligations, fulfils his destiny and is heroic.

   This project of the self is an ongoing vocation, a challenge to which the hero must rise time after time. Hence the answer to the question which ends 'Cuerpo veloz'—'¿Y aquel dominio celeste?' ('And that sublime dominion?')—is simply that such an ecstatic transcendence must be sought out again, just as Don Quixote, at

the end of Guillén's poem, seeks out a new adventure as soon as
the last is over:

> Allá va, prado arriba, disparada,
> La vocación de un hombre más que hombre. (p. 439)
>
> (There it goes, off up the meadow, shot forth,
> The vocation of a man more than a man.)

It is the *vocation* of the man which is shot forth or projected, not
strictly the man himself, for the ultimate meaning of Don Quixote
is that he has become his own vocation, which is to say, 'más que
hombre' ('more than a man'), heroic. In this understanding of heroism everyone is potentially heroic, as Ortega said, 'Todos, en varia
medida, somos héroes' (ibid., p. 319) ('We are all, to varying degree,
heroes'), for it is but a question of how much one is committed
to the project of one's own being, to pushing oneself to the limit
in one's chosen way. The way of chivalry makes patent this commitment and is an emblem of what Ortega calls man's 'naturaleza fron-
teriza' (ibid., p. 382) ('frontier nature'). The way of the poet is hardly
any less committed, as Guillén showed by entitling his major poem
on poetry 'Vida extrema' ('Extreme Life'), a title which suggests
that for Guillén poetry is an intense, quintessential, frontier form
of life. In short, for Guillén poetry is not merely a medium through
which to analyse his response to life, it is rather an all-pervading
vital vocation which subsumes his identity and energizes his commitment to being. This almost mystical coming together of poetry and
being is clear in Guillén's final dedication of *Cántico* to his friend
Pedro Salinas, a dedication which ends:

> HOMBRE COMO NOSOTROS
> ÁVIDO
> DE COMPARTIR LA VIDA COMO FUENTE,
> DE CONSUMAR LA PLENITUD DEL SER
> EN LA FIEL PLENITUD DE LAS PALABRAS.

> (A MAN LIKE OURSELVES
> EAGER
> TO SHARE OUT LIFE LIKE A FOUNTAIN,
> TO CONSUMMATE THE PLENITUDE OF BEING
> IN THE FAITHFUL PLENITUDE OF WORDS.)

Poetry and being are one, for Guillén; indeed, poetry is life in its
plenitude, it is where the life-enhancing integration or consummation
of being takes place.

On this note of reverence, so startling in a twentieth-century writer, we might pause to take stock of *Cántico* and its author. Clearly, we are dealing with a work of rare profundity and a poet of no mean intellectual bent. Guillén in fact epitomizes a certain brand of poet, the poet-professor. As an academic whose career took him to the Sorbonne (1917–23), to Murcia (1926–29), Oxford (1929-31), Seville (1931-38) and, with the Civil War, to the United States where he taught mainly at Wellesley College, Massachusetts, Guillén devoted his entire life to literature, as teacher, critic and poet, having the time and opportunity besides to familiarize himself with literatures other than Spanish. The influence of Valéry has already been mentioned, while, in connection with English, strong points of contact are to be found with Walt Whitman whom Guillén probably came to by way of Vielé-Griffin. Broadly speaking, as we shall see, Valéry's influence decreased and Whitman's increased as *Cántico* itself evolved at unhurried pace. Begun in 1919, *Cántico* was not published until 1928 when it contained seventy-five poems, and, in fact, though Guillén was next oldest to Salinas among his famous generation, he was the last to publish a volume. The original *Cántico* was expanded in the successive editions of 1936, 1945 and 1950 when as a finished work it comprised 334 poems. This imposing total represents a creative output of just over ten poems a year, the majority of them short poems, a remarkably steady growth indicative of the care and thought Guillén put into a work which developed in accord with his own life. The relative comfort provided by a professional career and the normality of a married life with two children suggest more a bourgeois than bohemian disposition. Indeed, it is the everyday nature of his topic which some readers find disconcerting. But if catastrophe and personal anguish are largely absent in *Cántico*, the advantages of such bourgeois normality are many, it seems to me, not least being the freedom which it allows the poet. With no social axe to grind and no compelling subjective dilemma to explore, Guillén looks starkly at man in his universal condition. His poetic voice, free from anecdote and idiosyncrasy, asks only generic questions, or rather, *the* question: what is being? Yet, as we have seen, the question applies only to the individual, intensely so. As readers we are doubly involved, for we are at once absorbed in the existential challenge by *Cántico*'s collective voice and evangelized by the ethical didacticism implicit in Guillén's centralization of man and affirmation of life on this earth. Even the most sceptical might find themselves persuaded by the secular yet transcendental faith which Guillén fervently advocates through the powerful mix of metaphysics and poetic language. These twin intensifiers of *Cántico*'s everyday world are inseparable not only for the way they embellish and conceptualize Guillén's thesis but also because the fundamentally simple and even axiomatic metaphysic of being-in-the-world relies heavily for its signification upon the primary unit of poetry, the metaphorical image.

Before turning to certain key images a few points on influence need to be clarified. I have mentioned Ortega, Valéry and Whitman. As regards Ortega, firstly, it is curious that Guillén makes no acknowledgement of his signal influence, especially when he is so charitable in *Homenaje* (*Homage*) to a host of other writers who inspired him much less. It could be said that Ortega is so formidable an influence as to be beyond simple acknowledgement, that, furthermore, it is more difficult to acknowledge the source of ideas than, say, of style. But the decisive reason for this omission may well be that Guillén had no wish to be associated with a man who in spheres other than metaphysics was much discredited. Ortega's Germanic political elitism, for which he is still unfortunately best known, made him something of a bogeyman, while, secondly, his description of the new cerebral art of the 1920s as 'dehumanized' gave particular offence to Guillén who was in the intellectual vanguard. Years later, in his major critical study, *Lenguaje y poesía* (*Language and Poetry*), Guillén rejected Ortega's analysis, showing a decided prickliness about the tags of coldness and abstraction which had so unfairly stuck to him.[5] The point was that when Ortega's theory of dehumanization came out in 1925 Guillén was already widely known as 'the Spanish Valéry', a label which suggested that he followed the calculating, almost scientific compositional principles of *poésie pure*. Guillén freely admits to the profound influence Valéry exerted on him in the early twenties (ibid., p. 244), typified by the fact that in 1923 he was considering giving his work the very reflexive title *Rigor* (*Rigour*).[6] But Guillén insists that he grew away from Valéry's inveterate narcissism and he describes *Cántico*, the much more outgoing title he settled on, as an 'anti-*Charmes*'.[7] Some indication of his progressive departure from Valéry is found in the versification of the three motor-car poems we have considered: the earliest, 'Profunda velocidad' of 1928, is a *décima* similar to the French *dizain* whose ten taut lines Valéry delighted in; chronologically second is 'Cuerpo veloz' of 1945, a vigorous and flowing *romance* or traditional Spanish ballad; last is 'Vario mundo' of 1950, an irregular and expansive poem, much closer in spirit to Whitman. By and large this is typical of *Cántico*'s trajectory, of its increasingly worldly and less self-consciously literary orientation. In short, knowingly or not, Guillén seems to have heeded Ortega's warning about dehumanization and, what is more, it was Ortega's metaphysic which led him towards the vitalism he found poetically voiced in Whitman. For other reasons, ironically, Guillén was unable to acknowledge Ortega—whose volumes he was rereading one by one in the late forties, a colleague recounts[8]—though one is inclined to believe that 'Noche del caballero', being such a faithful poeticization of *Meditaciones del 'Quijote'*, is in fact a form of tacit acknowledgement.

Let us now try to relate these points to the poems themselves. Earlier on I suggested that one of the tenets of *poésie pure* which adapted quite readily to Guillén's increasingly outward vision was linguistic compression, both because it links with phenomenology's essentialism and because it conveys the ecstatic, near mute surprise of the onlooker's response to the world. Another equally important feature of *poésie pure* which makes the same transition and comes to assume metaphysical value is the attachment to form. In Valéry as in Góngora form has a double importance, there being poetic form and the form of the world's objects. The hallmark of Valéry's work especially is the integration of these two types of form. When Valéry takes pomegranates, palm trees and columns as his subject-matter, he explores their beauty of form in such a way as to refer implicitly to poetic form. Similarly, in the early Guillén there are numerous poems on flowers, trees and such artistic subjects as statues ('Estatua ecuestre') or the painterly nude, 'Desnudo'. Again, a favourite topic of Valéry is the emergence of form from water—found in 'Naissance de Vénus', 'Baignée' and at the end of 'Aurore'—and Guillén takes up the subject in 'El manantial' (p. 46) ('The Spring') where the delightful spectacle of a girl's body emerging from chaotic waves not only parallels the classical myth of creation but is a stunning metaphor of poetry's natural propensity towards form. However, it is the transition from this kind of self-referential form to the metaphysical use of form which interests us. The transition can be conveniently charted in the short *décima*. Typical of the reflexive Guillén are the early poems 'La rosa' ('The Rose'), appropriately dedicated to the Neoplatonic Juan Ramón Jiménez, and 'El ruiseñor' ('The Nightingale'), dedicated to Góngora, which reads:

> El ruiseñor, pavo real
> Facilísimo del pío,
> Envía su memorial
> Sobre la curva del río,

Lejos, muy lejos, a un día
Parado en su mediodía,
Donde un ave carmesí,
Cenit de una primavera
Redonda, perfecta esfera,
No responde nunca: sí.   (p. 232)

(The nightingale, peacock
Of most fluent song,
Sends forth his petition
On the curve of the river,
Far, far away, to a day
Stopped in its midday,
Where a crimson bird,
The zenith of a round
Perfect sphere of Spring,
Never replies: yes.)

Let us be clear, there is nothing metaphysical in this poem which belongs to the early Guillén in his most precious mood of literary introversion. The poem is a tribute to Góngora, for the nightingale's song is a metaphor of poetry itself, a stylized motif by which Guillén evokes the unreal, magical world of the baroque master's verse. It is a world of form and stillness, of beauty halted in its noon perfection, and the symmetrical form of the *décima* with its centralized couplet is an inseparable part of the total harmony which the poem images. How far we seem from the vitalist Guillén! Yet it is only a short step from such reflexivity to the metaphysical application of form found in the following *décima*, 'Perfección' ('Perfection'):

Queda curvo el firmamento,
Compacto azul, sobre el día.
Es el redondeamiento
Del esplendor: mediodía.
Todo es cúpula. Reposa,
Central sin querer, la rosa,
A un sol en cenit sujeta.
Y tanto se da el presente
Que el pie caminante siente
La integridad del planeta.   (p. 250)

(Fixed in its curve the firmament
Is compact blue above the day.
It is the rounding
Of splendour: midday.
All is dome. Resting,
Unintentionally central, the rose
Lies subject to a sun in zenith.

And so much present abounds
That the travelling foot can feel
The integrity of the planet.)

The poem compares closely with the previous *décima* in its exquisite formal beauty and noon stillness. The 4—2—4 verse distribution again reinforces the now insistent concentricity of 'curve', 'rounding', 'midday', 'dome', 'central', 'rose', 'zenith' and 'planet'. But there is an additional implication: the circular forms are all, like monads, interconnected. The rose is linked to the sun, and man, the one mobile element, perceives the startling wholeness of the planet. Ortega had in fact developed the very same theme in his *Meditaciones*:

¿Cuán poca cosa sería una cosa si fuera sólo lo que es en el aislamiento? ¡Qué pobre, qué yerma, qué borrosa! Diríase que hay en cada una cierta secreta potencialidad de ser muchas más, la cual se liberta y expansiona cuando otra u otras entran en relación con ella. Diríase que cada cosa es fecundada por las demás; diríase que se aman y aspiran a maridarse, a juntarse en sociedades, en organismos, en edificios, en mundos. Eso que llamamos Naturaleza no es sino la máxima estructura en que todos los elementos materiales han entrado. Y es obra de amor naturaleza, porque significa generación, engendro de las unas cosas en las otras, nacer la una de la otra donde estaba premeditada, preformada, virtualmente inclusa.[9]

(How small would a thing be if it were only what it is in isolation? How poor, how barren, how indistinct! It might be said that in each thing there is a certain secret potential to be much more, which is released and expanded when another or other things enter into relation with it. One might say that each thing is fertilized by the rest; one might say that they love one another and wish to marry, to join together in societies, in organisms, in edifices, in worlds. This thing we call Nature is nothing but the maximum structure in which all material things have entered. And nature is a work of love, because it signifies generation, the engendering of one thing in another, the birth of one from another where it was premeditated, preformed, virtually included.)

We can now see that the poem 'Perfección' is a very accurate illustration of this theme of reality's interconnectedness. Its repeated circular motif indicates how one object is 'premeditated, preformed, virtually included' in another and the poem in its entirety evokes the sense of reality's 'maximum structure'. Hence form is now of metaphysical import and we have already gone a long way towards the vitalist theme of circumstantial plentitude or being-in-the-world which *Cántico* develops. To complete the transition we need only turn to another noon poem, 'Las doce en el reloj' ('Twelve by the Clock), also of 1936, which specifies the theme of the loving interrelationship of the world's objects and at the same time promotes the presence of the onlooker who appeared so fleetingly in 'Perfección':

> Dije: Todo ya pleno.
> Un álamo vibró.
> Las hojas plateadas
> Sonaron con amor.
> Los verdes eran grises,
> El amor era sol.
> Entonces, mediodía,
> Un pájaro sumió
> Su cantar en el viento
> Con tal adoración
> Que se sintió cantada
> Bajo el viento la flor
> Crecida entre las mieses,
> Más altas. Era yo,
> Centro en aquel instante
> De tanto alrededor,
> Quien lo veía todo
> Completo para un dios.
> Dije: Todo, completo.
> ¡Las doce en el reloj!   (p. 485)

> (I said: everything full now.
> A poplar shook.
> Its silver leaves
> Resounded with love.
> Greens were greys,
> Love was sun.
> Then, midday,
> A bird sank
> His song into the wind
> With such adoration
> That under the wind
> The flower felt itself sung
> As it grew among the tallest
> Corn. It was I,
> Centre at that moment
> Of so much surrounding,
> Who saw it all
> Complete for a god.
> I said: Everything, complete.
> Twelve by the clock!)

The very literary themes of noon stillness and rapturous birdsong persist, we note, but the poem is shorn of reflexivity. Reality itself has burst through, the real beauty of its real phenomena taking precedence over poetic beauty. The concentric motifs of sun, midday, flower and the implied clock also persist, but they now have the specific purpose of locating man at the godlike centre where the equation *man = god* suggests the heroic increment 'un hombre más que hombre' ('a man more than a man') noted earlier. The conclusion of 'Las doce en el reloj' indicates two important points about Guillén's use of form. First we note how literally Guillén's circle illustrates Ortega's theory of circumstance. Ortega had said, '¡La circunstancia! ¡*Circum-stantia!* ¡Las cosas mudas que están en nuestro próximo derredor!'[10] ('Circumstance! *Circum-stantia!* The silent things that are in our immediate surrounding!'), where the etymological point is that circumstance is precisely that which is or stands *around* us. It is this very *aroundness*, coupled with the centralization of the protagonist, which Guillén's ubiquitous circle draws. The second point to be made is that form, even the most abstract form, always has psychical value. The early Guillén had written abstract poems of the most extreme austerity that one can imagine, as is testified by titles such as 'Redondez' ('Roundness') and 'Perfección del círculo' ('Perfection of the Circle') and by the stark geometry of poems such as 'Gran silencio' ('Great Silence'), 'Ciudad de los estíos' ('City of Summers') and several more. Poems of this kind were very much in the artistic spirit of the twenties when painters such as Picasso and especially Kandinsky were exploring the inner properties of abstract form. The energy of form is also Guillén's concern in 'Perfección del círculo', for example, when, after describing the circle's perfectly uniform shape, the poem concludes:

> Misteriosamente
> Refulge y se cela.
> —¿Quién? ¿Dios? ¿El poema?
> —Misteriosamente . . .   (p. 90)

> (Mysteriously
> It shines out and conceals itself.
> —Who? God? The poem?
> —Mysteriously . . .)

Guillén's analysis indicates that a two-way movement is implicit in the static form of the circle, its circumference and centre being indicative of centrifugal and centripetal energy—'Refulge y se cela' ('It shines out and conceals itself')—which in its counterpoise and self-sufficiency is unfathomable and godlike. Though such a poem seems to justify Ortega's point about dehumanization, let us also remember that the artist Kandinsky[11] and the psychologist Jung[12] were unanimous in their view that the circle is essentially a psychical projection of its author. In fact Jung analysed the recurrence in dreams of what he called the *mandala* symbol and he considered the circle to be the archetype of the human desire for well-being. As far as we are concerned, it is not difficult to see the link between the abstract harmony of 'Perfección del círculo' and the human plenitude of 'Las doce en el reloj'. While the two poems share a transcendental conclusion in their reference to 'dios' ('god'), which continues the religious tradition of representing god at the centre of harmony, what happens typically in *Cántico* is that modern man in his newfound plenitude usurps that centre. What is more, the circle's dualistic movement of 'Refulge y se cela'—a dualism frequently found in *Cántico* and which we saw twice in the poem 'Vario mundo'—is itself indicative of how transcendental plenitude is achieved. The vitalist thesis of *Cántico*, as already suggested, is that by going out into the world man discovers his own inner self. Thus the circle's dual movement of outwardness and inwardness is a paradigm of the process which is summed up in a line from 'Más allá' ('Beyond'): 'Voy por él a mi alma' (p. 32) ('I go through it'—i.e. the world—'to my soul').

Form, then, has a multiplicity of values in *Cántico*. There is the form of everyday objects by which man perceives reality. There is the repetition of form from object to object by which man perceives the interconnectedness of reality. There is the pre-eminent form of the circle which expresses the round circumstance in which man is centrally located. And finally, supplementing the latter, there is the psychical value of form as a projection of man's transcendental aspiration. What is remarkable about Guillén's extensive use of form is that its ultimate metaphysical value seems to have evolved quite naturally out of his initial concern for poetic form. In other words, though the reflexivity of *poésie pure* was in time rejected, Guillén found that Valéry's compositional principles had valid application in the expression of his vitalist theme. Indeed, in *Cántico* the rigorous pursuit of literary craft is continually transposing before our eyes into a rigorous pursuit of being. While we shall continue to remain alert to this fundamental coincidence, it is time now to look at certain images which are especially important in the articulation of *Cántico*'s theme. Three we may consider are: air, water and the image of sexual union.

Air is one of the most thematic motifs in Guillén's entire work, as is testified by the title he gave to the tripartite volume which includes *Cántico*, *Clamor* and *Homenaje: Aire nuestro (Our Air)*. The communal nature of air, which this title indicates, is the key to its meaning in *Cántico*. Essentially, air, together with its inseparable twin, *luz* (light), signifies the contiguousness of reality. It is 'en tanta alianza / Con todo' ('in so much alliance / with everything') as the poem 'Presencia del aire' (p. 95) ('Presence of Air') puts it, binding and interlocking the items of reality with its real presence. The shimmering lustre of light-filled air embellishes reality—'Todo el aire en realce' (p. 95) ('All the air in splendour')—and at the same time it renders incongruous any notion of isolation or nothingness. Poem after poem shows how space is replete with the presence of air-light. 'La luz sobre el monte' ('Light on the Mountain') begins:

> ¡Oh luz sobre el monte, densa
> Del espacio, sólo espacio ... (!)   (p. 237)
>
> (Oh light on the mountain dense
> With space, only space ... (!))

'Meseta' ('Tableland') begins with the exclamation '¡Espacio!' (p. 501) ('Space!'), suggesting the grand vistas of three-parts sky to be seen on the Castilian plain, while the similar 'El horizonte' ('The Horizon') depicts the vast space of air as 'Trasparencia cuajada' (p. 187) ('Thickened transparency') which again suggests its substance and repleteness. This theme of spatial contiguousness results in images of most unassuming beauty, as at the beginning of 'Cima de la delicia' ('Crest of Delight'), where 'pájaro' (bird) and 'mozo' (youth) are located in three-dimensional splendour:

> ¡Cima de la delicia!
> Todo en el aire es pájaro.
> Se cierne lo inmediato
> Resuelto en lejanía.
>
> ¡Hueste de esbeltas fuerzas!
> ¡Qué alacridad de mozo
> En el espacio airoso,
> Henchido de presencia!   (p.85)
>
> (Crest of delight!
> Everything in the air is a bird.
> The close at hand soars
> Transformed into distance.
>
> A host of graceful forces!
> What briskness of a youth
> In the airy space,
> Crammed with presence!)

The linking facility of air is apparent in the roundly generic second line which indicates the spatial coexistence of air and bird, while the human youth of the second stanza similarly makes his way through a cubical aerial perspective. It might be said that Guillén's use of air and light again recalls painting, for instance the translucent depth of Cézanne's skies. But there is no aesthetical mannerism in this; it is simply a question of perceiving the full implications of physical phenomena. Ortega had described the same implications of space and light in 'Adán en el Paraíso', an article prompted by the contemporary Spanish painter Zuloaga:

El espacio es el medio de la coexistencia ... La construcción de la coexistencia, del espacio, necesita de un instrumento unitivo, de un elemento susceptible de diversificarse en innúmeras cualidades, sin dejar de ser uno y el mismo. Esta materia soberana de la pintura es la luz.[13]

(Space is the medium of coexistence ... The construction of coexistence, of space, requires a unitive instrument, an element which can diversify into innumerable qualities without ever not being its own single self. This sovereign material in painting is light.)

The human implications of this unitive instrument, air-light, are only embryonic in the above poems which all belong to the first *Cántico*. But Guillén was already aware of the deeper possibilities, as a letter to Lorca in 1927 reveals:

Cada vez me penetra más agudamente lo que yo llamo la felicidad atmosférica: es que nos viene en el aire, y en la luz del aire, cuya tranquila respiración—solamente *respiración*—calma nuestra inseguridad de vivir. Sólo así estoy seguro de la totalidad de mi existencia: respirando esta luz.[14]

(I am struck ever more sharply by what I call atmospheric happiness: which comes to us in the air, and in the light of the air, whose quiet respiration—no more than *respiration*—calms the anxiety of our living. Only thus am I sure of the totality of my existence: breathing this light.)

Such metaphysical implications were developed in the later editions of *Cántico*, notably in the major poem 'El aire' ('The Air') of 1945. The thirty-five quatrains of unchanged assonance in e-o which comprise this poem amount to a remarkably exhaustive treatment of a motif which, as the poem's first line indicates, is apparently so insubstantial: 'Aire: nada, casi nada' (p. 518) ('Air: nothing, almost nothing'). From this single invisible phenomenon, traditionally prized by poets such as Bécquer for its elusiveness, Guillén elicits a whole body of meaning. In particular the motif aptly conveys *Cántico*'s theme that ordinary reality has a stunning, even enigmatic beauty that we take for granted or completely fail to see, for, despite being all around us, air is 'un ser muy secreto ... / Con sigilo se difunde. / Nadie puede ver su cuerpo' (p. 518) ('is a very secret being ... / It diffuses secretly. / Nobody can see its body). This transposes easily into a transcendental implication, *aire* (air) = *cielo* (heaven), as in 'apenas terreno' ('scarcely earthly') and 'Hasta el espíritu el aire ... va ascendiendo ... / ¡Qué celeste levedad!' (p. 518) ('Towards the spirit air ever ascends ... / What heavenly lightness!'). At the same time, more inventively, it accommodates a notion of humility so important to *Cántico*'s protagonist, 'Ocultando su belleza / No quiere parecer nuevo' (p. 519) ('Hiding its beauty / It wishes not to seem new'), and it readily expresses the peace stressed in the letter to Lorca: 'Aire claro, buen silencio' (p. 518) ('Clear air, fine silence'). When the poem eventually expands to embrace reality at large, the motif assumes its customary extensive and integrational force, both in the spatial sense—'Aire noble que se otorga / Distancias, alejamientos' (p. 519) ('Noble air that confers / Distances, remotenesses')—and in the temporal sense, 'Aire que respiro a fondo / De muchos soles muy denso ... / Aire en que respiro tiempo' (p. 519) ('Air that I breathe deeply / Dense with many suns ... / Air in which I breathe time'), thereby integrating these two basic components of reality, time and space. Here we note that air is imbued with time because it partakes of cosmic duration and, subjectively, because it has lit up a whole storehouse of sensations which remain with the poet, 'En los altos del recuerdo' ('In the heights of memory'). A vast gloriole embellishing each item in reality, air is also a spatially interlocking agent as the insistent prepositions stress: 'Bajo el aire, por el aire', 'Entre el chopo y la ribera, / Entre el río y el remero ... / Un aire que nunca es término' ('Under the air, through the air', 'Between the poplar and the shore, / Between the river and the rower ... / An air that is never an end'). In thus unifying reality it banishes loneliness, 'Profundizando en el aire / No están solos, están dentro / Los jardinillos, las verjas ...' (p. 521) ('Deepening in the air / They are never alone, but rather inside / Gardens, railings ...'), an *insideness* which applies also to the poet who is similarly exempt from loneliness, 'Más allá del solilo-

quio' ('Beyond soliloquy'), and in fact surrounded or circumscribed
by air:

> Con su creación el aire
> Me cerca: divino cerco.   (p. 523)
>
> (With its creation the air
> Surrounds me: divine circle.)

Through the simple act of breathing—'Respirando, respirando'
(p. 520)—man enjoys a primordial, immediate and continuous contact with this quintessential phenomenon of life, 'la vida ... / Es
aire, simple portento' (p. 520) ('life ... / Is air, marvel of simplicity').
His being is thus as total and as transcendentally purified as the
substance of air itself, from which, as the last stanza concludes, he
is inseparable: 'Soy del aire' (p. 523) ('I am of the air').

A word, finally, on the poem's execution, which is also remarkable
for its simplicity. Each stanza is presented as a separate unit ending
in a full-stop, which is unusual in a poem of this length and does
much to create the mood of candour. There is an almost ingenuous
insistence on the word *aire* which occurs twenty-one times, while
a similar guilelessness is to be found in the syntactical linking:

> Vida, vida, nada más
> Este soplo que da aliento,
> Aliento con una fe.
> Sí, lo extraordinario es esto.
>
> Esto: la luz en el aire,
> Y con el aire un anhelo.
> ¡Anhelo de trasparencia,
> Sumo bien! Respiro, creo.   (p. 520)
>
> (Life, life, nothing but
> This gust that gives breath,
> Breath and with it a faith:
> Yes, the extraordinary thing is this.
>
> This: the light in the air,
> And with the air a panting desire.
> A desire for transparency,
> Absolute good! I breathe, I believe.)

Here the linking of ideas is done through an utterly plain repetition
of 'aliento', 'esto', 'aire' and 'anhelo' (meaning both 'to pant' and
'desire'). This straightforward syntax is a virtual metaphor of the
theme of interlocking, but its execution seems the very opposite of
poetic artifice, Guillén's point being that what he has to say is

self-evident rather than ingenious. The end effect of such a simple treatment is to render the poem's argument as pellucid as its compendious air motif, while the innocent, candid tone complements the sense of faith and revelation.

The above poem's conclusion, 'Soy del aire' ('I am of the air'), reminds us of the circumstantial theme which is at the heart of *Cántico*. The same point is most sharply made in a last poem on the air motif that we shall consider, 'Viento saltado' ('Jumped Wind'), one of *Cántico*'s key poems. Written entirely between exclamation marks, fourteen pairs in all, this poem expresses an intense physicality which seems scarcely intelligible at times:

> ¡En el viento, por entre el viento
> Saltar, saltar,
> Porque sí, porque sí, porque
> Zas!   (p. 134)

> (In the wind, between the wind
> Jumping, jumping,
> That's why, that's why, because
> Bang!)

Onomatopoeic and even childlike in its physical innocence, the poem expresses the ecstatic, uncontrollable joy of one who has experienced an immediate revelation, '¡Oh violencia de revelación ...!' ('Oh violence of revelation!'), a revelation of the world's wholeness and of his own certain place within it. So violent is the revelation as to make him jump for joy, the leap being both physical and, metaphorically, metaphysical. Reality's unbrokenness had been perceived in the first stanza, '¡El día plenario profundamente se agolpa / Sin resquicios!' ('The whole day crowds profoundly in / Without a crack!'), while the interrelationshp of reality's phenomena is suggested in the third: '¡Esa blancura de nieve salvada / Que es fresno ...!' ('That whiteness of rescued snow / Which is an ash tree ...!'). The intuition of wholeness recalls 'Perfección', '¡Mis pies / Sienten la Tierra en una ráfaga / De redondez!' ('My feet / Feel the Earth in a gust / Of roundness!'), and the poet is locked in his physical circumstance by the familiar encircling motif of air, here 'viento' (wind). Once again immersion is reinforced by prepositions, 'por', 'con', 'sobre', 'entre' (through, with, above, between) and the eight times repeated 'en' (in). This interlocking of man and circumstance through the act of breathing compares with Whitman's 'Song of the Open Road' where it is used to similar expansionist effect:

I inhale great draughts of space,
The east and the west are mine, and the north and the south are mine,
I am larger, better than I thought.

If anything, however, Guillén's conclusion is even more expansive,
with greater emphasis on outwardness:

> ¡Cuerpo en el viento y con cuerpo la gloria!
> ¡Soy
> Del viento, soy a través de la tarde más viento,
> Soy más que yo!   (p. 135)
>
> (Body in the wind and, with body, glory!
> I am
> Of the wind, I am, through the afternoon, more wind,
> I am more than myself!)

The conclusion in the last line is truly startling. By comparison Whitman's 'I am larger, better than I thought' seems quite mild. But
the transcendental force of Guillén's 'Soy más que yo!' (I am more
than myself!') derives logically from the theme of an absolute immersion in reality. Furthermore, it is an utterly faithful rendering of
Ortega's famous formula, 'Yo soy yo y mi circunstancia' ('I am
I and my circumstance'), i.e. I am myself *plus* my circumstance,
which, by simple mathematics, makes the first plenitudinous *I* greater
than the simple self or isolated *I*. The aggregate self indicated by
'Soy más que yo!' ('I am more than myself!') compares with the
expansionist *hombre<dios* (*man<god*) of 'Las doce en el reloj', also
with the 'hombre más que hombre' ('man more than a man') of
'Noche del caballero'. Guillén was to condense this worldly transcendentalism of self-plus-circumstance into just four syllables in 'Más
allá' (Beyond'):

> Soy, más, estoy.   (p. 28)
>
> (I am, more, I am [here and now].)

Exploiting a facility of Spanish with its two verbs 'to be', *ser* and
estar, Guillén argues that the circumstantial being indicated by *estar*
is greater (*más*) than the simple being of *ser* which has no reference
to time and place.

Turning now to the two other images I mentioned, water and
sexual union, we find that the same metaphysical points apply. We
shall therefore consider them more briefly, and, as far as possible,
together. Water, evidently, provides a very literal metaphor of
immersion and, like air, it has overtones of purity. An early instance
of the motif is found in 'La salida' ('Going Out'), which describes

a bather launching himself into waves, thrilled by the total contact
of his body with water as he swims:

> A través de la aurora
> Central de un paraíso,
> Ahogarse en plenitud
> Y renacer clarísimo . . .   (p. 490)

> (Across a dawn
> At the centre of paradise,
> Drowning in plenitude
> And being reborn afresh . . .)

Even formless water has its implied circle, we note, as did air in
'El aire', while the religious implication of a baptismal rebirth is
unmistakable. Linguistically, the poem's striking feature is that all
its verb forms are infinitives, eight in its twenty lines, and this lack
of subject specification effectively suggests repetition, even ritual,
as well as the idea that such a primordial experience is available
to everyone. The motif is given fuller development in 'El aparecido'
('The Appeared') of 1936, a much longer *romance* which describes
the uninterrupted narrative event of a diver plunging into a teeming
underwater world from which he soon emerges breathless. The proli-
fic world he discovers suggests reality's abundance and its hidden,
mysterious energy, while the constant movement of 'Irrupciones'
('Irruptions'), 'Eses de móviles algas' ('S's of mobile algae'), visibly
demonstrates the primordial vitality of protoplasmic phenomena:

> Aquí se ve a los relámpagos
> Que en zigzag definitivo
> Viven, red de nervaduras
> Lívidas, dentro del frío.   (p. 475)

> (Here are seen lightning flashes
> That in definitive zigzag
> Live, like a mesh of livid
> Veins, inside the cold.)

The world into which the subject plunges 'fascinado' ('fascinated')
is 'un más allá ofrecido / Sin cesar, irresistible' ('a beyond offered /
Endlessly, irresistibly'), a dynamically composite world which, with
its 'Vigor de una confluencia' ('Vigour of confluence'), engulfs him
totally:

> Siento en la piel, en la sangre
> —Fluye todo el mar conmigo—
> Una confabulación
> Indomable de prodigios.   (p. 476)

> (I feel on my skin, in my blood
> —The whole sea flows with me—
> An indomitable
> Confabulation of marvels.)

The thematic prefix *con* (with) of 'conmigo' ('with me') and 'confabulación' suggests again that it is the sum and aggregate of man and reality which is so startling, fabulous or transcendental. Strictly, it is the perception of reality's oneness and then of one's own supreme place within it—'dentro de él, colmándolo' (p. 476) ('inside it, crowning it')—which induces *asombro* (wonder) and which prompts an ecstatic, supraliminal singing:

> Asombro de ser: cantar,
> Cantar, cantar sin designio.
> ¡Mármara, mar, maramar,
> Confluyan los estribillos!

> (Wonder of being: to sing,
> Sing, sing without plan.
> Sea-o, oh sea, sea-o,
> Let the choruses flow as one!)

As regards the poem's title, it is clear that 'El aparecido' ('The Appeared') refers to the diver's act of bursting into view after having explored the waters below, 'Arrojarse . . . Para tajante emerger / Con felicidad de filo' (p. 475) ('To dive . . . So as to emerge cuttingly / With the joy of a blade'). But this physical reappearance is also a metaphor of the metaphysical notion of an emergence and manifestation within the subject of his true being:

> Yo quiero sólo flotar,
> Aparecer, un suspiro.
> ¡Aparecer en el ser . . . !   (p. 475)

> (I wish only to float,
> To appear, a breath.
> To appear in my being . . .!)

Flushed with his immediate experience of essential life in the underwater world, the subject responds in like manner by displaying his true self. In this novel attribution of the act of *appearing* to a human subject Guillén complements Ortega's phenomenological theme of objects appearing to man and in so doing further stresses the parity of being and reality.

The ecstasy of 'El aparecido' is virtually indistinguishable from the tone of Guillén's love poems and, clearly, the notion of reality's contiguousness with the subject's flesh applies intensely in sexual union. For this reason love in *Cántico* is not so much a separate theme as a further and supreme illustration of the metaphysic of being, as may be seen in its finest expression 'Salvación de la primavera' ('Salvation of Spring') which was written in 1931, only shortly after 'El aparecido'. The poem opens with three stanzas which give a stunningly lucid description of the beloved's presence in relation to her circumstance:

> Ajustada a la sola
> Desnudez de tu cuerpo,
> Entre el aire y la luz
> Eres puro elemento.

> ¡Eres! Y tan desnuda,
> Tan continua, tan simple
> Que el mundo vuelve a ser
> Fábula irresistible.

> En torno, forma a forma,
> Los objetos diarios
> Aparecen. Y son
> Prodigios, y no mágicos.   (p. 103)

> (Adjusted to the single
> Nakedness of your body,
> Between the air and the light
> You are pure element.

> You are! And so naked,
> So continuous, so simple
> That the world is once more
> An irresistible fable.

> All around, form by form,
> The daily objects
> Appear. And they are
> Prodigious, and not magical.)

The limpid beauty of these lines is well worth savouring. They seem to bear out Guillén's comment of 1926, 'Poesía pura—poesía simple, prefiero yo'[15] ('Pure poetry—simple poetry, I prefer'), and they illustrate to what advantage Guillén has adapted linguistic compression to the purpose of a stark, phenomenological view of reality. But the spareness which his Castilian language carries so majestically also holds a wealth of meaning: the beloved is literally well adjusted in her physical presence, the beauty of her body lit up by the light-filled air which surrounds her; she is further surrounded by objects which display themselves in their form, *appearing* in this way; finally, there is the now standard conundrum of reality being fabulous and yet not at all magical, which is to say, transcendental but real, a contradiction which might be termed a conceit if it were not so literally intended. Once again reality congregates around a human figure, though in this case it is the *amada* or beloved who is central and the poet simply observes at first. Essentially what he sees is her coexistence and contiguousness with reality: 'Por tu carne / La atmósfera reúne / Términos. Hay paisaje ... ¡Qué cerrado equilibrio / Dorado, qué alameda!' (p. 104) ('Through your flesh / The atmosphere joins / Its ends. A landscape is visible ... What a closed and golden / Harmony, what a grove of poplars!'). Thus, when in the third part the subject joins with his *amada* to make the single *coniuncto*—'¡Amor: ni tú yo, / Nosotros' (p. 105) ('Love: neither you nor I, / Us')—he enters into union not simply with the *amada* but with her as an extended being, a being-in-the-world, a being with the complement of her circumstance. In short, he experiences through the *amada* a direct sensation of reality in all its plenitude—'Se colma el apogeo / Máximo de la tierra' (p. 105) ('The earth's maximum apogee is fulfilled')—and reality responds in its own dynamic fashion:

> ¡Oh realidad, por fin
> Real, en aparición!   (p. 105)
>
> (Oh reality, finally
> Real, in appearing!

The *amada* is thus explored as an abundant, vital reality in much the same way as the subject had explored the mysterious aquatic world of 'El aparecido', and in this way Guillén's treatment not only by-passes sentimentality but even transcends sexuality. She is a phenomenon to whom the subject is fabulously conjoined in the act of love and with whom he experiences the same surfacing or manifestation of being:

> Henos aquí. Ten próximos,
> ¡Qué oscura es nuestra voz!
> La carne expresa más.
> Somos nuestra expresión.   (p. 106)
>
> (Behold us here. So close.
> How dark is our voice!
> The flesh expresses more.
> We are our expression.)

The union of two is of course a radical example of enlargement of being, 'Amar, amar, amar, / Ser más, ser más aún' (p. 108) ('To love, love, love, / To be more, to be still more'), and its vehemence at the point of climax is articulated with astounding precision:

> Furia aun no, más afán,
> Afán extraordinario,
> Terrible, que sería
> Feroz, atroz o . . . Pasmo.   (p. 109)

> (Beyond fury, more desire,
> Extraordinary, terrible
> Desire, that would be
> Ferocious, atrocious or . . . Shock.)

Here and in the previous stanza the Spanish contains such a high incidence of fricatives (notably the *f*, *th* and *s* sounds) that an illusion of breathless panting is created, all of which is brought to an end with the plosive—one might say ejaculatory—*p* of 'Pasmo'. By the poem's close the poet is content to apostrophize the 'tú' ('you') who has brought together the phenomenal and human constituents of his world, '¡Tú, tú, tú, mi incesante / Primavera profunda . . . (!)' (p. 113) ('You, you, you, my unending / Profound Spring'), and in the host of images applied to her one notes an insistence on form, even concentricity:

> ¡Tú, ventana a lo diáfano:
> Desenlace de aurora,
> Modelación del día:
> Mediodía en su rosa . . . !   (p. 113)

> (You, window on the diaphanous:
> Fulfilment of dawn,
> Outline of day:
> Midday in its rose . . . !)

Love, then, is a hyperextension of *Cántico*'s metaphysic: the *amada* epitomizes the wholesome beauty of reality's forms and through her the subject experiences its plenitude directly. Bearing in mind Ortega's statement that 'la reabsorción de la circunstancia es el destino concreto del hombre'[16] ('the reabsorption of circumstance is the concrete destiny of man'), we can see that the image of sexual union is the clearest emblem of the way man and reality are involved in mutual absorption, reabsorption.

In the foregoing I have tried to show that the whole of *Cántico* converges on the theme of being, fullness of being, but this is not to say Guillén is unaware of life's darker side. An array of negative forces is treated in *Cántico*. However, inasmuch as they represent the anti-life which conspires to prevent fullness of being, they too are related to *Cántico*'s central theme. In the personal context pain and death are two features of the negative. Pain, as we see in 'Aguardando' ('Waiting'), 'Ser' ('To Be') and 'Muchas gracias, adiós' ('Thanks a Lot, Goodbye'), is an intruder which disturbs man's normally harmonious relationship with reality. It has to be suffered, however, and, once its visitation is over, the subject returns with renewed zest to the business of being. The positive value of death is even clearer, as we see in the justly famous sonnet 'Muerte a lo lejos' ('Death in the Distance'). Here, much as in Heidegger's view of man as a *being-unto-death*, Guillén argues that the shadow which death casts over man's existence only reinforces his conviction that what matters is to live, live fully: 'Lo urgente es el maduro / Fruto' (p. 291) ('What is urgent is the mature / Fruit'). Similarly, in 'Su persona' ('Her Person'), the poet admonishes himself for having indulgently mourned the loss of a loved one, that is, for losing himself in a world of fantasy and pitiful isolation, when it is his clear duty to accept what has happened, to accept reality as a whole, the rough with the smooth: 'Quiero toda la adorable / Desigualdad imperfecta / De las cosas que así son' ('I want all the adorable / Imperfect inequality / Of things such as they are'). Here we note a new emphasis: the world is not, after all, all roses and circles, but ugly too. The second facet comes through more strongly in poems of social reference, especially later poems written in America. Typical is 'A vista de hombre' ('Man's Eye View'), a skyscraper perspective on New York, where the poet asks and then answers:

> ¿Quién la hizo
> Terrible, quién tan bella?
> Indivisible la ciudad: es ella.   (p. 224)

> (Who made it
> So terrible, who so beautiful?
> Indivisible, the city is what it is.)

In short, he accepts the city and, by extension, reality, for what it is, a composite of good and bad.

The bad has to be squared up to, 'Cara a cara' ('Face to Face'), as the title of *Cántico*'s last poem puts it. Here, perhaps to silence those who might have thought *Cántico* excessively joyous, Guillén shows full cognizance of the negative forces which beseige man, 'El círculo de agresión / General' (p. 524) ('The circle of general aggression'), which is witnessed, deplored and finally resisted, 'Yo no cedo' ('I refuse to surrender') being the poem's virtual refrain. But what is the method of resistance, and how is evil defeated? Not, we discover, by addressing evil itself, which is by implication impervious to direct assault in Guillén's opinion. Resistance lies in the essential self, in the furthering of one's own being and in the steadfast preservation of this being in the face of the evil that would destroy it. Paradoxically, then, it is to positive reality that man turns his face in order to combat evil, as 'Cara a cara' insists:

> Así sueño frente a un sol ...   (p. 531)
>
> (Hence I dream facing a sun ...)
>
> el día / Realísimo que yo afronto   (p. 532)
>
> (the utterly real day which I confront)
>
> Palpo el concierto que sólido
> Permanece frente a mí ...   (p. 530)
>
> (I touch the harmony that remains
> Solidly facing me ...)
>
> Entre tantos accidentes
> Las esencias reconozco ...   (p. 531)
>
> (Amidst so many mishaps
> I recognize the essences ...)

This is no escapism, no Epicurean retreat, but rather, a question of emphasis, *Cántico*'s chosen emphasis. Evil is recognized, but so is good, more so, triumphantly so. Thus in 'Luz natal' ('Native Light'), the very last poem Guillén wrote for *Cántico* on his brief return to Spain in 1949, the poet surveys the barren environs of his hometown of Valladolid from the mountain height of San Cristóbal, pondering as he does so on the good and the bad in his nation's history. As in Machado, the stark plains seem to image the waste and bellicose imperialism of Castile, and at one point a strutting caricature of a dictator is drawn, the likely reason why *Cántico* was banned in Franco's Spain. In what seems a deliberate opposition to the '98 emphasis, however, Guillén chooses to dwell on the positive aspects of his heritage, especially the heritage of language, and the poem ends with the poet rejoicing in the confluence of two rivers and in the pockets of cornfields, woodland and spring greenery which are also visible from his vantage point. Poems like 'Luz natal' and 'Cara a cara' indicate the extent of *Cántico*'s increasingly outward projection. But the work as a whole, as even these two poems confirm, is essentially metaphysical, with a focus upon the individual rather than society. Its message is that salvation lies in the self, in the individual's indomitable will to overcome adversity, to maximize the gift of being and to follow through his own unique vocation. Inasmuch as this is presented as a goal available to every living person, *Cántico* has a strong ethical tenor in the democratic, Christian tradition. A psalmist song in praise of life and creation, *Cántico* offers its own secular faith which centres on the self but which is not, as it were, self-centred. The protagonist's humility is the key. The things of this world, he realizes in 'Más allá', are far more important than he:

> Dependo
> Del total más allá,
> Dependo de las cosas.
> Sin mí son y ya están
> Proponiendo un volumen ...   (p. 33)

> (I depend
> On the totality out there,
> I depend on things.
> They exist without me and even now
> They put forward their volume ...)

It is reality's input, its 'afluencias amantes' (p. 35) ('loving inflows'), which gives the protagonist his stature. At the same time reality has need of this human subject and it is by converging on him that it attains its own fulfilment: 'Pero el día al fin logra / Rotundidad humana' (p. 34) ('But the day finally attains / Human roundness'). Humility is again the key to *Cántico*'s longest poem, 'Tiempo libre' ('Free Time'), which is a deliberate counter to Valéry's narcissism. Here, as the poet walks leisurely through parkland, attending closely to a host of visible objects, he comes suddenly upon a pond and wonders briefly if he should look into it to see his own reflection. Rejecting that as '¡Contemplación risible de sí mismo ... !' (p. 171) ('Laughable contemplation of oneself'), he turns away from the pond and describes his commitment to reality in his most definitive and at the same time most Ortegan terms:

> ¡Ay! Ya sé que ese esbozo sin final
> Temblando con las ondas me diría:

Quiéreme.—¡No! Así yo no me acepto.
Yo soy, soy . . . ¿ Cómo? Donde estoy: contigo,
Mundo, contigo. Sea tu absoluta
Compañía siempre.
                    ¿Yo soy?
                          Yo estoy
—Aquí, mi bosque cierto, desenlace
De realidad crujiente en las afueras
De este yo que a sí mismo se descubre
Cuando bien os descubre: mi horizonte,
Mis fresnos de corteza gris y blanca . . .
                          Rico estoy
De tanta Creación atesorada.
Profundamente así me soy, me sé
Gracias a ti, que existes.
Me predispone todo sobre el prado
Para absorber la tarde.
¡Adentro en la espesura!
Como una vocación que se decide
Bajo esa estrella al propio ser más íntima,
Mi destino es salir.   (pp. 171–2)

(Oh! I know very well what that indistinct sketch
Trembling on the waves would say to me:
Love me.—No! I can't accept myself like that.
I am, I am . . . How? Where I am: with you,
World, with you. May your absolute
Company always be.
                    I am?
                    I am now
—Here, my certain wood, an unfolding
Of rustling reality in the outskirts
Of this I that discovers itself
When it truly discovers you: my horizon,
My ash-trees of grey and white bark . . .
                    I am rich
With so much treasured Creation.
Thus profoundly am I myself, do I know myself
Thanks to you, your existing.
Everything in the meadow is predisposed
For my absorbing of the afternoon.
Let's go into the thicket!
Like a vocation resolved
Under that star most personal to one's own being,
My destiny is to go out.)

    These magnificent lines synthesize the essential points in Guillén's
metaphysic. In particular: firstly, coexistence, 'contigo, / Mundo,
contigo' ('with you, / World, with you'), a being in or with the world

which is again pointed up by the distinction between 'soy' ('I am')
and 'estoy' ('I am here now'); secondly, reality as an extension of
being, 'las afueras / De este yo' ('the outskirts / Of this I'); thirdly,
self-discovery through perception of reality, 'que a sí mismo se descubre / Cuando bien os descubre' ('which discovers itself / When
it truly discovers you'); fourthly, possession of reality, as indicated
by the possessives, 'mi bosque cierto', 'mi horizonte, / Mis fresnos'
('my certain wood', 'my horizon / My ash trees'), which is further
specified as an absorption, 'Para absorber la tarde' ('To absorb the
afternoon'); fifthly, humility and gratefulness, 'Gracias a ti' ('Thanks
to you'); and finally, a restatement of the commitment to outwardness, which is the *vocation* and *destiny* of being, 'Mi destino es salir'
('My destiny is to go out'). This last point reminds us of the importance of that title 'La salida' ('Going Out'), of Don Quixote's sallies
and of Guillén's motor car. But while the commitment to outwardness
as opposed to narcissism is total, it is balanced by the sense of inward
penetration suggested by the line '¡Adentro en la espesura!' (literally:
'Inwards into the thicket!'), which is itself a quotation from one
of Guillén's most cherished poets, the sixteenth-century mystic, St
John of the Cross, whose poem, 'Cántico espiritual' ('Spiritual Canticle'), contains the line: 'entremos más adentro en la espesura' ('let
us enter more inwards into the thicket'). Once again, then, we come
upon the religious dimension of Guillén's *Cántico* and its implicit
transcendentalism. Indeed, the whole of *Cántico* strangely parallels
St John's most famous metaphor of the soul leaving the body in
order to join in union with God, though, naturally, in Guillén the
body is not discarded and the god he discovers is the modern—one
might say Jungian—god of psychical wholeness, plenitude.

It is not only as a man, but also as a poet, that Guillén projects
himself out into the world, which is why his vocation as a poet is
inseparable from his vocation as a man. The projection has two
clear implications: First, his poems, as missives, have the express
purpose of furthering the collective well-being, in which regard few
modern writers could match Guillén for commitment. Second, as
distilled statements of his understanding of reality *vis-à-vis* the self,
Guillén's poems demand from their maker a continuously sustained
and heightened awareness of reality, in which sense the poems have
developed alertness and attentiveness as a way of life in the poet,
'el atento' ('the attentive one'), as he calls himself in 'Vida extrema'
('Extreme Life'). Thus the dialogue of poetry enhances the positive
world-orientation of both reader and poet and it is in itself an

integrational activity bent on plenitude. Poetry has two further values related to *Cántico*'s metaphysic of being, as 'Vida extrema' shows. First, by way of a magical metamorphosis which transforms reality into language, the poem saves reality from fugitive time:

> No ha de quedar aquella tarde trunca.
> Para el atento erige su palacio.   (p. 398)

> (That afternoon will not be left to waste.
> Its palace is built for the attentive.)

And, endorsing Valéry on this occasion:

> Correctamente,
> El atentado contra el cementerio.
> —Se salvará mi luz en mi futuro.   (p. 404)

> (Absolutely right,
> The prudent one opposes the cemetery.
> —My light will be saved in my future.)

Both reality and the poet, then, the observed and the observer, are saved by the poem's transcendence of time. Here we note that in using the verb *salvar* (to save) Guillén keeps utterly faithful to Ortega, 'Yo soy yo y mi circunstancia, y si no la salvo a ella no me salvo yo' ('I am myself and my circumstance, and if I do not save it I do not save myself'); similarly, he continues to parallel Don Quixote whose task in 'Noche del caballero' was precisely 'Para salvar la noche y su concierto' (p. 433) ('To save the night and its harmony'). The last major value of poetry in relation to being is, quite simply, that poetry adds to the world's store; it increases the human lot by making a new world which comes to life when the reader reads:

> Entonces crearás otro universo
> —Como si tú lo hubieras concebido—
> Gracias a quien estuvo tan inmerso
> Dentro de su quehacer más atrevido.   (p. 404)

> (Then you will create another universe
> —Just as if you had conceived it yourself—
> Thanks to one who was so immersed
> In his most daring occupation.)

Here the parallel between the poet's daring and the heroism of Don Quixote is clear, and when, out of modesty, the poet then asks the rhetorical question,

> ¿El hombre es ya su nombre?

> (Is man now his name?)

it is equally clear that *hombre* (man) is thought insufficient to describe one whose life-enhancing occupation has made him, like Don Quixote, 'un hombre más que hombre' ('a man more than a man'). In short, the vocation of poetry has led Guillén to the rare, sublime and, as Ortega says, heroic achievement of fulfilment of being. It is this coherence of poetry and being, so boldly proclaimed, which gives *Cántico* a stature larger than any work of its time.

V

Pedro Salinas

The Poetics of Motion

Orilla

¿Si no fuera por la rosa
frágil, de espuma, blanquísima,
que él, a lo lejos se inventa,
quién me iba a decir a mí
que se le movía el pecho
de respirar, que está vivo,
que tiene un ímpetu dentro,
que quiere la tierra entera,
azul, quieto, mar de julio?[1]

Shore

(If it weren't for the fragile
rose of purest white surf
which it distantly invents,
how would I have ever known
that it was moving its own chest
by breathing, that it is alive,
that it has an impetus within,
that it desires the whole earth,
this blue, tranquil, July sea?)

Natural, spontaneous, refreshingly light of touch, the simple form
of Pedro Salinas's poetry masks a penetrating metaphysic. Less challenging at first sight than his great friend Jorge Guillén, whose rigour

seems chiselled into *Cántico*'s momumental architecture, Salinas writes slim volumes of mostly brief poems, colloquial in diction, free in technique and so unassuming in motif that, especially in his love poems, we may be reminded of pop songs: 'Yo no puedo darte más. / No soy más que lo que soy' (p. 259) ('I can't give you any more. / I am no more than what I am').

But this air of instant intelligibility is deceptive, and Salinas, as easily underrated as he is misunderstood, is a poet of rare subtlety whose lightness is never lightweight and whose playfulness never merely frivolous.

A scholar in the humanist tradition, a professor and fine critic of Spanish literature, an avid reader of French and English, Salinas was every inch the cosmopolitan sophisticate, and, in the final analysis, his poetry centres on the intellectual concerns of his remarkably lively, inquisitive mind. Why he chose to reject rhyme, conventional stanza patterns and other trappings of poetic form becomes quite clear when we realize that his abiding theme and metaphysical base is motion, a motion which reflects all the elasticity of human thought and feeling. Unlike Guillén, who championed poetic form as a means of confirming a view that form is the essence of reality, Salinas logically regarded form as the antithesis of his ideal of flux. For him form is but a surface manifestation of reality which, moreover, gives the erroneous impression that reality is static. Nothing could be further from Guillén's paralyzed noon symmetry than Salinas's simple images of fleeting motility, for instance the wave in the above poem. In this Salinas is Béquer's natural heir, though in fact he goes further than Béquer since he will have no truck with linguistic patterning in his pursuit of the elusive texture of flux. His knowledge of Bergson, who held that language has an in-built tendency to solidify and therefore misrepresent human sensations, was a signficant factor in shaping his ideas. No less important was Ortega's theory of perspectivism, which gave Salinas conceptual insight into the motion-based nature of reality. Strangely, Bergson and Ortega influenced Salinas in ways quite unlike their respective influence on Machado and Guillén, and, as we shall see, a different set of emphases helped determine Salinas's problematic view of language and reality. From this dual metaphysical source flowed his characteristic interest in spontaneity, randomness, chance, freedom, irrationality and illumination, all of which may be conveniently condensed into the equation: *motion* = *vitality*. The brief poem 'Orilla' ('Shore') is a good example of this equation.

'Orilla' tells us quite simply that we are mistaken if we look at the sea and see only stillness. It is true that on a calm day perhaps only a ribbon of surf will give evidence of the sea's motion, but this is enough to undeceive us and make us think of the vast storehouse of mobile energy which lies beneath the surface. Guillén, typically, would have concentrated on the horizon's firm line or, as in 'En lo azul, la sal'[2] ('In the Blue, Salt'), searched for the sea's substantial essence. But Salinas highlights the purely transitory evidence of 'la rosa / frágil, de espuma' ('the fragile / rose ... of surf') as the kind of elusive sign we must be alert to if we would understand reality's vital motility. In addition to its quality of transience the wave also has direction: it moves towards the shore where the poet stands. This amorous projection of reality towards the onlooker recalls the two-way phenomenological synthesis we found in Guillén, but there are important differences in Salinas. In particular, he argues that it is *only* the ribbon of surf which gives evidence of motility and that otherwise—'Si no fuera por la ... espuma' ('If it weren't for the ... surf')—the reality he witnesses would have misled him into thinking it were motionless. Hence it is not a question of reality imposing its truths—'evidencias', as Guillén would say—upon him in the phenomenological manner; rather, it is a question of reality being largely deceptive, above all in the visual or perspectivist sense, and of man having to decipher truth from a host of misrepresentations. For Salinas truth will always come in such fleeting and random forms as the wave in 'Orilla', which, as an image, accords with his view that proper perception is momentary, intuitive, even fortuitous, which is to say, illuminative: 'Iluminación, todo iluminaciones'[3] ('Illumination, nothing but illuminations') was his succinct description of his own poetic-metaphysical purpose. Such illuminism casts Salinas in the role of the poet-seer, on which basis his work has been related not unfairly by Rupert C. Allen to oriental values.[4] But of more immediate relevance is Salinas's close correspondence on this point with Ortega who argued the quasi-rational virtues of *alétheia* or momentary insight:

> Esa pura iluminación subitánea que caracteriza a la verdad, tiénela ésta sólo en el instante de su descubrimiento. Por esto su nombre griego, *alétheia* ... es decir, descubrimiento, revelación, propiamente desvelación, quitar de un velo o cubridor.[5]

> (That pure, sudden illumination which characterizes truth, which is experienced only at the moment of its discovery. Hence its Greek name, *alétheia* ... that is, discovery, revelation, strictly an uncovering, a removing of a veil or cover.)

Salinas's poetic practice and vocation can be best understood, I believe, in this sense of a striving for luminous perception, a perception which pierces and transcends the limitations imposed by our perspectival relationship with reality. Shortly we shall explore this theme further, but for the moment let us simply note the central point in 'Orilla': that the bulk of reality remains hidden beyond one's visual scope, like the inner depths of the sea, and that we rely on fleeting insights to intuit its mysterious profundity.

Turning briefly to the linguistic system of 'Orilla', we find several telling indications of Salinas's attitude towards, and handling of, language. The poem's most obvious feature is that its nine lines—a typically unrounded or irregular length—comprise just one sentence, a unitary scheme which has some metaphysical bearing on the topic discussed since the sea is treated as a single, living entity. However, the way this one sentence is put together is not as straightforward as it might at first seem. Fundamentally the sentence is governed by the linking syntactical device of '¿Si no fuera por ... quién me iba a decir a mí ...' ('If it weren't for ... how would I have ever known ...'); but this, clearly, is a false interrogative and a rhetorical interlocking formula which, as we have already noted, functions primarily as an emphatic, i.e., 'Es sólo la espuma que me dice que está vivo el mar' ('It's only the surf that tells me that the sea is alive'). From here we can break the sentence down further to what Chomski calls its 'deep structure':

Ella me lo dice

(It tells me it)

This is a simple and dogmatic declaration of the type Guillén frequently makes, yet when we turn back to the poem and see again how Salinas has voiced it we are struck by its complexity. 'Ella' (the first 'It') is rendered by 'la rosa, / frágil, de espuma, blanquísima' ('the fragile / rose of purest white surf'), a compound subject in which the noun unit 'rosa ... de espuma' ('rose ... of surf') is dispersed by adjectival placement. It is this subject, 'Ella' (It), which informs the poet; indeed it informs him of no less than four things about the sea, i.e. 'Ella me lo dice que el mar ...' ('It tells me that the sea ...'):

1. se le movía el pecho / de respirar
   (was moving its own chest / by breathing)

2. está vivo
   (is alive)

3.   tiene un ímpetu dentro
      (has an impetus within)

4.   quiere la tierra entera
      (desires the world earth)

—all of which give vitality and even, in 'pecho' and 'quiere' ('chest', 'desires'), a human dimension to the sea. When the poet finally names his subject in the last line it is not simply 'mar' ('sea'), such as we should expect to find in Guillén's triumphant nominalization, but rather another compound—'azul, quieto, mar de julio' ('blue, tranquil, July sea')—whose specifications imply that the sea is an ever changing reality. Here the foregrounding of adjectives—'azul, quieto' ('blue, tranquil')—diminishes the generic force of the noun and points to temporary qualities, as does the noun unit itself, 'mar de julio' ('July sea'), which echoes the temporality implicit in the poem's first noun unit, 'rosa de espuma' ('rose of surf'). Thus we see that the poem's simple statement, 'Ella me lo dice' ('It tells me it'), is expanded by the hanging interrogative, the adjectival development and the cluster of dependent clauses into something which is not simple at all. What was a declaration is now an interrogative which conveys the poet's quizzical, even sceptical attitude towards reality, and what was a simple theme—the sea is all motion—is given in such a synchronic, fluid and, as it were, desubstantialized way that in the very texture of the language we experience or intuit the kind of complex motility which Salinas prizes. He was to be more demanding in the context of the love theme, where, indeed, he often found that language only insufficiently met his needs.

The two points we have made give a foretaste of Salinas's bristling argumentative buoyancy: in the first place there is reality, which is not what it seems, at least not to the eyes, and which must be sifted if its true, vital nature is to be perceived; secondly, language, which also has to be scrutinized and even radically adapted if it is to meet the challenge of vitality, for, in particular, an elastication of its syntax and of its denominative, solidifying force is imperative. Both points stem from the same metaphysical preoccupation and thus form a remarkably unified, coherent poetics. For the sake of clarity, however, we shall need to approach them separately, beginning with Salinas's view of reality and looking first at early poems which anticipate the full flowering of his metaphysic in his volumes of love poetry.

Most indicative of Salinas's abhorrence of form is the poem 'Escorial I', the first of three poems in *Fábula y signo* (*Fable and Sign*) of 1931 to focus on the monastic palace of the Escorial. Built by Philip II in the sixteenth century, the palace, which stands some thirty miles north-west of Madrid, is the most magnificent reminder we have of Hapsburg splendour and of Spain's zealous imperial days. But while the size and geometry of this 'edificio de granito' ('granite edifice') impress Salinas, he is ultimately chilled by its awesome, inhuman completeness:

> Está hecho.
> No es un afán por el aire.
> ... Se puede medir, exacto,
> mayor que el ansia y el vuelo.
> Vive en el paradisíaco
> más acá de su proyecto.
> ... De estar tan hecho
> ya se le acabó el querer.
> Lo que quiso es ahora piedra
> dimensión, forma. Y da miedo
> de que esté ya más arriba
> del vivir, al otro lado.
> Porque no le falta nada:
> está hecho.   (p. 190)

> (It's finished.
> It's no airy desire.
> ... It can be measured, exactly,
> far better than anguish or fancy.
> It lives in a paradisal
> hitherland of its conception.
> ... In being so finished
> it has lost all aspiration.
> What it once desired is now stone,
> dimension, form. And one fears
> it's already way above
> the living, on the other side.
> Because it lacks nothing:
> it's finished.)

In contrast to the humanized sea of 'Orilla', a natural force constantly unfolding before our eyes, the Escorial epitomizes the static and the sterile, an anti-life force which is anathema to the poet. The perfection of such an object excludes the poet, or, as Salinas argued

in an earlier poem, 'Vocación' ('Vocation'), reduces his role to that
of a mere witness:

> Abrir los ojos. Y ver
> ... perfecto el mundo, completo.
>   Pero yo ...
> Tú, de sobra. A mirar,
> y nada más que a mirar
> la belleza rematada
> que ya no te necesita.   (p. 110)

> (To open one's eyes. And to see
> ... the world, perfect, complete.
>   But me ...
> You, superfluous. Looking,
> merely looking
> at the finished off beauty
> which no longer needs us.)

Salinas might well have written this last poem with Guillén in mind,
as González Muela suggested,[6] for it certainly polarizes the two poets'
very different attitudes. Essentially, as we see, perfection for Salinas
is the equivalent of death, 'belleza rematada' (literally a 'killed off'
beauty). The only way it can be saved or resuscitated is by the
onlooker bestowing vitality on it, which, in the case of the Escorial,
is no mean challenge. However, in the second poem on this topic,
'Jardín de los frailes' ('The Monks' Garden'), Salinas views the great
palace from an adjacent garden and he hits upon the ingenious device
of looking at its reflection in a pond. This instantly mollifies its austere
geometry and returns the palace to the land of the living:

> Enorme
> deber de piedra gris.
> Pero el agua
> —¿por qué te fuiste a mirar?—
> te bautizó de temblor,
> de curvas, de tentación.
> Se te quebraron las rectas,
> los planos se te arqueaban
> para vivir, como el pecho.
> ¡Qué latido
> en ansias verdes, azules,
> en ondas, contra los siglos
> rectilíneos! ...
> El agua te sacó el alma.   (p. 193)

> (Enormous
> work of duty in grey stone.

But the water
—why did you go to look?—
baptized you with its quivering,
with curves and temptation.
Your straight lines were broken,
your planes were made to arch
so you could live, like a heart.
And how you throbbed
in green and blue longings,
in waves, against
the rectilinear centuries! . . .
The water brought out your heart.)

Together the two Escorial poems show what David L. Stixrude describes as the poet's central theme, 'his urge to escape finality',[7] that is, his rebellion against the fixity of things, his objection to 'cada cosa en su sitio, como siempre . . . / esa orden / que al nacer entendí, sin nada nuevo' (p. 92) ('everything in its place, as always . . . / that order / which I understood at birth, with nothing new'). But while the poems are clear evidence that Salinas is 'diciendo siempre que no / a las formas y a los tiempos' (p. 214) ('always saying no / to form and time'), as the volume *Fábula y signo* ends, it may be thought that to see the Escorial reflected in water is no more than a trick which evades the real issue of reality's form. How, then, does Salinas look at reality unaided by his mobilizing liquid agent?

First it must be said that a good many poems draw attention to the insufficiency of sight. When, for instance, Salinas looks at reality through a window he complains—once again in marked contast to Guillén—that its grille compartmentalizes what he sees:

Desde hace ya muchos años
la reja
me tiene partido el mundo
que se ve por la ventana,
en cuatro partes iguales.   (p. 102)

(For many years now
the frame
has split up the world
which I see from my window
into four equal parts.)

This kind of mathematical dissection provokes the poet and he is tempted to break the grille in response to 'el ansia esta / de ver todo el mundo entero' (p. 102) ('this burning desire / to see the whole world fully'). Other poems are chary of the visual faculty and some suggest that the sense of touch is superior. In the early poem which begins,

> Mis ojos ven en el árbol
> el fruto redondo y fresco   (p. 55)
>
> (My eyes see in the tree
> the round and fresh fruit)

the fruit is clasped by a hand which 'tiene / ambiciones más profundas / que las de los ojos' ('has / more profound ambitions / than do the eyes'). The hand in fact has 'eterna ambición de asir / lo inasidero' ('an eternal ambition to grasp / the ungraspable'), which again recalls Bécquer. In 'Don de la materia' (p. 124) ('Gift of Matter') it is by virtue of 'luz del tacto' ('the light of touch') that the poet confirms the presence of a pitcher on a table in a dark room, his hand discovering its 'realidad profunda' ('profound reality'). Similarly, in 'Yo no te había visto / amarillo limón escondido' (p. 80) ('I hadn't seen you, / hidden yellow lemon') the fruit which had escaped the poet's eyes in daylight is discovered by touch at night:

> te tengo en las manos,
> limpio limón escondido,
> limpio limón descubierto.   (p. 80)
>
> (I hold you in my hands,
> clean hidden lemon;
> now a lemon clean and uncovered.)

This insistence on touch recalls Ortega's statement: 'Es cosa clara que la forma decisiva de nuestro trato con las cosas es, efectivamente, el tacto'[8] ('It is clear that the decisive form of our relationship with things is, effectively, touch'). But, interesting as the tactile theme is, it has severe limitations both as a philosophic idea and as a poetic motif, and its primary use in poet and philosopher alike is to illustrate the shortcomings of the visual.

Returning more properly to the visual and continuing with poems on the fruit motif, we find in the poem begining 'Hoy, te han quitado, naranjo, / todas las naranjas de oro' (p. 75) ('Today, orange tree, they've stripped you / of all your golden oranges') that it does not matter to the poet that the tree is bare of fruit for he retains an impression in his mind more lasting than the original purely visual perception. Thus he is able to say of the tree, '¡Mentira, naranjo mío!' ('You lie, orange tree!'), a point which recalls Bergson's theory of memory. Finally on this motif we turn to a most indicative poem,

'El zumo' ('The Juice'), in which the poet is even sceptical that
the orange which his eyes see is in fact an orange:

> Le ven todas las miradas . . .
> '. . . Si parece una naranja.'
> . . . Pero el secreto se defiende
>   . . . dentro.
> Lo que da son disimulos,
> redondez, color, rebrillo,
> solución fácil, naranja,
> a la mirada y al viento.   (p. 112)

> (Everyone's eyes see it . . .
> '. . . It certainly looks like an orange'.
> . . . But its secret is well guarded
>   . . . inside.
> What it shows are dissimulations,
> roundness, colour, sheen,
> that's a facile solution, orange,
> to the eyes and to the wind.)

And here we come to the crux of the matter. First, evidently, the
orange serves in the above poem in much the same way as the sea
served in 'Orilla', for the mysterious juice of the orange remains
invisible to the eyes, latent and profound. But the poet also argues
that the visual perception he has of the orange is a misleading, 'facile
solution', for it makes him believe he sees something which in fact
he does not see. This is entirely consistent with Ortega's theory of
the perspective; moreover, it can hardly be coincidental that while
Salinas wrote so many poems on the motif of fruit, notably the orange,
Ortega's most celebrated exposition of his theory is given in a succinct
statement which uses the same motif:

> 'Nadie ha visto jamás una naranja'[9]

> (No one has ever seen an orange)

This at first puzzling statement makes a very simple point: the individual's perspective is strictly limited. Ortega went on to explain as
follows:

> Es ésta un cuerpo esférico, por tanto, con anverso y reverso. ¿Preten-
> derán tener delante a la vez el anverso y el reverso de la naranja?
> Con los ojos vemos una parte de la naranja, pero el fruto entero no
> se da nunca en forma sensible: la mayor porción del cuerpo de la naranja
> se halla latente a nuestras miradas.   (ibid.)

> (This is a spherical body which therefore has an obverse and a reverse
> side. Could anyone hope to have the obverse and the reverse side of

the orange in front of him at the same time? With our eyes we see a part of the orange, but the whole fruit is never offered to us in sensible form: the greater part of the body of the orange remains latent to our vision.)

Deceit, as Claudio Guillén has shown,[10] is traditionally associated with perspectivism, and it is this same deceit which lies at the heart of Salinas's sceptical approach to reality, the poet having once written: 'El mundo es infinito, / profusión de mentira' (p. 119) ('The world is infinite, / a profusion of lies'). The deceit in question has a lot to do with form: we see an outline of the orange, a silhouette, and we take this for the whole when all we have in its 'roundness', as Salinas said in 'El zumo', is a 'facile solution', 'dissimulations'. From here it is a short step to appreciate the importance of motion, that is, of motion as an answer to the deceit of form, for the fundamental point is that if we are to see the whole orange we need to adopt a variety of viewing positions by moving from one place to another, or else the orange will have to move as we view it. In passing we might note that much the same idea underlies the kind of artistic theory prevalent in Salinas's formative years, as instanced in Marcel Duchamp's seminal painting *Nude Descending a Staircase* or the many paintings of Picasso, for instance, which simultaneously depict a figure in full-face and in profile.

But the idea also contains the most basic of metaphysical issues, the polarization of form and motion. The eclectic Ortega, who championed form in a phenomenological context, was not unaware of a different visual emphasis: 'El Espectador lleva una segunda intención: él especula, mira—pero lo que quiere ver es la vida según fluye ante él'[11] ('The Spectator has a second purpose: he speculates, he looks—but what he wants to see is life as it flows before him'). Here the verb 'fluye' (flows) has a long philosophic history which takes us back to Heraclitus's river of flux into which man cannot step twice; and we remember that the Platonic-Aristotelian rationalization of form evolved at least in part as an answer to the scepticism which had derived from motion-based thinking. In more modern times, briefly, the opposite seems to have happened, with Cartesian logic suffering a series of assaults from those who preferred to place more emphasis on the life force, movement and change, namely the evolutionists, vitalists and so-called irrationalists, amongst whom Bergson was to have most influence on the creative arts. This age-old polarity is precisely what Ortega outlines in *El tema de nuestro tiempo* (*The Theme of Our Time*) of 1923, summarizing: 'El racionalismo se

queda con la verdad y abandona la vida. El relativismo prefiere
la movilidad de la existencia a la quieta e inmutable verdad'[12] ('Rationalism keeps to truth and abandons life. Relativism prefers the
mobility of existence to truth's tranquil stillness'). Ortega, though
German-trained, was susceptible to vitalist arguments and found
much to admire in Bergson. There was no escaping the evident fact
that 'la vida [es] esencialmente esto, acción y movimiento' (ibid.,
p. 192) ('life [is] essentially this, action and movement'), and the
key vitalist factor, spontaneity, had been praised from his earliest
essays: '¡Lo espontáneo! ... Es decir, si no entiendo mal, la última
intimidad del carácter'[13] ('Spontaneity! ... That is, if I'm not mistaken, the most intimate level of the personality'). It remains to
be shown that spontaneity, relativism and perspectivist thinking are
key factors in Salinas's vitalist conception of reality.

The conclusion drawn from the orange illustration was that either
the object or the onlooker must be mobilized. Many poems, in the
manner of 'Jardín de los frailes', play metaphysical games with the
first alternative of mobilizing a static object. Three examples will
suffice: in 'Underwood Girls' (p. 203) the keys of a typewriter are
'Quietas, dormidas' ('motionless, asleep') until awoken by rapid
fingers which turn the keys into 'treinta, eternas ninfas' ('thirty,
eternal nymphs') whose music fills the world's emptiness; in 'Madrid.
Calle de ...' (p. 132) ('Madrid. So and So Street') a mirror in the
street—'inmóvil / en el asfalto' ('static / on the asphalt')—is dramatically mobilized when it picks up the reflection of clouds and birds
in the sky above; a last example, which again shows how well modern
inventions adapt to this theme, is found in 'Cinematógrafo' (p. 133)
('Cinema') where the harsh rectangle of the screen is given 'dulzura
... ondulación' ('sweetness ... undulation') when moving images
are projected on it. While these poems are typical of Salinas's kinetic
tendency, it is the second alternative, that of the onlooker becoming
mobile, which leads us more specifically into the theory of perspectivism. A clear example is found in one of the poet's favourite motifs,
the driver or passenger in a car, a motif which shows just how much
Salinas entered into the playful spirit of the Roaring Twenties. Salinas had a passion for cars, especially fast cars; what stuck in his
mind about his meeting with Paul Valéry was their dazzling cab
ride through Paris,[14] while his own dubious skills behind the wheel
had not escaped Rafael Alberti who saw Salinas as one who diced
with death, pedestrians and the police every morning in his Fiat
A5.[15] Four poems on the car motif lead us progressively into the

topic. First the thrill of riding out alone in a car is captured in 'Navacerrada, abril' (p. 116) ('Navacerrada, April'), where Salinas delights
in having climbed to the Guadarrama pass high above Madrid. Man
and machine make a perfect team, 'Los dos solos ... Alma mía
en la tuya / mecánica' ('Just the two of us ... My soul in your /
mechanic soul'), and the poet is energized by the mountain air, crisp
snow and sheer adventure of it all, 'aventura de arranque / eléctrico'
('an adventue of electric thrust'). The element of risk is part of the
thrill and in 'Aviso' (p. 150) ('Warning') his relish for speed is shaken
by a sudden glimpse of death on the road, the RAC rescue vehicle
forcing him to brake hard and meditate on his narrow escape. Simple
as they are, these first two poems allude to deeper thematic attitudes
in Salinas, for the gusto of the first reflects his vital impulse, his
desire to possess reality,

> ... la mañana.
> Se rinde, se me rinde.
> Ya su silencio es mío:
> posesión de un minuto.   (p. 116)

> (... the morning.
> It surrenders itself, surrenders to me.
> Now its silence is mine:
> a momentary possession.)

—while the hazard which shocks him in the second is a reminder
of the fragility and the limitations of human life.

The two points find keener definition in 'Route Nationale' (p. 130).
Here the poet is disorientated by nightfall, 'Un negror ... me con-
funde la vida' ('a darkness ... confuses my life'); he laments the
loss of reality's riches, 'variedad / amada' ('beloved variety'), a reality he once possessed, '¡Colores, colores míos ...!' ('Colours, my
colours ...!'), and he panics at the thought of being left alone: 'no
me dejas solo / en lo negro' ('don't leave me alone / in the dark').
He is saved, however, by the car's lights:

> Con una vuelta a la llave,
> en visiones de cien metros,
> fragmentado, alegre, vivo,
> los faros
> me devolvieron el mundo.   (p. 130)

> (At the turn of a key,
> in hundred metre visions,
> fragmented, happy, alive,
> the headlamps
> gave me back my world.)

Despite the facile resolution, two important points have been made: first, that reality was temporarily lost or invisible, and second, when recovered it is seen only in partial or fragmented form. Though gratefully accepted in the circumstance, his 'hundred metre visions' are a clear sign of man's visual limitations. All of which prepares us for a most revealing poem. 'Pasajero apresurado' ('Passenger in a Rush') deals with the exhilarating topic of speeding through a city in a car, but there is a deep metaphysical point to the poem's opening question, a question which the remainder of the poem attempts to answer:

Ciudad, ¿te he visto o no?
La noche era una prisa
por salir de la noche.
Tú al paso me ofreciste
gracias vagas, en vano.
Aquella catedral
que disparaba piedras
a la niebla ... No sé
qué agua turbia, raptora
de luces a los puentes.
Inaccesibles entre
su guardia de cristales
perla, flor o pintura,
corazón de las tiendas.
Y hubo una pantorrilla
tersa en la media fina,
cuando el asfalto ofrece
sucio azogue a las nubes.   (p. 111)

(City, have I seen you or not?
The night was in a rush
to leave the night behind.
You, passing by, offered me
blurred attractions, in vain.
That cathedral
which shot stones
at the mist ... Some
murky water or other, thieving
lights from bridges.
Inaccessible behind
their glass screens,
pearls, flowers or paintings,
the very heart of shops.
And there was a smooth calf
in an elegant stocking,

as the asphalt offers
grimy quicksilver to the clouds.)

Though linguistically disjointed to match the poet's chaotic ride
through the city, the idea in the poem is clear enough: in answer
to the initial question as to whether or not the city has been seen,
Salinas catalogues a good many things which he has glimpsed of
the city, all these being fragments, snapshots or perspectives of its
total reality. He cannot give an absolutely affirmative answer to the
question because the city's reality is multiple and inexhaustible.
What he can do is give an impression of the city's exquisite vitality:
not only a stockinged leg but the cathedral too is animated, shooting
stones at the mist, while the river mischieviously steals the bridges'
lights. In short, the city is all movement, and, if much of it remains
latent to his peception—like the inaccessible items in a shop-win-
dow—at least the way in which Salinas attempts to perceive reality
is in perfect accord with its own nature, which is to say, mobile.
The moving car is thus a device which accentuates the inherent vital
motility of the reality perceived, much as it did for Guillén, but
it also mobilizes the perceiver in such a way as to enable him to
enter into the spirit of the reality he would perceive. This treatment
of reality and this manner of perception inevitably recall Bergson
whom Salinas no doubt read when at the Sorbonne, 1914–17, for
Bergson, besides insisting upon reality's motility—'Le mouvement
est la réalité même'—also spoke of an intuitive as opposed to anlayti-
cal way of perceiving reality's flux, this being achieved through a
sympathetic coincidence with the vital nature of reality: 'Il suit de là
qu'un absolu ne saurait être donné que dans une *intuition*, tandis
que tout le reste relève de *l'analyse*. Nous appelons ici intuition la
sympathie par laquelle on se transporte à l'intérieur d'un objet pour
coïncider avec ce qu'il a d'unique et par conséquent d'inexprimable'.[16]
It is, then, as a driver whose motility *coincides* with the city's vital
flux that Salinas intuits the true nature of the city. However, influential as Bergson's thought must have been on Salinas, the more exact
theoretical base underlying such a poem as 'Pasajero apresurado'
is found, not surprisingly, in Ortega.

To appreciate this we need to recall Ortega's second famous exposition of perspectivism which was given through the old adage, 'los
árboles no dejan ver el bosque'[17] ('you can't see the wood for the
trees'). Ortega explains:

Tengo yo ahora en torno mío hasta dos docenas de robles graves y de fresnos gentiles. ¿Es esto el bosque? Ciertamente que no: estos son los árboles que veo de un bosque. El bosque verdadero se compone de los árboles que no veo. El bosque es una realidad invisible. (ibid.)

(Presently I have around me some two dozen solemn oaks and graceful ash trees. Is this the forest? Certainly not: these are just the trees which I can see in the forest. The true forest consists of trees which I cannot see. The forest is an invisible entity.)

Naturally the same applies to the city, as Ortega immediately indicated, 'Selva y ciudad son dos cosas esencialmente profundas' (ibid.) ('Forest and city are two essentially profound realities'), and hence the point of Salinas's question: 'Ciudad, ¿te he visto o no?' ('City, have I seen you or not?'). To take it further we need to look at a short story Salinas wrote in the mid-1920s, 'Entrada en Sevilla'[18] ('Entry into Seville'), which, as an exploded version of 'Pasajero apresurado', is highly indicative of Salinas's Ortegan perspectivism.

In the story, Claudio, the protagonist, steps out one morning for the first time in Seville, having arrived in the dark the night before. But the car that awaits him is parked in such a narrow street that he is obliged to step straight into it without touching the 'blanda tierra andaluza' ('soft Andalusian ground'), and his *possession* of the city is playfully postponed. Then begins his heroic journey and Claudio experiences a thrilling bustle of movement over which he has no control, but which is beautifully caught in Salinas' chaotic prose:

La calle, inmóvil, pero poseída con la marcha del coche de una actividad vertiginosa y teatral, empezó a desplegar formas, líneas, espacios multi-colores y cambiantes, rotos, reanudados a cada instante, sin coherencia alguna, y con idéntica rapidez y destreza con que muestra un prestimano los colorinescos objetos que le van a servir en su juego, más que para el público los vea, con el malicioso propósito de que su rauda sucesión cree una imagen confusa y apta para cualquier engaño en la mirada del espectador. (ibid., p. 21)

(The street, immobile, but so taken with the car's movement as to have a giddy theatrical animation, began to unfold forms, lines, spaces, multicoloured and changing, breaking up and yet rejoining all the time, without any coherence and with the kind of speed and sleight of hand that a conjurer uses to show the bright objects of his trick, that is, less for the audience to see them than with the mischievous intention of creating in their rapid succession a confused image designed to deceive the spectator's eyes.)

Besides the typical theme of deceit, we note that Claudio, at this stage, is still thinking along conventional, rationalistic lines, and

he expects a formally organized image of the city to be offered him
at any moment:

> Sí, probablemente en cuanto todo aquello se aquietara, de esta confusión
> de colores iba a salir limpia y total, Sevilla, ofrecida como en la palma
> de una mano . . .   (ibid.)

> (Yes, no doubt as soon as things quietened down, there would emerge
> from this confusion of colours a sharp and complete Seville, as though
> shown in the palm of a hand . . .)

But no such neat image is forthcoming. Instead Claudio's eyes continue to be inundated with fragments, his rapid snapshots of the
city. Finally, overwhelmed by the rush of objects, he comes to the
decisive realization:

> Se le desvanecía a Claudio la Sevilla convencional de los panoramas,
> definición lejana en el paisaje con dos líneas—caserío, Giralda—que
> se cortan con una belleza estrictamente geométrica. La ciudad no se
> definía, lejos, depurada y distinta, sino que vivía cerca, complicadísima,
> esquiva siempre a la línea recta, complacida como un cuerpo de bailar-
> ina en gentiles quiebros y sinuosidades. Sus intenciones mudaban
> rumbo constantemente . . .   (ibid., p. 220.)

> (Claudio let go of the conventional, panoramic Seville, that remote
> definition in a two-lined landscape—houses, the Giralda—which is cut
> with a strictly geometric beauty. The city did not allow a distant, puri-
> fied, neat definition, for it lived intimately, complicatedly, ever fleeing
> from straight lines, happy as a ballerina's body in its spins and curves.
> It always took a different turn . . .)

Claudio realizes that there is no easy answer, that Seville cannot
be condensed into a simplistic visual image such as the Giralda—the
city's equivalent of Big Ben or the Eiffel Tower—which is akin to
the 'facile solution' of the orange's roundness. The city 'lives' and
'dances' and therefore evades all rational definition. By the same
token, Claudio, in his search for the city, finds it impossible to select
'una empresa racional' ('a rational undertaking') in the sense of
choosing somewhere definite to go. Rather,

> Había que andar por Sevilla, abandonado, como flotante, en aguas
> invisibles de estos cauces secos, marchar sin adonde, querer ir, pero
> sin ninguna llegada, arrastrado por estas corrientes sin caudal, en un
> automóvil, góndola sin rumbo, a la deriva.   (ibid., p. 23)

> (You had to abandon yourself to Seville, as though floating on invisible
> water in its dry river beds, going without direction, wanting to go,
> but never arriving, dragged along by its volumeless currents, in a car,
> a routeless gondola, adrift.)

The streets have been liquidized in accord with Salinas's favourite metaphor of constant change, and Claudio surrenders to the same spirit of volubility in a way that recalls Bergson's theme of sympathetic coincidence. But we have still to hear the final explanation of how the city is seen, apprehended. When the question is put again, a full answer is given:

> ¿Dónde estaría Sevilla? Sin duda por estas venas azules, que no tenían nombre de venas, sino de calles andaluzas—Aroma, Lirio, Escarpín—, se había de llegar a su corazón recóndito y difícil. Cada visión nueva era la aventura final, el último encantamiento, y, sin embargo, a cada visión se sustituía inmediatamente la de al lado ... Y era preciso que la imaginación juntase tal trozo de blanqueada pared, aquel zaguán, una cancela, con la perspectiva no suya—ésta ya se había evadido—, sino de la casa vecina, y poniendo sobre todo esos balcones y terrazas ajenos y un cielo visible, pero convencional, reconstruyese idealmente lo que por angostura de la calle y rapidez de la marcha no cabía, verdadero, en la visión. (ibid., p. 23)

> (Where could Seville be? No doubt in these blue veins, which did not bear the names of veins but of Andalusian streets—Aroma, Lirio, Escarpín—, one was sure to find its elusive, hidden heart. Each new view was the final adventure, the ultimate delight, and yet, each new view was immediately replaced by the one next to it ... And it was imperative that the imagination should join some fragment or other of whitewashed wall, that vestibule, an iron gate, with a different perspective—the first having already disappeared—of the house next door, and that, piling on top of it all those distant balconies and terraces and the visible though conventional sky, it should ideally reconstruct what the street's narrowness and the car's speed had not, in fact, allowed one's vision to contain.)

The mischievous complexity of Salinas's prose may drive us to distraction, but it is also an exact linguistic metaphor of his fundamental idea: just as we hold the fragments of a long sentence in our mind as we hear it out and come to understand it, so is the city seen or apprehended by mentally reconstructing the multiple, partial or individual perspectives of it into one whole. This idea of multiplicity is again consistent with Ortega's thinking:

> la perspectiva se perfecciona por la multiplicación de sus términos y la exactitud con que reaccionamos ante cada uno de sus rangos'.[19]

> (the perspective is perfected by the multiplication of its terms and by the exactitude with which we react to each one of its ranks.)

Thus the poem 'Pasajero apresurado', like 'Entrada en Sevilla' and indeed like a Picasso painting, tries to perfect a total perspective by multiplying individual perspectives of the same. Naturally the poet reacts as exactly as he can to its 'rangos' or hierarchical ranks, which in the case of the poem span from a cathedral to a stockinged leg. Returning to the same passage in the *Meditaciones* as quoted above, we note that Ortega says:

> ¿Cuándo nos abriremos a la convicción de que el ser definitivo del mundo no es materia ni es alma, no es cosa alguna determinada, sino una perspectiva?   (ibid.)

> (When will we allow ourselves to accept that the definitive being of the world is neither matter nor soul, nor anything determinate, but a perspective?)

In Ortega's view, then, reality, 'the definitive being of the world', is found neither in external objects nor in man but in what effectively is an interrelationship between the two, the perspective. The great virtue of this removal of emphasis from the thing-in-itself and from the being-in-himself, the great virtue of placing emphasis upon the fleeting and intermediary perspective, is, clearly, that it foregrounds the dynamic and changing nature of the relationship man-world. As Bergson argued, and as Ortega developed in his essay 'Verdad y perspectiva' ('Truth and Perspective') of 1916, it is only by keeping to an awareness of this motility, 'la vida espontánea' ('spontaneous life'), that truth can be arrived at:

> El Espectador ... especula, mira—pero lo que quiere ver es la vida según fluye ante él ... La verdad, lo real, el universo, la vida—como queráis llamarlo—, se quiebra en facetas innumerables, en vertientes sin cuento, cada una de las cuales da hacia un individuo. Si éste ha sabido ser fiel a su punto de vista, si ha resistido a la eterna seducción de cambiar su retina por otra imaginaria, lo que ve será un aspecto real del mundo ... La realidad, pues, se ofrece en perspectivas individuales.[20]

> (The Spectator ... speculates, looks—but what he wants to see is life as it flows before him ... Truth, the real, the universe, life—call it what you will—breaks up into innumerable facets, countless outpourings, each of which projects itself towards an individual. If the latter can keep faithful to his point of view, if he resists the eternal temptation to exchange his retina for another imaginary one then what he will see will be a real aspect of the world ... Reality, then, comes to us in individual perspectives.)

To conclude this theoretical and preliminary discussion, let us note that there are two ways of coming to terms with reality's flux: the ideal and the relative or real. The first, as stated, is by integrating

multiple points of view in accord with Ortega's theme that 'El punto
de vista crea el panorama'[21] ('The point of view creates the panorama'), an accumulative procedure which is relevant to the poet's
practice as Salinas indicated in the introductory poem to his first
volume:

> Forjé un eslabón un día,
> otro día forjé otro
> y otro.
> De pronto se me juntaron
> —era la cadena—todos.   (p. 51)

> (I forged a link one day,
> the next day I forged another
> and another.
> Suddenly there came together
> —it was the chain—all of them.)

Secondly, however, it is apparent from Ortega's remarks above that
the single perspective for all its limitations is a 'real aspect of the
world' and therefore true, and the onlooker's obligation is to keep
faith with it. Thus, finally, to Salinas's question in 'Pasajero apresurado' as to whether or not he has seen the city there seem to be
two kinds of answers: firstly, no, he probably has not, at least not
in its entirety, for the city is a latent, inexhaustible and ever-changing
reality, the total perception of which remains an ideal which can
only be approached rather than arrived at definitively; and secondly,
yes, he has, for his multiple perspectives of the city, finite and relative
as they are, are real perspectives of the city's real nature. Presumably
the gap between the real and the ideal can only be bridged by what
Bergson calls intuition, Ortega *alétheia* and Salinas illumination,
though we also note that locked into this dialectical tension is something highly characteristic of Salinas's sensibility, his fluctuation
between joy and frustration. This and the relevance of the foregoing
analysis will become increasingly apparent as we consider Salinas's
great poetry, his love poetry, where he deals with precisely the same
problems of perception and apprehension in the context not of a
city but of his love, the *amada*. The connection between the two
was made at the end of 'Entrada en Sevilla' where Claudio,

> [E]staba viendo Sevilla y aún tenía que seguir imaginándola, y la ciudad
> le era, tan dentro de ella, algo incierto e inaprehensible como una mujer
> amada . . .   (op. cit., p. 23)

(was seeing Seville and yet had to keep on imagining it, and so deep inside the city was he that to him it was something uncertain and inapprehensible like a beloved woman ...)

An even more profound reality whose apprehension is not restricted to the visual faculty, the *amada* is crucially endowed with the same essential ingredients of spontaneity and an endless capacity to change, as is clear from the first line of *La voz a ti debida* (*The Voice I Owe to You*):

Tú vives siempre en tus actos.   (p. 219)

(You are ever living in your acts.)

As we shall see, the *amada* is a reality which the poet discovers truthfully with each new vital perspective or poem on her, but whose mystery, often to his frustration, he can never exhaust.

☆   ☆   ☆   ☆   ☆   ☆

La voz a ti debida (*The Voice I Owe to You*) of 1933 is Salinas's masterpiece and one of the great volumes of love poetry in Spanish literature. It belongs to and borrows from a strong tradition of love poets which includes, in reverse chronological order, Bécquer, Espronceda (on whom Salinas wrote such a telling essay),[22] the mystics, notably St John of the Cross, and the courtly poets, Garcilaso de la Vega (the subject of another fine essay and the poet who provides Salinas's title) and Jorge Manrique. In his book on Manrique, Salinas, much in the spirit of T. S. Eliot, tirelessly argues the importance of tradition, 'la tradición es la habitación natural de un poeta'; '(E)l hombre inmerso en la tradición no sabe más; es más'[23] ('tradition is the natural habitat of a poet'; 'the man immersed in tradition does not know more, he is more'), and certainly one of the fascinations of *La voz* is the way it purposefully adapts tradition to its modern thesis. The latter, as we would expect, is subtle, intricate and, as many critics have pointed out, highly intellectual; but this does not mean the poetry is not felt. Here we come upon a totally fatuous stumbling block, for, not to mince words, a great disservice was done to Salinas by Leo Spitzer's early essay which, though brilliantly establishing the poet's link with *conceptismo* (the Renaissance tradition of arguing through conceits, called 'metaphysical poetry' in English), made the unforgiveable error of stating that the *amada* in *La voz* is not a woman at all but a figment of the poet's imagination.[24] Spitzer's essay was immensely influential, and subsequent critics like C. B. Morris have followed his suit by describing Salinas's poetry with such unhelpful phrases as 'mental surgery'.[25] Forewarned of Spitzer's thesis, Salinas was never able to bring himself to read his colleague's essay,[26] while it was left to close friends of the poet, Guillén and Stephen Gilman included, to defend him against the charge of cerebralism.[27] Though my essay concentrates on the metaphysical aspects of *La voz* this is because the volume's interpretative difficulties lie there and not because I share Spitzer's view. Far from it, as needs immediate clarification.

There are two reasons, it seems to me, why *La voz a ti debida* has been devalued as cerebral poetry. The first, ironically, is because its contemporaneity of thought and its particular debt to Ortega have not been appreciated, the result being that Salinas's borrowings from literary tradition have not been weighed against their proper counterbalance and have struck some as a pointless affectation, an academic indulgence. In addition it goes without saying that in missing the real ground of *La voz's* intellectual content critics have also missed its immediacy and vitality. The second reason is a more delicate biographical matter. To begin with, it is little wonder that those close to Salinas were the ones dumbfounded by Spitzer's view that there is no woman in *La voz*. Knowing Salinas and the outgoing life-style of one whose marriage would later break up was presumably enough to instil disbelief. Even Spitzer prefaces his theme with the words, 'no cometeré la indiscreción ... de querer penetrar el misterio biográfico de ese Tú feminino tan aéreo y tan emocionadamente cantado' (op. cit., p. 33) ('I will not commit the indiscretion ... of trying to penetrate the biographical mystery of that feminine You so airily and emotionally sung'), which virtually undermines the non-existence theme at the outset and suggests that the whole business of 'interior conceits' and narcissistic cerebralism came about by way of the critic's deference to the poet's private life. But neither do we need to pry, other than into the text, to appreciate that it was a real woman and a genuine love experience which inspired Salinas, no less than his car poems came from his passion for motoring. There is ample evidence of the *amada's* separate bodily presence—her 'tierno cuerpo rosado' (p. 219) ('soft pink body')—from *La voz's* first poem onwards. We are even given her age, submerged though it is in a Cupid image, 'tú ... arma de veinte años' (p. 230) ('you ... a twenty year old weapon'), which is corroborated more clearly later on:

> el tictac diminuto
> que hace veinte años
> sonó por vez primera
> en una carne virgen
> del tacto de la luz.   (p. 267–8)

> (the tiny tick-tock
> which first rang out
> twenty years ago
> from flesh virgin
> to the light's touch.)

And this of course is the problem: the *amada*, at twenty, is a good deal younger than the poet—'tú, tan joven, para mí' (p. 234) ('you, so young, for me')—as he constantly reminds us and himself in his descriptions of her: 'vestida de muchacha' (p. 231) ('dressed like a girl'), 'sonriendo / de niñez' (p. 272) ('smiling like a child'), 'iluminada / de joven paciencia honda' (p. 234) ('lit up with the deep patience of youth') and 'gacela ... infantil' (p. 302) ('childlike gazelle'). Not to make too fine a point of it, the *amada* is not the poet's wife (who was in fact five years older than Salinas), as the volume's fourth poem discreetly elucidates:

> ¡Si me llamaras, sí,
> si me llamaras!

> Lo dejaría todo,
> todo lo tiraría:
> los precios, los catálogos ...
> los telegramas viejos
> y un amor.
> Tú, que no eres mi amor,
> ¡si me llamaras!   (p. 224)

> (Were you to call me, yes,
> were you to call me!

> I'd leave everything,
> I'd throw it all away:
> prices, catalogues ...
> old telegrams
> and a love.
> You, who are not my love,
> were you to call me!)

La voz, then, is the diary of an affair, an affair with a beginning, middle and end, and which, to judge from other submerged indices, was short-lived. Brevity is a poignant theme in 'No en palacios de mármol, / no en meses .../ hemos vivido juntos' (p. 322) ('Not

in marble palaces, nor in months ... have we lived together') and
is confirmed by an early poem's dating of their first meeting in 'este
agosto que empieza' (p. 231) ('this beginning of August') while a
later poem on the affair's aftermath still speaks of 'esta noche de
agosto' (p. 326) ('this August night') and concludes 'todo eran
encuentros / fugaces' ('it was all brief encounters').

But is this narrative information, much of which is uncovered only
by sleuth reading, really significant? I believe so, and not merely
to refute Spitzer. Only when we appreciate that *La voz* deals with
an affair does it fall into place as a volume. This holds true as much
for its 'literariness' as for its metaphysical inquiry. With regard to
the former, the affair situation virtually explains and justifies Salinas's use of tradition, notably the prominent courtly tradition. The
point of connection is found in the essential ingredient of courtly
poetry, its illicitness, for as Salinas wrote 'El amor que canta el
trovador es, en su raíz, adulterino'[28] ('The love of which the troubadour sings is, at root, adulterous'). That courtly poets sang of *damas*
(ladies) who were unattainable in more ways than one applies directly to the situation in *La voz*, though with the stunning modification
that here it is the poet who is married! While Salinas's accommodation of this reversal is something we shall consider in a moment,
let us first note the key literary ingredient which arises from the
affair's illicitness: decorum. Feudal loyalty to the *dama* created an
ethic of decorum which strictly prescribed what the courtly poet
could and could not say in his poem, as Garcilaso bitterly complained
in his second sonnet:

> que aun aliviar con quejas mi cuidado
> como remedio m'es ya defendido.[29]

> (for even to ease my cares by moaning
> is a remedy now forbidden me.)

This prohibition largely explains why the *you* in *La voz* is, in Spitzer's
words, 'so airy', and why we have to play the detective to find out
what kind of person—let alone who—she is. Caught in the dilemma
of being 'o muy aventurado o muy medroso' ('either very bold or
very timid'), as Garcilaso put it (op. cit. p. 48), Salinas plays the
courtly game of identity for real, as it were, finally destroying the
amada and silencing her 'voz' (voice) because 'ya iba a traicionarnos'
(p. 307) ('It was about to betray us'). In these terms, though we
neither have nor expect a full descrition of her, the identikit we
can piece together is surprisingly sharp.[30]

As to what bearing the affair situation has on the volume's meta-physic, its basic principle can be stated in one word: freedom. When describing the courtly liaison as adulterous, Salinas added:

> Amor y matrimonio son incompatibles . . . El amor entre los cónyugues es cosa imposible. La razón es muy sencilla. El amor es la recompensa, libremente otorgada, por la dama, al que desde abajo la suplica. Y sólo se puede conceder ese galardón en estado de perfecta libertad.[31]

> (Love and marriage are incompatible . . . Love between husband and wife is impossible. The reason for this is very simple. Love is the reward, freely bestowed, by the lady, to the man who beseeches it from below. And that great prize can only be granted in a state of perfect liberty.)

Marriage, in this light, implies duty, bondage, while the extra-marital situation is based on choice, freedom, the thematic touchstone of *La voz*. Freedom is valued and sought by the poet in the *amada*,

> Te quiero pura, libre,
> irreductible: tú.   (p. 243)

> (I want you pure, free,
> irreducible: you.)

—and freedom is the root of the *amada*'s personality as she reveals herself in her spontaneity—'Tú vives siempre en tus actos' (p. 219) ('You are ever living in your acts')—and in her incorrigible change-ableness, depicted appropriately by Salinas in Petrarchan conceits:

> Fatalmente, te mudas
> sin dejar de ser tú,
> en tu propia mudanza,
> con la fidelidad
> constante del cambiar.   (p. 227)

> (Fatally, you change
> without stopping being you,
> even as you change,
> having the constant
> fidelity of changing.)

Since the well known paradox that the only constant is change stems from Heraclitus's theme that all is flux, the above lines give notice of how totally the *amada* embodies Salinas's metaphysical ideal. They also suggest an additional reason why the Renaissance poetic mode was of special appeal to Salinas: the verbal paradoxes which are part and parcel of the courtly and indeed mystic poets' articulatory system offered a very apt linguistic register to a poet who wished to explore the inbuilt contradictions which attach to such concepts

as change, motion, spontaneity, chance, etc. But here we are introducing a third topic and clarity demands further comment on Salinas's courtly pose and its crucial metaphysical implications before
we consider his view of language.

The integration of 'literariness', metaphysics and subjectivity (the
affair) is apparent throughout *La voz a ti debida* and here we note
some of the more important points of convergence. Starting with
the *sine qua non* of courtly poetry, the *amada*'s unattainability, we
know that the troubadour was obliged by circumstances to worship
his *dama* from afar; he elevates her to the level of goddess, assumes
the most servile role before her and suffers endless torment as he
awaits her merest token of affection. Well might we wonder how
such an artificial formula could apply to the modern situation in
La voz where the male breaks all courtly rules by erotically possessing
his *amada*. But, taking it by stages, the initial parallels are easy to
see. Salinas adopts the goddess-worshiper hyperbole as a metaphorical means of stressing the *amada*'s fabulous beauty and her shattering
impact upon his life. This is highly operational in the early poems,
for instance in the volume's opening stanza and in the poem beginning '¡Qué gran víspera el mundo!' (p. 240) ('How expectant is the
world!') which cast the *amada* in the role of Creator. The hyperbole
is of course so extravagant that it can lead to the delicious irony
of the mock-courtly (a tradition in itself),[32] as in the poem:

> Ha sido, ocurrió, es verdad.
> Fue en un día, fue una fecha
> que le marca tiempo al tiempo.
> Fue en un lugar que yo veo.
> Sus pies pisaban el suelo
> este que todos pisamos . . .
> Tan de verdad,
> que parecía mentira.   (p. 225)

> (It's happened, it took place, it's true.
> It was on a day, it had a date
> such as time marks down in time.
> It was in a place my eyes can see.
> Her feet trod upon this same ground
> that we all tread upon . . .
> So true,
> it seemed a lie.)

Far from being an indictment of the *amada* (Morris)[33] or proof of
her unreality (Spitzer),[34] this lovely passage expresses the poet's sheer
amazement that his beloved is real like any other woman, for he

had thought her divine, beyond the laws of gravity and other earthly ties. With regard to our present theme, however, the fact that the poet can indulge in the mock-courtly is itself an indication of how thoroughly entrenched the courtly proper is in *La voz*, and one only has to see the mileage Salinas gets from such images as the *amada*'s blinding eyes (e.g. pp. 269, 219) or the host of courtly clichés in both halves of the poem 'Miedo. De ti. Quererte' (p. 227) ('Fear. Of you. Loving you') to appreciate the point.[35] Besides this hyperbolic texture of adulation (such a standard feature, incidentally, of pop-songs: 'Venus in Blue Jeans', 'Teen Angel'), the courtly also works for Salinas without need of modification in the last third of the volume which is a post-mortem on the affair. From '¡Qué paseo de noche / con tu ausencia a mi lado!' (p. 289) ('What a night-time walk / with your absence at my side!') such standard courtly motifs as *dolor, pena, lágrimas, duda, memoria* (grief, suffering, tears, doubt, memory) are consistently developed. But that is safe ground, and both more interesting and revealing is the daring accommodation of the courtly which Salinas makes elsewhere.

Erotic possession of the *amada* does not, surprisingly, preclude the courtly ethic. Here we note firstly that the poet's possession of her is brief and that even at the high point of love he is acutely conscious of its temporality, '—hoy, nada más que hoy—' (p. 247) ('—today, just for today—') he poignantly reminds himself. He therefore suffers from the terrible awareness that total possession of her is impossible:

> Y siento
> que tu vivir conmigo
> es signo puro, seña
> en besos, en presencias
> de lo imposible, de
> tu querer vivir
> conmigo, mía, siempre.   (pp. 309–19)

> (And I sense
> that your living with me
> is a pure sign, an emblem
> in kisses, in presences
> of the impossible, of
> your wanting to live
> with me, as mine, always.)

The narrative level of the affair thus endows the situation with the same sense of impossibility which courtly lovers experienced.

But this soon overlaps into the thematic domain, for what is ultimately impossible and unattainable, above and beyond the permanence of love, is the *amada*'s true reality or deeper self which the poet
continually seeks in vain. The *amada*, we might think, can scarcely
be held responsible for this, and therefore it would seem that the
vital courtly ingredient of her indifference and cruelty towards her
suitor must be lacking. Not at all. The poet's possession of his *amada*
is thwarted by, of all things, his very physical possession of her!
What is more, she plays an active role in thus frustrating him:

> Entre tu verdad más honda
> y yo
> me pones siempre tus besos.
> La presiento, cerca ya,
> la deseo, no la alcanzo;
> cuando estoy más cerca de ella
> me cierras el paso tú,
> te me ofreces en los labios.
> Y ya no voy más allá.
> Truinfas. Olvido, besando,
> tu secreto encastillado.   (p. 303)

> (Between your deepest truth
> and me
> you always place your kisses.
> I glimpse it, drawing near,
> I want it, but I can't reach it;
> when I am closest to it
> you shut off my path,
> offering yourself to me in your lips.
> And then I can go no further.
> You triumph. And I, kissing you,
> lose track of your encastled secret.)

With scintillating irony the sequence implies that the *amada* takes
as much care to protect herself and frustrate her suitor as did the
medieval *dama*. And we note how deliberately evocative of that
period's famous 'batalla de amor' ('battle of love') is Salinas's diction
in 'Triunfas' and 'encastillado' ('You triumph ... encastled'), a point
continued in *La voz*'s next poem where 'frente' ('forehead') becomes
a 'fortaleza' ('fortress') and 'La defensa absoluta / del ser último'
(p. 304) ('The absolute defence / of the ultimate being'). But with
regard to the poem above we see that, paradoxically, it is by giving
herself so fully in the physical sense that the *amada* protects her
inner truth. Thus her 'cruelty' is the result of her inability to understand what the poet needs or feels. Here, evidently, we are coming

very close to the metaphysics of deception and the orange's roundness. Both points are apparent in the following sequence:

> Tú no puedes quererme:
> estás alta, ¡qué arriba!
> Y para consolarme
> me envías sombras, copias,
> retratos, simulacros,
> todos tan parecidos
> como si fueses tú.
> Entre figuraciones
> vivo, de ti, sin ti.   (p. 297)
>
> (You can't love me:
> you are too high, so remote!
> And to console me
> you send me shadows, copies,
> portraits, simulacra,
> all of such a likeness
> as if they were you.
> Amid semblances
> of you, do I live, without you.)

At the courtly level: he adores a literally elevated goddess while
she sends him discreet tokens of her affection not knowing that the
latter only increase his 'situación agónica' ('agonized situation') as
Salinas described the troubadour's predicament.[36] At another level,
at once intimate, psychological and metaphysical: he searches for
her deeper self, her latent or profound reality, while she frustrates
him by offering only sham imitations of this, as the orange offered
dissimulations. The *amada*'s obduracy and implacable indifference
to the poet's suffering reaches a peak in 'No, no puedo creer / que
seas para mí (p. 300) ('No, I can't believe / that you are meant
for me'), the most courtly poem of all in *La voz*,[37] but her inability
to understand his needs is a psychological theme prominent throughout the volume. At the narrative level of the affair, this communica-
tion problem stems directly from the age discrepancy between the
lovers: he is typically wise and mature, sometimes excusing himself
for his tutorly attitude towards her, 'Perdóname por ir así buscándote
... / Es que quiero sacar / de ti tu mejor tú' (p. 285) ('Pardon
me for seeking you like this ... / It's just that I want to bring out /
of you your best you'), while she is young and vivacious, which
also means to say (at least at times), superficial:

> Ahí detrás de la risa,
> ya no se te conoce.

Vas y vienes, resbalas
por un mundo de valses
helados, cuesta abajo;
y al pasar, los caprichos,
los prontos te arrebatan
besos sin vocación,
a ti, la momentánea
cautiva de lo fácil.
'¡Qué alegre!' dicen todos.   (p. 236)

(There behind your smile,
you are unrecognizable.
You come and go, gliding
through a world of frozen
waltzes, downhill;
and, passing by, caprices
and impulses snatch
meaningless kisses
from you, you, the momentary
prisoner of the facile.
'How happy she looks!' they all say.)

No doubt many a courtly poet fared similarly at a palace ball, darting behind a pillar or tapestry to hide his vexed frustration! On another level, as J. M. Aguirre has convincingly shown,[38] this kind of poem relates closely to Bergson's theory of two levels of being, *le moi fondamental* and *le moi superficiel*,[39] with the *amada* clearly having surrendered to the seductions of the latter in this instance. What is most striking, however, is that Salinas uses motility to illustrate both the negative and positive aspects of the *amada*'s being: as a dancer flitting through a crowded ballroom she epitomizes the fickle and the superficial; alternatively, as we have seen, motility is elsewhere the essence of her personality in the sense that 'Tú vives siempre en tus actos' (p. 219) ('You are ever living in your acts') depicts a spontaneous, ever-changing, vital being whose acts are an immediate reflection of her inner self. It is this latter positive connotation that we now need to explore in order to assess finally *La voz*'s metaphysic, but, in leaving the courtly behind, it is worth making one final point. The fact that Salinas uses motility to illustrate two different and indeed contradictory values is itself consistent with courtly practice. Salinas noted that the image of the castle, for instance, served Manrique as an illustration of his lady's inaccessibility, her rejection of his suit, and, conversely, as a metaphor of her steadfast, though pure, loyalty to his love. He described such *rhetorical resources* as 'recursos reversibles, que lo mismo se pueden llevar al revés que al derecho. Cosa después de todo naturalísima, ya que su papel es instrumental y serviciario, y lo que importa es que cumplan su menester de decir lo que siente el poeta'[40] ('reversible resources, which can be made to work one way or the other. All of which is only natural, since their function is instrumental and serviceable, and what is important is that they fulfil their duty of saying what the poet feels'). This, as we shall soon see, is highly relevant to the poet's view of language, but for the moment let us conclude more generally that Salinas adopted the courtly love formula for the same stylistic reasons hosts of poets did in the past: its hyperboles allow him poise in both irony and enthusiasm, its coded compactness gives his expression brilliant ease, *sprezzatura*, and its fantastic logic enables him to probe the most intricate and contradictory feelings.

Turning now to the theme of the *amada*'s positive motility, we find that the idea announced in the volume's opening line is echoed throughout *La voz*. Essentially she is a vital force, a blast of energy which overwhelms the poet, as he anticipated early on:

> Porque cuando ella venga
> desatada, implacable,
> para llegar a mí,
> murallas, nombres, tiempos,
> se quebrarían todos,
> deshechos, traspasados
> irresistiblemente
> por el gran vendaval
> de su amor, ya presencia.   (p. 222)

> Because when she comes
> unleashed, implacable,
> to seek me out,
> ramparts, nouns, times
> will all break up,
> destroyed, shot through
> irresistibly
> by the great hurricane
> of her love, made present.)

And when she does come the *amada* is—in pointed contrast to her role as Creator—a wild, random, anarchic force: she dwells in 'el desorden celeste' (p. 266) ('heavenly disorder'); the 'combustión de su ser' ('combustion of her being') startles the laws of physics and fills the world with ruins (pp. 244–5), and her impact on the poet's life is equally to wreak havoc. Supported by motifs of drunkenness and madness (e.g. p. 244), chaos is fundamentally a metaphor of love's irrationality—specifically, no doubt, of orgasm—and it represents an atavistic force which returns the lovers to primordial innocence. All this is found in the poem 'Amor, amor, catástrofe' (p. 248) ('Love, love, catastrophe') where the poet thrills to the retrogressive process of 'borrarse la historia' ('erasing history'), which includes the abolition of weights, measures and other impositions of civilization, and where, in a metaphorically blitzed landscape, he exclaims ecstatically '¡Que caiga todo!' ('Let it all crash down!'), as he and the *amada* go:

> a fuerza de besar
> inventando las ruinas
> del mundo, de la mano
> tú y yo
> por entre el gran fracaso
> de la flor y del orden.
> Y ya siento entre tactos,
> entre abrazos, tu piel
> que me entrega el retorno
> al palpitar primero,
> sin luz, antes del mundo,
> total, sin forma, caos.   (p. 249)

> (by dint of kissing,
> inventing the ruins
> of the world, hand in hand
> you and I
> through the great destruction
> of flower and of order.
> And already I sense in touching,
> in embracing, that your skin
> offers me a return
> to the first heartbeat,
> without light, prior to the world,
> total, formless, chaos.)

Amorality—a theme taken up more fully in the next poem, '¡Qué día sin pecado!' (p. 250) ('What a sinless day!')—and havoc are both reverberative of the affair's illictness, no doubt. But the main thrust of the above sequence is the depiction of love as an amorphous outpouring of energy, with the *amada* being the agent of its entropic force. Entropy, the tendency to increasing randomness, is perhaps the most apt term to describe Salinas's antipathy towards form and his championing of anarchic spontaneity. The poem which best expresses this is another from the middle section of *La voz* dealing with the lovers' ecstatic union, 'Extraviadamente' (p. 254) ('Aimlessly'). In essence the poem is an expanded conceit based on the paradox between its first word, 'Aimlessly', and its last word, 'acertar' (meaning, to hit the mark or succeed in reaching), for Salinas's point is that only by surrendering to the random, directionless force of love will lovers reach their specific goal. Just as Claudio realized that he had to *abandon* himself to Seville to experience the city truly so do the lovers throw away their maps and compasses:

> ¿Este camino, el otro,
> aquél? Los mapas, falsos,
> transtornando los rumbos,
> juegan a nuestra pérdida . . .
> . . . para querer
> hay que embarcarse en todos
> los proyectos que pasan . . .
> . . . llenos de fe
> en la equivocación . . .
> Con el júbilo único
> de ir viviendo una vida
> inocente entre errores . . .   (pp. 254–5)

> (This way, that way,
> the other? Maps are false
> and put us off the track,
> tricking us into getting lost . . .
> . . . to love
> you have to embark upon all
> possible projects . . .
> . . . full of faith
> in your blunders . . .
> With the single joy
> of living through your life
> innocently error-ridden . . .)

Entering into the spirit of the *amada* as Claudio entered into the spirit of Seville, the poet realizes and didactically affirms that love and life are not rational enterprises but fluid, haphazard activities which are constantly changing. 'Life is in the living', as they say, or, as Salinas stresses with his progressive present tense, in the 'ir viviendo' ('the process of living'). This clearly relates to Bergson's theme that life is not a series of definable states but 'une continuité fluide', 'une évolution', that 'les états de conscience sont des progrès et non pas des choses'.[41] In *L'Évolution créatrice* of 1907, in particular, Bergson argues that life is a *becoming*, 'un devenir' (in the sense that life occurs at the point of doing an action not as its completion), and this is precisely how Salinas described Claudio's abandon in Seville—'marchar sin adonde, querer ir, pero sin ninguna llegada' ('going aimlessly, wanting to go, but never arriving')—and how he situates the lovers in 'Extraviadamente':

> De alegría purísima
> de no atinar, de hallarnos
> en umbrales, en bordes
> trémulos de victoria,
> sin ganas de ganar.   (p. 255)

> (Having the pure joy
> of not concluding, of being
> on thresholds, on tremulous
> edges of victory,
> without wanting to win.)

The metaphor of chaos, then, with all its implications of chance, freedom and irrationality, refers essentially to the randomness of the doing, to the action in progress, and insofar as this is where Salinas and Bergson meet, it is not surprising to find that one critic of the latter believes his philosophy is best revealed in the light of the principle of entropy.[42] But if the link between Bergson and Salinas is clear, what of Ortega?

Does perspectivism apply in *La voz a ti debida*? We can see immediately that it does, at least in the broad terms of Salinas's method. The volume is an attempt to perceive a profound reality—the *amada*/ love—which is both mobile and latent, 'mi invisible' (p. 239) ('my invisible one') as Salinas calls her. The method employed is that of taking multiple perspectives of her, in which sense it is of further importance that the perspectives (or poems) are quite different and even, frequently, contradictory. Here we return to the randomness of 'Extraviadamente', 'hay que embarcarse en todos / los proyectos que pasan' ('you have to embark upon all / possible projects'), which parallels Claudio's method of perceiving Seville and, in turn, Ortega's theme that 'la perspectiva se perfecciona por la multiplicación de sus términos' ('the perspective is perfected by the multiplication of its terms'). But at this point we remember that our analysis of perspectivism ran into a certain dialectical tension, for there were two possibilities open to the onlooker, the idealist and the relativist possibilities, and a consideration of *La voz* in this light provides a key to understanding its dialectical tension between the body and the spirit. The first idealist possibility, we remember, was the mental reconstruction of multiple perspectives into one whole. This amounts to an interiorization of the desired object and is precisely what Salinas attempts to do initially in *La voz*:

> Tengo que vivirlo dentro,
> me lo tengo que soñar.   (p. 225)
>
> (I have to live it inwardly,
> I have to imagine it.)

Forgetting the narrative intrusion (for it is of course the impossible situation of the affair which obliges sublimation), we find that this attempt to transcend the body and arrive at a mental or spiritual reconstruction of the *amada* is one of Salinas's most consistent ambitions in *La voz*:

> tu solo cuerpo posible:
> tu dulce cuerpo pensado.   (p. 308)
>
> (Your only possible body:
> your sweet body in my mind.)

Besides the last two poems mentioned, those which begin on pages 258, 276, 278, 304 and 309 all belong to the transcendental or idealist category. But while this gathers momentum in the latter part of the volume as Salinas attempts to fashion his ideal 'sombra' (shadow) of the *amada* in his own imagination, the end result of the transcendental trajectory is frustration, a frustration akin to Espronceda's, and Salinas is obliged in the final poem to seek a return to the bodily presence of the *amada*:

> el retorno
> a esta corporeidad mortal y rosa
> donde el amor inventa su infinito.   (p. 329)
>
> (the return
> to this mortal and pink corporality
> where love invents its infinity.)

Here the adjective 'mortal' indicates the limitations and relativism of the real, but the last line adds that it is precisely from such limitation in the bodily and the concrete that the idealistic absolute—infinity—comes. Hence *La voz* ends by reconciling the spirit-body dichotomy in accord with perspectivism's truce between idealism and relativism: Salinas 'resists the temptation of the imaginary', as Ortega advocated, knowing that 'La realidad . . . se ofrece en perspectivas individuales' ('Reality . . . comes to us in individual perspectives'), but this adhesion to the real does not mean the poet must give up his idealism for he also knows that 'El punto de vista crea el panorama'[43] ('The point of view creates the panorama'). By holding to this Salinas avoids Espronceda's despair.

Language is a crucial and constant theme in Salinas. His sceptical, often antagonistic attitude towards language is interwoven with all his major themes and is directly related to what we have described as his metaphysic. The problem which language poses may be briefly put: if reality is in essence motion and flux, how is it possible to reflect this in language which, when the poem is written, is as finished and definitive as the Escorial monastery? Again, if life is spontaneous, random and irrational, how is it to be expressed by language which is governed by rules and logic? In one early poem Salinas rejoices at the way his baby daughter describes everything with the words 'Tatá, dadá', for this illogicality captures his ideal:

> 'Todo lo confunde' dijo
> su madre. Y era verdad.
> Porque cuando yo la oía
> decir 'Tatá, dadá',
> veía la bola del mundo
> rodar, rodar ...   (p. 56)

> ('She mixes everything up', said
> her mother. And that was right.
> For when I heard her
> say 'Ta-ta, da-da',
> I saw the whole globe of the world
> spinning, spinning ...)

Such a bias towards irrationalism links Salinas with the avant-garde movements of Dada and Surrealism which not only cultivated the incongruous but also abused language in terms of its laws of grammar and syntax. At the same time Salinas's preoccupation with the deficiency of language recalls Bécquer's theme of the 'mezquino idioma' ('miserly language') and his hope for a miraculous transmutation of language 'con palabras que fuesen a un tiempo / suspiros y risas, colores y notas' ('with words that were at once / sighs and laughter, colours and notes'). Salinas similarly desires a 'Lengua de paraíso' (p. 353) ('paradisal language'), the kind of sublime use of words he experiences with the *amada*:

Palabras sueltas, palabras,
deleite en incoherencias,
no eran ya signo de cosas,
eran voces puras, voces
de su servir olvidadas.   (p. 398)

(Words freed, words,
in a joy of incoherencies,
that were no longer signs of things,
but pure sounds of words, words
released from their servitude.)

Salinas's view of the 'servitude' of language is eminently Bergsonian. In stating his theme that 'la pensée demeure incommensurable avec le langage',[44] Bergson argued that the unique and changing experiences of an individual cannot be adequately rendered by language for the latter is not only static but impersonal, belonging to the public realm:

> En d'autres termes, nos perceptions, sensations, émotions et idées se présentent sous un double aspect: l'un net, précis, mais impersonnel; l'autre confus, infiniment mobile, et inexprimable, parce que le langage ne saurait le saisir sans en fixer la mobilité, ni l'adapter a sa forme banale sans le faire tomber dans le domaine commun ... Nous tendons instinctivement à solidifier nos impressions, pour les exprimer par le langage.   (ibid., pp. 85–6)

And:

> Pour lutter à armes égales, celles-ci (i.e. les impressions délicates et fugitives de notre conscience) devraient s'exprimer par des mots précis; mais ces mots, à peine formés, se retourneraient contre la sensation qui leur donne naissance, et inventés pour témoigner que la sensation est instable, ils lui imposeraient leur propre stabilité.   (ibid., p. 87)

The twofold obstacle of language's fixity and of its impersonal as opposed to unique reference is the subject of many of Salinas's poems. A clear example is found in *La voz* in the poem beginning:

¿Por qué tienes nombre tú,
día, miércoles?
¿Por qué tienes nombre tú,
tiempo, otoño?
... ¿por qué tienes nombre: amor?

... Si tú no tuvieras nombre,
todo sería primero,
inicial, todo inventado
por mí,
intacto hasta el beso mío.   (p. 233)

(Why do you have a name,
day, Wednesday?
Why do you have a name,
season, autumn?
... Why do you have a name: love?

... If you had no name,
everything would be fresh,
initial, all invented
by me,
even my kiss would be intact.)

Evidently the inadequacy and banality of language is most acutely
felt in the context of love's uniqueness where it intrudes destructively
upon the lovers' intimacy: 'Nombre: ¡qué puñal clavado / en medio
de un pecho cándido ...!' (p. 233) ('Name: what a dagger thrust
/ into the midst of a candid heart ...!'). The same point is more
subtly made in a later poem in *La voz*, 'Tú no las puedes ver' (p. 314)
('You can't see them'), where the poet refrains from using the word
'lágrimas' ('tears') to describe what he sees on his *amada*'s face on
the basis that to name them would be to destroy their mystery.
When the poem concludes with delightful irony,

(Si las llamara lágrimas
nadie me entendería.)   (p. 315)

(Were I to call them tears
no one would understand me.)

we can surmise that the poet objects to the word because it condenses
with erroneous simplicity a phenomenon he considers to be infinitely
complex and hence unfixed, and again because in using a word everyone knows he invites a standardized interpretation remote from his
unique experience of the *amada*'s tears. This refusal to name—that
is, to imprison and solidify—reaches its apogee in the title Salinas
gave to his volume of 1946, *El contemplado* (*The Contemplated*), for
while the topic of the volume's fifteen poems is in fact the 'Mar
de Puerto Rico' (p. 607) ('Sea of Puerto Rico') Salinas avoids such
rigid denomination and indeed chooses a title which subjectivizes
his topic in the individualistic spirit of perspectivism. But if this
is the theory underlying Salinas's antagonism towards language, how
does it in practice effect his writing of poems and the language he
uses?

Though not outlandish in the manner of the Surrealists, Salinas's
rebelliousness *vis-à-vis* his medium is much more sustained than Bécquer's. In Salinas, theory becomes practice and the poet employs

a number of what might be called counter-language techniques which
ultimately define his unique style. In the first place, bearing in mind
that his main grievance is the solidifying force of nouns/names
(*nombre* meaning both 'noun' and 'name' in Spanish), *La voz a ti
debida* is remarkable for its high incidence of pronouns which, as
it were, replace nouns: *pronomen* is a word that stands instead of
a noun. This is treated thematically in the lovely poem,

> Para vivir no quiero
> islas, palacios, torres.
> ¡Qué alegría más alta:
> vivir en los pronombres!
> ... Te quiero pura, libre,
> irreductible: tú.
> ... Y cuando me preguntes
> quién es el que te llama,
> el que to quiere suya,
> enterraré los nombres ...
> Y vuelto ya al anónimo
> eterno del desnudo,
> de la piedra, del mundo,
> te diré:
> 'Yo te quiero, soy yo'.   (p. 243)

> (To live I don't need
> islands, palaces, towers.
> What sublime joy:
> to live in pronouns!
> ... I want you pure, free,
> irreducible: you.
> ... And when you ask
> who it is who calls you,
> who wants you for his own,
> I'll bury all names (/nouns) ...
> and restored to the eternal
> anonymity of nakedness,
> of stone, of world,
> I will say to you:
> 'I am the one who loves you, it is I'.)

The pronoun, then, is prized as a word which denotes essence without
imposing restrictions in the manner of nouns, the essence of love
and of the *amada* being, as we know, freedom. But much as *La voz*
reflects this linguistic ideal in its lexicon, it is not of course devoid
of nouns. Remarkably, however, even in his use of nouns Salinas
often manages to undermine their denominative force. A typical
device is that described by Leo Spitzer as the 'chaotic enumeration',[45]

a haphazard listing of nouns. In '¡Qué gran víspera el mundo!' ('How expectant is the world!'), for example, we find:

> No, el pasado era nuestro:
> no tenía ni nombre.
> Podíamos llamarlo
> a nuestro gusto: estrella,
> colibrí, teorema,
> en vez de así, 'pasado';
> quitarle su veneno. (p. 240)

> (No, the past was ours:
> it didn't even have a name.
> We could call it
> what we liked: star,
> humming-bird, theorem,
> instead of just 'past';
> extracting its poison.)

In keeping with their free spirit the lovers choose whichever words they like to express an idea the rest of us convey by the word *past*, the unconnectedness of the list 'star, humming-bird, theorem' indicating the randomness of their choice. A few lines later we find another haphazard list, 'minas, / continentes, motores' ('mines, / continents, motors'), in another poem 'la luz, la vida, el mar' (p. 252) ('light, life, sea'), and in the one we looked at a moment ago, 'islas, palacios, torres' ('islands, palaces, towers'). This system of random recitation denies the nouns a proper connotative context and virtually destroys them as denominatives, as Spitzer noted by describing them as words which 'cease to be words' (ibid.).

Another distinctive feature in Salinas's counter-language is one we have already met in the poem 'Orilla' and the short story 'Entrada en Sevilla', the long meandering sentence of labyrinthine syntax. To thread one's way through such a sentence, deflected constantly by tangential thoughts and surprising images, requires the reader's sympathetic surrender to a new process. One further illustration will suffice:

> Te vi, me has visto, y ahora,
> desnuda ya del equívoco,
> de la historia, del pasado,
> tú, amazona en la centella,
> palpitante de recién
> llegada sin esperarte,
> eres tan antigua mía,
> te conozco tan de tiempo,

que en tu amor cierro los ojos,
y camino sin errar,
a ciegas, sin pedir nada
a esa luz lenta y segura
con que se conocen letras
y formas y se echan cuentas
y se cree que se ve
quien eres tú, mi invisible.   (pp. 238–9)

(I saw you, you've seen me, and now,
having been stripped of error,
of history, of the past,
you, an Amazon in a lightning flash,
with a heart throbbing
at its unannounced new arrival,
are so anciently mine,
I have known you for such a time,
that in your love I close my eyes,
and I make my way unerringly,
blindly, without needing anything
from that slow and certain light
by which one recognizes letters
and forms and adds up sums
and believes one can see
who you are, my invisible one.)

Close analysis is not required to affirm that this is a most complex sentence. Moreover, despite anaphora and other forms of repetition, the sentence gives an impression of patternlessness, or, at most, of random patterning. Similarly, while the sentence is contained within a conceit—'Te vi . . . mi invisible' ('I saw you . . . my invisible one')— we lose track of this on account of the two units being separated by such a wealth of apparently spontaneous thoughts. Salinas uses the conceit as an extensive apparatus and exploits its basic illogicality as a means of subverting the narrative progression of his sentence. Reading the sentence, with all its flashing insights, we realize that the poet is concerned more with the multiplicity of experience as it unfolds, or *becomes*, and that his syntax has been radically adapted to convey the fluctuating intricacies of his thoughts.

Salinas's whole purpose is to destabilize language, in its lexicon, its syntax and in its rhetorical resources. Supreme amongst destabilizing devices is the paradox or conceit, which no doubt explains its plentifulness in Salinas. It destabilizes by virtue of being based on an illogicality, as for instance in the poems in *La voz* beginning 'La materia no pesa' (p. 291) ('Matter doesn't weigh') and '¡Qué paseo de noche / con tu ausencia a mi lado!' (p. 289) ('What a night-time walk / with your absence at my side!'). In the conceit two contradictory ideas—matter/weightlessness, presence/absence—are held in a state of continuous opposition and their interaction has a decidedly unsettling effect upon the words' connotations and the reader's method of linguistic apprehension. Here we might also remember the destablizing effect of Salinas's deliberate contradictoriness in his use of *reversible* motifs, as in the case of motility expressing both essence and superficiality. The same contradictoriness can be found in contrasting entire poems, as for instance '¡Qué entera cae la piedra! (p. 281) ('How fully the stone falls!') with 'La materia no pesa' (p. 291) ('Matter doesn't weigh'), or 'Horizontal, sí, te quiero' (p. 271) ('Horizontal, yes, that's how I love you') with 'Despierta. El día te llama' (p. 261) ('Wake up. The day calls you') which praises a 'virgen vertical' ('vertical virgin'), or, finally, the poem which begins 'No, no te quieren, no. / Tú sí que estás queriendo' (p. 275) ('No, they don't love you. / You are the one who loves') with 'La forma de querer tú / es dejarme que te quiera' (p. 282) ('Your way of loving / is letting me love you') and also with 'Tú no puedes quererme' (p. 297) ('You can't love me'). These 'contradictory' poems are part of the paradoxical system of *La voz* and are further expansions on the conceits which, as we noted, can govern whole stanzas—'Te vi ... mi invisible' ('I saw you ... my invisible one')—or even entire poems, 'Extraviadamente ... acertar' ('Aimlessly ... to hit the mark'). But the ultimate level of contradictoriness is the volume itself and an indication that Salinas intended paradox on such a large scale is found in two of his titles, *Serguro azar* (*Certain Chance*) and *Razón de amor* (*Love's Rationale*), which are contradictions in themselves. Salinas's counter-language is most evident in the second of these volumes to which we now turn by way of conclusion.

Razón de amor of 1936 is nearly as impressive as *La voz a ti debida* though it lacks the latter's narrative urgency. What distinguishes it is its highly argumentative tone which ostensibly attempts to advocate the case for love. Thus *razón* (which can also mean 'right' or 'reason') is best understood in the old rhetorical sense of an argument conducted through the logic of language, the volume's poems being *razones* or individual rationales. Here we see the contradiction, for, as we know from *La voz*, love is not at all rational and simply cannot be rationalized. The delicious irony is exaggerated by Salinas's perverse use of all the linguistic formulae proper to the domain of logical argument: noteworthy is the high frequency of the question-answer pattern (eleven poems begin with questions), the repeated use of *porque* (because), *por eso* (that is why), of the conditional *si* (if), of refinements, *pero, aunque* (but, although), of equations, *igual que, lo mismo que* (just as, the same as) and of the concluding *así* (hence, therefore).[46] These and other devices combine to create an unmistakable impression of logical discourse, of reason working through the mechanism of language. But Salinas's purpose is subversive. Closer inspection shows that the poems' arguments hinge upon dubious premises which in fact are only logical in a poetic sense; they hinge, namely, upon such poetic contrivances as metaphor, conceit and personification. These render the logic specious, mock the pretensions of language to rationality, and, in so doing, deviously point up the essential irrationality of love.

This subversive, destablizing technique can be readily shown. The volume's first poem begins:

> Ya está la ventana abierta.
> Tenía que ser así
> el día.
> Azul el cielo, sí, azul ...   (p. 335)

> The window is now open.
> The day
> had to be just like this.
> The sky blue, yes, blue ...)

Soon we are told why the sky had to be blue and the day so clear:

> porque anoche tú quisiste
> que tú y yo embarcáramos
> en un alba que llegaba.
> Tenía que ser así.   (p. 335)

> (because last night you wanted
> the two of us to embark
> upon a dawn that was drawing near.
> It had to be just like this.)

The logic of this first *porque* (because) is purely verbal since it is based upon the linking motif of *alba* (dawn) which is strictly metaphorical in the context of love and the lover's fulfilment. In fact Salinas is making an irrational claim that the sky is blue and the world bright because it responds to the activity of the lovers and because love has the power to transform and beautify the world. The 'reason', psychological rather than meteorological, is later repeated with the utmost explicitness, 'el mundo es hoy como es hoy / porque lo querías tú, / porque anoche lo quisimos' (p. 335) ('the world is today as it is today / because you wanted it so, / because we wanted it last night'), and the logic of this argument is resolved near the poem's end:

> Un día
> es el gran rastro de luz . . .
> Es lo que quieren dos seres
> si se quieren hacia un alba.
> Porque un día nunca sale
> de almanaques ni horizontes:
> es la hechura sonrosada,
> la forma viva del ansia
> de dos almas en amor,
> que entre abrazos, a lo largo
> de la noche, beso a beso,
> se buscan su claridad.   (p. 336)

> (A day
> is the great trace of light . . .
> It is what two beings want
> when they love each other towards dawn.
> Because a day never comes
> out of almanacs or horizons:
> it is a flesh-coloured creation,
> the living form of the desire
> of two souls in love,
> who amidst embraces, through the length
> of the night, kiss by kiss,
> seek out in each other their clarity.)

Though feeding implicitly on the notion of love's procreativity, this final *explanation* rests on the word 'claridad' ('clarity') which in the one sense refers to light as a physical phenomenon and in the other is a metaphor of the lovers' enlightenment. Hence, the day is bright because:

(i)   the day is what two lovers want (it to be)
(ii)   what two lovers want is (their own) clarity.

The whole poem is really an exploded metaphor of 'alba-claridad' ('dawn-clarity') presented with the categorical assertion of a philosophic treatise. In this masquerade of logic the poetic truth remains intact—indeed is charmingly persuasive in its theme of (day)light coming from (lovers') dark—but its edifice of reason has collapsed into irrationality.

The explanatory force of *porque* is most severely tested in poems built around conceits, for here it has to explain a contradiction. In the volume's second poem Salinas argues that when two lovers say goodbye it is not to separate but to be together:

> Si se estrechan las manos, si se abraza,
> nunca es para apartarse,
> es porque el alma ciegamente siente
> que la forma posible de estar juntos
> es una despedida larga, clara.
> Y que lo más seguro es el adiós.   (pp. 337–8)

> (If hands are shaken, embraces made,
> it is never to part from one another,
> it is because the soul blindly senses
> that the only possible form of being together
> is in a long, clear farewell.
> And that the most certain thing is the goodbye.)

This surprising conclusion has been prepared with consummate clarity. First the poet argued that since we are all fated to be alone one day, presumably in death, then 'Vivir, desde el principio, es separarse' ('Living from the beginning, is a growing apart'). And if we are always growing apart it cannot be said that the separation comes right at the end, in the goodbye, 'es de antes, de después' ('it comes earlier, later'). The act of separation is but the material sign of what was always there implicitly. Furthermore, since the state of being separate is the only *permanent* state of either living or love, the act of separation is a sign of the lovers' wish to enjoy a state of permanence, to make their love 'seguro' ('certain'). In this way logic turns love's worst disaster into its triumph and the final revelatory *porque* obliterates the fact that the poet has fallaciously confused two separate concepts, namely, the end of an affair and death. In another poem Salinas argues that one should not rely on memory if one wishes to recall the experience of being in love, arriving at the conceit:

> Si quieres recordarlo
> no sirve el recordar.   (p. 351)

> (If you want to remember it,
> remembering is no use.)

The reason behind this is more straightforward:

> Ha sido tan hermoso
> que no sufre memoria,
> como sufren las fechas
> los nombres o las líneas.
> Nada en ese milagro

podría ser recuerdo:
porque el recuerdo
es la pena de sí mismo,
el dolor del tamaño,
del tiempo, y todo fue
eternidad: relámpago.   (pp. 350–51)

(It was so beautiful
it doesn't suffer memory,
as dates, nouns
or lines suffer.
Nothing in that miracle
could be memory:
because memory
is the grief of its own self,
the pain of measurement
and of time, and it was all
eternity: a lightning flash.)

Love cannot be recalled because, firstly, recollection of it is painful and love was not at all painful; secondly, because recollection implies the measuring out of temporal distance, while love was instantaneous and beyond time. The delightful punning on *sufrir* (meaning both 'to suffer' and 'to permit', as in English) assists in the central confusion which assumes an equation between memory and the past experience *relived*. Insofar as the poem says that memory is not the experience itself, it offers the same kind of undeniable truth which the previous poem offered in saying separation is more permanent than union, but when the poems go on to deny the function of memory and to deny the state of union—the one because it is inexact and the other because it is impermanent—then they indulge in irrational leaps which not only confound logic but make a burlesque of it. The point being, of course, that in so doing they approach the spirit of love's playfulness.

For a final example we turn to one of the longer and titled poems found at the end of *Razón de amor* which shows how logic interacts with a further typical poetic device, personification. 'Destino alegre' ('Joyful Destiny') is probably the volume's most tenaciously argumentative poem, having nine instances of *por eso* ('that's why') concentrated into its first half. The poem begins:

Por eso existen manos largas, sólidas,
fuertes nudillos, y la palma, donde
descansan frentes y se esconden sinos.
Por eso existen pechos, y en el pecho
esa tabla del pecho dura y lisa,

proa del ser en el mar y la pena.
Por eso existen ojos,
azules, verdes, grises, zarcos, negros.
Sí. Ojos azules, ojos verdes, ojos grises,
ojos zarcos, ojos negros, ojos, existen,
sí, por eso.   (p. 430)

(That's why hands exist, long, solid hands,
strong knuckles, and the palm, where
foreheads rest and fates hide.
That's why chests exist, and on the chest
the flat part of the chest, hard and smooth,
the prow of being in the sea and in sorrow.
That's why eyes exist,
blue, green, grey, light blue, black.
Yes. Blue eyes, green eyes, grey eyes,
light blue eyes, black eyes, eyes, exist,
yes, that's why.)

The poem's forty opening lines continue in this vein to catalogue
parts of the human body and rationalize their existence through
the evasive linguistic facility of *por eso* which in fact leaves a proper
rationale in abeyance. Teasing the reader mercilessly, the successive
por esos elicit an expectancy which is not relieved when the long
awaited 'reason' is finally given, for it is given in no less a devious
form than that of a hypothetical question, the main import of which is
further delayed until the end of a long, intricate sentence. They exist,

Porque si no existieran ellos
¿qué iba a ser de vosotras,
arrebatadas fuerzas, vendavales
del mundo . . .
madres de bien y mal,
malditas y benditas, hierro y pluma,
alba y desolación, duras hermanas,
que no pueden matarse y que se odian
eternamente unidas:
tú, tú, felicidad, tú, tú, desgracia?   (p. 431)

(Because if they didn't exist
what would become of you,
raging forces, the world's
storms . . .
mothers of good and evil,
cursed and blessed, iron and feather,
dawn and desolation, you harsh sisters,
who can't destroy each other yet hate each other so,
eternally united:
you, you, happiness, you, you, misfortune?)

If we had anticipated that the body and its parts exist simply 'to make love', then we certainly underestimated Salinas and his tendency to obfuscate. The body and its parts exist, we are now told in the development of the hypothesis, because if they did not exist those dual forces, *felicidad* and *desgracia* ('happiness' and 'misfortune'), 'no tendrían donde saciar su sed de carne y vida' ('would have nowhere to quench their thirst for flesh and life'), and their collective frustration would be such that they would turn violent and devastate the world, with the result that the world itself 'tendría que asumir el gran deber / humano: ser feliz, quererlo ser, / o recibir desgracia' (p. 432) ('would have to assume the great human / duty: being happy, wanting to be happy, / or else accepting misfortune'). Rounding off his argument with the most wicked irony, the poet then claims that the world would not be equal to this burden:

> Se rompería—es débil, inocente.
> Porque el mundo no puede resistir
> lo que resisten ellos, labios, ojos,
> sangre, piel, pecho, alma.   (p. 432)

> (It would break apart—being weak, innocent.
> Because the world cannot resist
> what they resist, lips, eyes,
> blood, skin, heart, soul.)

Therefore it is the human body, notably in the context of love—'dos seres lado a lado, / por besarse, besándose, besados' ('two beings side by side, / by kissing each other, kissing, kissed')—which must free the world from this terrible responsibility and lay its own self bare to the ultimate risk of receiving either 'felicidad. O su gran sombra' ('happiness. Or its great shadow'), as the poem concludes.

Reflecting on this superb poem, several points stand out clearly. First, it is entirely structured on the basis of argument. Second, its argument is expressly designed to prove that human love is the supreme factor in the constitution of our world. Third, the intricacies of the argument are followed through with compelling cohesion. Fourth, and last, the argument is patently and wilfully bereft of logic. To prove a proposition (p) by showing that its negative proposition (not p) leads to a contradiction or impossibility is to pursue the well-known logical fallacy *reductio ad absurdum*. Here:

(p)	the body (hands, lips, eyes …) exists to save the world because
(not p)	if the body did not exist

(deduction)   the world would have (would have had) to assume
                     the human duty of being happy or of accepting mis-
                     fortune

(impossibility)   the world is weak and would be
                     (would have been) destroyed

(conclusion)   the original proposition (p) is proven

What logic the poem has is again a kind of poetic logic, for it is
the device of personification—treating *felicidad* and *desgracia* (happiness, misfortune) as living entities, e.g. *hermanas* (sisters)—which is
the nucleus of the poem's argument as well as the error in its defective
logic. The fallacy is compounded in that, of all things, it is human
emotion which is personified. Happiness and misfortune are first
extricated from the human context and treated as natural forces—
'vendavales del mundo' ('the world's storms')—only to be re-
endowed with human qualities, 'sed', 'cólera' (thirst, anger) and
the like, in the process of personification. To personify human elements in this way is to carry through full circle the poetic contrivance
of personification to its most literal—hence most logical—but certainly its most absurd conclusion.

Poetry's triumph in *Razón de amor* is that of having debunked a
two-headed monster, logic-language, and of having preserved intact
love's essential irrationality. In destabilizing the scientific or mathematical apparatus of language, Salinas compares with Bécquer in
the disruptiveness of his purpose: both poets invite their worst enemy
to parade in the open, either to be ambushed by one in violent mood
or just as mercilessly ridiculed by the other in a poetic carnival.
Naturally, not all the poems in *Razón de amor* fall into this tongue-in-
cheek category; some are more typically entropic in their motifs,
as for intance 'Suicidio hacia arriba' (p. 440) ('Skybound Suicide'),
which develops the idea of an airy, weightless dispersion, or the
lovely poem which begins in familiar fashion: 'Mundo de lo prome-
tido, / agua. / Todo es posible en el agua' (p. 387) ('The land of
promise, / water. / Everything is possible in water'). But whether
reverent of motion or iconoclastic towards form, Salinas is consistently entropic and firm in his emphasis upon flux, spontaneity, irrationality and chance. It is chance, one of the many implications
of motion, which Salinas focuses upon when elucidating his own
poetics. His purpose in *La voz* is to 'Convertir todo en acaso, / en
azar puro' (p. 225) ('turn all into possibility, / into pure chance'),
while in 'Seguro azar' ('Certain Chance') the poem which provides

the volume's title also gives his poetics in nucleus, 'Fe mía' ('My Faith'):

No me fío de la rosa
de papel,
tantas veces que la hice
yo con mis manos.
No me fío de la otra
rosa verdadera,
hija del sol y sazón,
la prometida del viento.
De ti que nunca te hice,
de ti que nunca te hicieron,
de ti me fío, redondo
seguro azar. (p. 158)

(I put no faith in the paper
rose,
for I have made it often enough
with my own hands.
I put no faith in the other
true rose,
the daughter of sunshine and seasons,
fiancée of the wind.
In you whom I have never made,
in you whom no one has ever made,
in you I put my faith, round
certain chance.)

Puzzling as the poem admittedly is, I suggest that the first two roses which the poet rejects correspond respectively to the literary rose or rose-word—in Guillén's sense of a word incarnating the thing it denotes, cf. 'Los nombres' ('Names')—and secondly, the real rose which exists as a phenomenon in the world. Salinas rejects both the rose-word and the rose-thing in favour of something much more mysterious, something hypothetical and imminent, whose existence or *becoming* is entirely governed by chance. Yet we are told that this chance creation is *certain*, or inevitable, which we can understand in the light of 'Extraviadamente', 'Aimlessly ... hitting the mark'; that is: if the poet surrenders like the lovers to chance, he is certain to succeed, it is a question of letting go. Once again Salinas follows Bécquer who described himself or the spirit of poetry in the fifth *rima* as 'Saeta voladora ... / arrojada al azar, / sin adivinarse dónde / temblando se clavará' ('A flying arrow ... / shot at random, / without knowing where / it will tremblingly come to rest'), concluding:

eso soy yo, que al acaso
cruzo el mundo, sin pensar
de dónde vengo, ni adónde
mis pasos me llevarán.

(that's what I am, as I cross
the world at random, not thinking
whence I come, nor whither
my steps will take me.)

For Salinas too the spirit of poetry is free, its inspiration depending upon things beyond the poet's control, as the title *La voz a ti debida* (*The Voice I Owe to You*) implies. The important thing, however, as Salinas argued in his *Poetica*, is to surrender to its caprice:

La poesía es una aventura hacia lo absoluto. Se llega más o menos cerca, se recorre más o menos camino; eso es todo. Hay que dejar que corra la aventura, con toda esa belleza de riesgo, de probabilidad, de jugada. 'Un coup de dés jamais n'abolira le hasard'.[47]

(Poetry is an adventure towards the absolute. One comes more or less close, one covers more or less ground; that's all. But you have to let the adventure run, with all its beautiful risk, probability, gamble. 'Un coup de dés jamais n'abolira le hasard'.)

The reference to Mallarmé's poem which celebrates chance is apt, for the French poet, possibly the most calculating of all poets, knew full well that a poem's secret was beyond calculation.[48] For Salinas the poem is pure chance, inevitably so, since like the perspective it is struck between the world and the poet's mind, both of which are in motion.

Federico García Lorca

The Poetics of Dream

> Verde que te quiero verde.
> Verde viento. Verdes ramas.
> El barco sobre la mar
> y el caballo en la montaña.
> Con la sombra en la cintura
> ella sueña en su baranda,
> verde carne, pelo verde,
> con ojos de fría plata.
> Verde que te quiero verde.
> Bajo la luna gitana,
> las cosas la están mirando
> y ella no puede mirarlas.[1]

> (Green, how I want you green.
> Green wind. Green branches.
> The ship on the sea
> and the horse on the mountain.
> With shadow round her waist
> she dreams on her balcony,
> green flesh, hair of green,
> with eyes of cold silver.
> Green, how I want you green.
> Under the gypsy moon,
> things are looking at her
> and she cannot see them.)

It is now fifty years since Lorca was murdered by Franco's military police shortly after the outbreak of the Spanish Civil War in 1936 when the poet was just thirty-eight years old. That his phenomenal popularity in Spanish and non-Spanish-speaking countries continues undiminished suggests there is something of lasting quality in his work aside from the mystique of martyrdom. Everyone responds to Lorca, and it is not hard to see why: his imagery is stark and physical, rooted in his native Andalusia, the province of sunbaked Moorish towers, flamenco song, bullfighters and gypsies; his themes offer a raw mix of violence and sexuality which gives fatalistic relief to the poet's problematic personality. Reading Lorca we enter an instinctual world where, curiously, even the most mystifying images seem not to obscure meaning but only to lead more directly into the dark fundamentals of human experience. The lines quoted above, enigmatic and obsessional as they are, open what is probably Lorca's most famous poem, 'Romance sonámbulo' ('Somnabular Ballad'), and one suspects that the exceptional renown of its haunting first line—'Verde que te quiero verde' ('Green, how I want you green')— owes more to subliminal than rational understanding. This is perhaps one of the secrets of Lorca's appeal: his poems are made of images that we all understand at a certain level, the level of the unconscious, or, we might say, of dream. Oneiric elements are present in Lorca from his earliest traditional songs, as Dámaso Alonso pointed out,[2] and, since they are conspicuous in the avant-garde Lorca of the later 1920s, a constant feature in his work is its concentration of meaning into symbolic units which, like dreams, are expressive of inner, psychic tensions.

The source of this tension is plain: Lorca was a homosexual who lived in an extremely reactionary, moralistic, macho-orientated society, a society in which he simply could not be himself. His poetry is thus essentially a projection of the inner conflict and neurosis which develops when the quest for self-identity is frustrated by society's taboos. Here, inevitably, Freud comes to mind, and there is little doubt that the author of *The Interpretation of Dreams* is relevant both as a tool for understanding Lorca and in terms of his thought being a very likely influence on Lorca's conception of poetry. By the mid-1920s, when Lorca's poetry began to undergo change, many of his closest friends such as Luis Buñuel and Salvador Dalí had read and been deeply influenced by Freud, whose works were translated into Spanish and published by the Biblioteca Nueva from 1922– 34. Bearing in mind Lorca's years at the culturally aware Residencia de Estudiantes in Madrid, his long vacations with Dalí in Catalonia in 1925 and 1927, the loud championing of Freud by the French

Surrealists who published in Spain and, in the case of Luis Aragon, lectured at the Residencia,[3] it is certain that Lorca would have been well acquainted with Freud, whose thesis that dreams express the wishes of the unconscious could have no clearer literary rendering than the first line of the above poem, 'Verde que te quiero verde' ('Green, how I want you green'). However, though Lorca's poetry became increasingly psychical and dreamlike in texture, he continued to use those images which had come to him from traditional sources, and 'verde' ('green') is a typical example of this. Indeed 'Romance sonámbulo', written in July 1924,[4] is an ideal point of departure for discussion of Lorca since in this poem the traditional folkloric poet and the poet of the unconscious are one.

'Romance sonámbulo' belongs to Lorca's most celebrated volume of poems, *Romancero gitano* (*Gypsy Ballads*), which appeared in 1928. By that time the poem was already well known to friends such as Jorge Guillén, who had heard Lorca recite it many times,[5] and Rafael Alberti, who was deeply moved on hearing Lorca read it one autumn evening in the garden of the Residencia on the first occasion the poets met.[6] Alberti was impressed by the poem's 'mysterious dramatic quality', as was Dalí when on another occasion he exclaimed, '¡Parece que tiene argumento, pero no lo tiene!'[7] ('It seem to have a logical plot, but in fact it doesn't!'). Lorca himself was not certain of the poem's meaning. When explaining that his intention in *Romancero gitano* had been to revitalize Spain's most ancient genre of the ballad, he said:

Yo quise fundir el romance narrativo con el lírico sin que perdieran ninguna calidad, y este esfuerzo se ve conseguido en algunos poemas del *Romancero*, como el llamado 'Romance sonámbulo', donde hay una gran sensación de anécdota, un agudo ambiente dramático, y nadie sabe lo que pasa, ni aun yo, porque el misterio poético es también misterio para el poeta que lo comunica, pero que muchas veces lo ignora.[8]

I wanted to fuse the narrative and the lyrical ballad without either losing their special quality, and this ambition was realized in some of the *Gypsy Ballads*, as in the one called 'Somnambular Ballad', where there is a strong impression of anecdote, a sharp dramatic atmosphere, and yet nobody knows what's going on, not even I, for poetic mystery is also a mystery to the poet who communicates it, but who very often is unaware of it.

The mystery that puzzles the poet clearly has nothing to do with the external trappings of poetry but centres on the symbolic meaning of the poem in terms of its narrative and images. Indeed, Lorca might just as well be talking about a dream he has tried to decipher on waking up. That the poem is related to dream is explicit in its title, for somnambulism or sleep-walking is regarded by psychoanalysts as a neurotic reaction in which the sleeper, as in a dream, engages in activity designed to fulfil a wish or release tension. While Buñuel later used somnambulism as a specific motif in *Viridiana*, the interesting thing about Lorca's poem is that there is no somnambulist as such, even though the girl mentioned in the first stanza is said to be dreaming and the youth we meet later in the poem has a decidedly purposeful mobility. Despite the absence of a sleepwalker, the word *somnambular* is a masterly and fitting choice for the poem's title since it perfectly describes the poem's mood of psychic automatism. Before considering its psychic level, however, we ought to begin by trying to pin down the poem's narrative, which was so important to Lorca and which Dalí said is and is not there.

The first stanza, as we saw, introduced a mysterious girl of green hair and green skin who is enveloped in shadow and is dreaming on her balcony. The second fragment, also of twelve lines, continues to sketch in a most ominous nocturnal environment by means of a vigorous animation of natural elements. It now appears that the girl is waiting for someone to come to her:

> Pero ¿quién vendrá? ¿Y por dónde...?
> Ella sigue en su baranda,
> verde carne, pelo verde,
> soñando en la mar amarga.   (p. 430)

> (But who will come? And from where...?
> She remains on her balcony,
> green flesh, hair of green,
> dreaming of the bitter sea.)

The mention of the sea recalls images at the poem's opening, 'El barco sobre la mar / y el caballo en la montaña' ('The ship on the sea / and the horse on the mountain'), and we are led to suppose that the person she awaits is making a dangerous journey which perhaps, in good gypsy tradition, is connected with smuggling. The third fragment moves on abruptly and consists entirely of a dialogue between two men, namely the 'compadre' ('friend'), who is the owner of the house where the girl waits, and the newly arrived 'mocito' ('young man'), the one she is presumably waiting for. In this the poem's longest section we learn that the young man has escaped with terrible wounds from a mountainous region, the passes of Cabra, and that he comes to the other's house to seek shelter or to die a decent death. He says that he wishes to exchange the items of his dangerous way of life—'caballo', 'montura', 'cuchillo' ('horse', 'saddle', 'knife')—for the other's more comfortable things, 'casa', 'espejo', 'manta' ('house', 'mirror', 'blanket'). This request is twice refused, the older man making the strange reply:

> Si yo pudiera, mocito,
> este trato se cerraba.
> Pero yo ya no soy yo,
> ni mi casa es ya mi casa.   (p. 431)

> (If I only could, young man,
> this deal would be sealed.
> But I am no longer myself,
> nor is my house my house any more.)

The younger man, despairing now, asks if he may at least be allowed to go up to the high balcony or verandah. In the fourth section we learn that this last request is granted for the two men ascend together, 'Dejando un rastro de sangre. / Dejando un rastro de lágrimas' (p. 431) ('Leaving a trail of blood. / Leaving a trail of tears'). On arrival at the balcony the young man discovers that the girl is no longer there, and the other can only lament that she had waited for him on many occasions. In the poem's final fragment there is simply an image of the green girl, now described as a gypsy, being held over water by an icicle of the moon; she has apparently drowned, or has drowned herself, and her body lies on the surface of the water as though supported by a moonbeam or its reflection. Below the verandah, some drunken Civil Guards who have evidently been in pursuit of the young male beat on the door. The poem closes with a reiteration of its opening four lines:

> Verde que te quiero verde.
> Verde viento. Verdes ramas.
> El barco sobre la mar
> y el caballo en la montaña.

> (Green, how I want you green.
> Green wind. Green branches.
> The ship on the sea
> and the horse on the mountain.)

If nothing else this outline should warn us that we cannot hope to understand the poem in merely narrative terms. The dangers of thinking along the lines of a tight formal plot have been shown by Rupert Allen who offers a most unlikely interpretation of events.[9] What we have is the nucleus of a plot: a smuggler or fugitive from the law attempts to find asylum at a gypsy home; he is unsuccessful in this and in his apparently secondary wish to reach the green and bitter girl. But these bare bones hardly explain the profound mystery which the poem works on us, and clearly the narrative is little more than a vehicle for the poem's symbolic values. In the terms Freud used in dream analysis, the narrative is the poem's *manifest content* which conceals its *latent content* or true psychic value for the poet-dreamer. In one sense all poems follow this broad pattern insofar as they overtly say one thing and covertly mean another; but that practice is generally deliberate and the poet remains conscious of the other meaning of his 'objective correlative', while in 'Romance sonámbulo', by Lorca's own admission, he is not so cognizant and his role is thus similar to that of a dreamer. Also highly reminiscent of dream is the fact that the narrative is presented in a condensed, disjointed form, its linking sequences having been deleted. Here we note a happy coincidence between the old ballad technique and the Freudian theory of dream. Briefly the point is that the ballad form evolved from the ancient epic, and, this being an oral form passed down from generation to generation, in the course of time many parts of the original long poem were forgotten, indeed, only the best or literally most memorable parts were retained. This natural process, known as *fragmentismo*, was later cultivated by more sophisticated poets who realized that abruptly excerpted sequences often made intriguing, engimatic poems. In 'Romance sonámbulo' Lorca exploits the old technique of *fragmentismo* to the full, but with the specific purpose of creating the texture of dream, for of the five primary characteristics which Freud distinguished in dreams— namely, condensation, dramatization, displacement, symbolization and secondary revision—the first two are directly relevant to the presentation of 'Romance sonámbulo', namely, condensation, the laconic nature of the manifest content, and dramatization, the connecting of visual images into an apparently coherent dramatic sequence which on waking seems incoherent or mysterious. The mystery in 'Romance sonámbulo' ultimately centres on the green and bitter girl who is the object of the young man's quest—a decidedly erotic object too, in accord with Freud's thesis—but disjunction comes from the seeming unrelatedness of this quest to the young man's perilous way of life and persecution by the law. While we shall shortly consider the key synthetic symbol, *verde* ('green'), which occurs twenty-four times in the poem, let us prepare for this by looking first at other important images.

One aspect of condensation noted by Freud is that a single image or idea in the manifest content of a dream can stand for many separate though frequently overlapping associations in the latent content. With this in mind we approach the two lines found at the beginning and end of the poem:

> El barco sobre la mar
> y el caballo en la montaña.
>
> (The ship on the sea
> and the horse on the mountain.)

Here the laconic nature of the images no doubt invites a variety of interpretations, but, for my part, two notions impress themselves most forcefully: the first is propriety, in the sense that a ship *should* be on the sea and a horse *should* be on the mountain; the second is loneliness, for both images portray a single entity—ship, horse—against a vast spatial background—sea, mountain. Assuming the validity of these associations, the most obvious point to make about them is that they are contradictory or ambivalent, for while propriety would seem to be a positive notion, loneliness evidently is not. Such ambivalence, in addition to being regarded by Freud as a characteristic symptom of neurosis, is, as we shall soon see, fundamental to the poem's latent content. But, moving on, further and more specific interpretations of the two images could be hazarded. The horse is a well-known symbol of virility and one frequently used by Lorca, while the ship, like any vessel or container, is in Freudian terms a symbol of the female organ. Thus the images might well represent a polarization of gender, whereupon our thoughts return to the previous associations of propriety and loneliness. We might ask: do the lines indicate isolation/loneliness in a sexual context? Is the separation of male and female proper or improper? Is sexuality itself a fugitive from the law? At this point associations overlap at such a pace and analysis becomes so speculative that we are probably well advised to read on. But as we do so, we note that the second stanza is increasingly explicit in the erotic connotations of its imagery:

> Verde que te quiero verde.
> Grandes estrellas de escarcha
> vienen con el pez de sombra
> que abre el camino del alba.

La higuera frota su viento
con la lija de sus ramas,
y el monte, gato garduño,
eriza sus pitas agrias.
¿Pero quién vendrá? ¿Y por dónde...?
Ella sigue en su baranda,
verde carne, pelo verde,
soñando en la mar amarga.   (p. 430)

(Green, how I want you green.
Huge stars of frost
come with the fish of shadow
that opens the way to dawn.
The fig tree rubs its breeze
with the sandpaper of its branches,
and the mountain, a thieving cat,
stands its sour agaves on end.
But who will come? And from where...?
She remains on her balcony,
green flesh, hair of green,
dreaming of the bitter sea.)

Erotic images are now so plentiful that the stanza might be fairly said to follow the pattern of an erection dream. We note: the repeated desire (line 1); the phallic fish (3); its penetrating motion (4); the phallic tree, combining an allusion to the female genital in the implicit fig (5); the tree's reflexive, masturbatory action (6–7); the duplicated erection motifs of bristling cat fur and upstanding agaves (7–8), complemented by the persistent height-erection of stars, mountain and balcony. In all, eroticism virtually erupts here through the poem's manifest content, though it is an eroticism tinged with various negative associations, being harsh—'escarcha' (frost), 'lija' (sandpaper)—and of course bitter—'pitas agrias' (sour agaves), 'mar amarga' (bitter sea). But to whom is the eroticism attributable? The girl, who is the only person to have appeared so far, certainly waits and dreams in unwholesome isolation; though, being already green, she could hardly be the one to say 'Verde que te quiero verde', except in a reflexive, narcissistic sense. If the poem were in fact a dream there could only be one answer: the dreamer. This is the key to the decisive central section which follows:

Compadre, quiero cambiar
mi caballo por su casa,
mi montura por su espejo,
mi cuchillo por su manta.
Compadre, vengo sangrando

desde los puertos de Cabra.
Si yo pudiera, mocito,
este trato se cerraba.
Pero yo ya no soy yo,
ni mi casa es ya mi casa.
Compadre, quiero morir
decentemente en mi cama.
De acero, si puede ser,
can las sábanas de holanda.
¿No ves la herida que tengo
desde el pecho a la garganta?
Trescientas rosas morenas
lleva tu pechera blanca.
Tu sangre rezuma y huele
alrededor de tu faja.
Pero yo ya no soy yo,
ni mi casa es ya mi casa.
Dejadme subir al menos
hasta las altas barandas,
¡dejadme subir!, dejadme
hasta las verdes barandas.
Barandales de la luna
por donde el agua retumba.   (p. 431)

(Friend, I want to change
my horse for your house,
my saddle for your mirror,
my knife for your blanket.
Friend, I come bleeding
from the passes of Cabra.
If I only could, young man,
this deal would be sealed.
But I am no longer myself,
nor is my house my house any more.
Friend, I want to die
decently in my bed.
One made of steel, if possible,
with fine Holland sheets.
Can't you see the wound I have
from my chest to my throat?
Three hundred dark roses
cover your white shirt front.
Your blood oozes pungently
around your belt.
But I am no longer myself,
nor is my house my house any more.
Let me go up at least
to the high balustrades,
let me go up!, let me,

to the green balustrades.
Balustrades of the moon
where water resounds.)

If we accept that the initial imperative is to read the poem as a dream—as the title virtually instructs and the hypnotic rhythms persuade—we can penetrate the objective superficies of narrative and characterization by seeing the poem as an imagistic presentation of the poet's own psychic dichotomy. In particular we will see that the two males introduced here are not separate individuals at all, but external projections of key elements within the same psychic experience, forming, as it were, a dual persona. Indicative of their union is the omission of punctuation to clarify a change of speaker in the above dialogue, a marked contrast with the ballad tradition which, being oral, always took great care to introduce and distinguish between speakers. In addition, the sympathetic tone of the conversation—'Compadre ... Si yo pudiera, mocito' ('Friend ... If only I could, young man')—and the fact that they eventually ascend together in mutual pain and grief towards the high balcony underlines the sense of a natural bondage between the two. The excessive and bloody wounds of the younger male conform to Lorca's way of imaging psychic pain—and indeed the psychoanalytical term *trauma* originally meant 'wound' in Greek—while in literary terms this technique may be traced back to such traditional images as that of the wounded stag representing the suffering of a passionate male whose love is unrequited. The wounded male makes three requests of the other, though the requests are not all for the same thing, as Rupert Allen suggests, but for two very different things. The first request, which is repeated, is that he be allowed to change his way of life for the more conventional way of life of the houseowner, so that he may die 'decentemente' ('decently') in bed. As J. M. Aguirre has shown,[10] the features that represent his previous way of life—'caballo', 'montura', 'cuchillo' ('horse', 'saddle', 'blanket')—all point towards erotic motifs and at the same time situate the young man as an 'outsider', the person who lives, by implication, *indecently*, beyond the frontiers of a conventional environment. What this first request amounts to, then, is a tragic plea for asylum and acceptance—*inside* the boundaries of social normality—by one who has been hounded and persecuted to such an extent that his only solution seems to be to change his way of life. Here we inevitably recall the trials and tribulations which beset Lorca in his own life, the rumours he faced both in Granada and Madrid, his deep-seated fear that his parents would learn the truth about him, his later estrangement from his brother Francisco, not to mention the ultimate persecution of his murder.[11] But, to return to the poem, while the younger man represents one aspiration, the older man embodies the faculty of understanding or wisdom of the very same psyche, and the answer he provides is negative, indicating that there is no possibility of change: 'Pero yo ya no soy, / ni mi casa es ya mi casa' ('but I am no longer myself, / nor is my house my house any more'). The reply points towards a loss of will or self-control, in which connection 'casa' (house) might be understood as an image of the body as traditionally used for instance by St John of the Cross in his famous 'Noche oscura del alma' ('Dark Night of the Soul'). There is no possibility of change in the conventional life-pattern because the persona is possessed by a force he cannot subdue, which, as always in Lorca's work, is that of a violent, incurable passion.

In Freudian terms, the poem offers a fairly consistent representation of the psychic battle that goes on between the id, the ego and the super-ego, these being represented respectively by the young man, the older man and the police. The id, or instinctual drive, in the form of the young man, has been battered into submission by the super-ego's social conscience which continually exerts or introjects notions of guilt and fear which have their base in a long-standing acceptance of parental/social authority. But the ego, which is awareness of self, as represented by the older man, knows full well that the desire to change is unreal and futile. Here we note that it was precisely because the ego is accosted on both sides by the id and the super-ego that Freud made his famous statement, 'The ego is not master of its own house',[12] which is strikingly paralleled by the older man's plaintive and repeated line: 'ni mi casa es ya mi casa' ('nor is my house my house any more').

Having been told twice that there is no possibility of change, the young man makes his last request:

> Dejadme subir al menos
> hasta las altas barandas
>
> (Let me go up at least
> to the high balustrades)

The key here, I believe, is 'al menos' ('at least'), for this indicates that the speaker has accepted his destiny as being outside that of the norm, that he has indeed understood the truth expressed by his ego, the older man, and that finally he now has a certain determination to salvage something from his essentially tragic inner reality. The request to ascend to the high balcony—fundamentally erotic in its erection motif—is quite different from the earlier request to enter the house and, strictly, need not involve entry. But in the poem's last fragments even these compromised ambitions are frustrated, for the impure object of his quest, imaged in the young and green girl, proves to be elusive. In this sense we see that the poem is totally despondent in its view of the situation: the poet-dreamer is successively unable to change his way of life and is denied even minimal consolation on surrendering himself to his destined impulse. Inevitably the poem concludes with a correlation of love and death, while the accumulation of images which connote sterility—'fría plata', 'luna', 'escarcha', 'mar amarga', 'hojalata', 'cristal', 'carámbano de luna' ('cold silver', 'moon,' 'frost', 'bitter sea', 'tinplate', 'glass', 'icicle of moon')—reinforce the mood of comprehensive frustration. With the appearance of the Civil Guards, the instruments of law and order who are there to persecute those who live outside society's required behavioural standards, the poem closes with an intensification of the dominant mood of remorse. Finally, with the repetition of 'El barco sobre la mar / y el caballo en la montaña' ('The ship on the sea / and the horse on the mountain'), the notions of propriety and loneliness take on added force.

Into this complex and even schizophrenic fabric of psychic experience, the traditional colour symbol *verde* ('green') is woven with startling precision. Extensive repetition of the word is itself instrumental in creating a dreamlike atmosphere, a dream-screen. The five instances of 'Verde que te quiero verde' indicate a fixation, while the allocation of the colour to many physical aspects in the poem— 'viento', 'ramas', 'carne', 'pelo', 'barandas' ('breeze', 'branches', 'flesh', 'hair', 'balustrades')—serves to bring about a total integration of scene and psychic experience. The colour's immediate association is with youth, personified in the young girl who is the real object of the dreamer's quest. In the opening fragments the colour preserves its normal chthonic associations of springtime and fertility which apply in all cultures. This holds out a prospect of freedom, though it is again problematic whether freedom would be intended in the sense of a release from pain, as in the young man's first request, or as a more positive appeal for freedom of expression such as we find voiced by the sympathetic woodcutter in *Bodas de sangre* (*Blood Wedding*) who comments on the illicit lovers, 'El mundo es grande. Todos pueden vivir en él' (p. 1245) ('The world is large. There's room for everyone in it'). As for the girl in 'Romance sonámbulo', it is apparent that she too assumes contradictory values; for while her intimate association with the colour green initially suggests the positive notions of youth and fertility, there is a warning in the cold silver of her eyes that this is only an illusion. By the end of the poem, though still *verde*, she is described as 'amarga' ('bitter'), and this restates the specifically Iberian symbolism of the green citrus fruits which is often used by Lorca and is generally presented in a negative, nocturnal atmosphere:

> Nadie come naranjas
> bajo la luna llena.
> Es preciso comer
> fruta verde y helada.   (p. 393)

> (No one eats oranges
> under the full moon.
> One has to eat
> green and frozen fruit.)

Here we have the fundamental polarization between positive and negative love, which is to say, between the sweet orange and the bitter unripe fruit. This system of equations—*luna = verde, helada* (moon = green, frozen)—and of oppositions—*naranja × luna, verde, helada* (orange × moon, green, frozen)—is the basis of much of Lorca's early poetry and, naturally, its allusive condensation is highly reminiscent of the symbolic thinking of dream. The positive value of the orange is shown in 'Cancioncilla del primer deseo' ('Little Song of the First Desire'):

> (Alma,
> ponte color naranja.
> Alma,
> ponte color de amor.)   (p. 407)

> (Soul,
> dress yourself in the colour of orange.
> Soul,
> dress yourself in the colour of love.)

But green, by contrast, is the colour of sterile or unrequited love, as in the poem beginning:

> Arbolé arbolé
> seco y verdé.   (p. 381)

> (Tree-o tree-o
> dry and green-o.)

The positive value of the orange can be negated, as in that remorseful poem of sexual guilt 'Canción del naranjo seco' (p. 420) ('Song of the Dry Orange Tree'). But the natural antithesis to the orange and the standard representative of bitter fruit is the lemon. So well established is the symbolic meaning of the lemon that its coded messages can be amazingly brief, as is the case in the ballads on Antoñito el Camborio. In the first ballad, 'Prendimiento de Antoñito el Camborio' ('Arrest of Antoñito el Camborio'), the young and handsome gypsy is seized by Civil Guards on his way to see the bullfights in Seville. The crime he has committed seems very harmless:

> A la mitad del camino
> cortó limones redondos,
> y los fue tirando al agua
> hasta que la puso de oro.   (p. 445)

> (Mid way on his journey
> he cut some round lemons,
> and he threw them into the water
> until it was turned to gold.)

One could read the poem literally and say that Antoñito's arrest for such a trivial offence is a measure of the police harassment gypsies had to endure. But this would not take into account the lemon's natural reference to sexual matters, and we would be left to wonder why the poet stressed Antoñito's handsome appearance, his 'empavonados bucles' ('brilliantined locks'), his fine willow cane and jaunty gait. In the second ballad, 'Muerte de Antoñito el Camborio' ('Death of Antoñito el Camborio'), we learn that the gypsy is set upon and killed by four of his own cousins. The ostensible reason for this brutality is that the cousins feel Antoñito has brought shame on the family by not resisting police arrest. But Antoñito himself gives another reason, turning our attention back to his appearance:

> Lo que en otros no envidiaban
> ya lo envidiaban en mí.
> Zapatos color corinto,
> medallones de marfil,
> y este cutis amasado
> con aceituna y jazmín.   (p. 448)

> (What in others they did not envy
> they certainly envied in me.
> Shoes the colour of raisins,
> medallions of ivory,
> and this skin that is smoothed
> with olives and jasmin.)

The unmistakable implication is that Antoñito is effeminate. Indeed, he smacks of the extrovert, dandy, Quentin Crisp type of homosexual. This is why he has brought shame on the family and why he has to be killed. Thus his picking of lemons refers perforce to a sexual misdemeanour he indulged in on his way to Seville. Of this we can be as certain in symbolic terms as we are that the gallant who, in a traditional poem,

> en huerta de monjas
> limones cogía[13]
>
> (in a convent orchard
> picked lemons)

had his irreverent way with a nun. Furthermore, one stunningly condensed description of Antoñito which occurs in both ballads— 'moreno de verde luna' (pp. 445, 447) ('dark-skinned from green moon')—tells us all we need to know about his sensuality (*moreno* + *verde*) and its inevitably tragic consequences (*verde* + *luna*), where the symbolism of 'green' links both concepts.

The extent to which Lorca identifies with the bitter fruit complex is plain in one remarkably oneiric and equational poem of 1921:

> Limonar.
> Momento
> de mi sueño.
>
> Limonar.
> Nido
> de senos
> amarillos.
>
> Limonar.
> Senos donde maman
> las brisas del mar.
>
> Limonar
> Naranjal desfallecido,
> naranjal moribundo,
> naranjal sin sangre.
>
> Limonar.
> Tú viste mi amor roto
> por el hacha de un gesto.
>
> Limonar,
> mi amor niño, mi amor
> sin báculo y sin rosa.
>
> Limonar.   (p. 591–2)

(Lemon grove.
Moment
of my dream.

Lemon grove.
Nest
of yellow
breasts.

Lemon grove.
Breasts where suckle
the breezes of the sea.

Lemon grove.
Decrepit orange grove,
moribund orange grove,
bloodless orange grove.

Lemon grove,
you saw my love broken
by the hatchet of a gesture.

Lemon grove,
my childlike love, my love
without staff and rose.

Lemon grove.)

The dream of breast-like lemons, sea-water, infertility—'sin sangre'
('bloodless')—castration—'amor roto / por el hacha' ('love broken /
by the hatchet')—impotence—'sin báculo' ('without staff')—and
aversion to the female, 'sin rosa' ('without rose'), is totally consistent
in its sexual diagnosis. One of the poem's most typical equations—
Limonar = *mar* (lemon grove = sea)—which is based on the bitterness
of the liquids involved, reminds us of 'Romance sonámbulo' where
a similar equation is implicit: 'Ella sigue en su baranda, / verde
carne, pelo verde, / soñando en la mar amarga' ('She remains on
her balcony, / green flesh, hair of green, / dreaming of the bitter
sea'). Lorca had used the traditional symbol of the sea frequently,
notably in 'Mar' ('Sea') of 1919, which begins,

> El mar es
> el Lucifer del azul.
> El cielo caído
> por querer ser la luz.   (p. 276)

> (The sea is
> the Lucifer of the blue.

The sky which has fallen
through aspiring to be light.)

He used it again in 'La balada del agua del mar' (p. 263) ('The Ballad of the Sea's Water'), another despairingly erotic poem which appeared in his first volume, *Libro de poemas* (*Book of Poems*) of 1921. Inevitably the sea's bitterness suggests unwholesomeness or even, as above, devilish aspiration, and always in the context of love. Thus in 'Romance sonámbulo' the sea complements the negative implications of *verde* and, inasmuch as the young girl dreams of the sea, she reciprocates the poet-dreamer's desire—'Verde que te quiero verde'—and is his prospective partner in illicit love. At the same time it is important to appreciate that these negative connotations of *verde* coexist with the positive chthonic associations of the life-force. They underline or subvert the attractiveness of *verde* and create an ambivalent, metamorphic symbol which ultimately forecasts the futility of the ascent towards the love object and leaves the poet in its wake as one betrayed.

Reflecting on 'Romance sonámbulo', we find that ambivalence is ultimately its key note, an ambivalence which stems from two contradictory desires. On the one hand there is the wish to change, as the younger man wishes to change from outsider to insider, and this motif which we shall call the transformation motif is one we shall meet frequently in Lorca. It may take innocuous form, as in 'Canción tonta' ('Silly song'):

> Mamá.
> Yo quiero ser de plata...
>
> Mamá.
> Yo quiero ser de agua...   (p. 375)
>
> (Mummy.
> I want to be silvery...
>
> Mummy.
> I want to be watery...)

Or, as in 'Muerte' ('Death') from *Poeta en Nueva York* (*Poet in New York*) of 1930, it may be seen more lugubriously as a fatal aspiration which applies to all living things:

> ¡Qué esfuerzo!
> ¡Qué esfuerzo del caballo por ser perro!
> ¡Qué esfuerzo del perro por ser golondrina!
> ¡Qué esfuerzo de la golondrina por ser abeja!
> ¡Qué esfuerzo de la abeja por ser caballo!   (p. 506)

(What striving!
What striving from the horse to be a dog!
What striving from the dog to be a swallow!
What striving from the swallow to be a bee!
What striving from the bee to be a horse!)

The cyclical nature of this series, from horse back again to horse, naturally suggests that the aspiration is futile. But we can be sure that the source of the aspiration to change is guilt, the sexual guilt of 'Canción del naranjo seco' ('Song of the Dry Orange Tree'):

> Leñador.
> Córtame la sombra.
> Líbrame del suplicio
> de verme sin toronjas.
>
> ¿Por qué nací entre espejos?
> El día me da vueltas.
> Y la noche me copia
> en todas sus estrellas.
>
> Quiero vivir sin verme...   (p. 420)

> (Woodcutter.
> Cut me some shadow.
> Free me from the anguish
> of seeing myself fruitless.
>
> Why was I born between mirrors?
> The day makes me dizzy.
> And the night copies me
> in all its stars.
>
> I want to live without seeing myself...)

The guilt-ridden poet struggles against what the second stanza unmistakably defines as a narcissus complex, which is the subject too of the poem 'Narciso', 'Narciso. / Mi dolor. / Y mi dolor mismo' (p. 411) 'Narcissus. / My suffering. / And my suffering itself'), and we scarcely need Freud's confirmation to know that narcissim is closely related to homosexuality. Thus we might say that the transformation motif found in 'Romance sonámbulo' and other poems reflects a desire on the part of the guilt-ridden poet to escape the reflexive self, a self in which he feels hopelessly trapped.

On the other hand, 'Romance sonámbulo' expresses a second or alternative desire which, as opposed to the flight mechanism of transference, is the desire to be true to the self, to follow through on the fatal attraction of the bitter fruit. This idea is also found in other poems, from the early 'Cancioncilla del primer deseo', where we read,

> En la mañana viva
> yo quería ser yo.
> Corazón. (p. 407)
>
> (In the bright morning,
> I wanted to be myself.
> Heart.)

to the powerful poem from *Poeta en Nueva York* entitled 'Poema doble del lago Edem' ('Double Poem of Lake Eden') where the poet attempts to listen to the 'voz de mi verdad' ('voice of my truth'):

> ¡Ay voz antigua de mi amor,
> ay voz de mi verdad,
> ay voz de mi abierto costado...! (p. 498)
>
> (Oh, ancient voice of my love,
> oh voice of my truth,
> oh voice of my open side...!)

This second, contrasting desire creates ambivalence in 'Romance sonámbulo' and throughout Lorca's work, the poet's dichotomy or split personality being apparent in the very title 'Poema doble...' ('Double Poem...'), a poem we shall look at in detail shortly. Such a symptomatic polarization is found again in the sonnet 'Adán' ('Adam') where, after first evoking the sense of a vibrant, virile Adam, Lorca concludes by referring to his impotent opposite:

> Pero otro Adán oscuro está soñando
> neutra luna de piedra sin semilla
> donde el niño de luz se irá quemando. (p. 353)
>
> (But another dark Adam is dreaming
> a neutral moon of seedless stone
> where the child of light will depart burning.)

Polarization is also fundamental to 'Baladilla de los tres ríos' ('Little Ballad of the Three Rivers') which opens the volume *Poema del cante jondo* (*Poem of the Deep Song*) of 1921. This poem's lucid structure consists of a series of simple contrasts between Seville, with its single majestic river, the Guadalquivir, and Granada, which has two insignificant rivers, the Dauro and Genil:

> El río Guadalquivir
> va entre naranjos y olivos.
> Los dos ríos de Granada
> bajan de la nieve al trigo.

¡Ay, amor
que se fue y no vino!

El río Guadalquivir
tiene las barbas granates.
Los dos ríos de Granada,
uno llanto y otro sangre.

¡Ay, amor
que se fue por el aire!

. . . Guadalquivir, alta torre
y viento en los naranjales.
Dauro y Genil, torrecillas
muertas sobre los estanques.

¡Ay, amor
que se fue por el aire! . . .   (pp. 295–6)

(The river Guadalquivir
flows between orange and olive trees.
The two rivers of Granada
come down from the snow to the wheat.

Oh, love
that left and never came back!

The river Guadalquivir
has garnet-coloured beards.
The two rivers of Granada,
grief the one and blood the other.

Oh, love
that was borne away on the wind!

. . . Guadalquivir, a tall tower
and breeze among the orange groves.
Dauro and Genil, puny towers
lying dead upon the pools.

Oh, love
that was borne away on the wind! . . .)

Seville's associations—orange groves, garnet beards, tall towers and a single powerful river—are all positive and impressively virile, while Granada's—from the cold snow melting on the Sierra Nevada to the stumpy towers reflected in stagnant pools—are quite the opposite and suggest impotence. It is scarcely necessary to know that Lorca was from Granada—where indeed he often felt claustrophobic[14]—to appreciate that he associates himself with that city's values and above all with its two dichotomizing rivers.

The ambivalence we have found in 'Romance sonámbulo' and elsewhere is consistent with Freud's view expressed in *Totem and Taboo* of 1914 that ambivalence is deeply inherent in obsessional neurosis. In that volume's second essay, 'Taboo and Emotional Ambivalence', Freud describes the characteristic indecision and contradictoriness of those who suffer from 'taboo sickness', which is to say, those who are guilt-ridden from the conviction that they have broken the rule of the totem or the institutionalized tribal code. For Freud the strongest taboo in all cultures, especially primitive cultures, was incest, and the first essay in *Totem and Taboo* is entitled 'The Horror of Incest'. Significantly, one of the most powerful ballads in *Romancero gitano* is 'Thamar y Amnón' which retells the biblical tale of Tamar's rape by her half-brother Amnon found in the Second Book of Samuel, chapter 13. It is instructive to compare Lorca's treatment with the original, noting certain differences.

The Bible gives a matter of fact account of how Amnon, a son of David, being strongly attracted by his half-sister Tamar, a beautiful virgin, took the advice of Jonadab, 'a very crafty man', and feigned illness so that Tamar might come to tend him in his chamber. There, ignoring Tamar's plea—'No, my brother, do not force me, for such a thing is not done in Israel; do not do this wanton folly'—'he forced her, and lay with her'.[15] Amnon then sent Tamar away, filled with hatred for her, and it was not until two years later than Absalom, Tamar's full brother, exacted revenge by killing Amnon. In Lorca's version we are not told that Tamar is half-sister to Amnon; she is described as 'su hermana' ('his sister'), an omission which increases the degree of consanguinity and thereby our abomination of the crime. At the end of the poem, rather than Tamar being sent away in shame, it is Amnon who flees David's city on his horse while 'Negros le dirigen flechas / en los muros y atalayas' (p. 467) ('Blacks shoot arrows at him / from the battlements and watchtowers'). Thus not only does the crime seem greater in Lorca's poem but persecution of its perpetrator is also more immediate, there being a sense of a spontaneous, collective response on the part of an outraged society. While these features tend to highlight Amnon's culpability, other differences from the Bible are less condemnatory. In particular, there is no mention of the crafty Jonadab, so that when Amnon lies on his bed of pain we feel that his sickness is real, if psychosomatic, and not a ruse:

Toda la alcoba sufría
con sus ojos llenos de alas ...
Linfa de pozo oprimida
brota silencio en las jarras.
En los musgos de los troncos
la cobra tendida canta.
Amnón gime por la tela
fresquísima de la cama.
Yedra del escalofrío
cubre su carne quemada.   (p. 465)

(The whole chamber suffered
with his fluttering eyes ...
Oppressed water from the well
sprouted silence in the pitchers.
In the moss of tree trunks
the stretched-out cobra sings.
Amnon groans between the chilling
sheets of his bed.
The ivy of a shiver
covers his burnt flesh.)

Tormented by sexual desire, a desire he is powerless to repress though he knows it is wrong, Amnon's sickness is 'taboo sickness' in advance of the act. The pain in his body mirrors the feverish pain of the parched moonlit land described in the first stanza:

La tierra se ofrece llena
de heridas cicatrizadas,
o estremecida de agudos
cauterios de luces blancas.

(The land shows itself covered
with the scars of wounds,
or shot through with the intense
searing of white lights.)

And this parallel suggests a universal rather than idiosyncratic aspect to Amnon's torment. Had we not read the biblical version we would have thought that Tamar comes uninvited to her sick brother's room. Indeed, reflecting on the poem's second stanza which depicts Tamar singing naked on her flat roof at night in full view of Amnon in his phallic tower, we might even think that an element of seductive provocation applies and that this culminates in a demure, knowing entry by Tamar into her brother's room. The sequence prior to the 'rape' is again ambivalent:

Thamar entró silenciosa
en la alcoba silenciada,

color de vena y Danubio,
turbia de huellas lejanas.
Thamar, bórrame los ojos
con tu fija madrugada.
Mis hilos de sangre tejen
volantes sobre tu falda.
Déjame tranquila, hermano,
Son tus besos en mi espalda
avispas y vientecillos
en doble enjambre de flautas.
Thamar, en tus pechos altos
hay dos peces que me llaman,
y en las yemas de tus dedos
rumor de rosa encerrada.   (pp. 465–6)

(Tamar entered silently
into the silenced chamber,
the colour of vein and Danube
she was mixed with distant traces.
Tamar, blot out my eyes
with your fixed dawn.
The threads of my blood weave
flounces on your lap.
Let me be, brother.
Your kisses on my shoulder
are wasps and windy breezes
in a double swarm of flutes.
Tamar, in your high breasts
there are two fishes calling me,
and in your fingertips
the murmur of an enclosed rose.)

Tamar's association with coldness and more northerly climes—
'Danubio'—suggests her chastity, but this had assumed masochistic
overtones in the previous stanza: 'Su desnudo en el alero, / agudo
norte de palma, / pide copos a su vientre / y granizo a sus espaldas'
(p. 464) ('Her naked body on the rooftop, / like a sharp pointer
of palm, / asks for snowflakes on her belly / and hailstones on her
back'). Her coolness is of course the only possible antidote to
Amnon's feverish passion; but Amnon's first words to his sister,
quoted above, are both a tragic supplication and a warning to her
of his sexual need. Her reply—'Déjame tranquila, hermano' ('Let
me be, brother')—is a rejection, though perhaps not a forceful rejection,

and indeed, in view of her following remarks, may even be construed as token modesty:

> Son tus besos en mi espalda
> avispas y vientecillos
> en doble enjambre de flautas.   (p. 466)
>
> (Your kisses on my shoulder
> are wasps and windy breezes
> in a double swarm of flutes.)

The contrasting images of wasps with their implicit stings and the seductive 'windy breezes' marvellously capture an erotic intimacy of pain mixed with pleasure, and in so doing they suggest Tamar's own confusion as she is both aroused and repelled by a 'doble enjambre de flautas' ('double swarm of flutes'). Tamar, admittedly, is taken violently,

> Ya la coge del cabello,
> ya la camisa le rasga.   (p. 466)
>
> (Now he grasps her by the hair,
> now he rips her slip.)

but the doubts that may already be in our minds, together with the absence of further protestations, do not encourage an outright condemnation of Amnon. Even the image of resistance,

> Sol en cubos resistía
> la delgadez de la parra.   (p. 466)
>
> (The slenderness of the vine
> resisted a downpour of sun.)

—is not unequivocal, for while the female vine is said to resist the male onslaught there is a sense in 'parra' ('climbing vine') of clinging. Whichever way we read the poem, I think we must at least admit that Lorca gives Amnon's character a more sympathetic or empathetic treatment than did the Bible. Even if we reject any form of complicity on Tamar's part, we at least know that Amnon suffered torment too, the torment of conscience in its typically futile resistance to libidinal forces. In my view Lorca's subtle shifts of emphasis, symbolic hints and thought-provoking deletions—for once again *fragmentismo* works wonderfully well—turn what was originally a straightforward narrative into an ambiguous one.

We can be confident that the poem's taboo theme is a projection of that other taboo found in 'Romance sonámbulo' and the ballads on Antoñito el Camboro, and that Amnon's sickness is a projection of Lorca's own neurosis or emotional ambivalence. A similar if more muted projection is found in other poems in *Romancero gitano* that we may briefly mention. The ballad 'La monja gitana' ('The Gypsy

Nun' depicts the plight of a young nun who has been shut away in a convent—no doubt for her sins—there to pass her time in such harmless activity as embroidering the altar cloth. As she sews, however, she engages in a kind of waking dream, a dream which is blatantly erotic:

> Por los ojos de la monja
> galopan dos caballistas.
> Un rumor último y sordo
> le despega la camisa,
> y al mirar nubes y montes
> en las yertas lejanías,
> se quiebra su corazón
> de azúcar y yerbaluisa.
> ¡Oh, qué llanura empinada
> con veinte soles arriba!
> ¡Qué ríos puestos de pie
> vislumbra su fantasía!   (pp. 433–4)

> (Through the nun's eyes
> two horsemen gallop.
> One last mute sigh
> heaves at her smock,
> and, seeing clouds and hills
> in the barren distance,
> her heart of sugar
> and verbena breaks.
> Oh, what a tall plain
> with twenty suns on high!
> What upstanding rivers
> does her fantasy visualize!)

The excess of 'twenty suns' and flooding phallic rivers measures the response of the nun's imagination to the oppression of the convent and its barren surroundings, fantasy being her only sexual release. We can guess that her religious vocation was as weak as that of the girl who complained disbelievingly in a traditional poem,

> ¿Agora que sé d'amor me metéis monja?
> ¡Ay, Dios, qué grave cosa!
> Agora que sé d'amor de caballero,
> agora me metéis monja en el monasterio.
> ¡Ay, Dios, qué grave cosa!16

> (Now that I know about love you'll make me a nun?
> My God, that's a terrible thing!
> Now that I know about a man's loving,
> you'll make me a nun and shut me in a convent.
> My God, that's a terrible thing!)

And her wishful indulgence behind closed doors is as futile and reflexive as the activity of another traditional nun:

> ¡Cómo lo tuerce y lava,
> la monjita el su cabello;
> cómo lo tuerce y lava,
> luego lo tiende al hielo.[17]
>
> (How she washes and wrings
> her hair, the pretty young nun;
> how she washes and wrings it,
> and then lays it out on the ice!)

Lorca's nun suffers from the same icy oppression under the totem
church which had been imaged most unfavourably earlier in the
poem: 'La iglesia gruñe a lo lejos / como un oso panza arriba' (p. 433)
('The church growls in the distance / like a bear on its back'). We
might also note that the contrast between taboo morality and libidinal drive is already evident in the poem's title, 'La monja gitana',
where nun and gypsy are a virtual contradiction in terms.

Other poems in *Romancero gitano* which have bearing on the sexual
theme include: 'La casada infiel' ('The Unfaithful Wife'), which deals
in flamboyantly heterosexual vein with the illicit situation of adultery
and, most likely, prostitution, and 'Romance de la pena negra' ('Ballad of the Black Suffering'), which, like 'La monja gitana', depicts
the frustration of a passionate but isolated woman whose name is
'Soledad' ('Loneliness'). Following a traditional pattern, Soledad
comes down from the mountains to seek her satisfaction, not wanting
her fine clothes and her 'muslos de amapola' (p. 437) ('poppy thighs')
to waste away for no good reason. Alone she had cried tears that
were like 'zumo de limón / agrio de espera y de boca' ('lemon juice /
bitter to the tongue from waiting'), but now, despite the poet warning
her of the dangers of the sea to which she descends, her mind is
set:

> Vengo a buscar lo que busco,
> mi alegría y mi persona.   (p. 436)
>
> (I come to seek what I seek,
> my joy and my being.)

Soledad is thus an admirable Lorquian heroine, for, whether frustrated from widowhood or simple isolation, she shamelessly puts
her human needs before the demands of social mores; nonetheless,
in search of her self, her sexual self, she suffers the same torment
and sickness as all Lorca's transgressing personae. While Soledad

leaves her lonely mountain bed to descend in sleep-walking fashion towards her goal, the male in 'Romance del emplazado' ('Ballad of the Doomed Man') lives in a waking nightmare of the imminent death predicted for him in 'naipes helados' ('frozen cards') and 'un sueño de trece barcos' (p. 451) ('a dream of thirteen boats'). We cannot be sure why this man has been singled out by his fellows for such a curse, but the fact that he does die on the stipulated day, without any violence being done to him, points to the power of the gypsies' voodoo-like superstition and to the connection of this with hypnotic auto-suggestion. His name, 'el Amargo' ('the Bitter One'), inevitably evokes immoral love, while the homosexual tones in the poem's second stanza may well be a clue to his tribal ostracism:

> Los densos bueyes del agua
> embisten a los muchachos
> que se bañan en las lunas
> de sus cuernos ondulados.
> Y los martillos cantaban
> sobre los yunques sonámbulos
> el insomnio del jinete
> y el insomnio del caballo.   (p. 451)

> (The heavy oxen of the water
> rush upon the boys
> who bathe in the moons
> of their undulating horns.
> And the hammers sang out
> on somnambular anvils
> the insomnia of the rider
> and the insomnia of the horse.)

The reduplicated curve in moons, horns and implicit waves creates a synthetic image of phallicism and fate which infers that the young lads' sexual penchant is as predetermined and irreversible as the heavy water's flow. The youths have come under the moon's perverse spell and will be carried off just as the infant boy in the haunting lullaby ballad, 'Romance de la luna, luna' ('Ballad of the Moon, Moon'), is abducted by the moon from the safety of the smithy before the gypsies can rescue him. Here we recall that the ubiquitous moon symbol essentially combines two notions: namely, sterility—'sus senos de duro estaño' (p. 425) ('her breasts of hard tin')—and death, paralleled in this instance by the sleep-inducing lullaby. Once again it would seem natural to assume that the mixing in of death and sterility is a projection of the poet's own sexually-based anxiety. Finally, the theme of abduction, so typical of anxiety dreams, appears

again in 'Preciosa y el aire' ('Preciosa and the Wind') where a young
girl flees from the lascivious 'viento-hombrón' ('wind-man'):

> Niña, deja que levante
> tu vestido para verte.   (p. 427)
>
> (Child, let me lift
> your dress to see you.)

The bogey-man wind is described also as 'viento verde' ('green
wind'), reinforcing the perverse connotations of that colour.[18] But
Lorca's preoccupation with the abduction of children and pederasty,
besides introducing another potent taboo, shows his sensitivity to
the theme of sexual corruption at formative ages, a theme he was
to explore most purposefully and psychoanalytically in *Poeta en Nueva
York*. Before considering that second major volume, however, we
turn first to a short but brilliant cinematic skit, *El paseo de Buster
Keaton* (*Buster Keaton's Ride*), which is largely based on the theme
of corruption and which, stylistically, provides a useful stepping stone
to the avant-garde Lorca of New York.

El paseo de Buster Keaton, written in July 1925, is a four-page piece
of hybrid genre. Classified as *Teatro breve* (*Short Theatre*) in Lorca's
Obras completas, it has clear cinematic characteristics besides having
been inspired by one of the most famous comics of the silent-movies.
Lorca referred to it as a 'diálogo fotografiado'[19] ('photographed dialogue'), and it contains the odd cinematic allusion such as 'gros plan'
(p. 895), ('close up'). Yet much of the piece is neither stageable nor
filmable, but only readable, its images having a distinctly poetic
resonance. Not strictly a film-script, then, *El paseo de Buster Keaton*
rather feeds off the cinema, and the rush and inventiveness of its
images capture the texture of celluloid gymnastics and the mood
of the flickering 'dream-house' which so entranced Lorca, Buñuel
and Dalí in their Residencia days. In its oneiric atmosphere, its
brevity and its simple focus on the predicament of one character,
the piece is not far removed from the ballads of the *Romancero gitano*;
indeed, Keaton's bicycle ride has much the same momentum and
sense of quest as found in the ballads. Its plot, as such, depicts
Keaton on an afternoon ride in a city park (Philadelphia is mentioned), and, after the incongruous opening in which Keaton kills
his four children with a wooden dagger (presumably a movie prop),

the comic hero goes off chasing butterflies, sighs disconsolately—'¡Ay amor, amor!' (p. 894) ('Oh love, love!')—and is accosted in turn by two women, the second of whom promptly faints on being told that she is speaking to no less a person than Buster Keaton. Finally, in a manner unmistakably reminiscent of 'Romance sonámbulo', the piece closes with an image of a police car's shining light, leaving us to wonder if the police come for Keaton, and, if so, whether for the intial unexplained filicide or for his later encounters. Thus, while ostensibly humorous and slapstick in the riotous fashion of silent movies, *Buster Keaton* is also a disconcerting work in which Lorca treats familiar themes in a most innovative way. What is more, in Keaton, a film star renowned for his stone-face reaction to the constant battering he receives from his environment, Lorca redefines a ready-made character who may well be the most precise of all his male personae.

Looking first at the way Lorca depicts the urban environment, we find a typically complex and intriguing image at the start of Keaton's ride:

(*Entre las viejas llantas de goma y bidones de gasolina, un Negro come su sombrero de paja.*) (p. 893)

(*Amid old rubber tyres and gasoline cans, a Black eats his straw hat.*)

Visually the image makes a lucid statement about urban's man's oppression. The negro, who was to figure prominently in *Poeta en Nueva York*, represents a class and racial concept, much as the gypsy did in *Romancero gitano*. The negro is similarly at the bottom of the social heap and, being historically much closer than the white man to nature, has associations with the pure primitive. The victimized Black might well have to eat his straw hat to stay alive in the harsh economic reality of the 1920s. But his straw hat is also the emblem of his caricature as coon and minstrel, the very symbol of his degradation; thus his eating of it could be taken as submissive acceptance of his role, or, alternatively, as a prophetic statement of revolt via destruction. The image very likely carries erotic connotations too, since *comer paja* ('to eat straw') is Granada slang for masturbation, a theme which is picked up later in the piece. Certainly Lorca presents the negro in a state of total frustration, besieged by junk and alienated from the human dimension, all of which anticipates the love theme that is soon to develop. Continuing on his way, Keaton next sees a variety of birds. Surprisingly the initial dawn motif of 'Kikirikí' ('Cock-a-doodle-doo') from the *Gallo* (*Cock*)—which incidentally recalls the trumpeting opening of *Pathe News*—is followed almost immediately by the 'Chirrrrrrrr' of the presumably disorientated *Búho* (*Owl*). We later find that this is consistent with the condensing of time-scale in the reference to autumn's 'sudden invasion' of the park, a foreshortening device which evokes cinematic trickery. Consistency is also apparent in that Lorca continues the bird or winged motif throughout, there being mention of a *parrot, ostrich, swan, nightingale, butterflies, angels, seraphim* and *wasp* in addition to the *Cock* and *Owl*. The image of the parrot provides a clue to this pattern:

> (*Un loro revolotea en el cielo neutro.*) (p. 893)

> (*A parrot flutters about in the neutral sky.*)

A surprising choice of bird for an urban setting, the parrot develops the sense of incongruity begun with the murder. The sky in which it flies is *neutral*, indicative of the unsympathetic response of the environment; though here too we remember the sexual implications of the word neutral found in 'Adán' ('Adam'): 'Pero otro Adán oscuro está soñando / neutra luna de piedra sin semilla' (p. 353) ('But another dark Adam is dreaming / a neutral moon of seedless stone'). However, the two primary points made by the parrot/sky image— incongruity and uncongeniality—soon become thematic. Incongruity receives impetus from further exoticisms: the *cabeza de ruiseñor* (*nightingale head*) of the *Joven* (*Young Girl*) her *piernas ... como dos cebras agonizantes* (p. 896) (*legs ... like two zebras in the throes of death*), Keaton's *ojos de avestruz* (p. 894) (*ostrich eyes*). In addition there is the distortion of dimension, notably of time-scale, as already mentioned, and of the spatial dimension: *El paisaje se achica entre las ruedas de la máquina ... La bicicleta tiene una sola dimensión. Puede entrar en los libros y tenderse en los hornos de pan* (p. 894) (*The landscape grows small between the machine's wheels ... The bicycle has just one dimension. It can get into books and stretch out in bread ovens*). Finally, incongruity is also present in the actions and statements of Keaton which will be considered presently.

The second thematic pattern, that of urban environment's negative and oppressive force, displays itself in a variety of ways. Fundamentally, society is seen as predatory, feeding off nature, as explicit in the description of the shoes worn by the *Americana* (*American Woman*): '¡Oh, qué zapatos! No debemos admitir esos zapatos. Se necesitan las pieles de tres cocodrilos para hacerlos' (p. 895) ('Oh, what shoes! Such shoes ought not to be allowed. It would take the skins of three crocodiles to make them'). This notion of an all-devouring city will reach its peak in 'New York. Oficina y denuncia' ('New York. Office and Denunciation') in *Poeta en Nueva York*:

> Todos los días se matan en Nueva York
> cuatro millones de patos,
> cinco millones de cerdos,
> dos mil palomas para el gusto de los agonizantes,
> un millón de corderos
> y dos millones de gallos
> que dejan los cielos hechos añicos.   (pp. 515–6)

> (Every day in New York they kill
> four million ducks,
> five million pigs,
> two thousand pigeons to please the dying men,
> one million cows,
> one million lambs
> and two million cocks
> who leave the skies in shreds.)

Besides having a voracious appetite, the city also perverts both nature and man. In the following sequence from *Buster Keaton* the artificially enlarged roses suggest an abuse of nature, while man is presented as so vulgarized and corrupted by his environment that he has literally lost his senses:

> *Los habitantes de esta urbe ya saben que el viejo poema de la máquina Singer puede circular entre las grandes rosas de los invernaderos, aunque no podrán comprender nunca qué sutilísima diferencia poética existe entre una taza de te caliente y otra taza de te frío.*

> (*The inhabitants of this city know very well that the old poem about the Singer sewing-machine can mix with the huge roses of the greenhouses, but they will never understand what an extremely subtle poetic difference exists between a hot cup of tea and a cold cup of tea.*)

The song of the Singer sewing-machine, notorious for its gross allusions to female masturbation, is allowed by the relaxed mores of American society in the 1920s. But the end result of such warped permissiveness, Lorca goes on to imply, is a complete obliteration of the senses, an inability to tell hot from cold. Now we can see that Lorca's system of incongruous images and his theme of the city's oppression are really complementary ideas. The surprise of the parrot and other exoticisms are no longer surprising in the context of a modern American city where anything goes. In the line of Huysmans, Lorca's point is that the city, in offering exotic but denying simple experiences, perverts man and turns his values upside-down. Only the extreme registers with his dimmed faculties, only the incongruous makes sense: *Adán y Eva correrían asustados si vieran un vaso lleno de agua, y acariciarían, en cambio, la bicicleta de Keaton* (p. 894) (*Adam and Eve would run away in fright if they saw a glass full of water, and they would caress, instead, Keaton's bicycle*). This last image is an effective means of stressing the simplicity or innocence of Keaton's bicycle, but it is also an ironical comment on the idea that modern man has to base his values on mechanical objects for points of reference. Man is as far removed from nature and from true values as the exotic animals are from their natural habitat. The city is in fact a zoo for the one and a prison for the other. This same double theme appears in Lorca's sketch, 'Perspectiva urbana con autorretrato' (p. 1845) ('Urban Perspective with a Self-Portrait'), where a number of strange and nightmarish animals stand between highrise towers, one of them kicking out his hind legs in frustration, as the equally tormented poet weaves amongst them. Now we can appreciate Keaton's tragic sigh, '¡Ay amor, amor!' ('Oh love, love!'), for if the city's excesses have dimmed man's senses they have also deprived him of his one means of salvation. Without the proper capacity to communicate, man is trapped, isolated from human contact, related only to mechanical props, as the Black to the junk-yard, Keaton to his bicycle and the young girls to their Singer machines. It is in the light of this distortion of values that Keaton's murdering of his children begins to make sense.

In this unwholesome environment the figure of Buster Keaton has a most apt function and eminently Lorquian role to perform. His stone face appears amidst Lorca's hostile props as the epitome of passivity. Apart from his first action everything he does is innocuous. His statements are idiotically simple: 'Uno, dos, tres y cuatro' ('One, two, three and four'), he counts his dead children; 'Da gusta pasearse en bicicleta' ('It's nice to ride about on a bicycle'), he says like a child, and again, ingenuously, 'Esto es un jardín' ('This is a park'), all of which are the kind of clipped remarks that could be flashed on screen. But we soon know that Keaton's vacant disposition stems from frustration, and we gather from his mumbling to himself that this is rooted in love, a point supported by the cliché image of his frantic gropings after elusory butterflies. With the suggestion of an erotic dilemma Lorca superimposes his own preoccupations, and in the main description the poet's empathy with the sad clown is manifest:

(*Sigue andando. Sus ojos, infinitos y tristes, como los de una bestia recién nacida, sueñan lirios, ángeles y cinturones de seda. Sus ojos, que son de culo de vaso. Sus ojos de niño tonto. Que son feísimos. Que son bellísimos. Sus ojos de avestruz. Sus ojos humanos en el equilibrio seguro de la melancolía...*)   (p. 894)

(*He goes on his way. His eyes, infinite and sad, like the eyes of a new-born beast, dream of lilies, angels and silk girdles. His eyes, which are like the bottom of a glass. His silly child's eyes. Which are terribly ugly. Which are terribly beautiful. His ostrich eyes. His human eyes in the sure equilibrium of melancholy...*)

The clear implication is of an heroic character bearing a tragedy to which he has been fated since birth. In this context of inherited suffering we can infer that the initial infanticide was really an act of euthanasia, freeing youth from the disease of corruption that awaits them. All that is left of value in Keaton himself is his eyes, which still have the capacity to dream. They are revealing, sensitive, with a childlike innocence and vulnerability which suggests by contrast that the remainder of his stone-faced appearance, besides its connotations of numbness, is a protective mask he has learn to grow as a means of combating the vulgar aggression of his environment.

Soon this aggression is emphatically represented in the Americana, a tart, who puts purity to the test with her direct propositioning and strikes at Keaton's tenderest spot by inquiring about his sexual leanings:

AMERICANA: ¿Tiene usted una espada adornada con hojas de mirto?
(*Buster Keaton se encoge de hombros y levanta el pie derecho.*)
AMERICANA: ¿Tiene usted un anillo con la piedra envenenada?
(*Buster Keaton cierra lentamente los ojos y levanta el pie izquierdo.*)
AMERICANA: ¿Pues entonces?

AMERICAN WOMAN: Do you have a sword adorned with myrtle leaves?
(*Buster Keaton shrugs his shoulders and lifts his right foot.*)
AMERICAN WOMAN: Do you have a ring with a poisoned stone?
(*Buster Keaton closes his eyes slowly and lifts his left foot.*)
AMERICAN WOMAN: Well then?

In symbolic terms that are as crude as befits the speaker, the tart's questions alternate between the phallic *espada* (*sword*)—with accessory connotations of love in *mirto* (*myrtle*)—and the vulviform *anillo* (*ring*), which, with the perversion motif *envenenada* (*poisoned*), suggests the homosexual. Keaton's mime, evoking the actions of a dog, is also consistent with the vulgarity of the encounter. It may be argued that Keaton does not commit himself to a response, that he remains neutral, but there is a definite progression from the shrugging of his shoulders in answer to the first question to the slow closing of his eyes in answer to the second, clearly an act of resignation. In any event the subsequent images of *serafines con alas de gasa celeste* (*seraphims with wings of heavenly gauze*), *flores* (*flowers*) and piano music seem in their parody of Hollywood romanticism to imply a successful conclusion to the soliciting. Now Keaton has to withstand all kinds of contrived, seductive stimuli: *El vals, la luna y las canoas estremecen el precioso corazón de nuestro amigo* (p. 895) (*The waltz, the moon and the canoes make our friend's lovely heart tingle*). But the situation is relieved by a sudden temporal jump which Lorca expresses in one of his most precise and beautiful images:

> (... *Con gran sorpresa de todos, el Otoño ha invadido el jardín, como el agua al geométrico terrón de azúcar.*)   (p. 895)

> (... *To everyone's great surprise, Autumn has invaded the park, like water on a geometrical cube of sugar.*)

Here visual exactness evidently lies in the way that the simile captures the idea of disintegration and even of colour change, both associated with autumn. But also admirable is the integral quality of the image in relation to the whole piece: sustaining the distortion of both time and space, the image comments too on urban man's sad plight of only being able to understand nature—*Autumn*—in relation to what is man-made, *terrón de azúcar* (*cube of sugar*). Hinting at the kind of urban tedium explicit in Eliot's 'I have measured out my life with coffee spoons' ('The Love Song of J. Alfred Prufrock'), the *geometrical* quality of the cube of sugar is also evocative of urban form, while its disintegration recalls the Black's destruction of his stereotype in his eating of his hat.

Thematically the piece culminates in the next sequence where we find Keaton alone, his melancholy unrelieved, dreaming of release:

> BUSTER KEATON (*suspirando*): Quisiera ser un cisne. Pero no puedo aunque quisiera. Porque ¿dónde dejaría mi sombrero? ¿Dónde mi cuello de pajarita y mi corbata de moaré? ¡Qué desgracia!   (pp. 895–6)

> BUSTER KEATON (*sighing*): I would like to be a swan. But I can't, much as I'd like to be. Because, where would I leave my hat? Where my high collar and my silky tie? What a shame!

We are back to the characteristic desire for a transformation of identity, in which context the swan presumably represents purity. Once again the speaker realizes the impossibility of his wish, though the reasons given seem at first ridiculous, in keeping only with Keaton's role as a 'niño tonto' ('silly child'). Change is impossible because, at face value, the persona is laden with the showy trappings of urban society which he is reluctant to surrender. At a more subjective level, this implies that Keaton cannot decontaminate himself from the depravity which has seduced him, that he has a kind of narcotic dependence on luxury, and secondly that he cannot free himself from the stereotype he has become. The detail of fine items of clothing suggests a dandy figure, developing the point of the American Woman's second question. When Keaton then inadvertently causes Joven (Young Girl) to faint, presumably because he is a film-star, we suspect that part of the problem of being imprisoned in one's own identity is fame, which was no doubt Lorca's own experience too, increasingly so. Keaton can only excuse himself with the childish ellipsis, '¡perdóneme, que yo no he sido!' (p. 896) ('Excuse me, but I'm not the one to blame!'), and the piece closes in ritualistic formula with the prospect of the police arriving. The cinematic Keaton would no doubt set them a comic chase, but Lorca's Keaton is as likely to pay for his indiscretions as was Antoñito el Camborio and the younger man in 'Romance sonámbulo'. By the end Lorca has converted the superficial frivolity of the silent-movie world into a sombre work of his own. And in Keaton, with the rich symbolism of his handsome mask-like face, with his bicycle as a tragicomic and disembowelled inversion of the old *jinete* (horserider) motif, Lorca found a perfect projection of his own sense of alienation.

It was personal problems that drove Lorca to New York in June 1929. As early as 1926 he had spoken in a letter to Guillén of 'una gana aguda de alejarme de España (p. 1609) ('an acute longing to get away from Spain'), but things had come to a head by 1929, the year in which Dalí met Gala and, more significantly, when Emilio Aladrén—the young Madrilenian sculptor to whom 'Romance del emplazado' ('Ballad of the Doomed Man') was dedicated—broke off his affair with Lorca after meeting the woman he would marry.[20] Lorca was now an extremely well known figure; the *Romancero gitano* had come out to great acclaim in July 1928 and his first successful play, *Mariana Pineda*, had been staged in Barcelona and Madrid. When Margarita Xirgu, Spain's most famous actress, took the play to Granada in May 1929, Lorca made a gracious speech at the banquet in their mutual honour, thanking the people of Granada for their tribute, but ending with a remarkably candid statement about how he was now engaged in a 'duelo a muerte' ('fight to the death') with his poetry and with his own heart:

> Con mi corazón, para librarlo de la pasión imposible que destruye y de la sombra falaz del mundo que lo siembra de sol estéril; con la poesía, para construir, pese a ella que se defiende como una virgen, el poema despierto y verdadero donde la belleza y el horror y lo inefable y lo repugnante vivan y se entrechoquen en medio de la más candente alegría. (p. 130)

> (With my heart, in order to free it from the impossible passion which destroys it and from the world's fallacious shadow which plants seeds of a sterile sun in it; with poetry, in order to construct, though it defends itself like a virgin, the true and vital poem in which beauty and horror and the ineffable and the repugnant live and collide together in the most candescent joy.)

That Lorca could speak at such a time and such a place about his 'impossible passion'—impossible, we note, because of the 'world' or society at large—is a measure of his new resolution, a resolution which, we also note, incorporated an intention to deal more openly with certain matters in his poetry. He had already been speaking in his letters about 'mi nueva manera *espiritualista*' (p. 1654) ('my new *spiritualist* style') and of writing 'una poesía de abrirse las venas' (p. 1664) ('a poetry of an opening of the veins'). While this new poetry was no doubt partly born from his offence at having been branded by some as a folkloric Andalusian poet of *gitanería* ('gypsy culture'), it was also plainly an expression of an inner need, a need to resolve what he had recognised ten years earlier as the 'enigma de mí mismo'[21] ('enigma of my own self'). His decision to go to New York, ostensibly to study English at Columbia University, was similarly a response to a deep psychological need. On the one hand it was a flight—the classical defence mechanism—an escape from himself, his past, his fame and his recent calamities, for he confided to a friend that his soul had been 'estremecida como un pequeño antílope por las últimas brutales flechas'[22] ('shaken like a small antelope by the recent brutal arrows'). At the same time it was also a search for something new, a new experience, a new identity, perhaps his true self which might be found in the meditation that relative anonymity allows. Yet New York was hardly the ideal retreat, and, given Lorca's preconceptions about American cities noted in *Buster Keaton*, one cannot help thinking, finally, that there was a punitive

element in this self-imposed exile. Lorca himself was determined
to go but unclear about his motives, as he wrote immediately prior
to his departure, 'Yo estoy muerto de risa por esta decisión.
Pero me conviene y es importante en mi vida' (p. 1673) ('I'm dying of
laughter at this decision. But it's the best for me and is important
in my life'). And shortly after, from the boat that had left Southamp-
ton, he wrote: 'No sé para qué he partido; me lo pregunto cien veces
al día. Me miro en el espejo del estrecho camarote y no me reconozco.
Parezco otro Federico'[23] ('I don't know why I've left; I ask myself
a hundred times a day. I look at myself in the mirror in my cramped
cabin and I don't recognize myself. I seem a different Federico').

He was to look hard at himself in New York too, and, as Derek
Harris rightly observes of Lorca's most intriguing, confessional and
self-analytical work, *Poeta en Nueva York*, 'The fundamental subject
of the book is the poet not the city'.[24] Indeed, there is nothing really
new or unexpected in its depiction of the city, nothing that was
not already anticipated in *Buster Keaton*. Rather there is a lot more
of the same, perhaps too much in strictly artistic terms, as Lorca
seemed to recognize in saying of the book he would never publish
in his own lifetime: 'Es un libro enorme, larguísimo. Un libro para
matar a uno' (p. 1730) ('It's an enormous book, extremely long.
A killing sort of book'). In it we see in epic scale the same junk,
filth, corruption and oppression of human values, the same down-
trodden Negro, dislocated exoticisms, frenetic stimuli, the same abuse
of nature and unnatural abuse of man as we glimpsed in *Buster Keaton*;
in short, the same prison and the same zoo. But if Lorca found
New York just as he had expected, he vented his anger and disgust
upon it with a vengeance and in a tirade of acid images he had
hitherto been unable to unleash. And this, surely, is the point,
especially if we bear in mind his comment prior to departure, 'New
York me parece horrible, pero por eso mismo me voy allí' (p. 1637)
('New York seems horrible to me, but that is precisely why I am
going there'), the point being that Lorca used New York as a pretext
and as a whipping boy, that is, in literary terms, metonymically,
or, in dream terms, as a displaced object upon which to transfer
and vent his anger. It was not New York itself that Lorca hated—
hateful as the city probably was to him—but rather society at large,
society with a big 'S', which the great metropolis so manifestly epitomizes, the society or 'world' which had made his love and his life
'impossible'. At the same time the nightmare of New York is clearly
a projection of Lorca's own nightmare, notably with regard to its

depravity *vis-à-vis* the poet's sexual guilt. Thus the city has a dual function: it is a cathartic facility which enables the poet to release a flood of repressed emotions and protestations which he felt unable to release in Spain where the seeds of his frustration were sown, and it is at once a mirror image which objectivizes his inner hell and lays open his worst dream to therapeutic analysis. There are new emphases, of course, significantly a religious emphasis in which Lorca expresses a bitter sense of having been betrayed by the Church. This culminates in the near hysterical 'Grito hacia Roma' (p. 520) ('Shout at Rome'), which curses the Pope for having signed in 1929 a concordat with Mussolini, but which is so bilious and scathing that not only could it not have been written in Spain but, we suspect, the wrath which it vents is rooted in a personal rather than political anguish. In these religious poems we are already encroaching upon the real substance of *Poeta en Nueva York*, the poet himself. Without wishing to decry the city poems, ferociously evocative and deeply personal as they ultimately are, the poems most germane to our present discussion are those of self-contemplation and retreat, a handful of which we now consider by way of conclusion.

Poeta en Nueva York begins with four poems which have the collective title 'Poemas de la soledad en Columbia University' ('Poems of Solitude in Columbia University'), and the first of these, 'Vuelta de paseo' ('Return from a Walk'), is indicative of the volume's system in which the poet contemplates the disaster of his own personality against the horrific backcloth of the city. Describing himself in the poem's first and last lines as 'Asesinado por el cielo' (p. 471) ('Assassinated by the sky'), Lorca announces his desperate psychic state and—in 'cielo' ('sky' or 'heaven')—points an accusing finger at God, the Church, totemic morality. The rapid images at the poem's centre reinforce the idea of destruction and mutilation—especially 'árbol de muñones' ('tree of stumped branches'), 'animalitos de cabeza rota' ('little animals with broken heads') and 'mariposa ahogada en el tintero' ('butterfly drowned in the inkwell')—then the poem closes with an image that pinpoints Lorca's identity crisis:

> Tropezando con mi rostro distinto de cada día.
> ¡Asesinado por el cielo!   (p. 471)

> (Stumbling across my face that is different every day.
> Assassinated by the sky!)

The multiple faces suggest a schizoid, disintegrating self, a disintegration treated in later poems such as 'Nocturno del hueco' (p. 507)

('Nocturne of the Hollow Man'). But what is the source of this neurosis and how does Lorca attempt to come to terms with it? The volume's second poem, '1910 (Intermedio)' ('1910 (Intermediate)'), provides an answer, it being one of several in which the poet recalls his youth, specifically here the age of twelve. The opening stanza suggests improbably that he was then still unaware of death, but we learn from subsequent images that death has to be understood in the context of sexuality, that is, as a metaphor for the loss of innocence. Thus the poet refers to that critical phase when he was on the threshold of puberty and sexual awareness, a delicate, 'intermediate' stage. The second and third stanzas consist of a series of images in free association which recollect the twelve-year-old's decisive impressions about sexuality, their unmistakable inference being that of a developing antipathy on the part of the youth towards the female:

> Aquellos ojos míos de mil novecientos diez
> vieron la blanca pared donde orinaban las niñas,
> el hocico del toro, la seta venenosa
> y una luna incomprensible que iluminaba por los rincones
> los pedazos de limón seco bajo el negro duro de las botellas.

> Aquellos ojos míos en el cuello de la jaca,
> en el seno traspasado de Santa Rosa dormida,
> en los tejados del amor, con gemidos y frescas manos,
> en un jardín donde los gatos se comían a las ranas.　　　　(p. 472)

> (Those eyes of mine of nineteen ten
> saw the white walls where the girls pissed,
> the bull's snout, the poisonous mushroom
> and an incomprehensible moon that lit up in corners
> pieces of dry lemon beneath the hard black of bottles.

> Those eyes of mine on the horse's neck,
> on the pierced heart of the sleeping Saint Rose,
> on the rooftops of love, with groanings and cool hands,
> in a garden where the cats ate up the frogs.)

From the first degrading image of girls to the last predatory association—which derives, it has been suggested, from Lorca having been told as a child that the sound of cats copulating in the garden came from cats eating frogs[25]—we have a complex and cryptically personal catalogue of the boy's disgust, fear and confusion. The dual orifices of the bull's nostrils suggest the female with overtones of *vagina dentata*; the 'seta' ('mushroom') is a taboo word for vagina and again has a negative complement in 'venenosa' ('poisonous'); the bottles in corners suggest a bar scene and prostitution, reinforced this time by the oneiric fatalism of 'moon' and 'lemon'; the phallic 'horse's neck', plus the erection motif and possible clandestine implications of 'rooftops of love', combine with 'groaning and cool hands' to suggest masturbation; finally in the martyrdom of Saint Rose we have the typically confusing image of woman as presented by the Church, it being at once horrific, sado-masochistic, bloody or menstrual, and yet untouchably pure and remote.

In saying that these two convincing and authentically personal stanzas consist of images in 'free association', we come close to describing their author as a Surrealist, free association being central to the Surrealists' theory of spontaneity and automatic writing. Yet it is often said that Lorca stops short of this last critical step which requires a complete surrender to the irrational forces of the unconscious. Luis Buñuel, for instance, would not admit Lorca to the Surrealists' coterie, saying caustically in 1928: 'Federico quiere hacer cosas surrealistas, pero falsas, hechas con la inteligencia, que es incapaz de hallar lo que halla el instinto'[26] ('Federico wants to make Surrealist things, but they are false, made with the intelligence, which is not capable of finding what the instinct finds'). From Lorca's own comments of the same year, however, we saw that he had no wish to gatecrash that inner sanctum and his view of his own poems partly accepts Buñuel's distinction:

> Responden a mi nueva manera *espiritualista*, emoción pura, descarnada, desligada del control lógico, pero, ¡ojo!, ¡ojo!, con una tremenda lógica poética. No es surrealismo, ¡ojo!, la conciencia más clara los ilumina.
>
> (p. 1654)

> (They reflect my new *spiritualist* style, a pure, lean emotion detached from logical control, but—be warned!—with a tremendous poetic logic. It's not Surrealism—be warned!—for a very clear consciousness informs them.)

We might protest that the didactic and often heavy-handed director of *L'Age d'or* also made things with his intelligence, but it would be pointless to deny Lorca's rider about poetic logic. The real issue, however, centres upon free association and the extent to which this is possible in art, be it poetry, painting or film. What we need to remember is that free association was a Freudian idea picked up by the Surrealists; that for Freud it referred to the way in which the unconscious mind worked, notably in dreams, and that it thus became the key to his interviewing technique in sessions which attempted to reach the pyschogenesis or root of a patient's disturbance. In these terms, the main distinction between Lorca and

Buñuel, it seems to me, is that Lorca uses free association actively and earnestly for his own therapy in such a poem as the last one read, while Buñuel in his films uses it more flamboyantly as a theoretical exegesis of Freudian ideas and with little or no reference to personal neurosis. In short, though Lorca is probably not to be described strictly as a Surrealist, he is closer than Buñuel to the fundamental premises on which Surrealism was based. When we also bear in mind Freud's point that one of the features of dream-work is 'secondary elaboration'—an attempt by the dreamer to systemize and make sense out of his dream either upon waking or during the dream—it becomes even more difficult to make categorical distinctions of the kind Buñuel made about Lorca. One assumes that any art form would have an element of secondary elaboration, and, what is more, that there would be a lot more time for such elaboration or revision when painting a canvas or constructing a movie set than when putting pen to paper.

The foregoing is more a warning about the pitfalls inherent in Surrealist ideology than an attack upon Luis Buñuel, who, in the end, for all the predictability of his surprises and gags, is a brilliant film-maker. As for Lorca, he clearly had no time for the niceties of theory and manifesto when, as we have stressed, he was living through the kind of sexually-induced neurosis that Freud had described so well. Let us return, then, to those poems in which Lorca looks back at his youth and in which free association plays an important part in creating a release—an abreaction, in Freudian terms—of long-buried emotions. The third poem in *Poeta en Nueva York*, entitled 'Fábula y rueda de los tres amigos' (pp. 473–5) ('Fable and Ring of the Three Friends'), is based on a children's game in which the players drop out of a circle in turn. The game is given a sinister twist by Lorca in that the three boys involved are said to die—once again no doubt in the sense of losing their innocence upon gaining sexual awareness—and there is a steady progression in the stanzas which depict them as 'helados', 'quemados', 'enterrados' and 'momificados' ('frozen', 'burnt', 'buried', 'mummified'). Different reasons are given for the deaths in each case, though images of sexuality, corruption and social oppression are prominent. But when Lorca says 'Fueron los tres en mis manos' ('The three were in my hands') and 'Los vi perderse llorando y cantando' (p. 474) ('I saw them disappear crying and singing') and, in the last stanza, 'comprendí que me habían asesinado' (p. 475) ('I understood that they had killed me'), there is little room for doubt that the three boys are, as Derek

Harris suggests,[27] projections of Lorca's own youth and further fragments of his being.

In the last of the opening group of poems, 'Tu infancia en Menton' ('Your Infancy in Menton'), Lorca takes a celebratory line by Guillén—'Sí, tu niñez ya fábula de fuentes' ('Yes, your childhood now a fable of fountains')—and almost perversely reinvests this with negative values as he explores his own 'dolor de Apolo' (p. 476) ('grief of Apollo') or homosexuality. In the lines 'pasto de ruina, te afilabas / para los breves sueños indecisos' ('fodder of ruin, you sharpened yourself / for brief indecisive dreams'), there is a suggestion of being hell-bent on destruction for the sake of ephemeral sexual pleasure, but in 'yo he de buscar por los rincones / tu alma tibia' ('I have to seek in corners / for your mild soul') and again in 'Alma extraña de mi hueco de venas, / te he de buscar pequeña y sin raíces' ('Strange soul of my hollowed veins, / I have to seek you out small and rootless'), there is an urgency to discover the original, uncorrupted and prepubescent self upon which the new self is to be constructed or resurrected. A last example of poems of childhood is 'El niño Stanton' ('The Boy Stanton'), which rejoices in the innocence of a ten year old—'Tu ignorancia es un monte de leones, Stanton' (p. 502) ('Your ignorance is a mountain of lions, Stanton')—a boy who is, like Keaton, 'idiota y bello entre los pequeños animalitos' ('stupid and beautiful amongst the tiny little animals'). Lorca sees the boy as one threatened by the death values of society, that is, by the six times repeated cancer, 'vivísimo cáncer' (p. 501) ('most living cancer'), which is again based on imminent sexuality, 'el agrio cáncer mudo que quiere acostarse contigo' (p. 502) ('the bitter, silent cancer that wants to sleep with you'). By the end of the poem, having advised the boy to fight off this metaphorical death and hold fast to the values of nature, Lorca identifies so closely with the boy that he finds in him his own defence against corruption:

> Y yo, Stanton, yo solo, en olvido,
> con tus caras marchitas sobre mi boca,
> iré penetrando a voces las verdes estatuas de la Malaria.   (p. 503)

> (And I, Stanton, all alone, in oblivion,
> with your withered faces on my lips,
> will make my way loudly through the green statues of Malaria.)

These poems on childhood prepare us for one of Lorca's finest and most moving poems, 'Poema doble del lago Edem' ('Double Poem of Lake Eden'),[28] with which we conclude. It was written

in late August or early September of 1929, when, after having spent
six weeks or so in New York, Lorca went to stay at a lakeside cabin
in Vermont which belonged to the family of Phillip Cummings, a
young American he had befriended the year before at the Residencia
in Madrid. This idyllic retreat was no doubt a welcome respite from
the hurly-burly of the city, and, in his letter to Angel del Río from
Eden Mills, Lorca writes, 'Muy divertido. Es un paisaje prodigioso,
pero de una melancolía infinita' (p. 1668) ('Very pleasant. It is a
prodigious landscape, but infinitely melancholy'). He goes on to say
that he is able to spend the whole day writing and that the family
with whom he stays—including the young boy Stanton and his sister
Mary who is the tragic subject of 'Niña ahogada en el pozo'
(p. 504) ('Girl Drowned in the Well')—are extremely kind. Having
plenty of time to himself in the vast and damp landscape—'No cesa
de llover' (p. 1668) ('It doesn't stop raining')—Lorca finds that 'toda
mi infancia viene a mi memoria envuelta en una gloria de amapolas
y cereales ('my whole infancy comes to my mind swaddled in a
glory of poppies and cereals'), and he ends the letter by describing
himself as 'Perseguido en Eden Mills por el licor del romanticismo'
(p. 1669) ('Pursued in Eden Mills by the liquor of Romanticism').
Indeed the poem does have a plaintive Romantic ring, though the
free association of some of its images and, in particular, the
psychical or schizoid texture announced in the word 'doble'
('Double') of the title make it very much a poem of its time. The
duality stems from a contrast between the poet as he is now, a desperately unhappy adult, and the poet as he was as a child, for the
child's voice surfaces in his mind and reminds him, as Stanton did,
of his true self:

> Era mi voz antigua
> ignorante de los densos jugos amargos.
> La adivino lamiendo mis pies
> bajo los frágiles helechos mojados.
>
> ¡Ay voz antigua de mi amor,
> ay voz de mi verdad,
> ay voz de mi abierto costado,
> cuando todas las rosas manaban de mi lengua
> y el césped no conocía la impasible dentadura del caballo!   (p. 498)
>
> (It was my former voice
> ignorant of the thick bitter juices.
> I divine it licking my feet
> beneath the wet and fragile ferns.

Oh former voice of my love,
oh voice of my truth,
oh voice of my open side,
when all the roses flowed from my tongue
and the grass had no knowledge of the horse's impassive teeth.)

In a way strangely reminiscent of Antonio Machado the poem's opening lines set the mood of dreamlike recollection. As distinct from Machado, however, a sexual emphasis is immediately if negatively apparent in the child's ignorance, which is specifically an ignorance of semen (line 2) and of the relentless, all-devouring libido symbolized by the horse. The former pre-pubescent voice is, in its innocence, the voice of the poet's 'love' and 'truth', but also the voice of his 'abierto costado' ('open side') since his innocence has been crucified in the process of growing up. The third stanza depicts the coming together in the poet's present of these two different voices or temporal selves, while the fourth sees regression to the paradise of childhood as the only possible salvation:

Estás aquí bebiendo mi sangre,
bebiendo mi humor de niño pesado,
mientras mis ojos se quiebran en el viento
con el aluminio y las voces de los borrachos.

Déjame pasar la puerta
donde Eva come hormigas
y Adán fecunda peces deslumbrados.
Déjame pasar hombrecillos de los cuernos
al bosque de los desperezos
y los alegrísimos saltos.[29]   (p. 498)

(You are here now drinking in my blood,
drinking in my temperament of a tiresome child,
as my eyes split in the wind
with the aluminium and with the voices of drunks.

Let me pass through the door
where Eve eats ants
and Adam fertilizes dazzled fish.
Let me pass little fellows with horns
to the forest of stretchings
and the most joyous jumps.)

Notable in the last stanza quoted is that, in addition to its evocation of childhood games, there is a very strong awareness of physical life and even—in 'peces', 'desperezos' and 'saltos' ('fish', 'stretchings', 'jumps')—of sexuality. This is entirely consistent with Freud's analysis of infantile sexuality—his notion of 'polymorphous perversity'—which views the child as an extremely erotic subject but one

in whom eroticism is innocent and undifferentiated, that is, total
or polymorphous, its entire body being erogenous in contrast to the
adult's concentration upon genitalia. What the stanza thus suggests
is not a desire to escape sexuality but rather a desire to return to
the unbounded, joyful and ignorant sexuality of the child. Two stanzas later, the plea for freedom incorporates homosexuality:

> Pero no quiero mundo ni sueño, voz divina,
> quiero mi libertad, mi amor humano
> en el rincón más oscuro de la brisa que nadie quiera.
> ¡Mi amor humano!   (p. 499)

> (But I want neither world nor dream, divine voice,
> I want my freedom, my human love
> in the darkest corner of the breeze that no one needs.
> My human love!)

The lines are plain enough in their twofold rejection of 'mundo'
('world' in the sense of 'society') and of 'sueño' ('dream' in the sense
of 'fantasy') and in their plea for freedom of sexual pursuit at least
in privacy. Unfortunately, as we see in the next stanza, not only
does society hound the homosexual, it also corrupts him, perverting
his once innocent love and creating the abominable pansy:

> Esos perros marinos se persiguen
> y el viento acecha troncos descuidados.
> ¡Oh voz antigua, quema con tu lengua
> esta voz de hojalata y de talco!   (p. 499)

> (Those sea dogs chase each other
> and the wind stalks unguarded tree-trunks.
> Oh former voice, burn with your tongue
> this voice of tinplate and talcum.)

Here the reflexive chasing of 'perros marinos' ('sea dogs') might
well infer promiscuity, while the stalking wind recalls the pederasty
of 'Preciosa y el aire'. Certainly Lorca condemns his present self
in the last line where the associations of 'hojalata' ('tinplate') and
'talco' ('talcum') respectively suggest sterility and effeminacy. It is
precisely the pansy type of homosexual that Lorca attacks in 'Oda
a Walt Whitman' (p. 522) ('Ode to Walt Whitman'), a long and
magnificent poem which catalogues the failings and perversities of
'maricas' ('queers'), their worst failing being that they are not men
at all:

¡Maricas de todo el mundo, asesinos de palomas!
Esclavos de la mujer, perras de sus tocadores ...   (p. 526)

(Queers all over the world, you murderers of doves!
Slaves of woman, bitches of her boudoir ...)

By contrast, it is the extremely masculine—though homosexual—
American poet, Walt Whitman, whom Lorca idealizes. Whitman
is described as 'Adán de sangre, macho' (p. 524) ('a full-blooded
Adam, a real man'), where the well known Spanish word 'macho'
(male) conveys an ideal of power and virility lacking in the English
equivalent. There is no contradiction for Lorca, then, between homosexuality and manhood, at least not in theory; but, returning to
'Poema doble', we find in practice that it is his own lack of Whitman-
esque pride and virility that is so troubling:

Quiero llorar porque me da la gana
como lloran los niños del último banco,
porque yo no soy un hombre, ni un poeta, ni una hoja,
pero sí un pulso herido que sonda las cosas del otro lado.

Quiero llorar diciendo mi nombre,
rosa, niño y abeto a la orilla de este lago,
para decir mi verdad de hombre de sangre
matando en mí la burla y la sugestión del vocablo.[30]   (p. 499)

(I want to cry because I feel like crying
just as the boys in the back row cry,
because I am not a man, nor a poet, nor a leaf,
only a wounded pulse that sounds out things on the other side.

I want to cry saying my name,
rose, boy and fir tree on the shore of this lake,
and speak my truth as a full-blooded man
killing in me the jibe and innuendo of the word.)

These two stanzas represent the emotional climax of 'Poema doble'
and they poignantly express the poet's mental agony. It is the agony
of a man who is not able to call himself a man—'hombre de sangre'
('full-blooded man')—the agony of a man who has lost faith in himself
and who has come to look upon himself, after years of indoctrination
by society, as a dirty joke. Instead of holding to his own truth he
has accepted the verdict of society and of his super-ego, with devastat-
ing consequences. The 'niños del último banco' ('boys in the back
row') is a cryptic allusion to Lorca's own childhood which shows
just how long this process of subjugation to totemic morality has
been going on: a fellow pupil at the secondary school Lorca attended
in Granada from the age of ten informs that the future poet was

ostracized by the boys in his class who considered him effeminate
and called him Federica—which has an insulting feminine ending—
and that one particularly macho teacher consigned Lorca to the
back row of the class.[31]

'Poema doble' closes with a further plea for freedom in its penultimate stanza and then, in the last stanza, on a note of despair and
futility, the poet sensing that his time has run out:

> Así hablaba yo.
> Así hablaba yo cuando Saturno detuvo los trenes
> y la bruma y el Sueño y la Muerte me estaban buscando.
> Me estaban buscando
> allí donde mugen las vacas que tienen patitas de paje
> y allí donde flota mi cuerpo entre los equilibrios contrarios.
>
> (p. 499)
>
> (So I spoke.
> So I spoke when Saturn stopped the trains
> and mist and Dream and Death were looking for me.
> They were looking for me
> there where cows with page-boy feet bellow
> and there where my body floats between opposite balances.)

Lorca's therapeutic self-analysis is interrupted by the exigencies of
daily life. He will, for instance, have to make his way back to New
York, and, in practical terms, at a time when the holiday season
is coming to an end and transport services are less regular. The
opening line, 'Así hablaba yo' (literally, 'Thus spoke I'), has an
oracular tone in the manner of *Thus Spake Zarathustra*, and indeed
it is Lorca's 'voz divina' ('divine voice') which has been interrupted,
his visionary perception of truth terminated. The reference to Saturn
is consistent with the volume's strange tendency to interject classical
allusions. Here Saturn appears in his ominous role and one suspects
that, in addition to associations with libidinousness—i.e. saturna-
lia—Lorca has in mind the destructive giant as painted by Goya
in the thematically germane 'Saturn Devouring One of His Children',
a nightmarish canvas he would have seen in the Prado, Madrid.
In then describing himself as being sought after by 'bruma', 'Sueño'
and 'Muerte' ('mist', 'Dream', 'Death') Lorca interlocks three related
concepts. The first, 'mist', figuratively evokes the lakeside setting
at the onset of autumn and at the same time is consonant with the
recollective mood of the poem, both of which ideas appear in the
letter to Angel del Río: 'me ahogo en esta niebla y en esta tranquilidad
que hacen surgir mis recuerdos de una manera que me quema'
(p. 1669) ('I am drowning in this mist and tranquillity which make

my memories loom up in a way that scalds me'). Thus the poet is literally hunted down by childhood memories which, as we have seen, painfully remind him of how badly astray his adult life has gone. Second, the poet is sought out by 'Sueño' ('Dream'), personified in its capital letter, and while this partly continues the theme of recollection it also looks forward—in the Freudian sense of an anxiety dream—towards some imminent catastrophe. Here, then, it is not the dream of transformation that is uppermost, not the ideal dream that Walt Whitman dreamt and realized—'soñabas ser un río' (p. 524) ('you dreamt of being a river')—rather it is the terrifying dream of suffering and persecution which is described in that same poem:

> Agonía, agonía, sueño, fermento y sueño.   (p. 525)

> (Agony, agony, dream, ferment and dream.)

Naturally the ultimate persecution comes in the form of the third element said to be seeking the poet, 'Muerte' ('Death'), and again we cannot fail to be moved by the lamentable accuracy of Lorca's often repeated prophecy of his own death, especially since it was to be administered by the forces of social order, the Civil Guard. Turning to the poem's last two lines, we have, firstly, a typically unexpected visual link between cows' and a page-boy's feet, an image that works well thematically in two ways: the cows' bellow evokes the poet's terrible agony while the page-boy carries the suggestion of youth being contained inside the suffering of the mature animal or adult. The magnificent last line restates the poem's essential duality and refers to the unresolved psychic dichotomy we first met in 'Romance sonámbulo', a warring tension from which Lorca's highly dramatic poetry springs.

But though the dilemma is unresolved, that is largely society's fault and is now recognized as such, while, in personal terms, 'Poema doble', like *Poeta en Nueva York* as a whole, has brought about a release or an abreaction of emotional complexes that could not fail to be beneficial. Indeed, upon returning to New York, Lorca was shortly able to write: 'Estoy sereno y alegre. Ha vuelto a nacer aquel Federico de antes' (p. 1674) ('I am serene and happy. That old Federico has been born again'). Thus, while the rancorous city poems provided a necessary catharsis, the poems of mnemonic introspection discovered a truth to which the poet could hold, the truth of his childhood innocence, and they were of course liberating in accord with Freud's doctrine that anything which cannot be remembered cannot be left behind. Lorca left a lot behind when he finally departed America in March 1930 and there ended what he called 'la experiencia más útil de mi vida'[32] ('the most useful experience in my life'). Indeed, he was to embark upon an extremely productive phase, especially as a dramatist, though it is arguable whether as a poet he ever achieved again the same degree of intensity. The seething inner tension which accumulated through the 1920s and the poet's own twenties seems to have reached its point of combustion in New York. In *Poeta en Nueva York* we see the culmination of Lorca's persistent tendency as a poet to work out his inner dilemma through oneiric symbolism, and we also see most clearly the three aspects of dream in Lorca: dream as therapeutic recollection; dream as wish-fulfilment, incorporating the desire for a transformation of the self; and dream as anxiety, horror and prophetic nightmare. It is Lorca's ability to express his deepest inner self in an oneiric poetic idiom that makes a reading of his poems such a moving and unforgettable experience.

VII

Rafael Alberti

The Transcendental Poetics of Surrealism

Buscad, buscadlos:
en el insomnio de las cañerías olvidadas,
en los cauces interrumpidos por el silencio de las basuras.
No lejos de los charcos incapaces de guardar una nube,
unos ojos perdidos,
una sortija rota
o una estrella pisoteada.

Porque yo los he visto:
en esos escombros momentáneos que aparecen en las neblinas.
Porque yo los he tocado:
en el destierro de un ladrillo difunto,
venido a la nada desde una torre o un carro.[1]

(Look hard, look hard for them:
in the insomnia of forgotten pipelines,
in drains blocked by the silence of rubbish.
Not far from puddles that cannot contain a cloud,
a pair of lost eyes,
a broken ring
or a trampled star.

Because I have seen them:
in those momentary piles of rubble that appear in mists.
Because I have touched them:
in the isolation of a defunct brick,
fallen into the void from a tower or truck.)

Spain's finest and most authentic Surrealist poet is Rafael Alberti, another Andalusian, who was born in Puerto de Santa María in

1902 but who moved reluctantly to Madrid with his family at the age of fourteen. This move was a momentous event in Alberti's life, as he recounts in his autobiography *The Lost Grove*,[2] and a core theme in the poetry he would write is the contrast between a lost paradise of youth which he enjoyed on the shores of the Bay of Cadiz and the kind of urban dereliction depicted in the above lines, the hellish dereliction of adulthood when meaning or salvation is hard to find. Alberti's need to find meaning in objects—worthless, random objects—is what makes him a Surrealist. This ultimately metaphysical dimension to his work, rather than the over-emphasized question of technique, is what distinguishes him from Lorca for instance. Technique is not unimportant, of course, for it relates to the poet's mental instability or paranoia in the face of the world and it also has bearing on the way in which meaning is found or rediscovered in the world. But the decisive issue is the quest and need for meaning. In the above lines—which form the first half of the poem 'Los ángeles muertos' ('The Dead Angels') found near the end of Alberti's great volume, *Sobre los ángeles* (*Concerning the Angels*)—it is presented in no less stark a guise than a search for angels in rubbish. Since the angels are dead and have to be resurrected, this amounts to an attempt to restore a religious sense of transcendence to the material world which Alberti, as an atheist, accepts as finite. His search for meaning in matter, subjective meaning in objective matter, accords with Surrealism's integrational metaphysic of materio-mysticism, and it is in this context that Alberti, more than any other Spanish poet, reaches the transcendental level of the surreal. Not surprisingly, when Alberti discovered his new road to salvation he proclaimed it with all the didactic and proselytizing commitment that is typical of new converts and especially of Surrealists, as we see in his above exhortations. But the road that led him to his Surrealist pulpit and turned him into a poet-prophet was not direct, and Alberti became a Surrealist by stages.

Four years younger than Lorca, whom he greatly admired, Alberti began his career in similar vein as a traditional poet. His first volume, *Marinero en tierra* (*Sailor on Land*) of 1924, was a lyrical recollection of the Atlantic waters he had left behind:

> El mar. La mar.
> El mar. ¡Sólo la mar!
>
> ¿Por qué me trajiste, padre,
> a la ciudad?

¿Por qué me desenterraste
del mar?

En sueños, la marejada
me tira del corazón.
Se lo quisiera llevar.

Padre, ¿por qué me trajiste
acá?   (p. 51)

(The sea. The sea.
The sea. Only the sea!

Why did you bring me, father,
to the city?

Why did you uproot me
from the sea?

In dreams, the rip tide
pulls at my heart.
It wants to take it back.

Father, why did you bring me
here?)

The blunt answer to Alberti's question is that his father had to go
to Madrid to make a living. The Alberti family, once important
wine merchants in Puerto de Santa María, had come down in the
world and his father was now a mere employee of one of the new
big-name companies that would export the fortified wines of Jerez
to the whole world. The decline of his family would deeply trouble
Alberti and it is an important factor in the bitter nostalgia of his
later poetry. But for the most part *Marinero en tierra* lacks the anger
and remorse that would surface later and Alberti is content to develop
simple topoi along the lines of traditional poetry:

¡Qué blanca lleva la falda
la niña que se va al mar!

¡Ay niña, no te la manche
la tinta del calamar!   (p. 69)

(How white is the skirt
on the girl who goes to sea!

Watch it doesn't get stained,
girl, by the ink of the squid!)

Though Lorca's phenomenal success in this idiom has partly eclipsed
Alberti's early verse, one can only admire the lightness and innocence
of the latter's rhythms which in this sense are even closer in spirit
to the oral tradition.

After a further two short collections Alberti briefly turned baroque
with *Cal y canto* (*Lime and Song*), written in 1926–7 for the tercentenary
celebrations of Góngora. Stylistically the cultured intricacies of the
baroque are as distant from traditional poetry as from the Surrealist
verse that Alberti would write next, but there is a certain common
ground and Alberti's poetic development is not as erratic as it might
seem. The point of connection is that in *Cal y canto*, which as a
colloquial phrase also means 'robust' or 'strong', Alberti, like Góngora himself, focuses on the concrete world of objects, objects which
are no less robust in their concreteness than the 'pipelines', 'drains'
and 'rubble' we met in the first poem. As Jorge Guillén said in
his fine commentary on Góngora: 'The solid world of Góngora takes
refuge in robust quietness . . . Images and metaphors are drawn primarily from the concrete world. In Góngora's poetry there will always
be many more things, or ideas of things, than abstract ideas . . .
Objective poetry it is, through its fondness for the physical world
. . . the object among objects, the most beloved of all'.[3] And so it
is with the baroque Alberti, whose poems on the bullfight, a railway
station and even a tram ticket are teeming with substantives. On
the same basis one could argue that what characterizes traditional
poetry above all else is the persistent concreteness of its nouns and
objects. Though undeniably symbolical and allusive, its motifs are
taken from a real and circumscribed world of things, be they oranges
or squids, and this 'thinginess' is never lost in authentic traditional
poetry. But concreteness is more marked in the baroque, as it would
be in Surrealism, and, for all their differences, the same objective
worldliness that is so evident in the lines that began this chapter
is to be found in Góngora and in Alberti's impressive imitation of
him:

> El viento, ya empinado,
> tromba la barba y mar veloz de nieve
> la cola, al peregrino extraviado,
> haciendo de su sombra puntería,
> le enseña, al par que la borrasca mueve
> de los árboles fría,
> la del verde aguacero artillería.   (p. 223)

(The wind, now reared up high,
beard a-whirl and tail a speedy sea
of snow, to the lost peregrine,
taking aim at his shadow,
shows, as it meanwhile stirs
the cold tempest of the trees,
the green downpour's artillery.)

Out of context, the meaning of the above stanza may escape us, but its plasticity does not. The syntax is another challenge, though, as Guillén says of Góngora's syntax, its muscularity and architectural quality is largely intended to reinforce the sense of solidity, especially when, as in the last line, it produces two consecutive substantives. Admittedly, the 'wind', 'whirl', 'beard', 'sea', 'snow', 'tail', 'trees', 'downpour' strike a different chord than the 'pipelines', 'drains', 'rubbish', 'rubble' and 'brick' of the Surrealist poem, but this is a question of selection or environment, nature as opposed to the city. Moreover, there is a common underlying purpose to the torrent of substantives found in both. Guillén refers us to the 'fitting formula' by which Pedro Salinas describes Góngora's purpose as 'the exaltation of reality', and he quotes Salinas's telling lines: 'Góngora is enamoured of the real. But he exalts it, ennobles it in such a way that the world becomes a marvelous feast for the imagination and the senses'.[4] Clearly this is what happens in the baroque Alberti, for instance in 'Madrigal al billete del tranvía' (p. 226) ('Madrigal to the Tram Ticket') where the humble object becomes a 'flor nueva' and 'pétalo' ('new flower' and 'petal') through a kind of poetic alchemy summarized in the title of another poem, 'Metamorfosis y ascensión' (p. 220) ('Metamorphosis and Ascension'). But this worldly metamorphosis is precisely what happens too in the Surrealist Alberti whose search for transcendence hic et nunc similarly exalts the real. He is not exactly enamoured of pipelines and rubbish, it is true, but he does tell us that what transcendence there is, is to be found only in such real things. Naturally it is not the thing in itself that is transcendent; it has to be metamorphosed and resurrected by man. Hitherto, in Góngora and in the poem on a tram ticket, for instance, the agent of change was poetry, poetic imagination, and the poet brought his inventiveness to bear catalytically upon objective reality. But in the late 1920s the Surrealist poet has learnt to identify his imagination with what he now calls his unconscious, and, in place of inventiveness or even talent, it is his unconscious—complete with its neuroses—that he brings to bear upon objective reality. Not any man can do this; only the Surrealist, only the man who has been through hell to emerge a paranoiac. At least, if not clinically paranoiac, the Surrealist is a man who has undergone traumatic and ultimately liberating psychical changes, changes which allow him to put his anguished mental life to a new and penetrating creative use. This is the crucial link which Surrealism makes, the link between mental anguish and transcendentalism. In this it completes the cycle begun by Romanticism.

Sobre los ángeles, written in 1927–8, charts Alberti's mental crisis and with it his final steps towards Surrealism. It is a Surrealist work, but also a work which becomes progressively more Surrealist. This we can appreciate by relating the work to the development of Surrealism itself, determined and validated as this was by André Breton and his circle in Paris, and signposted as it was by Breton's manifestos of 1924 and 1930. What we need to remember is that whereas Freud was the guiding light in the first manifesto this role was taken over by Hegel in the second. It was Freud's influence which had been largely responsible for the way in which Dada's nihilist revolt was redirected by Surrealism towards the potentially creative domain of the unconscious with its dream images and free association. But the point of divergence between Freudian and Surrealist thinking is found in the latter's more positive view of the unconscious. Though Surrealists continued to accept Freud's thesis that the unconscious is a disorderly world of repressions, anxieties and neuroses, they also argued that the verbal and image projections which came from that world in dream or psychic dictation were indicative of the richness of the human mind, not merely of its disintegration. Contrary to Freud, the Surrealists exalted the imaginative faculty of the unconscious and even attributed prophetic powers to dream. Above all they rejected Freud's distinction between psychic and material reality, and instead, noting the remarkable concreteness of dream images, took this as confirmation of the mind's tendency towards synthesis. Specifically, they saw in the Surrealist image—which treats the object as an object, never an abstraction—a confirmation of Hegel's metaphysic of the phenomenology of mind, that is, of materio-mysticism, which Breton described in the second manifesto as 'the penetrability of subjective life by "substantial" life'.[5] Thus, while the bizarre and the incongruous remained the most readily indentifiable features of Surrealism, by the late 1920s the movement had assumed a deeper metaphysical purpose under the ascendancy of Hegel, one that envisaged man's highest faculty—his imaginative unconscious—being directed towards and united with the objects of this world.[6] This second Surrealist phase is reflected in 'Los ángeles muertos' and it would be the theme of the short, underrated volume which Alberti wrote next, *Sermones y moradas* (*Sermons and Dwelling Places*) of 1929–30. But *Sobre los ángeles* also reflects the initial Freudian phase of Surrealism and, in large part, like Lorca's *Poeta en Nueva York*, it is a psycho-dynamic work of self-analysis in which the poet seeks to effect a catharsis or abreaction of the deep-seated tensions that have caused his neurosis. In order, then, to appreciate the transcendental thrust of Alberti's Surrealism we must consider his mental crisis which was in effect his conduit and 'open sesame' to Surrealism proper.

Alberti's mental crisis in 1927–8 was real enough, however, and not the simulation of a paranoiac state which Salvador Dalí would soon advocate. In the end there would be significant points of contact between Alberti and Dalí, as we shall see, which is hardly surprising since not only was Alberti's first vocation to painting rather than poetry—he had exhibited his work in Madrid as early as 1920—but during the period he was writing *Sobre los ángeles* he was for a time involved with Maruja Mallo, an artist then renowned for her depiction of Madrid squalor. Yet familiar as Alberti must have been with the emerging theories of Surrealist painting, theories that would crystallize with Dalí's essays of the early 1930s,[7] there is no reason to doubt the genuineness of the crisis which he described eloquently in *The Lost Grove*. It was as real as Lorca's crisis, though its nature was more diffuse:

> I could not sleep, the roots of my hair and my nails ached as I drowned in a sea of yellow bile, biting my pillow in an attempt to overcome the pulsating pain. How many real things in the semi-darkness had been pushing me in that direction, making me fall into that deep precipice like a crackling bolt of lightning! An impossible love that had been bruised and betrayed during moments of confident surrender; the most rabid feelings of jealousy which would not let me sleep and caused me to coldly contemplate a calculated crime during the long sleepless nights; the sad shadow of a friend who had committed suicide pounded against my brain like the mute ringing of bells. Unconfessed envy and hate struggled for expression, only to explode like a bomb buried deep beneath the ground. With empty pockets that could not even warm my hands, I took interminable and directionless strolls in the wind, the rain and the heat. My family remained silent or indifferent in the presence of this terrible struggle that was reflected on my face and in my very being, wandering like a somnambulist through the rooms of our house and coming to rest occasionally on street benches.

Waves of infantile fears that created even greater pangs of conscience, doubt, fears of hell, somber echoes of that Jesuit school on the shores of the Bay of Cadiz where I had loved and suffered; my displeasure with my earlier work; my sense of panic which urged me on, leaving me no time to concentrate on anything nor allowing me a moment of respite—all this and more, contradictory, inexplicable, labyrinthine. (*LG*, p. 259).

This catalogue of Alberti's problems reads like the contents page to *Sobre los ángeles* where amongst other titles we find: 'El ángel falso' ('The False Angel'), dedicated to Maruja Mallo, 'El ángel mentiroso' ('Lying Angel'), 'El ángel rabioso' ('The Rabid Angel'), 'El ángel de la ira' ('The Angel of Wrath') and 'El ángel envidioso' ('The Envious Angel'). Alberti begins this last poem with a warning that no one or nothing, not even himself, is safe from his venomous tongue:

> Leñadoras son, ¡defiéndete!,
> esas silbadoras hachas
> que mueven mi lengua.
>
> Hoces de los vientos malos,
> ¡alerta!,
> que muerden mi alma.   (p. 269)
>
> (These whistling axes
> that move my tongue
> —watch out!—are treefellers.
>
> Sickles of evil winds,
> —take cover!—
> that eat into my soul.)

The point was that Alberti had come upon an uncontrollable— though systematic—way of discharging his unconscious:

And then there was a kind of angelic revelation—but not from the corporeal, Christian angels found in all those beautiful paintings and religious icons, but angels representing irresistible forces of the spirit who could be molded to conform to my darkest and most secret mental states. I released them in waves on the world, a blind reincarnation of all the cruelty, desolation, terror and even at times the goodness that existed inside of me but was also encircling me from without. (*LG*, pp. 259–60).

Alberti's angels are nothing less than external projections of his embittered mind. They are a purely cathartic facility which isolates and gives concrete form to the amorphous, warring forces of his psyche, making them surface one by one. Some of the concepts they represent are easily defined: betrayal in love, for instance, suicidal thoughts, his own poverty, even his envy, which includes envy of

fellow poets, 'those who had been more successful', like Lorca, or
'were living off their family's money', like Vicente Aleixandre, or
'had careers . . . [as] teachers, visiting professors at universities' (*LG*,
p. 260), like Salinas and Guillén. But these bitter feelings are more
symptomatic of Alberti's neurosis than strictly its cause. There is
another deeper source of anguish already mentioned by Alberti which
is the binding theme of both *The Lost Grove* and *Sobre los ángeles*:

> I had lost a paradise, the Eden of those early years: my happy, bright
> and carefree youth. I suddenly found myself cut off from my past without
> the consolation of those soothing shades of blue. (*LG*, p. 260).

This theme of a lost childhood and a lost faith, which recalls Lorca
and Rosalía de Castro in particular, gives shape and metaphysical
unity to *Sobre los ángeles* from first to last. In its 'Entrada' or introductory poem, 'Paraíso perdido ('Lost Paradise'), the theme is expressed
with perhaps too much clarity and too much shape to impress us
as Surrealist:

> A través de los siglos,
> por la nada del mundo,
> yo, sin sueño, buscándote.
>
> Tras de mí, imperceptible,
> sin rozarme los hombros,
> mi ángel muerto, vigía.
>
> ¿Adónde el Paraíso,
> sombra, tú que has estado?
> Pregunta con silencio.
>
> Ciudades sin respuesta,
> ríos sin habla, cumbres
> sin ecos, mares mudos.
>
> . . . ¡Paraíso perdido!
> Perdido por buscarte,
> yo, sin luz para siempre.   (pp. 247–8)
>
> (Across the centuries,
> through the world's void,
> me, sleepless, looking for you.
>
> Behind me, imperceptibly,
> without touching my shoulders,
> my dead angel, on watch.
>
> Where is Paradise,
> shadow, you who have been there?
> Question unanswered.

Cities without response,
rivers without speech, hilltops
without echoes, silent seas.

... Paradise lost!
And lost through looking for you,
me, without light for ever.)

The submerged lyricism of the above will surface more expansively in the poem which begins the volume's third section, 'Tres recuerdos del cielo' (p. 278) ('Three Memories of Heaven'), which anticipates the mood of Lorca's 'Poema doble del Lago Edem'. But between these two extremes of a hellish present and a past paradise recalled, Alberti gives expression to his mental chaos with a harshness and directness we will not find in *Poeta en Nueva York*. Outstanding is the long poem 'El cuerpo deshabitado' ('The Uninhabited Body'), which begins:

Yo te arrojé de mi cuerpo,
yo, con un carbón ardiendo.

—Vete.

Madrugada.
La luz, muerta en las esquinas
y en las casas.
Los hombres y las mujeres
ya no estaban.

—Vete.

Quedó mi cuerpo vacío,
negro saco, a la ventana.

Se fue.

Se fue, doblando las calles.
Mi cuerpo anduvo, sin nadie.   (p. 250)

(I cast you out from my body,
me, with a burning coal.

—Get out.

Dawn.
The light, dead on street corners
and in the houses.
Men and women
were not yet about.

—Get out.

My body stood empty,
a black sack, at the window.

It made off.

It made off, turning corners.
My body walked, with no one.)

Here the lines are so stark we can only guess what the pronoun
'te' (you) represents and what Alberti has expelled. But to judge
by the great vacuum it leaves behind, as well as the spiritual tone of
the following imagery, the most likely candidate is religion or faith:

Llevaba una ciudad dentro.
La perdió.
Le perdieron.

Solo, en el filo del mundo,
clavado ya, de yeso.
No es un hombre, es un boquete
de humedad, negro,
por el que se ve nada.   (p. 253)

(He once carried a city within.
He lost it.
They lost him.

Alone, on the world's edge,
stuck, with gypsum.
He is not a man, but a hole
of dampness, black,
through which nothing can be seen.)

These lines, like so many in the volume, evoke a sense of profound
despair. Much in the spirit of their times, they recall T. S. Eliot's
'The Hollow Men' of 1925 and, in Spain, Luis Cernuda's poems
on the void, while at the same time there is an unmistakable kinship
between this post-war urban malaise and the metaphysical crisis
that foreshadowed Romanticism a hundred years before. For Alberti
the crisis is double-edged since not only has he lost the paradise
of youth but, it seems, he has himself rejected the faith that was
its mainstay. His paradise has been both taken away and given away,
and thus his bitterness is directed both at others and at himself.
In several poems Alberti depicts the magnitude of his desolation
in meteorological or even cosmic terms, as in 'Los ángeles bélicos
(Norte, Sur)' ('The Bellicose Angels (North, South)') which begins:

Viento contra viento.
Yo, torre sin mando, en medio.   (p. 256)

(Wind against wind.
Me, a tower without control, between.)

This poem, like 'El ángel ceniciento' ('The Ashen Angel') and especially 'Can de llamas' ('Dog of Flames'), is densely structured, though its parallelisms and repetitions suggest confrontation rather than balance, an impasse rather than harmony. Indeed, in 'Can de llamas', which has a similar north–south polarization, the poet asks the mythical centralized dog to unite the warring opposites, '¡Únelos, sombra del perro!' (p. 271) ('Join them, shadow of dog!'). Again in 'Los ángeles de la prisa' ('The Speedy Angels'), the poet is powerless in the face of elemental forces that crowd and jostle him without respite. His sleep is broken by 'los rápidos giros de los cielos' ('the sky's rapid spinning') and by 'los veloces, espirales pueblos, / rodadoras montañas, / raudos mares ...' ('the headlong, spiralling towns, wheeling mountains, rushing seas'), all of which bump him mercilessly:

> Me empujaban.
>
> Enemiga era la tierra,
> porque huía.
> Enemigo el cielo,
> porque no paraba.
>
> ... No querían
> que yo parara en nada. (p. 265)
>
> (They shoved me about.
>
> The earth was an enemy,
> because it ran away.
> The sky an enemy
> because it wouldn't be still.
>
> ... They wouldn't let
> me be still for a second.)

These cosmic images are an important feature in *Sobre los ángeles* for not only do they suggest the scale of Alberti's crisis, and indeed its religious or heavenly source, but they also tend to dwarf the poet and thereby give a real sense of his psychic disintegration and his panic. Essentially they point up the persecution complex which Alberti had expressed so crisply in 'El cuerpo deshabitado':

> Contra mí, mundos enteros,
> contra mí, dormido,
> maniatado,
> indefenso. (p. 251)

> (Against me, entire worlds,
> against me, asleep,
> handcuffed,
> defenceless.)

Clearly too, the hyperbole inherent in this type of imagery is indicative of a hallucinatory element in Alberti's developing paranoia. Hallucinations go hand in hand with a persecution complex. The idea of persecution is strong, for instance, in 'El alma en pena' ('The Soul in Torment') which begins:

> Ese alma en pena, sola,
> ese alma en pena siempre perseguida
> por un resplandor muerto.
> Por un muerto.   (p. 274)

> (That soul in torment, alone,
> that soul in torment forever persecuted
> by a dead splendour.
> By a dead person.)

Here it is the splendour of Alberti's dead past which 'pursues' or 'persecutes' him, its joy contrasting so markedly with his present as to make it, like Rosalía's present, all the more unbearable. His desolation prompts him, in the fashion of biblical prophecies, to have visions of terrible destruction:

> Sísmicos latigazos tumban sueños,
> terremotos derriban las estrellas.
> Catástrofes celestes tiran al mundo escombros ...

> (Seismic lashes flatten dreams,
> earthquakes shatter stars.
> Heavenly catastrophes cast debris on earth ...)

But though his spirit seems bent on gloom and ruin—'No hay entrada en el cielo para nadie. / En pena, siempre en pena, / alma perseguida' ('There is no way in to heaven for anyone. / In torment, forever in torment, / persecuted soul'—we can already sense the metamorphic potential of this mental chaos:

> las perdidas batallas en los trigos,
> la explosión de la sangre en las olas.   (p. 275)

> (the lost battles in wheat fields,
> the explosion of blood in the sea's waves.)

The supreme point of connection between persecution and hallucination, however, is found in Alberti's identification with Christ. There is an inevitable logic about this in a volume that is so deeply marked with religious patterns. Christ represents the ultimate form of persecution, of course, even of self-inflicted persecution, while his resurrection parallels that emergence from the depths of despair which Alberti will experience. Significantly, it is immediately after the poem 'Ascensión' ('Ascension')—which echoes the theme of the 'Tumba rota' (p. 273) ('Broken tomb'), or the removal of Christ's body from its tomb—that Alberti, in 'Los ángeles mudos' ('The Dumb Angels'), presents himself as one who has returned and is looked upon with disbelief by people in the street. They had evidently thought he was dead and now can only gape at his resurrected form:

Inmóviles, clavadas, mudas mujeres de los zaguanes
y hombres sin voz, lentos, de las bodegas,
quieren, quisieran, querrían preguntarme.

—¿Cómo tú por aquí y en otra parte?
Querrían hombres, mujeres, mudos, tocarme,
saber si mi sombra, si mi cuerpo andan sin alma
por otras calles.
Quisieran decirme:
—Si eres tú, párate.

Hombres, mujeres, mudos, querrían ver claro,
asomarse a mi alma,
acercarle una cerilla
por ver si es la misma.
Quieren, quisieran . . .

—Habla.

(Motionless, transfixed, dumb women in doorways
and slow, speechless men from wine cellars,
want, would like, would dearly love to question me.

—And how are you here and somewhere else?
Men, women, struck dumb, would like to touch me,
to know if my shadow and my body walk with no soul
through other streets.
They would like to tell me:
—If it's you, stop.

Men, women, struck dumb, would like to see clearly,
look into my soul,
bring a wax taper to it,
to see if it is the same one.
They want, they would like . . .

—Speak.)

The passage has many biblical echoes, including Christ's having to prove to the doubting Thomas that he was the Risen Lord by letting him touch his hands and side (John, 20.27). This aptly parallels the concrete source of the poem which was the return visit Alberti made to Puerto de Santa María in 1928 when he spent 'several weeks' at the house of his Uncle Jesús (*LG*, p. 264), and well can we imagine how the local villagers would have stared at the 26-year-old poet and found him much changed from the youth they had once known. But the parallel is no mere ornamentation, for Alberti was changed, spiritually. He had recently suffered his own kind of death in Madrid and was returning to the Puerto precisely when he was coming out of his crisis (*LG*, pp. 261–4). What is more, just as the cross was central to Christ's purpose, Alberti's crisis and its attendant persecution complex was the meaningful and transforming factor in his life as a poet. Certainly in the latter part of *Sobre los ángeles* Alberti's tone changes. Essentially he begins to speak to an audience rather than to himself. Indeed, in at least six poems he addresses us in the familiar plural form of 'vosotros' (you), as used by Christ, by preachers and anyone who has a message to impart. Alberti did have a message, as we know, but before listening to him proclaim it loud and clear from his pulpit let us see how he describes his coming upon it. The following poem, 'El ángel de las bodegas' ('The Angel of the Wine Cellars') is indicative of his discovery, and, since it was also probably inspired by or written during his return to the Puerto, we can assume that this was an important moment in his rehabilitation. The first half of the poem reads:

Fue cuando la flor del vino se moría en penumbra
y dijeron que el mar la salvaría del sueño.
Aquel día bajé a tientas a tu alma encalada y húmeda.
Y comprobé que un alma oculta frío y escaleras
y que más de una ventana puede abrir con su eco otra voz, si
  es buena.

Te vi flotar a ti, flor de agonía, flotar sobre tu mismo espíritu.
(Alguien había jurado que el mar te salvaría del sueño.)
Fue cuando comprobé que murallas se quiebran con suspiros
y que hay puertas al mar que se abren con palabras.   (p. 281)

(It was when the flower of the wine was dying in shadows
and they said that the sea would save it from sleep.
That day I groped my way down to your limed and moist soul.
And I proved that a soul conceals cold and stairways

and that more than one window can another voice open with its
    echo, if it is good.
I saw you floating, flower of agony, floating on your own spirit.
(Someone had sworn that the sea would save you from sleep.)
It was when I proved that walls break up with sighs
and that there are doors to the sea that open with words.)

The poem draws heavily on aspects of the wine-making process
which Alberti knew intimately. In particular we need to know that
the dying 'flor del vino' ('flower of the wine') is the creamy froth
that appears on the surface of wine during fermentation. This
becomes the poem's central image when, in its second half, we are
told that the flower dies 'sin haber visto el mar' ('without having
seen the sea'), which is to say, before the wine is exported. And
here we find the connection with Christ and the theme of sacrifice,
for the flower of the wine has to die before the wine can mature,
that is, before the wine is wine. Thus fermentation, by which sugar
is turned to alcohol, provides Alberti with a powerful image which
combines the two concepts of agony and metamorphosis. It is not
surprising therefore that he should say at the poem's conclusion:
'He aquí paso a paso toda mi larga historia' (p. 282) ('You have
here, step by step, my whole life history'). Yet the poem does not
remain at the level of a neat viticultural allegory. For the point is
that Alberti is very close to the objects that appear in the poem;
he knows them intimately; they are part of his life. Thus, on going
down to the cellar, he had said in the first stanza: 'comprobé que
un alma oculta frío y escaleras' ('I proved that a soul conceals cold
and stairways'). He had in fact verified that the objects of his past
were inside him, checking his memories of the cellar against the
actual and same cellar he visited on his return. At the same time
he also proves or verifies the reciprocal point, namely that man has
the power to act upon objects: 'comprobé . . . que más de una ventana
puede abrir con su eco otra voz' ('I proved that more than one
window can another voice open with its echo') and 'comprobé que
murallas se quiebran con suspiros y que hay puertas al mar que
se abren con palabras' ('I proved that walls break up with sighs
and that there are doors to the sea that open with words'). In short,
Alberti's return to the Puerto was a significant event, for it was
then that he proved or became convinced of the notion that things
or objects are meaningful and inextricably bound up with man's
inner life.

A similar theme emerges in 'Invitación al arpa' (p. 286) ('Invi-
tation to the Harp'), where Alberti takes us into an old and dusty

room piled high with objects. This backward journey in time has a Romantic flavour which recalls Bécquer and Antonio Machado, but Alberti recharges it with the specifically Surrealist notion that objects in their relation to man have a sentient life. In the first stanza alone we find: 'las estancias olvidan . . .' ('rooms forget'), 'las consolas sueñan' ('consoles dream'), 'Un sombrero se hastía' ('A hat gets weary'), 'lazos sin bucles se cansan' ('ribbons without curls tire') and 'violetas se aburren' ('violets grow bored'). This is no mere stylistic device of personification. The poet actually presents objects as sentient and alive, or indeed, bored, in the above poem, where they have been deprived of man's presence. The message that Alberti wishes to proclaim, then, is that man's salvation lies in appreciating the interpenetration—however painful—of objective and subjective reality. This is the theme of the volume's penultimate poem, 'Los ángeles feos' ('The Ugly Angels'):

> Mirad esto también, antes que demos sepultura al viaje:
> cuando una sombra se entrecoge las uñas en las bisagras de las puertas
> o el pie helado de un ángel sufre el insomnio fijo de una piedra,
> mi alma sin saberlo se perfecciona.   (p. 292)

> (Note this too, before we say the journey is over and done:
> when a shadow catches its nails on the hinges of doors
> or the frozen foot of an angel suffers the unrelenting insomnia of a stone,
> my soul unknowingly grows more complete.)

The main thrust of the above lines clearly lies in its connecting of suffering and salvation, but we can also glimpse here the point at which they meet, namely in the interpenetration of man and objects. Let us try to ascertain broadly the logic behind this. First, we note that a two-way flow operates in the images of nails catching on hinges and a foot suffering the insomnia of stone, for while in the former image sentience resides in man, his fingernails, in the latter it resides in an object, a stone. Such reciprocity reminds us of Guillén's phenomenology, except that here it is based on pain. Naturally in Alberti pain is not merely physical, but mental, and the unrelenting images of pain keep before us a sense of the poet's anguish and mental disturbance. Strictly, one would have to be mentally deranged to think of a stone suffering insomnia. Yet we know that this is a projection, that the stone's insomnia is in fact the poet's. Such a projection amounts to a delusion typical of a disturbed man or paranoiac, the Surrealist poet, whose irrational mind will change the world. But the projections also invest the world of objects with psychical values which are deeply and inevitably relevant to the poet, their projector, and the objects will respond or return to him in such a way as it might be said that they enrich, complete or perfect his inner life. Thus, in his delusory psychical projections the paranoiac metamorphoses objects, absorbs them into his own mental life and makes the world his own. In short, his suffering leads to his salvation.

The fundamental egocentricity of the above bears comparison with the paranoiac method of Salvador Dalí who argued with characteristic flamboyance that all beauty was 'comestible' and that objects were so inviting they seemed to say to him, 'mange-moi'.[8] Edibleness in Dalí underlines the notion that the paranoiac consumes his reality and it also points towards Dalí's obsession with decay. In his paintings this is reflected in the famous soft—i.e. edible or faecal—objects, such as melting watches or a putrefying donkey. In Alberti there is of course ample evidence of decay and rubble, but one is also struck by such images as 'las tierras que se derriten' (p. 292) ('the lands that melt'), which ends 'Los ángeles feos' ('The Ugly Angels') on a disturbing note, and again 'la lentitud de una piedra que se dobla hacia la muerte' (p. 288) ('the slowness of a stone that folds towards death'). However, to develop the point of the egocentric or pananoiac consumption of reality we need only turn to the last lines of the poem with which we began, 'Los ángeles muertos' ('The Dead Angels'):

> Buscad, buscadlos:
> debajo de la gota de cera que sepulta la palabra de un libro
> o la firma de uno de esos rincones de cartas
> que trae rodando el polvo.
> Cerca del casco perdido de una botella,
> de una suela extraviada en la nieve,
> de una navaja de afeitar abandonada al borde de un precipicio.

> (Look hard, look hard for them:
> beneath the drop of wax that entombs the words of a book
> or the signature in some or other corner of a letter
> that comes spinning in the dust.
> Near the lost shell of a bottle,
> a stray shoe-sole in the snow,
> a razor abandoned on the edge of a precipice.)

Again we cannot help but be impressed by the concreteness and indeed hardness of the objects listed here. The fact that they are worthless, random and apparently lacking in reference to the poet seems only to promote their sheer physical presence. Yet on further consideration we begin to suspect that each object listed has a more than incidental link with the kind of personal problems Alberti enumerated in *The Lost Grove*. It hardly seems fanciful to connect the images beginning in the second line with, respectively, Alberti's struggles as a poet, his disappointment in love, a drink problem (if not his own, then that of a member of his family), his poverty ('I was ... forced to go everywhere on foot ... with the rain seeping through the torn soles of my shoes', *LG*, p. 260), and finally, in the image of a razor, his thoughts on suicide or on a friend's suicide. The same could be said of some of the objective images we met in the first lines of the poem where 'una sortija rota' ('a broken ring') is a sentimental, Romantic and, in this sense, soft image which suggests lost love, while 'una estrella pisoteada' ('a trampled star') evokes lost faith in similar vein. In both sequences the poet urges 'Buscad, buscadlos' ('Look hard, look hard for them'), where the sought objects are the dead angels of the title, that is, Alberti's past self now lost. Even allowing for a certain discrepancy in time-scale, we cannot fail to note the self-based nature of this reciprocity: effectively Alberti is looking for himself in objects which are projections of his own self. This is an infallibly logical process and it is not surprising that Alberti should urge it with a preacher's conviction. He has found a system whereby he can impose himself upon reality, subjectivize reality in his own terms or in terms of his own obsessions, and subsequently rediscover himself in reality. The person rediscovered is one intensely connected with the objects of reality, the Surrealist in fact, whose claims to transcendentalism are sufficient to replace the Christian faith of his remote boyhood. Alberti has been visited by what he entitles in one poem 'El ángel bueno' ('The Good Angel'), and the purpose of this angel of mercy was to 'hacerme el alma navegable' (p. 275) ('make my soul navigable'). By the end of *Sobre los ángeles* Alberti's soul was navigable and he was ready to explore new territory. Though necessarily 'alicortado' (p. 292) ('without wings'), that is, earth-bound and atheist, he was very much a survivor, as the title of this last poem—'El ángel superviviente' ('The Surviving Angel')—indicates. Indeed, the effect of Surrealism's metaphysic had been to turn his crisis into his triumph. All that remained was to cultivate and exploit this source, which he did most effectively in the first poem of his next volume.

'Sermón de las cuatro verdades' ('Sermon on the Fourth Truths') is Alberti's finest Surrealist poem and it climaxes his development as a Surrealist which *Sobre los ángeles* had not quite fully charted. Here Alberti continues his evangelism of materio-mysticism but does so with the absolute conviction of a poet-prophet and Christ-figure who urges us to throw away past idols and turn to a new faith and truth. His adoption of the role of Christ is, in the first place, indicative of his delusions and paranoia, the bedrock of Surrealist creativity, but it also gives some measure of the controlled channelling and systematization by which the paranoiac imposes his obsessions. It was no doubt important too that, having lost his Christian faith, Alberti had something substantial to fill the vacuum. Such a problem of reinhabiting the empty self was foreseen at the beginning of *Sobre los ángeles*: 'Te pregunto: / ¿cuándo abandonas la casa, / dime, / qué ángeles malos, crueles, / quieren de nuevo alquilarla?' (p. 249) ('I ask you: / when you abandon the house, / tell me, / what evil, cruel angels / will want to rent it again?'). When Alberti came upon his surprisingly positive answer it was virtually inevitable that he would see it in religious terms and present it in religious guise.

There was, however, another crucial reason why Alberti turned preacher: he wished to mock religion itself. The point is that the root cause of Alberti's neurotic state of mind in *Sobre los ángeles* was his religious upbringing and early education at the Jesuit school in Puerto de Santa María. Alberti is insistent on this in *The Lost Grove*. He recalls that, with his father away for long periods, he found himself as a boy 'in an endless nightmare of aunts, uncles, cousins, great-aunts and great-uncles' who displayed an 'ugly, inflexible, dirty and unpleasant bigotry' (*LG*, p. 27); while at school he was made 'to suffer a series of humiliations and bitter resentments' at the hands of 'severe and even cruel teachers' (*LG*, p. 40), teachers who were particularly hard on the sin of masturbation (*LG*, p. 54) and who gave him 'horrifying sermons' and more than one 'fiery lecture on the torments of hell' (*LG*, p. 84). The great irony in this account is that the Puerto was a place of extreme natural beauty, a beauty Alberti held on to desperately, but his Jesuit teachers were blind to this and focused all their attention on the other world, mostly hell. Their attitude is succinctly put in a line of Jesuit verse Alberti remembers: '¡Guerra al mundo!' ('War on the World!') (*LG*, p. 43). Only years later, he says, as an adult was he fully wounded by the 'hysterical tyranny' of 'the good fathers of the Society of Jesus'

(*LG*, p. 21), but when he realized the damage they had done he unleashed his hatred with uncompromising ferocity:

> I am compelled once again to put in writing the repugnance I feel for this Spanish Catholic spirit, this reactionary and savage Catholicism that darkened the blueness of the sky from the days of our childhood, covering us with layers and layers of grey ashes which only served to muffle any real creative intelligence we might have had ... What a hideous inheritance of rubble and suffocation! (*LG*, p. 35).

It was to these same ashes and rubble that Alberti returned in his late twenties to reconstruct a new set of values and a new faith in life. Moreover, it was in terms of things themselves, the things religion had rejected or denied, that Alberti would build his faith. His adoption of the role of preacher in *Sermones y moradas* was thus entirely appropriate and meaningful: not only did it suit the transcendental metaphysic of Surrealism but it allowed Alberti to present this as a rejoinder and counter-religion to the one he so clearly detested.

Turning now to the poem itself, which is long, bulky and frankly dazzling in its imagery and syntax, I shall for the sake of brevity adopt a tabular system of commenting on its itemized 'four truths' since this will allow for greater coverage of the multiple associations in Alberti's images, (it being understood of course that my comments are, to a greater or lesser extent, always speculative).

We begin with the title: 'Sermón de las cuatro verdades' (p. 295) ('Sermon on the Four Truths'). Number is an important feature in theological dogma, as for instance the Ten Commandments, the twelve disciples. 'Four' recalls the four gospels, which are variations on the same truth of Jesus: 'I am the way, and the truth, and the life' (John 14.6). It also recalls the doctrine of 'The Four Last Things', i.e., Death, Judgement, Heaven and Hell, and thereby the eschatalogical emphasis of the Jesuits. Enumeration gives rhetorical shape to discourse and predisposes the audience/readers to expect an orderly, logical account, even scientific proof, of the matter discussed. Alberti will both exploit and abuse this expectation in the course of the poem.

There now follow a dozen introductory lines which present the sermon's theme in the manner of an exordium. The first:

> En frío, voy a revelaros lo que es un sótano por dentro.

> (Coldly, am I going to reveal to you what a cellar is like on the inside.)

Coldness refers to the cellar's temperature and to the speaker's proposed manner of delivery. This pun suggests an element of mockery and alerts us to Alberti's subversive intentions in turning preacher. The idea of 'revelation' and the familiar plural form of address in *vosotros* ('you') are consistent with the preacher's role. 'Sótano' ('cellar') is the poem's key image. It represents the inner mind and spatializes this in the way the Bible spatializes heaven as a 'kingdom' or a 'house': 'In my Father's house are many rooms' (John 14.2). But 'cellar' takes us down rather than up, suggesting hell and torment and therefore contrasting pointedly with such orthodox religious locations as The Sermon on the Mount. It also prepares for the many associations with childhood that follow, cellars having been a haunt of the young Alberti. Thus Alberti announces he is going to show us the inside of his mind, with special reference to its formulation in childhood, a mind that is gloomy and enclosed, as 'cellar' suggests, not unlike the cave Alberti refers to at the time of writing *Sobre los ángeles*: 'I had to escape from that cave filled with demons, with long hours of insomnia and nightmares' (*LG*, p. 261). But there would be a creative element in it too, such as astounded Alberti in the caves of Altamira which he visited in the summer of 1928 (*LG*, p. 263). Next:

> Aquellos que al bucear a oscuras por una estancia no hayan derribado un objeto, tropezado contra una sombra o un mueble; o al atornillar una bujía, sentido en lo más íntimo de las uñas el arañazo eléctrico e instantáneo de otra alma, que se suelden con dos balas de piedra o plomo los oídos.

> (Those who on plunging darkly into a room have not knocked over an object, bumped against a shadow or a piece of furniture; or on screwing in a bulb have not felt in the quick of the nails the electric and instantaneous scratch of another soul, let them solder up their ears with two balls of stone or lead.)

The preacher's aggressive opening gambit is to tell those who do not share his faith that they need not listen to him. And his faith is nothing less than a belief that objects have vitality, that a living spirit exists in the inanimate world, that electricity has soul. Those who have not experienced this, says Alberti, can block up their ears. Such an exclusion of non-believers recalls the religious bigotry Alberti had known as a boy. It also reminds us of Christ's answer to his disciples when they asked why he spoke in parables: 'To you it has been given to know the secret of the kingdom of heaven, but to them it has not been given ... because seeing they do not see, and hearing they do not hear, nor do they understand' (Matthew 13.11, 13).

Both stress metamorphosis: religion, for instance, in the doctrine of transubstantiation of bread and wine, or again in the glorification of Christ. But whereas in religion this is typically an other-worldly projection, in Surrealism the change is effected *hic et nunc* in the suffering mind. The motif of fish brings to mind Christ's feeding of the multitude, a magical and even worldly transformation, while the thorn, 'shout for help' and the suffering body suggest the ultimate persecution of the cross. This identification with Christ—which the poem sustains even while it contradicts his teaching—is developed in the next lines which refer to his suffering:

> No le habléis, desnudo como está, asediado por tres vahos nocturnos que le ahogan: uno amarillo, otro ceniza, otro negro.   (p. 296)

> (Don't speak to him, naked as he is, beseiged by three nocturnal vapours which choke him: one yellow, the other ashen, the other black.)

The number three suggests the Trinity, which for the Surrealist would typify religion's erroneous procedure of conceptualizing the bodily or concrete. Alternatively, in the context of psychoanalysis, the 'three vapours' parallel Freud's division of the warring psyche into id, ego and superego.

We are now invited to listen to the voice of the oracle—the martyrized Surrealist—and the preacher offers a first textual reading from his bible-manifesto:

> Atended. Esta es su voz:

> —Mi alma está picada por el cangrejo de pinzas y compases candentes, mordida por las ratas y vigilada día y noche por el cuervo.

> Ayudadme a cavar una ola, hasta que mis manos se conviertan en raíces y de mi cuerpo broten hojas y alas.

> (Listen. This is his voice:
> —My soul is pierced by the crab of burning pincers and compasses, bitten by rats and watched night and day by the crow.

> Help me to dig a wave, until my hands are changed into roots and my body sprouts leaves and wings.)

The images of suffering are associated with Alberti's childhood, for the burning pincers and compasses of the crab evoke two locations prominent in *The Lost Grove*, namely the seashore and the school. Just as Christ appealed through suffering, the Surrealist martyr asks his followers to help him to do the impossible, 'cavar una ola' ('dig a wave'), that is, to bring about a transformation of the body, 'hasta que mis manos se conviertan en raíces ...' ('until my hands are changed into roots ...'), an image which merges human and non-human features in a way typical of paintings by Miró, Dalí, Max Ernst, Victor Brauner and other Surrealist artists. It similarly suggests the idea of the reduction of man to the level of things as well as the integration of man with things. Thus the transformation which the Surrealist envisages is not one from the body to the spirit, but from the body to something even more concrete and terrestrial. Clearly implicit in this process too is a notion of salvation and transcendence, as we see from the stock images of 'hojas' ('leaves') and 'alas' ('wings'), the former evoking verticality and the upward growth of a tree and the latter angelic flight. Christ had referred to the sprouting of a fig-tree's leaves as being equivalent to a sign of the coming of God's kingdom (Luke 21.29–31).

> Alguna vez mis ascendientes predijeron que yo sería un árbol solo en medio del mar, si la ira inocente de un rey no lo hubiera inundado de harina y cabelleras de almagra no azotaran la agonía de los navegantes.

> (Once my ancestors predicted that I would be a tree alone in the middle of the sea, had not the innocent wrath of a king flooded it with flour and trails of red ochre not whipped the navigators' agony.)

The coming of the Messiah had been predicted in the Old Testament. At the same time one presumes that Alberti's own ancestors, once powerful wine merchants in the Puerto, would have had high expectations for a male descendant. As regards the second of these associations, the 'árbol solo en medio del mar' ('tree alone in the middle of the sea') indicates the powerful status Alberti should have enjoyed had his immediate ancestors been more prudent, in which connection the reference to a king reminds us of Alberti's description of his great-grandfather as 'one of the principal kings ... of the juice from our vines', and of his reference to the area as 'the kingdom of Bacchus' (*LG*, pp. 58, 59). As to the biblical associations in the above images, a completely different set of values attaches to a 'tree alone in the middle of the sea'. Now we think of the isolation of Christ, particularly on the cross (tree), and we recall the unhappy predictions of his coming in the so-called 'Songs of the Servant': 'He was despised and rejected by men; a man of sorrows, and acquainted with grief ... he was despised, and we esteemed him not' (Isaiah 53.3). Christ had to explain to his apostles why it was necessary for him to suffer and how this confirmed the prophets' predictions (Luke 24.25–7), as did Paul to the Jews in Thessalonika (Acts 17.2–3). Now 'the innocent wrath of a king' evokes Herod and 'cabelleras de almagra' ('trails of red ochre'), with its suggestion of bleeding hair, even the crown of thorns.

> Ya podéis envaneceros de la derrota de aquel hombre que anduvo por el océano endurecido . . .
>
> (Well might you congratulate yourselves on the destruction of that man who walked through the hardened ocean . . .)

Alberti, with some irony, admonishes us by using a typically devious preaching ploy, that of identifying his audience with the unbelievers who scorned Christ. Alberti and Christ alike are associated with the sea. Alberti, or at least his father, should have made his fortune in maritime exports, whereas in fact his father was reduced to the role of a travelling salesman who tramped endlessly around Spain; hence perhaps 'océano endurecido' ('hardened ocean'), which, for similar reasons, makes us think too of Alberti's earlier title, *Marinero en tierra* (*Sailor on land*). Christ was associated with Galilee, did much of his teaching beside the sea (Mark 4.1), was a fisher of men and, indeed, walked on water. Yet the defeated man Alberti refers to, found only death, 'sólo consiguió que los moluscos se le adhirieran a la sangre' ('only succeeded in having molluscs stick to his blood').

We move on to the second truth:

> La segunda verdad as ésta:
>
> Una estrella diluída en un vaso de agua devuelve a los ojos el color de las ortigas o del ácido prúsico.
>
> Pero para los que perdieron la vista en un cielo de vacaciones, lo mejor es que extiendan y comprueben la temperatura de las lluvias.
>
> (The second truth is this:
>
> A star diluted in a glass of water brings back the colour of nettles or of prussic acid to one's eyes.
>
> But for those who lost their sight in a heaven of holidays, they might just as well stay where they are and check the temperature of rainwater.)

A contrastive, dialectical method is again apparent in the last two stanzas. The first suggests the need to dilute or dissolve stars, that is, to return our thinking from the other world to this world, for only then will our eyes recover their sight and will we be sensitive to things, as is our sense of touch responsive to nettles and our smell or taste to prussic acid. The next stanza refers to those who have lost the ability to see, through having taken a holiday in heaven, that is, by having switched off from this life and taken a holiday from truth. As for them, Alberti suggests they should get back to basics or real issues, starting while they are up there in the clouds by taking note of the rainfall! Two stanzas later Alberti reintroduces the Christ-figure:

> He aquí al hombre.

> (Here is the man.)

'So Jesus came out, wearing the crown of thorns and the purple robe. Pilate said to them, "Here is the man!"' (John 19.5).

> Loco de tacto, arrastra cal de las paredes entre las uñas ...
> No le toquéis, ardiendo como está, asediado por millones de manos
> que ansían pulsarlo todo.   (p. 297)

> (Mad from touch, he drags lime from the walls between his nails ...
> Don't touch him, burning as he is, besieged by millions of hands that
> long to feel him all over ...)

The paranoiac is indeed mad, though here madness is more an indication of the frenzy of his relationship with things. The limed walls along which he drags his nails indicate confinement—that of a punitive or rehabilitative institution perhaps—but also his febrile 'cellar' mind. The image of a man thronged by outstretched hands is at once nightmarish and evocative of Christ amid the multitudes. There now follows a second textual reading:

> Escuchadle. Esta es su voz:

> —Mi alma es sólo un cuerpo que fallece por fundirse y rozarse con
> los objetos vivos y difuntos.

> (Listen to him. This is his voice:

> —My soul is only a body that dies on merging with and rubbing against
> living and dead objects.)

The statement is a pure declaration of materio-mysticism in that the Surrealist's soul is absorbed by the objects with which he comes into contact. This is strengthened by a second possible reading of 'Mi alma ... fallece por' as 'My soul is dying to' / 'longing to', which appropriately echoes the mystic tradition proper and in particular the famous 'Muero porque no muero' ('I die because I do not die') of San Juan de la Cruz. But Alberti's thesis of 'fundirse ... con los objetos' ('merging with objects') is a complete reversal of San Juan's, for while the sixteenth-century saint wished to escape the body in order to enter into total spiritual union with the divine, the twentieth-century Surrealist argues that man's spiritual dimension is located in the body, is inseparable from the body, and can only express or fulfil itself through contact with other bodily or concrete things. These things are not merely things-in-themselves, however, but, by definition, things which are, will be or have been dynamically related to man: 'objetos vivos y difuntos' ('living and dead objects'). Here the adjective 'living', besides indicating actuality and presence, suggests the potential vitality of things in relation to man, while 'dead' introduces the important notion of the perdurability of things insofar as they are remembered by man. Thus, the Surrealist's desire to merge with 'living and dead objects', that is, with objects of his present and his past, is a highly integrational concept in temporal terms and one which parallels the undertaking of psychoanalysis to try to make sense of the whole personality.

Next comes a stanza which refers to the soul's 'inutilidad en este mundo' ('uselessness in this world'), which is argued on the basis that the soul has nothing in common with reality's objectivity. Then Alberti says he is going to tell us something surprising, which is:

> El hombre sin ojos sabe que las espaldas de los muertos padecen de insomnio porque las tablas de los pinos son demasiado suaves para soportar la acometida nocturna de diez alcayatas candentes.

> (The man without eyes knows that shoulders of dead men suffer from insomnia because the planks of pine are too smooth to resist the nightly assault of ten red-hot meat hooks.)

Though it may be a truism to say that man fears death, there is something terrible and shocking in Alberti's view that we are all— even blind, orthodox believers, i.e., 'los que perdieron la vista en un cielo de vacaciones' ('those who lost their sight in a heaven of holidays')—plagued by gruesome images of our corpse being devoured as it lies in the ground in its coffin. Such necrophobia recalls many Spanish authors from Quevedo to Unamuno, but above all the incipient Romantic Cadalso and his *Noches lúgubres* (*Lugubrious Nights*). The difference is that Alberti makes no attempt to soften, spiritualize or seek an abstract answer to death. Instead, contradicting the whole ethos of Christianity, he asks us to accept the real truth of our physical decomposition in death and the torment that this inspires in us, a torment we are wont to repress. Not only is it useless to look beyond the grave, but, we are now told, what infinity there is, is to be found only in such waste matter as birds' droppings:

Si no os parece mal, decid a ese niño que desde el escalón más bajo
de los zaguanes pisotea las hormigas ... que nunca olvide que en el
excremento de las aves se hallan contenidas la oscuridad del infinito
y la boca del lobo.

(If you think it fit, tell that boy who stamps on ants at the bottom
stair of hallways ... that he should never forget that in birds' excrement
is to be found the darkness of infinity and the wolf's mouth.)

Rather than chastizing the child for his cruelty, Alberti suggests
that his stamping on ants is an action innocently in keeping with
life's devouring nature, 'la boca del lobo' ('the wolf's mouth'). As
he matures, the child can do without instruction on such supposedly
higher things as religion and morality; what he should remember
is that life's meaning is there in its ephemeral and apparently insignificant objects, this being something he instinctively knew as a child.

The theme of death continues in the third truth where, after several
images of agony and suffering, Alberti argues that we should be
sensitive to the feelings of objects—'idlos aproximando cuidadosa-
mente' (p. 298) ('approach them with great care')—precisely because
the objects are themselves ever dying: 'las burbujas agonizantes se
suceden de momento en momento' ('the bubbles die successively
from second to second'), and ironically, because it is healthy for
us to witness such images of our own decomposition:

> Porque no existe nada más saludable para la arcilla que madura la
> muerte como la postrera contemplación de un círculo en ruina.

> (Because there is nothing healthier for this clay that death matures
> than the final spectacle of a circle in ruin.)

Here we suspect that the emphasis on death has a dual purpose:
it is a therapeutic cure to the lie of religion, which purports to conquer
death, and at the same time it promotes that state of anxiety and
paranoia deemed essential to the Surrealist mind. In keeping with
this double focus, the penultimate stanza of the third truth is at
once apocalyptic and an announcement of the coming of the kingdom:

> Yo os prevengo, quebrantaniños y mujeres beodas que aceleráis las
> explosiones de los planetas y los osuarios, yo os prevengo que cuando
> el alma de mi enemigo hecha bala de cañón perfore la Tierra y su
> cuerpo ignorante renazca en la torpeza del topo o en al hálito acre
> y amarillo que desprende la saliva seca del mulo, comenzará la perfec-
> ción de los cielos.

> (I warn you, childbreakers and female drunks that you are accelerating
> the explosions of planets and charnel houses, I warn you that when

my enemy's soul turned into a cannon ball perforates the Earth, and his ignorant body is reborn in the slowness of the mole or in the acrid, yellow breath that issued from the dry saliva of a mule, the perfection of heaven will be at hand.)

Christ had forecast destruction: 'Then he said to them: "Nation will rise against nation, and kingdom against kingdom; there will be great earthquakes, and in various places famines and pestilences and there will be terrors and great signs from heaven ..."' (Luke 21.10–11). But, for Alberti, destruction is wreaked by 'childbreakers and female drunks', that is, by parents intoxicated by other-worldly thinking who inculcate this in their children and destroy their natural and truthful understanding of reality. This parallels Freud's thesis that social pressures condition the maturing child to repress and sublimate instinctive psychical forces, thereby causing mental havoc. By contrast, when such an unbeliever is converted to phenomenology, when he willingly becomes part of the physical reality he normally seeks to transcend—'cuando el alma de mi enemigo hecha bala de cañón perfore la Tierra' ('when my enemy's soul turned into a cannon ball perforates the Earth')—and when he is thus 'reborn' into explosive or shattering awareness of life's physicality, then the kingdom of heaven or the liberated psychical state envisaged by the Surrealist will be at hand.

Until such time, Alberti continues in the last stanza of this section, we must forcefully denounce 'a esa multitud de esqueletos violentadores' ('that multitude of skeleton violators')—i.e., those who will not be satisfied with worldly reality, those unable to leave the dead to lie rotting in their corporal graves—for we are still lacking strength to do away with our enemies. This sense of being outnumbered by a philistine enemy recalls Christ's words to his disciples: 'they will lay their hands on you and persecute you ... This will be a time for you to bear testimony' (Luke 21.12–13). The enemy for Alberti, however, is the person who is 'casi desposeída ya del don entrecortado de la agonía' ('now almost dispossessed of the intermittent gift of agony'), which is to say, not the Surrealist, for he has the precious gift of agony or paranoia and is very much in touch with his unconscious, but the Christian, the person who has repressed such tormented thoughts as accompany an acceptance of definitive death in the body and is therefore 'dispossessed' of his true self or unconscious.

The fourth and last truth begins with a sentence-stanza of stunning complexity which leads us deeper into the poet's cellar mind:

La cuarta y última verdad es ésta:

Cuando los escabeles son mordidos por las sombras y unos pies poco
seguros intentan comprobar si en los rincones donde el polvo se desilu-
siona sin huellas las telarañas han dado sepultura a la avaricia del
mosquito, sobre el silencio húmedo y cóncavo de las bodegas se persiguen los diez ecos que desprende el cadáver de un hombre al chocar
contra una superficie demasiado refractoria a la luz.

(The fourth and last truth is this:

When footstools are bitten by shadows
and hesitant feet try to ascertain
if in corners where unmarked dust grows disillusioned
spiderwebs have laid to rest the mosquito's avarice,
in the moist and concave silence of wine cellars
ten echoes chase each other in issuing from a man's corpse
as it bumps into a surface too refractory to the light.)

This is an opportune moment to appreciate the power of Alberti's
language, notably its persuasive syntax. Though dazzling to the point
of bewilderment, a sentence like the above has an impeccable syntactical logic which is typical of Surrealist expression, as F. G. Sarriá
pointed out in a convincing discussion of *Sobre los ángeles*.[9] The logic
is more apparent if we read the sentence as free verse, there being
seven natural lines as I have indicated in the English translation.
Indeed, the sentence unfolds with an inexorable and even Gongor-
esque syntactical flow, reaching its main clause in the penultimate
line, 'se persiguen los diez ecos' ('ten echoes chase each other').
The last line tells us what initially caused the sound that was the
source of these echoes, while the first five lines sketch in the cellar
setting, telling us when and in what circumstances the echoes of
that sound can now be heard. This has the effect of integrating two
temporal planes: the 'hesitant feet' of the second line belong to the
present, Alberti's present, and the 'man's corpse' of the penultimate
line to his now dead past. As in 'El ángel de las bodegas' ('The
Angel of the Wine Cellars'), then, the sequence depicts a return
visit Alberti paid to a cellar he knew in his youth, though his technique is noticeably more free now. The nostalgic theme and temporal
synthesis recall Antonio Machado—for instance the poem 'El limo-
nero lánguido' ('The languid lemon tree')—but, if the primary requi-
site for such an excursion into the past is a sensitivity to objective
detail, it might be argued that Alberti even outdoes Machado by
virtue of his Surrealist thesis of intersubjectivity: 'el polvo se desilu-
siona sin huellas' ('unmarked dust grows disillusioned') attributes
to objects the capacity to feel solitude, while the idea of a man bumping

into surfaces suggests once again that painful or paranoiac relationship between man and objects. Naturally the last image might well be based on an actual event witnessed by the young Alberti of a drunken man reeling about in a wine cellar, the kind of tragicomic scene any number of his male relatives could have provided.

But the stanza as a whole admirably achieves that physical-temporal synthesis which Alberti described earlier as 'rozarse con los objetos vivos y difuntos ('rubbing against living and dead objects'). The single-sentence construction enhances the impression of synthesis, while the image of echoes reverberating in a disused cellar offers a very concrete representation of the poet's psyche. It is an image that stays with us as we read the remainder of the fourth truth:

> Es muy sabido que a las oscuridades sin compañía bajan en busca de su cuerpo los que atacados por la rabia olvidaron que la corrupción de los cielos tuvo lugar la misma noche en que el vinagre invadió los toneles y descompuso las colchas de las vírgenes.   (pp. 298-9)

> (It is very well known that into those solitary darknesses there descend in search of their body all those who attacked by rage forget that the corruption of heaven took place on the same night that vinegar invaded the casks and decomposed the virgin's mattresses.)

As a matter of axiomatic truth Alberti tells that certain types of person are wont to go down into the solitary darkness of wine cellars in search of their body. As usual this counters religion's upward trajectory in search of the soul, it being understood that the downward motion is one of inner or psychical penetration, that union with the body represents man's true goal and that those who go down are the paranoiacs or Surrealists, those 'attacked by rage'. At the same time, in this increasingly recollective section of the poem, 'rage' refers to Alberti's torment as a boy, for the 'corruption of heaven' took place precisely when vinegar ruined the wine, that is, when Alberti became bitterly conscious of his family's ruin, and when it 'decomposed the virgin's mattresses', when he became embarrassingly aware of girls and sexual sin. It is typical of Alberti to associate his family and early courtship disasters with the insidious influence of the church or the brotherhood; for, though they were not directly to blame for the financial ruin, his Jesuit teachers certainly exacerbated Alberti's awareness of it by favouring boys from rich families (LG, pp. 31, 36), while of course they hardly encouraged normal or healthy sexual attitudes.

> No abandonéis a aquel que os jura que cuando un difunto se emborracha en la Tierra su alma le imita en el Paraíso.

(Do not renounce the person who tells you that when a dead man gets drunk on Earth his soul copies him in Paradise.)

The Jesuits doubtless had many sombre sayings of the kind 'El que peca en la Tierra lo paga [or 'pagará'] en el Infierno' ('He who sins on Earth will pay for it in Paradise'), and here Alberti offers an irreverent parody that might well have come from the wine-soaked lips of one of his beloved uncles.[10] That such relatives were 'cranks' as well as 'drunks' (*LG*, p. 20) suggests an affinity between them and Surrealists. Apart from being rebellious and fantasy-prone, the drunk, like the Surrealist, essentially looks for his paradise on earth, for he is interested in wine itself rather than its transubstantiation. Accordingly, in the next stanza, Alberti sees the soul of such a person as remaining on earth after death, still attached to the objects it had valued most:

Pero la [= alma] de aquel hombre que yace entre las duelas comidas y los aros mohosos de los barriles abandonados, se desespera en el fermento de las vides más agrias y grita en la rebosadura de los vinos impuros.

(But the soul of that man who lies between the corroded staves and rusty hoops of abandoned barrels, grows desperate in the ferment of the bitterest vines and cries out in the overflow of impure wines.)

The decline of Alberti's family is again implicit in this picture of a derelict cellar. Hence the despair of that bygone person whose soul or spirit survives amid its junk objects, that is, strictly, whose soul is seen to survive there by the reflective poet. Since 'aquel hombre' ('that man') is a deceased person who now lives only in the poet's mind, the speaking voice which Alberti now introduces in his last textual reading is a curious amalgam of that of a defunct drunk, of himself as a boy, and again as a Surrealist:

Escuchad. Esta es su voz:

—Mi casa era un saco de arpillera, inservible hasta para remendar el agujero que abre una calumnia en la órbita intacta de una estrella inocente.

No asustaros si os afirmo que yo, espíritu y alma de ese muerto beodo, huía por las noches de mi fardo para desangrarme las espaldas contra las puntas calizas de los quicios oscuros.

(Listen. This is his voice:

—My house was a bag of sackcloth, useless even for mending the hole that a slander opens in the intact orbit of an innocent star.

Don't be shocked if I tell you that I, spirit and soul of that drunken deadman, used to flee at night from my bundle to bleed my shoulders against the limestone edges of dark doorjambs.)

In the first stanza 'house' has the meaning of 'body', as in San Juan de la Cruz, and 'sackcloth' suggests both poverty and religious penance. Thus the poet appears to say that his body was once a worthless and guilt-ridden bundle of rags useless even for stuffing the holes or psychological wounds opened in him by slander, that is, by accusations of immorality from his spying, gossiping teachers, accusations made against a child who was in fact pure in body and spirit, 'intact' and 'innocent'. For Alberti it is no doubt a measure of the peversity of such schooling that children should be taught to despise the body and be made aware of sexual sin even before reaching puberty. Essentially, then, the first stanza depicts the confusion this schooling has produced in a child's mind, a confusion Alberti later described as follows:

Chastity! Chastity! In that atmosphere of insane Catholicism and exaggerated bigotry, how was it possible not to always have before one's eyes, filled with fear and sweetness at the same time, the fleeting image of one's sister or mother undressing, or that of a cousin and a sister suddenly discovered urinating together, a broad smile on their faces, behind the rockroses in the Pinar del Obispo or half-hidden by the clumps of broom along the beach? God, how sinful! (*LG*, p. 57).

The last stanza above confirms Alberti's practice of identifying himself with dead relatives, 'yo, espíritu y alma de ese muerto beodo' ('I, spirited soul of that drunken deadman'), relatives who were like himself 'black sheep' (*LG*, p. 260). In both the alcoholic and Surrealist there is too a marked element of self-inflicted pain; indeed, the image of fleeing at night 'para desangrarme las espaldas contra las puntas calizas de los quicios oscuros' ('to bleed my shoulders against the limestone edges of dark doorjambs') connects variously with the staggering drunk's penchant for self-destruction, the mystic's self-flagellation and the adolescent's self-abuse or masturbation, while it is of course another telling illustration of the Surrealist theme of empathy between man and objects, an empathy based on mutual suffering. This latter point applies even in the apparent indifference of objects towards man's fate, which Alberti suggests in the poem's last, deliberately anti-climactic stanza:

Bien poco importa a la acidez de los mostos descompuestos que mi
alegría se consuma a lo largo de las maderas en las fermentaciones
más tristes que tan sólo causan la muerte al hormigón anónimo que
trafica con su grano de orujo.

En frío, ya sabéis lo que es un sótano por dentro.

(It matters little to the acidity of decomposed musts that my joy should
be consumed alongside timbers in the saddest fermentations which only
cause the death of the anonymous ant that traffics with his grain of
grape residue.

Coldly, you now know what a cellar is like on the inside.)

Death's unimportance recalls the Christian notion succinctly put
by Saint Paul, 'to die is gain' (Philippians 1.21). But Alberti's point
is that it is not surprising that living organisms such as those found
in wine cellars do not lament his death, or, strictly, the ebbing of
his life, 'alegría' (joy) being a reference to his now dead youth. Why
should they if they are themselves continually dying and are perennial
witnesses of death and decay? Life, like the process of making wine,
is a cycle of fermentation and waste; it cannot therefore be saddened
by the human predicament which is no different from its own. Rather
than indifference, then, the last stanza suggests a natural kinship
and compatibility between man and objects, that is, between everything that lives and dies. It is not the poet's passing life or 'joy'
that matters. Why should it be any more significant than that of
an ant? Like the ant, who comes and goes endlessly shifting bagasse
or grape refuse, 'orujo', man's activity is similarly pointless and just
as surely linked to life's waste. There is no cause for despair, however,
in this atheistic, even nihilistic conclusion. It is consistent with the
theme advanced throughout the poem that by attaching himself to
objects man comes to appreciate his true worth. The simple truth
is that life is perishable and that man is part of the cycle of fermentation and waste.

Appropriately, then, the poem ends quietly. Alberti the preacher
leaves his audience with the calm conviction of an absolute and
irrefutable truth, a truth which no longer seems terrible, but rather
natural, inevitable and even reassuring. In the course of the sermon
his emphasis has changed from suffering to acceptance. Much as
the orthodox preacher passes from the stirring example of Christ's
Passion to the implications this has for his congregation, Alberti
takes us from the torment, paranoia and materio-mysticism of the
Surrealist to the now not unpalatable truth that all we have is in

the body. His sermon is thus a sermon on Surrealism, but also, increasingly, on atheism, a fundamental tenet of Surrealism's dialectical materialism. Alberti preaches a message designed to counter the kind of lies he was fed in his youth, his sermon being an attempt to invest the cold message of atheism with the mystique of religion, complete with a charismatic messiah. His use of the Christ parallel, then, though naturally irreverent, is also deeply meaningful and not merely intended to shock as one suspects was largely the case with Luis Buñuel's parallel of Christ and the Marquis de Sade at the end of *Un Chien andalou*. Indeed, insofar as all religion is prompted by the need to appease man's fear of death, Alberti's sermon is religious too. On the one hand it stresses that the fear of death is real, vital and not to be glossed over; on the other it treats death reassuringly as an inevitability in which we all partake. The sermon does not offer four truths as such, in the sense of there being an orderly presentation of four separate points; but in retrospect we can distinguish four recurrent emphases: Alberti's problematic youth, his Surrealist present, the attachment to matter and the finality of bodily death. The free and spontaneous presentation of these points fully accords with Surrealist practice, the poem's expansive lines and sentences being an indication of the degree of therapeutic abreaction which has taken place. But this discharging of the unconscious is no longer passive or uncontrolled as was the case in psychic dictation and the dream images of Surrealism's first stage. The release of images is now strongly directed by the cultivation of a paranoiac state of mind which, as in Dalí, is designed to facilitate hallucinations and impose obsessions. At the same time this presentation, relying as it does upon the irrationality of the paranoiac mind, satirizes the presumed rationalism of orthodox preachers and implies that their holy rhetoric is mumbo-jumbo. Insofar as the preacher, like the poet, is a word-monger, his art in weaving magic spells of words that stir his audience irrationally is one that Alberti has matched and parodied in 'Sermón de las cuatro verdades', a rich and remarkable poem by any standards.

As a volume *Sermones y moradas* still awaits proper evaluation, but to judge by its first poem one could say that in its irreverent theme and masterly technique it bears comparison with Espronceda's *El estudiante de Salamanca*, and perhaps it is no less important an expression of Surrealism in Spain than was the other of Romanticism. What I hope to have shown is that the decisive feature in its first poem is the sermon-manifesto format, for this allowed Alberti to contrast the old with the new, that is, traditional Spanish with modern European thinking. It also provided a synthetic means of revealing the inner workings of his mind, a mind that was, like any genuine Surrealist's, clear thinking. As a poem 'Sermón de las cuatro verdades' confirms a view Breton expressed in his second manifesto, that Surrealism as it progressed would turn its attention 'to something other than the solution of a psychological problem, however interesting that problem may be'.[11] Indeed, as we have seen, the rubble of Alberti's mental life became the building blocks of a new credo. It may well be doubted, in view of its atheistic emphasis, whether this new credo is properly described as transcendental. That it is vociferously and adamantly earth-bound cannot be denied, yet, and this is the point, it is not frustratedly earth-bound as was Romanticism. There is much common ground between Romanticism and Surrrealism, as Breton himself argued. He in fact put Young's *Night Thoughts* first in his historical list of Surrealist texts, while Alberti saw Goya as the father of Spanish Surrealism.[12] No doubt the essential points of contact between Romanticism and Surrealism lie in their excessive subjectivity, or egocentricity, and in their rebellious championing of irrationalism. Yet one cannot fail to notice that a Romantic's transcendentalism is utlimately limited by its very otherworldliness and that Espronceda, on coming upon the wall of death, looks back on this life as a prison in which one is deprived knowledge. In short, for the Romantic the infinite remains unknowable and he is forever trapped in his earth-bound measurements. For the Surrealist, on the other hand, the earth and its objects offer the only prospect of extrication from the prison of the self. In his systematic subjectivization of the world he transfigures objects at will and *ad infinitum*, his hallucinations and free associations being not just mentally therapeutic but new creations which are enactments of his personal freedom. This, to use Anna Balakian's phrase, at least amounts to 'a vicarious sort of transcendence'.[13]

Conclusion

While this book should really have seven conclusions not one, it is not hard to find common threads in the very different poets discussed and even a sense of homogeneity in the century which distances Romanticism from Surrealism. Alberti recognized the spiritual affinity between his and the earlier age when he said that '[E]l surrealismo español viene de Goya'[1] ('Spanish Surrealism comes from Goya'), and we cannot fail to notice how the agony and neurosis, the rebellion and irrationalism of Romanticism is restated in Surrealism. But so too is its transcendental thrust, and here we find the link with the poets who came between. The challenge which Espronceda threw down in *El estudiante de Salamanca* was decisive. He challenged God and the old order, but also, in saying that man would no longer be submissive and satisfied with his lot, he announced the coming of an agnostic age and challenged each poet that followed to find meaning, spiritual meaning, in the here and now. In a country as religious and traditional as Spain this radical break with the past would have lasting repercussions and not a few casualties. Bécquer led the way by making a religion of his poetry and by indicating for the first time that poetry was the medium in which to probe the transcendental. This theme was taken up by three giant poet-metaphysicians, Machado, Guillén and Salinas, for whom the practice of poetry was a way of penetrating the self and of unlocking such perennial mysteries as time, being and freedom.

Each of them in their different ways showed how the individual in an enlightened state could transform contingent reality and find a way through the impasse which had frustrated Espronceda. In Rosalía and Lorca we have two casualties, for their respective stigmas of illegitimacy and homosexuality made the old order something more personal and much harder to struggle against. Yet both poets show the resilience of the self in the face of disintegration, and, even in their emotional turmoil, continue to search for the absolute: Rosalía not knowing quite what she searches for 'en la tierra, en el aire y en el cielo' ('on earth, in the air and in heaven'), and Lorca as 'un pulso herido que sonda las cosas del otro lado' ('a wounded pulse that sounds out things on the other side'). This perplexity is resolved by Alberti who quixotically turns the neurosis induced by a large dose of religion into a creative paranoia that allows him to explore the ultimate realms of worldly transcendentalism, the surreal, and in so doing he joins the ranks of the metaphysicians. A consistent feature, then, in these poets of Spain is their earnest endeavour to find meaning through poetry. This, I hope to have shown, results in poetry that is remarkably meaningful.

---

[1] Letter to V. Bodini, 1959, quoted by F. Aranda, *El surrealismo español* (Barcelona, 1981), p. 15.

Notes

I

1 Gustavo Adolfo Bécquer, *Obras completas*, 8th edition (Madrid, 1954), p. 449. All page numbers refer to this edition.
2 Matthew Arnold, 'The Study of Poetry' (1880), in *The Complete Works of Matthew Arnold*, IX (Ann Arbor, 1973), pp. 161–3.
3 D. L. Shaw, 'Towards the Understanding of Spanish Romanticism', *Modern Language Review*, LVIII (1963), p. 191.
4 See Alban Forcione, 'Meléndez Valdés and the "Essay on Man"', *Hispanic Review*, XXXIV (1966), pp. 291–306.
5 Juan Meléndez·Valdés, *Poesías selectas, La lira de marfil*, edited by J. H. R. Polt and Georges Demerson (Madrid, 1981), p. 199.
6 Ibid., pp. 131–5.
7 Pedro Salinas, *Ensayos de literatura hispánica* (Madrid, 1961), p. 315.
8 R. M. McAndrew, *Naturalism in Spanish Poetry* (Aberdeen, 1931), p. 81.
9 Edith Helman, *Trasmundo de Goya* (Madrid, 1963), 28, p. 146.
10 See Gwyn A. Williams, *Goya and the Impossible Revolution* (London, 1976), p. 173.
11 Quoted by Edith Helman, op. cit., 15, p. 35.
12 Ibid., index of plates, p. 21.
13 See F. D. Klingender, *Goya in the Democratic Tradition* (London, 1968), pp. 90–1.
14 Though sometimes called '*Proverbios* (*Proverbs* or *Sayings*), Goya always referred to them by the more appropriate term of *Disparates*, possibly in recognition of Bosch who was known in Spain as the painter of *disparates*. See F. D. Klingender, op. cit., p. 168.
15 Mariano José de Larra, *Obras*, vol. 2 (Madrid, 1960), p. 282.

16 Pedro Salinas, *Ensayos de literatura hispánica* (Madrid, 1961), pp. 259–67; Joaquín Casalduero, *Espronceda* (Madrid, 1983), p. 147.

17 José de Espronceda, *Obras poéticas completas* (Madrid, 1959), pp. 428–9.

18 Victor Brombert, *The Romantic Prison. The French Tradition* (Princeton, 1978).

19 On the parallels between Bécquer and Florentino Sanz's translations of Heine see, for instance, Dámaso Alonso, *Poetas españoles contemporáneos* (Madrid, 1958), pp. 26–35.

20 See Laura Hofrichter, *Heinrich Heine*, translated by Barker Fairly (Oxford, 1963), p. 78.

21 Jorge Guillén, *Lenguaje y poesía* (Madrid, 1962), p. 172.

22 J. M. Aguirre, 'Bécquer y "lo evanescente"', *Bulletin of Hispanic Studies*, XLI (1964), pp. 28–39.

23 See Rica Brown, *Bécquer* (Barcelona, 1963), pp. 295–304.

24 See chapter five in Dámaso Alonso and Carlos Bousoño, *Seis calas en la expresión literaria española* (Madrid, 1963), pp. 179–218.

25 Laura Hofrichter, op. cit., p. 27.

26 Ibid., p. 23.

27 Dámaso Alonso, 'Originalidad de Bécquer', in *Poetas españoles contemporáneos* (Madrid, 1958), p. 33.

II

1 Rosalía de Castro, *Obras completas*, 6th edition (Madrid, 1968), p. 621. All page numbers refer to this edition.

2 *Diccionario enciclopédico gallego-castellano*, III (Vigo, 1961), p. 320.

3 Alberto Machado da Rosa, 'Rosalía de Castro, poeta incompreendido', *RHM*, XX (1954), pp. 181–223.

4 Catherine Davies, 'Rosalía de Castro's Later Poetry and Anti-Regionalism in Spain', *MLR*, LXXIX (1984), pp. 609–19.

5 *Diccionario enciclopédico gallego-castellano*, pp. 319–20.

6 J. Rof Carballo, 'Rosalía, Anima Galaica', in *7 (Siete) ensayos sobre Rosalía de Castro* (Vigo, 1951), p. 123.

7 Hernani Cidade, ed., *Poesía medieval, I: Cantigas de amigo* (Lisbon, 1959), p. 4.

8 Mario Praz, *The Romantic Agony* (Oxford, 1951).

9 Kathleen Kulp-Hill, *Rosalía de Castro* (Boston, 1977), p. 98.

10 Norman O. Brown, *Life Against Death. The Psychoanalytical Meaning of History* (London, 1970).

11 Ibid., pp. 131–2.

12 Ibid., p. 48.

III

1 Antonio Machado, *Poesías completas* (Madrid, 1983), p. 119. All page numbers refer to this edition.

2 See J. M. Aguirre, *Antonio Machado, poeta simbolista* (Madrid, 1973).

3 See 'Autobiografía escrita en 1913 para una proyectada antología de Azorín' in Antonio Machado, *Soledades. Galerías. Otros poemas*, ed. Geoffrey Ribbans (Barcelona, 1975), p. 269.

4 Antonio Machado, *Obras, poesía y prosa* (Buenos Aires, 1975), p. 834.

5 Antonio Machado, *Los complementarios y otras prosas póstumas* (Buenos Aires, 1957), p. 23.

6 See, for instance, Serrano Poncela, *Antonio Machado. Su mundo y su obra* (Buenos Aires, 1954), p. 39; Aurora de Albornoz, *La presencia de Miguel de Unamuno en Antonio Machado* (Madrid, 1968), p. 29; A. J. McVan, *Antonio Machado* (New York, 1959), p. 22; Geoffrey Ribbans, op. cit., p. 12; even N. Glendinning, 'The Philosophy of Henri Bergson in the Poetry of Antonio Machado', *Revue de la Littérature Comparée*, XXXVI (1962), p. 51. One critic who allows a possible influence of Bergson on the early Machado is Eugenio Frutos, 'El primer Bergson en Antonio Machado', *Revista de filosofía*, XIX (1960), p. 119, but this is suggested only tentatively and in the main Frutos agrees with the argument of Sánchez Barbudo, *El pensamiento de Antonio Machado* (Madrid, 1974), that Machado was Bergsonian a priori, that is, without having read Bergson before 1911. The issue is discussed at greater length in my article, 'Antonio Machado's Knowledge of Bergson Before 1911', *Neophilologus*, LXVII (1983), pp. 204–14.

7 See J. R. Jiménez, *La corriente infinita (crítica y evocación)* (Madrid, 1961), p. 228; Miguel de Unamuno, *Obras completas*, I (Barcelona, 1958), p. 487.

8 See J. M. Palacios, 'Traductions espagnoles d'œuvres de Bergson, *Les Études Bergsoniennes*, IX (1970), 122.

9 See Ribbans, op. cit., p. 14.

10 From a letter written to Federico de Onís in 1932, quoted by Arthur Terry, *Antonio Machado: Campos de Castilla* (London, 1973), p. 77.

11 Henri Bergson, *Matière et mémoire*, in *Œuvres* (Paris, 1959), p. 221.

12 Ibid., p. 229.

13 Claudio Guillén, *Literature as System. Essays Toward the Theory of Literary History* (Princeton, 1971), p. 253.

14 Op. cit., *Œuvres*, p. 228.

15 Ibid., p. 251.

16 Ibid., p. 230.

17 Ibid., p. 233.

18 Machado's letter was first quoted by Unamuno in his 'carta abierta' ('open letter'), *Helios*, VIII (Madrid, August, 1903), and has since been quoted by several critics, for instance Aurora de Albornoz, 'Miguel de Unamuno y Antonio Machado' in *Antonio Machado*, ed. Ricardo Gullón and Allen W. Phillips (Madrid, 1973), p. 125.

19 See 'Welsh Landscape' in the volume *Song at the Year's Turning* in *Selected Poems 1946–1968* (London, 1973), p. 9.

20 H. Bergson, *Essai sur les données immédiates de la conscience*, in *Œuvres*, p. 85.
21 H. Bergson, *Introduction à la métaphysique*, an essay first published in 1903, *Œuvres*, p. 1395.
22 *Essai sur les données*, *Œuvres*, 67–8. See Bergson on music also in *La Perception du changement*, *Œuvres*, p. 1382–4.
23 See Claudio Guillén's thorough and convincing analysis of this poem in *Literature as System*, op. cit., to which I am inevitably indebted.
24 H. Bergson, *Time and Free Will*, translated by F. L. Pogson (London, 1910).
25 H. Bergson, *Essai sur les données*, *Œuvres*, p. 113.

IV

1 From the final *Cántico* collected in *Aire nuestro* (Milan, 1968), p. 479. Page numbers refer to this edition.
2 José Ortega y Gasset, *Obras completas*, I (Madrid, 6th edition, 1963), pp. 244–60.
3 *Obras completas*, I, p. 480.
4 *Obras completas*, I, p. 322.
5 Jorge Guillén, *Lenguaje y poesía* (Madrid, 1962), pp. 240-42.
6 See 'Siete cartas de Pedro Salinas a Jorge Guillén', *Buenos Aires Literaria*, no. 13, October 1953, p. 18.
7 *Lenguaje y poesía*, p. 244.
8 J. Ruiz de Conde, *El Cántico americano de Jorge Guillén* (Madrid, 1973), p. 266.
9 *Obras completas*, I, p. 350.
10 *Meditaciones del 'Quijote'*, *Obras completas*, I, p. 319.
11 See Marcel Brion, *Kandinsky*, translated from the French by A. H. N. Molesworth (London, 1961), p. 70; also Wassily Kandinsky, *Punto y línea sobre el plano* (Barcelona, 1971), pp. 29, 83.
12 See C. G. Jung, 'Archetypes of the Collective Unconscious' in *Complete Works*, translated by R. F. C. Hull (London, 1959), IX, pp. 42–3; also XII, p. 91.
13 *Obras completas*, I, pp. 487–8.
14 Jorge Guillén, *Federico en persona* (Buenos Aires, 1959), p. 129.
15 Jorge Guillén in *Revista de Occidente* (Madrid, November 1926), p. 234.
16 *Meditaciones del 'Quijote'*, *Obras completas*, I, p. 322.

V

1 Pedro Salinas, *Poesías completas* (Barcelona, 1975), p. 117. All page numbers refer to this edition.
2 Jorge Guillén, *Aire nuestro* (Milan, 1968), p. 249.

3 In Gerardo Diego, *Poesía española contemporánea 1901–1934* (Madrid, 1962), p. 303.
4 Rupert C. Allen, *Symbolic Experience: A Study of Poems by Pedro Salinas* (Alabama, 1982).
5 José Ortega y Gasset, *Meditaciones del 'Quijote'* (1914) in *Obras completas*, I (Madrid, 6th edition, 1963), pp. 335–36.
6 González Muela makes the point in both 'Poesía y amistad: Jorge Guillén y Pedro Salinas', *BHS*, XXXV (1958), 28, and in his introduction to Pedro Salinas, *La voz a ti debida, Razón de amor* (Madrid, 1969), p. 29.
7 David L. Stixrude, *The Early Poetry of Pedro Salinas* (Princeton, 1975), p. 12.
8 The passage is quoted and developed by A. R. Huéscar, *Perspectiva y verdad: el problema de la verdad en Ortega* (Madrid, 1966), p. 389. Though it belongs to a later period in Ortega's work, *El hombre y la gente, OC* VII, p. 124, these Madrid lectures of 1949–50 are essentially a summary of earlier ideas.
9 *Meditaciones del 'Quijote', OC*, I, p. 333.
10 Claudio Guillén, *Literature as System: Essays towards the Theory of Literary History* (Princeton, 1971), pp. 299 ff.
11 From 'Verdad y perspectiva' (1916), *OC*, II, p. 18.
12 *OC*, III, p. 163.
13 'Pidiendo una biblioteca' (1908), *OC*, I, p. 84.
14 Pedro Salinas, 'Lamparilla a Paul Valéry', *Sur*, Nos. 129–34 (1945), pp. 46–7.
15 'Itinerarios jóvenes de España. Rafael Alberti', *La Gaceta Literaria*, no. 49 (January 1929).
16 Henri Bergson, *La Pensée et le mouvant* in *Œuvres* (Paris, 1959), pp. 1378, 1395. Although *La Pensée et le mouvant* did not appear until 1934, the essays and lectures which it contains had been published much earlier, specifically, with regard to the two quotations above, 1911 and 1903 respectively.
17 *Meditaciones, OC*, I, p. 330.
18 Pedro Salinas, *Narrativa completa* (Barcelona, 1976), pp. 19–24.
19 *Meditaciones*, pp. 321–2.
20 'Verdad y perspectiva', *OC*, II, p. 19.
21 'Adán en el Paraíso', *OC*, II, p. 475.
22 Pedro Salinas, *Reality and the Poet in Spanish Poetry* (Baltimore, 1940).
23 Pedro Salinas, *Jorge Manrique o tradición y originalidad* (Buenos Aires, 1962), pp. 115, 123.
24 Leo Spitzer, 'El conceptismo interior de Pedro Salinas', *RHM*, VII (1941), pp. 37, 39.
25 C. B. Morris, *A Generation of Spanish Poets*. Cambridge, 1969), p. 164.
26 See Jorge Guillén's introduction to Pedro Salinas, *Poesías completas*, p. 11.
27 S. Gilman, 'The Proem to *La voz a ti debida*', *MLQ*, XXIII (1962), pp. 355–6. For Guillén's defence see note 26.
28 *Jorge Manrique*, ibid., p. 29.
29 Garcilaso de la Vega, *Poesías castellanas completas*, ed. E. L. Rivers (Madrid, 1969), p. 38.
30 It is also interesting to note that Salinas expunged certain details from

early drafts of the poems, as for instance a reference to a walk in the patios of Córdoba and to the *amada* being *morena* (*dark* in hair and complexion), see Diana Ramírez de Arellano, *Caminos de la creación poética en Pedro Salinas* (Madrid, 1956), pp. 114, 147.

31 *Jorge Manrique*, p. 30.

32 Courtly Love and Petrarchism were often attacked by those who practised it. Equally famous broadsides are Shakespeare's 'My mistress' eyes are nothing like the sun' (sonnet CXXX) and Lope de Vega's 'Señora mía, si de vos ausente / en esta vida duro y no me muero, / es porque como y duermo' ('My lady, if in being absent from you / I persist in this life and do not die, / it is because I eat and sleep'), Lope de Vega, *Poesías líricas*, I, ed. J. F. Montesinos (Madrid, 1960), p. 175.

33 C. B. Morris, 'Salinas and Proust', *RLC*, XLIV (1970), p. 210.

34 Leo Spitzer, loc. cit., p. 35.

35 Salinas's use of courtly clichés is examined more closely in my article 'Pedro Salinas and Courtly Love. The *amada* in '*La voz a ti debida*: woman, muse and symbol', *BHS*, LVI (1979), pp. 123–44.

36 *Jorge Manrique*, p. 15.

37 The poem is analysed in 'Pedro Salinas and Courtly Love', loc. cit., pp. 1345–5.

38 J. M. Aguirre, '*La voz a ti debida*: Salinas y Bergson', *RLC*, LII (1978), pp. 98–118.

39 Henri Bergson, *Œuvres*, pp. 83–92.

40 *Jorge Manrique*, p. 21.

41 *Œuvres*, pp. 284, 326, 129.

42 Satosi Watanabé, 'The concept of time in modern physics and Bergson's pure duration' in *Bergson and the Evolution of Physics*, ed. P.A.Y. Gunter (Tennessee, 1969), pp. 62–7.

43 *OC*, I, p. 475.

44 *Œuvres*, p. 109.

45 'El conceptismo interior', p. 41.

46 Something approaching a statistical count of these devices is given in my article, 'The Ironic Rationality of *Razón de amor*. Pedro Salinas: Logic, Language and Poetry', *OL*, XXXVIII (1983), pp. 254–70.

47 See Gerardo Diego, *La poesía española contemporánea*, p. 303.

48 See Wallace Fowlie, *Mallarmé* (Chicago, 1962), pp. 225–6.

VI

1 Federico García Lorca, *Obras completas* (Madrid, 6th edition, 1963), p. 430. All page numbers refer to this edition.

2 Dámaso Alonso, *Poetas españoles contemporáneos* (Madrid, 1958), p. 188.

3 A list of French Surrealist works which appeared in Spain and the text of Aragon's lecture are given in C. B. Morris, *Surrealism and Spain* (Cambridge, 1972).

4 See Ian Gibson, *Federico García Lorca. 1. De Fuente Vaqueros a Nueva York, 1898–1929* (Barcelona, 1985), p. 383.

5 See Guillén's prologue to F. G. Lorca, *Obras completas*, p. xlvii.

6 Rafael Alberti, *The Lost Grove* (Berkeley, 1976), pp. 168–9.

7 As reported by Jorge Guillén in his prologue to Lorca, *O.C.*, p. xlvii.

8 F. G. Lorca, *Romancero gitano*, edited by Mario Hernández (Madrid, 1981), pp. 143–4.

9 In his article 'An Analysis of Narrative and Symbol in Lorca's "Romance sonámbulo"' *Hispanic Review*, XXXVI (1968), 338–52, Allen suggests that the young man has been having an affair with the green girl, that this has been discovered by the other male who is her husband and that the latter has taken bloody revenge on the youth. This theory is refuted by several points in the text: there is no suggestion that the older man is husband to the young girl, in fact 'niña' (girl) is an improbable term for wife; there would be no need for the younger man to tell the other 'Compadre, vengo sangrando / desde los puertos de Cabra' ('Friend, I come bleeding / from the passes of Cabra') if he were in fact speaking to his assailant as suggested; lastly, there is nothing in the dialogue between the two men which suggests hostility, much less that they have recently fought, indeed the conversation is polite and sympathetic as one would expect from 'dos compadres' ('two friends').

10 J. M. Aguirre, 'El sonambulismo de Federico García Lorca' *BHS*, XLIV (1967), p. 285.

11 See Ian Gibson, op. cit., pp. 136, 364–6, 21, 153 respectively.

12 S. Freud, *Collected Papers*, IV, translated by Joan Riviére, (London, 1950), p. 335.

13 See Dámaso Alonso and José Manuel Blecua, *Antología de la poesía española, lírica de tipo tradicional* (Madrid, 1969), p. 44.

14 See his letters to Guillén in Jorge Guillén, *Federico en persona* (Buenos Aires, 1959).

15 *The Holy Bible*, revised standard version (London, 1952), p. 280.

16 See Alonso and Blecua, op. cit., p. 48.

17 Ibid., p. 122.

18 Compare the description of Pedrosa in Lorca's *Mariana Pineda* as 'un viejo verde', *O.C.*, p. 800 ('a dirty old man').

19 Letter to Guillermo de Torre, *O.C.*, p. 1630.

20 Ian Gibson has definite views about Lorca's relationship with Dalí, op. cit., p. 493, while there is no room for doubt about the Dionysian Aladrén (1906–44) whom all Lorca's friends, Dalí included, appear to have despised, ibid, pp. 544–9.

21 Letter to Adriano del Valle, 1918, in F. G. Lorca, *Epistolario*, vol. 2, edited by Christopher Maurer (Madrid, 1983), pp. 16–19, and in Ian Gibson, op. cit., p. 188.

22 Letter to Carlos Morla Lynch, 6 June 1929, Ian Gibson, op. cit., p. 605.

23 Carlos Morla Lynch, *En España con Federico García Lorca (Páginas de un diario íntimo, 1928–1936)*, (Madrid, 1958), p. 43, also Gibson, op. cit., p. 611.

24 Derek Harris, *García Lorca. Poeta en Nueva York* (London, 1978), p. 69.

25 C. Marcilly, *Ronde et fable de la solitude à New York* (Paris, 1962), p. 17.

26 See J. Francisco Aranda, *Luis Buñuel, biografía crítica* (Barcelona, 1969), p. 60.

27 D. Harris, op. cit., p. 28.

28 In his manuscript Lorca misspelt Eden, writing 'Edem' instead of the correct Spanish *Edén*, but the poem shows that he was fully aware of the word's connection with paradise.

29 There are problems surrounding the definitive text of *Poeta en Nueva York* which we cannot go into here; see F. G. Lorca, *Poeta en Nueva York. Tierra y luna*, edited by Eutimio Martín (Barcelona, 1981). While I have been content to follow the text of *Obras completas*, it may well be that in the case of 'Poema doble del lago Edem' the text given by Martín is more correct. With regard to the two stanzas quoted Martín gives not 'niño pesado' ('tiresome child') but 'niño pasado' ('child of old'), not 'voces de los borrachos' ('voices of drunks') but 'voces de los soldados' ('voices of soldiers'), and finally his second-last line reads 'Déjame salir, hombrecillo de los cuernos' (op. cit., p. 199) ('Let me out, little fellow with horns'), where the comma and the singular noun (little fellow, i.e. devil) seem appropriate.

30 Eutimio Martín gives '—rosa, niña y abeto—' ('—rose, girl and fir-tree—'), op. cit., p. 200, where the punctuation of parenthesis and comma seems more logical, suggesting in fact that the poet is speaking abstractedly to items of nature and a child that he sees near him at the lakeside.

31 Ian Gibson, op. cit., p. 95.

32 See Eutimio Martín, op. cit., p. 316.

VII

1 Rafael Alberti, *Poesías completas* (Buenos Aires, 1961), pp. 290–91. All page numbers refer to this edition.

2 Rafael Alberti, *The Lost Grove*, translated and edited by Gabriel Burns (Berkeley, 1976). Quotations from this text will be followed by *LG* plus the page of reference in parenthesis. Alberti's Spanish original was *La arboleda perdida* (Buenos Aires, 1959).

3 Jorge Guillén, *Language and Poetry, Some Poets of Spain*, (Cambridge, Massachusetts, 1961), pp. 51, 52, 55–6. There is also a Spanish version, *Lenguaje y poesía, Algunos casos españoles* (Madrid, 1961).

4 Jorge Guillén, *Language and Poetry*, p. 67.

5 André Breton, *Manifestos of Surrealism*, translated by Richard Weaver and Helen R. Lowe (Ann Arbor, 1972), p. 139.

6 For a full discussion of this point see Anna Balakian, *Surrealism, The Road to the Absolute* (London, 1972), especially pp. 123–39.

7 Dalí's 'Visage paranoïaque' appeared in *Le Surréalisme au service de la Révolution* in 1931, in number 3 of that year.

8 Salvador Dalí, 'De la beauté terrifiante et comestible de l'architecture modern style', *Minotaure*, no. 3–4 (1933), p. 76.

9 F. G. Sarriá, '*Sobre los ángeles* de Rafael Alberti y el surrealismo', *Papeles de Son Armadans*, XCI (1978–9), pp. 23–40. This excellent article argues the Surrealist case on the basis of Alberti's style and it also provides a penetrating synopsis of the various and often muddled approaches critics have made to the question of Surrealism in Alberti.

10 Alberti speaks for instance of the drinking habits of his Uncle Guillermo (*LG*, p. 60), while 'Uncle Ignacio was also immersed in a high tide of alcohol' (*LG*, p. 61) and his father 'was also a great lover and a great drinker of the liquids he represented, thus upholding an old, alcoholic family tradition' (*LG*, p. 59).

11 André Breton, *Manifestos of Surrealism*, p. 139.

12 See Francisco Aranda, *El surrealismo español* (Barcelona, 1981), p. 15.

13 Op. cit., p. 208.

Select Critical Bibliography

Bécquer and the Romantics

Aguirre, J. M., 'Bécquer y lo evanescente', *Bulletin of Hispanic Studies*, XLI, 1964.

Alonso, Dámaso, 'Originalidad de Bécquer', in *Poetas españoles contemporáneos*, Madrid, 1952.

Alonso Cortés, Narciso, 'Una nota sobre Bécquer', *Bulletin of Spanish Studies*, XXIV, 1947.

Benítez, Rubén, *Ensayo de bibliografía razonada de Gustavo Adolfo Bécquer*, Buenos Aires, 1961.

Bousoño, Carlos, 'Las pluralidades paralelísticas en Bécquer', in Dámaso Alonso and Bousoño, *Seis calas en la expresión literaria española*, Madrid, 1951.

Brown, Rica, *Bécquer: Gustavo Adolfo Bécquer en dos tiempos*, Barcelona, 1963.

Carpintero, Heliodoro, *Bécquer de par en par*, Madrid, 1957.

Casalduero, Joaquín, *Espronceda*, Madrid, 1983.

Demerson, Georges, *Don Juan Meléndez Valdés et son temps (1754–1817)*, Paris, 1961.

Díaz, José Pedro, *Gustavo Adolfo Bécquer, vida y poesía*, Madrid, 1958.

Entrambasaguas, Joaquín de, *La obra poética de Bécquer en su discriminación creadora y erótica*, Madrid, 1974.

Fogelquist, Donald, F., 'A Reappraisal of Bécquer', *Hispania*, XXXVIII, 1955.

Forcione, Alban, 'Meléndez Valdés and the *Essay on Man*', *Hispanic Review*, XXXIV, 1966.

Glendinning, Nigel, *Vida y obra de Cadalso*, Madrid, 1962.

—— 'New Light on the Text and Ideas of Cadalso's *Noches lúgbres*', *The Modern Language Review*, LV, 1960.

Guillén, Jorge, 'La poética de Bécquer', *Revista Hispánica Moderna*, VIII, 1942.

—— *Lenguaje y poesía. Algunos casos españoles*, Madrid, 1962.

Havard, Robert, 'The *romances* of Meléndez Valdés, in *Studies of the Spanish and Portuguese Ballad*, ed. N. D. Shergold, London, 1972.

—— 'Meaning and Metaphor of Syntax in Bécquer, Guillén and Salinas', *Iberoromania*, XIX, 1984.

Helman, Edith, *Trasmundo de Goya*, Madrid, 1963.

—— '*Caprichos* and *monstruos* of Cadalso and Goya', *Hispanic Review*, XXVI, 1958.

King, Edmund L., *Gustavo Adolfo Bécquer: From Painter to Poet*, Mexico, 1953.

Klingender, F. D., *Goya in the Democratic Tradition*, London, 1968.

Martínez Ruiz, José, (Azorín), *Rivas y Larra*, Madrid, 1916.

McAndrew, R. M., *Naturalism in Spanish Poetry*, Aberdeen, 1931.

McClelland, I. L., 'New Interpretations of Spanish Poetry. V. Bécquer: Rima XV', *Bulletin of Spanish Studies*, XIX, 1942.

Pageard, Robert, 'Le germanisme de Bécquer', *Bulletin Hispanique*, LVI, 1954.

Polt, J. R. H., and Demerson, Georges, (eds.), *Juan Meléndez Valdés, Poesías selectas, La lira de marfil*, Madrid, 1981.

Rees, Margaret A., *Espronceda: El estudiante de Salamanca*, London, 1979.

Salinas, Pedro, prologue and edition of Meléndez Valdés, *Poesías*, Madrid, 1925.

Schneider, Franz, 'Gustavo A. Bécquer as *Poeta* and his Knowledge of Heine's *Lieder*', *Modern Philology*, XIX, 1922.

Sebold, Russell P., *Cadalso: El primer romántico 'europeo' de España*, Madrid, 1974.

—— *Trayectoría del romanticismo español*, Barcelona, 1983.

Shaw, D. L., 'Towards the Understanding of Spanish Romanticism', *The Modern Language Review*, LVIII, 1963.

Varela, José Luis, *Larra y España*, Madrid, 1983.

Williams, Gwyn A., *Goya and the Impossible Revolution*, London, 1976.

Rosalía de Castro

Alonso Montero, Xesús, *En torno a Rosalía*, Madrid, 1985.

Bouza Brey, F., 'El tema rosaliná de *negra sombra* en la poesía compostelana del siglo XIX', *Cuadernos de Estudios Gallegos*, VIII, 1953.

— — 'La joven Rosalía en Compostela (1852–1856)', *Cuadernos de Estudios Gallegos*, X, 1955.

Carballo Calero, R., *Contribucion ao estudo das fontes literarias de Rosalía*, Lugo, 1959.

— — 'Problemas biográficos', in *Estudios rosalianos*, Vigo, 1979.

— — 'Machado desde Rosalía', *Insula*, XIX, no. 212–13, 1964.

Cernuda, Luis, *Estudios sobre poesía española contemporánea*, Madrid, 1957.

Costa Clavel, Javier, *Rosalía de Castro*, Barcelona, 1967.

Davies, Catherine, *Rosalía de Castro no seu tempo*, Vigo, 1987.

— — 'Rosalía de Castro's Late Poetry and Anti-Regionalism in Spain', *The Modern Language Review*, LXXIX, 1984.

Díaz, Nidia, *La protesta social en la obra de Rosalía*, Vigo, 1966.

González Alegre, R., 'Sobre una interpretación de Rosalía de Castro', *Papeles de Son Armadans*, VIII, 1958.

Havard, Robert, 'Image and Persona in Rosalía de Castro's *En las orillas del Sar*', *Hispanic Review*, XLII, 1974.

— — 'Saudades as Structure in Rosalía de Castro's *En las orillas del Sar*', *Hispanic Journal*, V, 1983.

— — 'Paralelos entre los sentimientos gallegos y galeses de la *saudade/hiraeth*: un espejo céltico de la neurosis rosaliana', in *Rosalía de Castro e o seu tempo*, Santiago de Compostela, 1986.

Kulp, Kathleen, *Manner and Mood in Rosalía de Castro*, Madrid, 1968.

Kulp-Hill, Kathleen, *Rosalía de Castro*, Boston, 1977.

Machado da Rosa, Alberto, 'Rosalía de Castro, poeta incompreendido', *Revista Hispánica Moderna*, XX, 1954.

— — 'Subsidios para la cronología de la obra poética rosaliana', *Cuadernos de Estudios Gallegos*, XII, 1957.

— — 'Heine in Spain (1856–67): Relations with Rosalía de Castro', *Monatshefte fur der deutsch Unterricht*, XLIX, 1957.

Mayoral, Marina, *La poesía de Rosalía de Castro*, Madrid, 1974.

— — (ed.) Rosalía de Castro, *En las orillas del Sar*, Madrid, 1978.

Montero, Eugenia, *Rosalía de Castro, la luz de la negra sombra*, Madrid, 1985.

Murguía, M., *Los precursores*, La Coruña, 1976.

— — prologue to Rosalía de Castro, *Obras completas*, Madrid, 6th Aguilar edition, 1968.

Nogales de Muñiz, María Antonia, *Irradiación de Rosalía de Castro*, Barcelona, 1966.

Placer, Fr. Gumersindo, 'La danza del demonio en las obras de Rosalía de Castro', *Grial*, XVII, 1967.

Poullain, C. H., *Rosalía Castro de Murguía y su obra literaria*, Madrid, 1974.

Rof Carballo, J., 'Rosalía, ánima galaica', in *Siete ensayos sobre Rosalía de Castro*, Vigo, 1951.

Schwartz, Kessel, 'Rosalía de Castro's *En las orillas del Sar*: A Psychoanalytical Interpretation', *Symposium*, XXVI, 1972.

Stevens, Shelley, *Rosalía de Castro and the Galician Revival*, London, 1986.

Tirrel, P., *La mística de la saudade*, Madrid, 1955.

Antonio Machado

Aguirre, J. M., *Antonio Machado, poeta simbolista*, Madrid, 1961.

Albornoz, Aurora de, *La presencia de Unamuno en Antonio Machado*, Madrid, 1967.

—— and Torre, Guillermo de, (eds.) Antonio Machado, *Obras: poesía y prosa*, Buenos Aires, 1964.

Alonso, Dámaso, *Poetas españoles contemporáneos*, Madrid, 1965.

Cano, José Luis, prologue to Antonio Machado, *Campos de Castilla*, Madrid, 1974.

Frutos, Eugenio, 'El primer Bergson en A. Machado', *Revista de Filosofía*, XIX, 1960.

Glendinning, Nigel, 'The Philosophy of Henri Bergson in the Poetry of Antonio Machado', *Revue de la Littérature Comparée*, XXXVI, 1962.

Guillén, Claudio, *Literature as System. Essays Towards the Theory of Literary History*, Princeton, 1971.

Gullón, Ricardo, and Phillips, Allen, W., (eds.) *Antonio Machado*, Madrid, 1973.

Jiménez, Juan Ramón, *La corriente infinita (crítica y evocación)*, Madrid, 1961.

Machado, Antonio, *Juan de Mairena*, Madrid, 1936.

McVan, A. J., *Antonio Machado*, New York, 1959.

Pérez Ferrero, Miguel, *Vida de Antonio Machado y Manuel*, Madrid, 1947.

Ribbans, Geoffrey, *Niebla y soledad. Aspectos de Unamuno y Machado*, Mardid, 1971.

—— prologue to Antonio Machado, *Soledades, Galerías, Otros poemas*, Barcelona, 1975.

Sánchez Barbudo, A., *Estudios sobre Unamuno y Machado*, Madrid, 1959.

— — *El pensamiento de Antonio Machado*, Madrid, 1974.

Serrano Poncela, Segundo, 'Borrosos laberintos', in *La Torre* (*Homenaje a Antonio Machado*), XII, 1964.

Sesé, Bernard, *Antonio Machado (1875–1938). Madrid, 1980.*

Terry, Arthur, *Antonio Machado: Campos de Castilla*, London, 1973.

Zubiría Ramón de, *La poesía de Antonio Machado*, Madrid, 1955.

Jorge Guillén

Alonso, Amado, 'Jorge Guillén, poeta esencial', *La Nación*, Buenos Aires, 21 April 1929, republished in B. Ciplijauskaité, *Jorge Guillén*, (see below).

Bobes Naves, María del Carmen, *Gramática de 'Cántico' (análisis semiológico)*, Barcelona, 1975.

Bousoño, Carlos, 'Neuva interpretación de *Cántico* de Jorge Guillén (El esencialismo guilleniano y juanramoniano)', in *Homenaje a Jorge Guillén, Wellesley College*, Madrid, 1978.

Casalduero, Joaquín, '*Cántico' de Jorge Guillén*, Madrid, 1953.

Ciplijauskaité, Biruté, editor, *Jorge Guillén*, Madrid, 1975.

— — *Deber de plenitud, la poesía de Jorge Guillén*, Mexico City, 1973.

Couffon, Claude, *Dos encuentros con Jorge Guillén*, Paris, undated.

Debicki, Andrew P., *La poesía de Jorge Guillén*, Madrid, 1973.

Dehennin, Elsa, '*Cántico' de Jorge Guillén, une poésie de la clarté*, Brussels, 1969.

Gil de Biedma, Jaime, '*Cántico': el mundo y la poesía de Jorge Guillén*, Barcelona, 1960.

Giovanni, N. T. di, (ed.) Jorge Guillén, *Cántico, A Selection*, London, 1965.

Guillén, Jorge, *El argumento de la obra*, Milan, 1961.

González Muela, Joaquín, *La realidad y Jorge Guillén*, Madrid, 1962.

Havard, Robert, *Jorge Guillén: Cántico*, London, 1986.

— — 'The Early *décimas* of Jorge Guillén', *Bulletin of Hispanic Studies*, XLVII, 1971.

— — 'Guillén, Salinas and Ortega: Circumstance and Perspective', *Bulletin of Hispanic Studies*, LX, 1983.

— — 'La metafisca de *Cántico*: Jorge Guillén, Ortega, Husserl y Heidegger', *Sin Nombre*, XIV, 1984.

Pleak, F. A. *The Poetry of Jorge Guillén*, Princeton, 1942.

Ruiz de Conde, Justina, *El 'Cántico' americano de Jorge Guillén*, Madrid, 1973.

Sibbald, K. M., Prologue and compilation, Jorge Guillén, *Hacia 'Cántico': escritos de los años 20*, Barcelona, 1980.

Silver, Philip W., prologue and edition, Jorge Guillén, *Mientras el aire es nuestro*, Madrid, 1978.

Zardoya, Concha, *Poesía española del 98 y del 27*, Madrid, 1968.

Pedro Salinas

Aguirre, J. M., 'La voz a ti debida: Salinas y Bergson', *Revue de la Littérature Comparée*, LII, 1978.

Allen, Rupert C., *Symbolic Experience: A Study of Poems by Pedro Salinas*, Alabama, 1982.

Costa Viva, Olga, *Pedro Salinas, frente a la realidad*, Madrid, 1969.

Crispin, John, *Pedro Salinas*, New York, 1974.

Darmangeat, Pierre, *Pedro Salinas et 'La voz a ti debida'*, Paris, 1955.

Feal Deibe, Carlos, *La poesía de Pedro Salinas*, Madrid, 1965.

Feldbaum, J., 'El trasmundo de la obra poética de Pedro Salinas', *Revista Hispánica Moderna*, XXII, 1956.

Gilman, S., 'The Proem to *La voz a ti debida*', *Modern Language Quarterly*, XXIII, 1962.

González Muela, Joaquín, 'Poesía y amistad: Jorge Guillén y Pedro Salinas', *Bulletin of Hispanic Studies*, XXXV, 1958.

— — prologue to Pedro Salinas, *La voz a ti debida, Razón de amor*, Madrid, 1969.

Guillén, Jorge, prologue to Pedro Salinas, *Poesías completas*, Barcelona, 1975.

Havard, Robert, 'The Reality of Words in the Poetry of Pedro Salinas', *Bulletin of Hispanic Studies*, LI, 1974.

— — 'Pedro Salinas and Courtly Love. The *amada* in *La voz a ti debida*: woman, muse and symbol', *Bulletin of Hispanic Studies*, LVI, 1979.

— — 'The Ironic Rationality of *Razón de amor*. Pedro Salinas: Logic, Language and Poetry', *Orbis Litterarum*, XXXVIII, 1983.

— — 'Fast Car Metaphysics: Jorge Guillén and Pedro Salinas', *Romance Studies*, VI, 1985.

— — 'Guillén, Salinas and Ortega: Circumstance and Perspective', *Bulletin of Hispanic Studies*, LX, 1983.

Marichal, Juan, *Tres voces de Pedro Salinas*, Madrid, 1976.

Morris, C. B., 'Salinas and Proust', *Revue de la Littérature Comparée*, XLIV, 1970.

Palley, J., *La luz no usada. La poesía de Pedro Salinas*, Mexico, 1966.

Ramírez de Arrellano, Diana, *Caminos de la creación poética en Pedro Salinas*, Madrid, 1956.

Spitzer, Leo, 'El conceptismo interior de Pedro Salinas', *Revista Hispánica Moderna*, VII, 1941.

Stixrude, David L., *The Early Poetry of Pedro Salinas*, Princeton, 1975.

Zubizarreta, Alma de, *Pedro Salinas: el diálogo creador*, (prologue by Jorge Guillén), Madrid, 1969.

Federico García Lorca

Aguirre, J. M., 'El sonambulismo de Federico García Lorca', *Bulletin of Hispanic Studies*, XLIV, 1967.

Allen, Rupert C., 'An Analysis of Narrative and Symbol in Lorca's "Romance sonámbulo" ', *Hispanic Review*, XXXVI, 1968.

—— 'Una explicación simbólica de "Iglesia abandonada" de Lorca', *Hispanófila*, XXVI, 1966.

—— 'A Commentary on Lorca's *El paseo de Buster Keaton*', *Hispanófila*, XVI, 1973.

—— *The Symbolic World of Federico García Lorca*, New Mexico, 1972.

Alonso, Dámaso, *Poetas españoles contemporáneos*, Madrid, 1958.

Campbell, R., *Lorca: An Appreciation of his Poetry*, Cambridge, 1952.

Correa, G., *La poesía mítica de Federico García Lorca*, Madrid, 1970.

Duncan, Bernice G., (trans.), F. García Lorca, 'Trip to the Moon', in *New Directions in Prose and Poetry*, XVIII, 1964.

Durán, Manuel, (ed.) *Lorca, A Collection of Critical Essays*, Englewood Cliffs, N.J., 1962.

García Posada, Miguel, *Lorca: Interpretación de 'Poeta en Nueva York'*, Madrid, 1981.

Gibson, Ian, *Federico García Lorca. Vol. 1. De Fuentevaqueros a Nueva York, 1898–1929*, Barcelona, 1985.

Gili, J. L., (trans.) *Lorca*, Harmondsworth, 1960.

Guillén, Jorge, *Federico en persona*, Buenos Aires, 1959.

—— prologue to Federico García Lorca, *Obras completas*, Madrid, 6th Aguilar edition, 1963.

Harris, Derek, *García Lorca: Poeta en Nueva York*, London, 1978.

—— 'The Religious Theme in Lorca's *Poeta en Nueva York*, *Bulletin of Hispanic Studies*, LIV, 1977.

Havard, Robert, 'The Symbolic Ambivalence of *Green* in García Lorca and Dylan Thomas', *The Modern Language Review*, LXVII, 1972.

—— 'Lorca's Buster Keaton', *Bulletin of Hispanic Studies*, LIV, 1977.

—— 'Dream and Nightmare in Lorca's *Poeta en Nueva York*', in M. A. Rees (ed.), *Catholic Tastes and Times (Essays in Honour of Father Michael E. Williams)*, Leeds, 1987.

Higginbotham, V., 'El viaje de García Lorca a la luna', *Insula*, 254, January, 1968.

—— 'Lorca's Apprenticeship in Surrealism', *Romanic Review*, LXI, 1970.

—— *The Comic Spirit of Federico García Lorca*, Austin and London, 1976.

Honig, E., *García Lorca*, New York, 1963.

Ilie, Paul, *The Surrealist Mode in Spanish Literature*, Michigan, 1968.

Laffranque, Marie, *Federico García Lorca*, Paris, 1966.

Marcilly, C., *Ronde et fable de la solitude à New York*, Paris, 1962.

Maurer, C., (ed.) Federico García Lorca, *Epistolario*, Madrid, 1983.

Morla Lynch, Carlos, *En España con Federico García Lorca (Páginas de un diario íntimo, 1928–1936*, Madrid, 1958.

Morris, C. B., *Surrealism and Spain, 1920–1936*, Cambridge, 1972.

Rafael Alberti

Alberti, Rafael, *La arboleda perdida. Libros I y II de memorias*, Barcelona, 1976 (first published Buenos Aires, 1959); *The Lost Grove*, Gabriel Burns (trans.), Berkeley, 1976.

Aranda, J. F., *El surrealismo español*, Barcelona, 1981.

Belitt, Ben, (trans.) Rafael Alberti, *Selected Poems*, Berkeley and Los Angeles, 1966.

Bergamín, J., 'De veras y de burlas', *La Gaceta Literaria*, no. 71, 1929.

Bodini, V., *I poeti surrealisti spagnoli. Saggio introduttivo e antologia*, Turin, 1963.

Bowra, C. M., 'Rafael Alberti, *Sobre los ángeles*', in *The Creative Experiment*, London, 1967 (first published, London, 1949).

Connell, G. W., 'The Autobiographical Element in *Sobre los ángles*', *Bulletin of Hispanic Studies*, LX, 1963.

—— 'The End of a Quest: Alberti's *Sermones y Moradas* and Three Uncollected Poems', *Hispanic Review*, XXXIII, 1965.

—— translator, Rafael Alberti, *Concerning the Angels*, London, 1967.

Durán, M., 'El surrealismo en el teatro de Lorca y de Alberti', *Hispanófila*, I, 1957.

González Muela, J., '¿Poesía amorosa en *Sobre los ángeles*?', *Insula*, no. 80, 1952.

Havard, Robert, 'Rafael Alberti's Sermon on Surrealism', *Bulletin of Hispanic Studies*, forthcoming.

Heisel, Margaret, 'Imagery and Structure in Rafael Alberti's *Sobre los ángeles*', *Hispania*, LVIII, 1975.

Horst, R., 'The Angelic Prehistory of *Sobre los ángeles*', *Modern Language Notes*, LXXXI, 1966.

Ilie, Paul, *The Surrealist Mode in Spanish Literature*, Michigan, 1968.

Marcial de Onís, Carlos, *El surrealismo y cuatro poetas de la generación del 27*, Madrid, 1974.

Morris, C. B., Rafael Alberti's '*Sobre los ángeles*': *Four Major Themes*, Hull, 1966.

— — '*Sobre los ángeles*: A Poet's Apostasy', *Bulletin of Hispanic Studies*, XXXVII, 1960.

— — *A Generation of Spanish Poets, 1920–1936*, Cambridge, 1969.

— — *Surrealism and Spain, 1920–1936*, Cambridge, 1972.

— — prologue, Rafael Alberti, *Sobre los ángeles, Yo era un tonto y lo que he visto me ha hecho dos tontos*, Madrid, 1981.

Pérez, C. A., 'Rafael Alberti: Sobre los tontos', *Revista Hispánica Moderna*, XXXII, 1966.

Popkin, Louise B., *The Theatre of Rafael Alberti*, London, 1976.

Proll, E., 'The Surrealist Element in Rafael Alberti', *Bulletin of Spanish Studies*, XVIII, 1941.

Sarriá, F. G., '*Sobre los ángeles* de Rafael Alberti y el surrealismo', *Papeles de Son Armadans*, XCI, 1978–79.

Sobejano, G., 'El epíteto surrealista: Alberti, Lorca, Aleixandre', in *El epíteto en la lírica española*, Madrid, 1956.

Index